Principles of Land Law in Uganda

John Tamukedde Mugambwa

Fountain Publishers

Fountain Publishers Ltd
P.O. Box 488
Kampala
E-mail:fountain@starcom.co.ug
Website:www.fountainpublishers.com

Distributed in Europe, North America and Australia by African Books Collective (ABC), The Jam Factory, 27 Park End St, Oxford OX1 1HU, United Kingdom. Tel: 44 (0) 1865-726686, Fax:1865-793298

First published 2002

ISBN 9970 02 287 3

1 2 3 4 5 06 05 04 03 02

Cataloguing-in-Publication Data

Mugambwa, John Tamukedde,
Principles of land law in Uganda/John Tamukedde Mugambwa – Kampala: Fountain Publishers, 2002
___ p. ___ cm
Includes index ISBN 9970-02-287-3
1. Property law – Uganda I. title
343.02'096761 – dc 21

Contents

Preface ix
Table of Cases xi
Table of Statutes xxii
List of Abbreviations xxv

1. **Introduction and Historical Background** **1**
Sources of Ugandan Land Law 1
Background to the tenure systems 2
Mailo tenure 2
Freehold tenure 3
Native freeholds 3
Adjudicated freeholds 3
Customary tenure 4
The *Land Reform Decree* 5
Constitutional reform of land tenure law 6

2. **Land Ownership** **7**
Government land 7
Freehold tenure 7
Leasehold tenure 8
Conversion of leases into freehold 9
Mailo tenure 10
'Lawful' and '*bona fide*' occupants 10
'Lawful' occupant 10
Bona fide occupant 12
Non-bonafide occupant 14
Tenant by occupancy 14
Termination of tenancy by occupancy 21
Customary land tenure 23
Certificate of customary ownership 23
Procedure for application 23
Effect of a certificate 25
Conversion of customary tenure and grant of freeholds 26
Communal Land Associations 30
Restrictions on ownership of land by non-Ugandans 32

3. **Land Administration Control and Dispute Settlement** **33**
Land administration 33
The Uganda Land Commission 33
Land Fund 33
District Land Boards 34
Functions of the Board 34
Land Committees 35
Control over land 36
Ownership of land by non-citizens 36
Protection of family land 37
Control over land use 38
Compulsory acquisition of land 38

	Compulsory acquisition under the *Land Act*	40
	Compensation from the Land Fund	41
	Land Disputes Settlement	42
	Land Tribunals	42
	District Land Tribunals	42
	Sub-county, Urban District and City Division Tribunals	44
	Alternative Dispute Resolution	45
	Customary dispute settlement and mediation	45
	Mediator	46
	Transitional jurisdiction	47
4.	**General Principles of Land Law**	**48**
	The doctrine of tenure and estates	48
	Doctrine of tenure	48
	Doctrine of estates	48
	Relevance of the doctrines of tenure and estates	49
	Meaning of land	50
	Rights above the surface	50
	Rights below the surface	51
	Fixtures	51
	Test for a fixture	52
	Right to remove fixtures	54
	Equitable and legal interests in Land	55
	Origin of the dual system	55
	Fusion of the courts of law and equity	56
	Nature of equitable interest	56
	Creation of equitable interests	57
	Priorities	58
	Priorities over registered land	60
	Adverse possession and limitation	61
	The concept of possession	61
	Power to evict squatters	61
	Limitation period	62
	Consequences of lapse of time	65
	Adverse possession, prescription and acquiescence	67
	Prescription	67
	Acquiescence	67
5.	**Registration of Titles**	**69**
	Introduction	69
	Scheme of the Act	69
	Essential features	70
	Title by registration	70
	Unregistered instruments	71
	Indefeasibility of title	73
	Exceptions to indefeasibility	74
	Exceptions within the Act	74
	Overriding statutory exceptions to indefeasibility	81
	Judicial inroads - *rights in personam*	82
	Protection of unregistered interests by caveat	83

Remedies for deprivation of land 86
Ejectment 86
Compensation 87

6. **Leases** **90**
Leases and licences distinguished 91
Essential features of a lease 91
Duration 91
Exclusive possession 92
Creation of a lease 94
Contract 94
Tenancy by estoppel 94
Registration requirement 95
Unregistered lease 95
Rights and obligations of a landlord and tenant 97
Conditions and covenants 97
Express covenants 98
Covenants implied under the general law against the landlord 98
Covenant implied against a tenant 99
Covenants implied under the *Registration of Titles Act* 100
Sublease and assignment 101
Enforcement of covenants in a lease 102
Assignment 102
Sublease 102
Registration of transfer 103
Assignment of a reversion 103
Remedies for breach of covenant 104
Tenant's remedies 104
Landlord's remedies 104
Termination of leases other than by forfeiture 110
Effluxion of time 110
Notice to quit 111
Surrender 112
Merger 113
Lessor's rights to fixtures 113

7. **Mortgages** **114**
Introduction 114
Creation of a mortgage 115
Registered mortgage 115
Equitable mortgage 115
Mortgage of customary land and tenancy by occupancy 116
Remedies of a mortgagee 116
Action on a personal covenant 117
Possession 117
Appointment of a receiver 118
Power of sale 119
Foreclosure 123
Remedies of equitable mortgagees 123
Remedies of mortgagee of customary land and tenancy by occupancy 124

Discharge of a mortgage by payment 125
Equity's protection of a mortgagor 125
Collateral advantage 127
Other grounds for judicial intervention 127

8. Servitudes over Land 129
Introduction 129
Easements 129
Essential features 129
Dominant and servient land 129
Creation of easements 131
Easement by Statute 131
Extinguishment of easements 136
Profits à prendre 136
Restrictive covenants 138
Enforcement of covenants at common law 138
Enforcement of covenants in equity 139
Scheme of development 140
Restrictive covenants and the *RTA* 141
Remedies for branch of restrictive covenants 141
Extinguishment of restrictive covenants 142
Licence 142
Types of licences 142
Customary rights 144

9. Co-ownership of Land 145
Introduction 145
Joint tenancy 145
The four unities 145
The right of survivorship (*jus accrescendi*) 146
Tenancy in common 147
Creation of joint tenancy and tenancy in common 147
Common law 147
Equity 147
Creation of co-ownership under the *RTA* 149
Right of enjoyment amongst co-owners 150
No liabilities for trespass or occupation rent 150
No compensation for improvements or repair 151
No liability to account for profits 152
Termination of co-ownership 152
Termination of joint tenancy 152
Termination of tenancy in common 154
Practical application of co-ownership 155

10. Expropriated Property 156
Historical background 156
Asians' economic dominance 156
Corrective measures 156
The expropriation 158
Cancellation of entry permits 158
Prohibition of new liabilities158
Declaration of assets 158

Agents for sale of properties to Ugandan citizens 159
Vesting of the properties in the board and government 159
Constitutionality of the expropriation 160
Management of expropriated property 160
Compensation to departed Asians 161
Reversing the expropriation 162
The pressure for repossession 162
The purpose of the *Expropriated Properties Act*, 1982. 162
Properties to which the Act applies 162
Re-vesting of property in government and nullification of dealings 164
Dealings by the minister 165
Dealing with incumbered properties. 167
Present tenants 167
Compensation 167
Appeal from the minister's decision 168
Conclusion 168

Index 169

Preface

In 1998, the Ugandan Parliament enacted the *Land Act,* which substantially changed the land tenure laws of the country. The Uganda Land Act Implementation Project, which was sponsored by the British Department for International Development ("DFID"), commissioned me to write a land law "handbook" to be used for the training of the members of land tribunals established under the Act. (The Act gives land tribunals exclusive jurisdiction over all land disputes.) The handbook was supposed to be a fifty-page description of the Act to assist members of the tribunal, most of whom will not have legal qualifications, to understand the Act. It soon became obvious to me that a handbook requires a textbook on Ugandan land law that readers can refer to for more information. Such a textbook I found wanting.

It is true that there are several well-known English textbooks, used by the legal profession and law students; however, I did not consider them suitable because they deal with land law in England. Although Ugandan land law is based on English land law, it differs from English law. The social-economic and political differences between the two countries, has in some instances, resulted in dissimilar legal principles. The fact that the land law of both countries is increasingly statutory based, will make the gap between their legal regimes even wider. The case in point is the *Land Act*, which is unique to Uganda. Clearly, English textbooks are no longer suitable tools for the teaching and the understanding of Ugandan land law. For this reason, with the blessing of Professor Patrick McAuslan of the University of London, then DFID Uganda Land Act Implementation Project administrator, I decided to write this textbook in lieu of a handbook.

In addition to the *Land Act*, the book deals with all major topics which traditionally are covered in land law textbooks. As much as possible the book uses Ugandan cases and materials to explain and illustrate the legal principles. Legal materials from other jurisdictions are used where they are particularly useful in explaining the law in Uganda or for comparative purposes. Readers will notice that the book refers to several Australian cases, which is unusual in Ugandan courts. The reference to Australian cases is justified on the grounds that the *Registration of Titles Act* (cap 205), which is one of the major land legislations in Uganda, is based on the Australian Torrens System of land registration. It makes more sense for the Ugandan courts to refer to the Australian case law for assistance in the interpretation of this Act than to the English common law cases, as tends to be the practice.

I make no pretence that this book is definitive of Ugandan land law. Rather, it is a platform for more and, hopefully, better textbooks on Ugandan land law. In conjunction with this book, I have compiled a cases and materials book entitled *Source Book of Uganda's Land Law.* The latter contains extracts of mainly Ugandan cases and other extracts on land law in Uganda. The two books are intended to complement each other.

Many people have assisted me in various ways to write this book. In particular, I wish to express my gratitude to the following: Dr Alex Amankwah, Evarist Mwesigye, Professor McAuslan, William Johnson, Rupert Johnson, Andrew McRobert, A K Lutaaya, Robina Lutaaya, Beatrice Kavuma-Kiwanuka, Peter Walubiri, Elijah Wante and Harriet Byenkya. In addition, I wish to express my appreciation to the following law students for their untiring research assistance: Flavia Nabakooza, Rashida Batanulwa and Joseph Isanga (Makerere University); Elvis Onyoru, David Markovich, Darrel Chia, Elouise Dellit (Murdoch University) and Sanyu Mugambwa (UTS). I am also grateful to a number of institutions for their support, in particular DFID, for its sponsorship of the original project, the Uganda Law Development Centre, for allowing me unlimited access to its library, and the School of Law, Murdoch University, for material and moral support of my research. Finally, I wish to express my gratitude to Juliet and our son, Paul, for their encouragement and patience. Needless to say, I am solely responsible for any imperfections in the book.

John T. Mugambwa
School of Law
Murdoch University
Perth, Western Australia
2002

Table of Cases

A.M. Dharas and Sons Ltd v Elys Ltd [1963] EA 573 98, 104
Adonia v Mutekanga [1970] EA 429 83
AG Securities v Vaughan [1988] 3 All ER 1058 (HL) 145, 146
A-G v Jacobs Smith [1895] 2 QB 341 59
Ahmed Farah and another v Kiwanuka CS No 687 of 1993 (unreported) 87,109
Aldin v Latimer Clark Muirhead & Co. Ltd [1894] 2 Ch 437 99
Alibhai and another v Karia and another CA No 52 of 1995 72, 75, 97
Alibhai and others v The Chief Registrar of Titles, Misc. Appn. No. 60 of 1992 108
Allen v Roughley (1955) 94 CLR 98 64
Amodu Tijani v Southern Nigeria [1921] 2 AC 399 48
Anderson V Bowles (1951) 84 CLR 310 at 325 105
Appah v Parncliffe Investments [1964] 1 WLR 1064 92, 93
Armour v Penrith Projects Pty Ltd [1979] 1 NSWLR 98 108
Ashburn Anstalt v Arnold and another [1988] 2 All ER 147 91, 142
Asher v Whitlock (1865) LR 1 QB I 61
Assets Company Ltd v Mere Roihi [1905] AC 176 75, 76, 80, 87
Attorney-General of Ontario v Mercer (1883) LR 8 App Cas 767 48
Austerberry v Oldham Corporation (1885) 29 Ch D 750 131, 138
Australian Hi-Fi Publications Pty Ltd v Gehl [1979] 2 NSWLR 619 78
Babiruga v Karegyesa and others D.R. CA No MKA 13 of 1993 (unreported) 11, 52, 61
Bahr and another v Nicolay and others (1988) 164 CLR 604 83
Balbir v Panesar [1972] EA 94 111
Barclays Bank (U) Ltd v Northcote and another C.S. No. 1467 of 1974 (unreported) 117, 123, 124, 125
Barclays Bank D.C.O. v Gulu Millers Ltd [1959] EA 540 56, 58, 69,115 116, 123, 124
Barclays Bank D.C.O. v Patel [1970] EA 88 (CA) 133, 134, 135, 136
Barclays Bank of Uganda Ltd v Livingstone Katende Lutu CA 22 of 1993 (unreported) 119
Barry v Haseldine [1952] 2 All ER 317 133
Barry v Heider (1914) 19 CLR 197 72
Baxter v Oaks Properties Ltd [1965] Ch 816 141
Bejoy Chundra v. Kally Prosonno (1878),4 Cal. 327 64
Berkley v Poulett (1976) 241 EG 911 54
Bernstein of Leigh (Baron) v Skyviews and General Ltd [1978] QB 479 50, 51
Berry v Heider and another (1914) 19 CLR 197 71
Bidandi Ssali v Attorney General, Civil Suit No. 834 of 1989 164
Biggs v Hoddinott (1898) 2 Ch 307 127
Billson and others v Residential Apartments Ltd [1992] 1 All ER 108
Bligh v Martin [1968] 1 WLR 804 63
Boyer v Warby [1953] 1 QB 234 104, 105
Boyes v Gathure [1969] EA 385 84, 85
Breskvar and another v Wall and others (1971) 126 CLR 376 87
British Anzani (Felixstone) Ltd v International Marine Management (UK) Ltd [1980] QB 137 73, 104
Brocklebank v Thompson [1903] 2 Ch 344 144

Browne v Flower [1911] 1 Ch 219	131
Bryant v Foot (1867) LR 2 QB 161	134
Buckby v Coles (1814) 5 Taunt.311	136
Buckingham City Council v Moran [1969] 2 All ER 225	63
Buganda Timber Co. Ltd v Mulji K Metha [1961] EA 477	115
Bull v Bull [1955] 1 QB 234	145, 147, 151
Burgess v Rawnsley [1975] 1 Ch 429	153
Butagira v Namukasa CA No. 69 of 1989	108, 109
Bweya Steel Works Ltd v National Insurance Corporation CS No 63 of 1985; [1985] HCB 58	90, 92, 110, 111, 112
Byaruhanga v Barclays Bank of Uganda Ltd CS 1327 of 1977 (unreported)	115
Calverley v Green (1984) 155 CLR 242	148, 149, 150
Calvert v Tate Argus 8th August 1867	79
Campbell v Holyland [1877] 7 Ch D 166	123
Canas Property Co. Ltd v Television Service Ltd [1970] 2 QB 433	108
Capelinha v Marchese Holdings (1995) 3 SR (WA) 261	107
Caunce v Caunce [1969] 1 ALL ER 722	59
Chan and another v Cresdon Properties Limited [1989] 168 CLR 242	72, 97
Chhagan v Manani [1964] EA 71	111
Citamong v Olinga [1988] HCB 86	36
Citamong v Olinga CA No 104 of 1982; (1985) HCB 86 (unreported)	29, 62, 67, 68
City & Metropolitan Properties v Greycroft [1937] 1 WLR 1085	103
City Council of Kampala v Mukibi [1967] EA 368	11, 17, 72, 92, 96, 101, 102
City Council of Kampala v Mukubira and another [1968] EA 497 (U)	92, 107, 110
City Council of Kampala v Odido CS No 232 of 1969	61
Cleaver v Mutual Reserve Fund Life Association [1892] 1 QB 147	154
Clifton Securities v Huntley [1948] 2 All ER 283	111
Cobb & another v Lane [1952] 1 All E R 1199	62
Colchester Borough Council v Smith [1991] Ch 448	62, 65
Corin v Patton (1990) 169 CLR 313	153
Crabb v Arun DC [1976] Ch 179	52
Crane v Morris [1965] 1 WLR 1104	93
Crow v Wood [1970] 3 All ER 425	131
Cruse v Mount (1932) All ER 781	99
Cuckmere Brick Co Ltd v Mutual Finance Co Ltd [1971] Ch 948	121
Custodian of Expropriated Property v Tedep (1964) CLR 318	144
Dalton v Angus (1881) 6 App. Cas 740	67, 134, 135
Davies v Davies [1983] WAR 305	154
De Souza Figueiredo v Talbot and another [1961] EA 167 (CA)	116
Dennis v McDonald [1981] 2 All ER 633	151
Desai v Cooper (1950) KLR 32	92, 93, 94
Di Masi v Piromalli [1980] WAR 57	78
Dickson v McWhinnie [1958] SR (NSW) 179	84
Dolphin's Conveyance, Re, Birmingham Corporation v Boden [1970] 1 Ch 654	141
Donoghue v Stevenson [1932] AC 562	121
Dr Nur Illahi s/o Nur Mohamed v Patel and others 1956 [EACA] 80	110
Driscoll v Church Commission for England [1957] 1 QB 330	108
Duke of Sutherland v Heathcote [1892] 1 Ch 475	136, 137

E.R Ives Investment Ltd v High [1967] 2 QB 379	62
East African General Insurance Co Ltd v Ntende and others CS No 1387 of 1975; (1979) HCB 225 (unreported)	147
Eastern Radio Service and another v R.J. Patel t/a Tiny Tots and another [1962] EA 818	105, 107, 110
Eaton v Swansea Waterworks Co (1851) 17 QB 267	135
Ediginton v Clark [1964] 1 QB 367	65
Elliston v Reacher [1908] Ch 374	140, 141
Elwes v Maw (1802) 3 East 38; 102 ER 510	54
English, Scottish & Australian Bank Ltd v Phillips (1937) 57 CLR 302	114
Errington v Errington and another [1950] 1 KB 290	93, 94
Esiroyo v Esiroyo & another [1973] EA 388 (K)	144
Esso Petroleum Co Ltd v Harper's Garage (Stourport) Ltd [1968] AC 269	127
Ex Parte Leathes (1833) Ch 112	140
Fairclough v Swan Brewery Company Limited [1912] AC 565 (PC)	126, 127
Fairweather v St Marylebone Property Co. Ltd [1963] AC 510	65
Federated Homes Ltd v Mill Lodge Properties Ltd [1980] 1 WLR 594	140
Fernandes v Houstein (1963) 4 FLR 355	84
Francis v Ibitoye (1936) NLR 1	51
Fraser v Walker [1967] AC 569	81, 83, 86
Freeth v Burr (1874) LR 9 CP 208	104
G A Investments Pty Ltd v Standard Insurance Co Ltd [1964] WAR 264	126
G and C Kreglinger v New Patagonia Meat Storage Co Ltd [1914] AC 25	127
G Colegrave v Dias Santos 107 ER 311	54
Gabriel Michel and another v Khoury (1944) 10 WALR 286	154, 155
Gaskin v Balls (1879) 13 Ch D 324	142
Gatare v Parkash Kaur and others HCCS 106 of 1995 (unreported)	81
Genrich v Maitland Holding Pty Ltd [1982] Qd R 58	84
Getobed v Pridmore (1970) 115 Sol Jo 78	21
Giella v Cassman Brown and Co. Ltd [1973] EA 358	122, 127
Gill v Lewis (1956) 1 All ER 844	109
Gokaldas Laximidas Tanna v SR Rosemary Munyinza Civil Appeal No. 12 of 1992, Supreme Court [1994-5]; HCB 53	82, 164
Goldsack v Shore [1950] KB 708	91
Gomba Marines & Contractors (Ltd) v Kiwana Misc. Appn. No. 131B/93	108, 109
Grangeside Properties Ltd v Collingwood Securities Ltd *et al* [1964] 1 WLR 139	125
Greenwood v Bennett [1973] 1 QB 195	52
Grigsby v Melville [1973] 3 All ER 455	131
Grindlays Bank (U) Ltd v Edward Boazi CA No 23 of 1992 (Supreme Court)	118
Grymes v Boweren 130 ER 1349	54
Guaranty Discount Co. Ltd v Credit Finance Corporation Ltd & another [1963] EA 345	115
Haji Musa Magala v Ondowa HCCC 360 of 1971	108, 109
Hanak v Green [1958] 2 QB 9	104
Hansraj Thakkar v The Vanik Mahajan [1960] EA 208	131
Harding v Crethorn 170 ER 278	100
Harmer v Jumbi (Nigeria) Tin Areas Ltd [1921] 1 Ch 200	64
Hasanali Mamuji v Dar & Sons (1935) 32 EACA 111	79
Hatim v Mohsin Bin Saleh [1957] EA 486	94
Hayward v Chaloner [1968] 1 QB 107	26

Haywood v Brunswick Permanent Benefit Building Society (1881) 8 QB D 403 — 139
Hemming v Stone Poges Golf Club [1920] 1 KB 720 — 106
Henderson v Eason (1851) 17 QB 701 — 150, 152
Henderson v Squires (1869) LR 4 QB 170 — 100
Hill v Tupper (1863) 2 H & C 121; 159 ER 51 — 91, 129, 130
Hodgson v Marks [1971] Ch 892 — 53
Holland v Hodgson (1872) LR 7 CP 328 — 65, 66
Hooke v Holland [1984] WAR 16 — 86
Hotel International Ltd v The Administrator of the Estate of the Late Robert Kavuma CA No 37 of 1995 — 70, 75, 77
Hudda & Ors v Nyanza Saw Mills (1947) Ltd & Ors High Court Miscellaneous Application No. 46 of 1987, unreported — 160
Hulme v Brigham [1943] KB 152 — 54
In Re: (An Application by) Bukoba Gymkhana Club (1963) EA 478 — 39, 66
In Re: Foley (Deceased); Public Trustee v Foley [1952] NZLR 702 — 150
In Re: Gibbs & Holder Brothers & Co. Ltd [1925] Ch 198 — 102
In re Ivan Mutaka Misc C No 81 of 1976 (unreported); [1980] HCB 27 — 87
In Re: Refund of Dues under Timber Regulations [1935] AC 184 — 165
In the Matter of Ruzhwengyibwa and In the Matter of Ruzigana Misc. C No 48 of 1976 (unreported) — 29
Industrial Properties (Barton Hill) and others v Associated Electrical Industries Ltd [1977] 1 QB 580 — 94, 95
International Drilling Fluids Ltd v Louisville Investments (Uxbridge) Ltd [1986] 1 All ER 3210 — 102
Inwards v Baker [1965] 1 All ER 446 — 143
Ismail Jaffer Alibhai and others v Nandala Harjivan Karia and another CA No 53 of 1995 (unreported) — 83
Ittappan v. Manavikrama (1897) 21 Mad. 153, p. 159 — 64
Jacobs v Seward (1872) LR 5 HL 464 — 150
Jaffer Alibhai and 2 others v Nandala H. Kaira and another Civil Appeal No. 53 of 1995, Supreme Court, unreported — 164
Jaffer Brothers Ltd v Bagalaliwo, Civil Appeal No.43 of 1997, unreported — 165, 166
Jaffer Brothers Ltd v Bagalaliwo, High Court Civil Suit No. 31 of 1995, unreported — 202
Jakana v Senkaali CS No 491 of 1984 (unreported); [1988-90] HCB 167 — 116, 124
Jama Noor Shakiya v Hassanali Ahmed Jusub (1965) EA 241 (U) — 94
James Jones & Sons Ltd v Earl of Tankerville [1909] 2 Ch 440 — 165, 137, 143
James v Stevenson [1893] AC 162 — 96, 64, 78, 136
Jandu v Kirpal and another [1975] EA 225 (K) — 64
Jani Mohammed Jaffer Ltd v Khemisa Senya, High Court Civil Suit No. 829 of 1992, unreported — 166
Jennings v Ward (1705) 2 Vern S20 — 127
Jones (AE) v Jones (FW) [1977] 1 WLR 438 — 150
Jones v Carter (1846) 15 M&W 718; 153 ER 1040 — 107
Jones v Pritchard [1908] 1 Ch 730 — 131
Jones v Smith (1841) 1 Hare 43; 66 ER 943 — 59
Jones; Farrington v Forrester [1893] 2 Ch 461 — 129, 151
Juma v Habibu [1975] EA 108 (T) — 113
Kalani v Kaur CA No. 22 of 1995 — 112
Kalsi v Commissioner of Lands [1958] EA 367 — 110

Kamanyire v Standard Bank (U) Ltd [1977] HCB 82	100, 104, 105, 111
Kampala Bottlers Ltd v Damanico (U) Ltd CA No 22 of 1992 (unreported)	73, 75
Kanjee Naranjee Ltd v Tulsidas Dharamshi Ghadialy [1965] EA	94, 95
Karamat Ali v Champion Shoe Company (1949) 16 EACA 15	92
Kassaja v Registrar of Titles Misc. Appn. No. 51 of 1993	160, 108
Katarikawe v Katwiremu and another CS No 2 of 1973; [1977] HCB 18737	29, 61, 72, 77, 83, 84, 97
Kawalya-Kagwa v Registrar of Titles [1974] EA 481	2
Kazzora v Rukuba CA No 13 of 1992 (unreported)	60, 70, 75, 83, 85
Keeves v Dean [1924] 1 KB 685	101
Kelson v Imperial Tobacco Co. of Great Britain and Ireland [1957] 2 QB 334	50
Kenny v Preen [1963] 1 QB 499	98
Khadir Juma et al v Abdul Juma Martin CS No 951 of 1990; (1988-90) HCB 154 (unreported)	85
Khoja Shia Jamat v Norman Godhino (1936-51) 6 ULR 47	106
Kikabhai N Mistry v Abdulla Mohamed (1956) 23 EACA 192	112
King v David Allen & Sons, Billposting Ltd [1916] 2 AC 54	143
Kisee Maweu and others v Kiu Ranching and Co-operative Society (1982-88) 1 KAR 746	67, 78
Kitiiza v Registrar of Titles Misc. Appn. No 82 of 1977	148
Kiwanuka-Musisi v Seggane [1973] EA 561	106, 108, 109
Knightsbridge Estate Trust Limited v Byrne and others [1939] Ch D 441	126, 127
Kulani v Satwant Kaur Civil Appeal No. 22 of 1995, Supreme Court, unreported	163
Kulubya v Singh [1963] EA 408	37
Kuper & Kuper v Keywest Construction Pty Ltd [1990] 3 WAR 419	84, 86
Kursell v Timber Operators and Contractors Ltd [1927] 1 KB 298	136
Kyazze v Eunice Busingye CA No 13 of 1990 (unreported)	76
La Martina v Penny [1968] SASR 41	84
Lace v Chantler [1944] 1 All ER 305	91, 92
Lake v Craddock (1733) 3 P Wms 158; 24 ER 1011	148
Lake v Jones (1889) 15 VLR 728	66
Lavery v Pursell (1888) 39 Ch 508	165
Leigh v Dickeson (1881-85) All ER Rep 1099	150, 151
Leros Pty Ltd v Terara Pty Ltd & another (1992) 106 ALR 595	85
Liverpool Corporation v Coghill & Sons Ltd [1918] 1 Ch 307	135
Loke Yew v Port Swettenham Rubber Co. Ltd [1913] AC 491	75
Lomolo v Kilembe Mines Ltd CS No 395 of 1976; (1978) HCB 157	51, 61, 107, 67, 68
London City Council v Allen [1914-15] All ER Rep 1008	139, 140
Lugogo Coffee Co (U) Ltd v Singo Combined Coffee Growers Ltd CS No. 554 of 1973; [1976] HCB 92	97, 106, 107, 108, 109
Lukwago v Bawa Singh and another [1959] EA 282	2, 20
Lumu v Sood CS No 1541 of 1972, unreported	149
Lusweswe v Kasule and Coulibally CS No 1010 of 1983 (unreported)	75
Lutakome v Sentongo (1988-90) HCB 95	57

Lutaya v H.G. Gandesha & Anor High Court Civil Suit No. 860 of 1982; [1986] HCB 46 163, 165
Lwanga v The Registrar of Titles Misc. Cause No 7A of 1977; (1980) HCB 24 (unreported) 73, 87
Lysaght v Edwards (1876) 2 Ch D 499 57, 58
Makerere Properties Ltd v Attorney General CA No 36 of 1996 82
Makerere University v St Mark Education Centre and another CS No 378 of 1996 77
Makumbi (Mrs E) & another v Puran Singh Ghana & another [1962] EA 331 78, 129
Malayan Credit Ltd v Jack Chia-MPH Ltd [1986] AC 549 (PC) 148
Malzy v Eicholz [1916] 2 QB 308 98
Management Committee of Rushasha Primary School v Nkorenta C.A. MKA 11/1993 (unreported) 77
Mancatter Developments Ltd V Garmansa Ltd [1986] QB 1212 55
Marshall v Green (1875) 1 CPD 35 138
Martin v Martin (1959) 110 CLR 297 149
Matambulire v Kimera CA No 37 of 1972 (unreported); [1975] HCB 150 3, 114, 116, 117, 123, 125
Matovu and others v Sseviri and another CA No 7 of 1978 (unreported); [1979] HCB 174 30, 75
Matthews v Smallwood [1910] 1 Ch 777 110
Mayanja-Nkangi v National Housing Corporation [1972] 1 ULR 37 94, 111, 153
Mayfair Property Co. Ltd v Johnson [1894] 1 Ch 508 154
Mbazira v Abasagi Nansubuga CA No 14B of 1992; (1992-93) HCB 241 62
McLernon v Connor [1907] 9 WALR 141 133
McManus v Cooke (1887) 35 Ch D 681 58
Mercer v Denne [1905] 2 Ch 538 144
Mercier v Mercier [1903] 2 Ch 98 149
Midland Rly Co v Miles [1886] 33 Ch D 632 133
Miller v Encer Products Ltd [1956] Ch 304 131
Miller v Minister of Mines and another [1963] 1 All ER 109 82
Mills and another v Stokman and another (1967) 116 CLR 61 138
Mills v Stockman (1967) 116 CLR 61 136, 137
Milmo v Carreras [1947] KB 306 at 310 101
Milroy v Lord (1862) 4 De GF & J 264; 45 ER 1185 153
Mohamed Mohamedi v Athman Shante [1960] EA 1062 127
Moore v Ullcoats Mining Co Ltd [1908] 1 Ch 575 107
Morley v Bird (1798) 3 Ves. 628; 30 ER 1192 147, 148
Moule v Garrett (1872) LR 7 Ex 101 103
Mpalikamanya v Sempiira CS No 571 of 1976 (unreported) 154,155
Mubiru v Uganda Credit & Savings Bank (1978) HCB 109 117, 121, 122
Municipal District of Concord v Coles (1906) 3 CLR 96 84, 85
Musisi v Grindlays Bank (U) Ltd and others CA No 37 of 1995 (unreported) 75
Musoke Bafirawala v Jogga CS No 33 of 1973; (1976) HCB 26 (unreported) 52, 64, 65
Musumba v Haji Kasaka and Mbarara Auction Mart (1971) 1 ULR 105, 111
Muwereza v Mbusye CA No 118 of 1975 (unreported) 66
Naluswa v Luswabi Misc. C No. 5 of 1974 107,108
Nambalu Kintu v Efulaimu Kamira CA No 26 of 1973 (unreported); [1975] HCB 221 12, 13, 62, 64, 65, 66, 67, 78, 124

Namusisi and others v Ntabazi CS No 887 of 1988 84
Nandala Harjivan Karia and another CA No 53 of 1995 (unreported) 83
National and Grindley's Bank (K) Ltd v P.T. Punater [1965] EA 648 (K) 100,104
National Carriers Ltd v Panelpina (Northern) Ltd [1981] AC 675 104
National Guarantee Manure Co v Donald (1859) 4 H & N 8 131
Nazarali Hassanali Sayani v Edward Mperese Nsubuga CS No 364 of 1993 (unreported) 73, 86, 166
Ndigejjerawa v Isaka Kizito and Sabane Kubulwamwana (1953) 7 ULR 31 61, 70
Nelson v Hughes [1947] VLR 227 78
New Windsor Corporation v Mellor [1975] Ch 380 144
New Zealand Government Property Corp v HM & S Ltd [1982] 1 QB 1145 54
Njuki v Musisi Nyanzi HCCS No 0434 of 1996 (unreported) 83, 85
Noakes and Co Ltd v Rice [1902] AC 24 127
Noor Hassan v Mukiibi CA No. 103 of 1977; [1978] HCB 162 90, 110
Nordin Charania Walji v Drake Semakula Civil Appeal No. 40 of 1995, Supreme Court, unreported 164
Norman Godhino V Virani cc 224 of 1938, High Court Digest P. 256 105
Norton V Kilduff (1974) QDR 47 141
Northern Counties of England Fire Insurance Co v Whipp (1884) 26 Ch D 482 58, 59, 114
Northern Counties of England Fire Insurance Co v Whipp Co (1884) 26 Ch D 482 Supreme Court, unreported 199
Nsubuga and another Mutawe (1974) EA 487 (CA) 106
Obiero V Opiyo et al [1905] 2 Ch 538 144
Olinda De Souza V Kassamali Namji [1962] EA 756 73
Olojo V Rajab CS No 1241/86 (unreported) 85
Onapa V Muhammed Rashid Punjani Civil Appeal No. 5 of 1995, Supreme Court, unreported 163
Opinya v Mukasa CC No 167 of 1964, High Court Digest, p 514 98, 104
P&A Swift Investments (a firm) v Combined English Stores Group PLC [1988] 3 WLR 313 102
Pardhan Jivraj v Dudley-Whelpadale (1920-29) 3 ULR 193 94, 95
Patel v Lalji Makanji [1954] EA 314 75
Patzak v Lytton [1984] WAR 532 187
Perry v Clissold [1907] AC 73 61, 65
Pilcher v Rawlins (1872) 7 Ch App 259 57, 59
Plimmer v Mayor of Wellington (1884) 9 AC 699 143
Poole's Case (1703) 1 Salk 368; 91 ER 320 54
Popatlal Hirji v L.H. Lakhai & Co (EA) Ltd [1960] EA 437 (U) 72, 95
Powell v McFarlane (1977) 38 P& CR 452 62
Progressive Mailing House Pty Ltd v Tabali Pty Ltd (1985) 157 CLR 17 104
Proudfoot v Hart (1890) 25 QBD 42 100
Prudential Assurance Co. Ltd v London Residuary [1992] 3 All ER 504 90, 91
Public Trustee v Evans [1985] 2 NSWLR 188 154
Pyrali Abdul Resul Esmail v Adrian Sibo, Constitutional Petition No. 9 of 1997, Constitutional Court, unreported 167
Queen's Club Gardens Estate Ltd v Bignell [1924] 1 KB 117 111, 112
Radaich v Smith (1959) 101 CLR 209 92, 93, 142
Rains v Buxton (1880) 14 Ch D 537 63, 64
Rajan Nanji v Jadowji Dewji 1 EALR 91 112
Ramji v Rattansi [1969] EA 309 84

Ramsden v Dyson (1866) LR 1, HL 129	51, 52, 68, 143
Randall v Stevens 118 ER 907	65
Rashad Moledina Co (Mombasa) Ltd and others v Hoima Ginners Ltd [1967] EA 645 CA (K)	104
Rasmanis v Jurewitsch (1968) 88 WN (Pt 1) (NSW) 59	154
Re: a Caveat; Ex P The Canowie Pastoral Co Ltd [1931] SASR 502	84
Re: Beavan [1912] 1 Ch 196	65
Re: Caines [1987] 1 WLR 546	152
Re: De Falbe; Ward v Taylor [1901] 1 Ch 523	54
Re: Ellenborough Park [1956] 3 All ER 667	130, 131
Re: Forrest Trust Trustee's Executors & Agency Co Ltd v Anson [1953] VLR 246	114
Re: Habib Lubwama (1991) HCB 74 (unreported)	87
Re: Murram Murtor 18 KLR 65	147
Re: Refund under Timber Regulations [1935] AC 184	136, 137
Re Stone [1989] 1 Qd R 251	154
Reeves v Lisle [1902] AC 461	126
Registered Trustees of Kampala Institute v Departed Asians Property Custodian Board Civil Appeal No. 21 of 1993	162, 163
Registrar of Titles v Franzon (1975) 132 CLR 611	87, 88
Reynolds v Ashby & Sons [1904] AC 466	54
Rice v Rice (1854) 2 Drew 73; 61 ER 646	60
Robertson v Fraser (1871) 6 Ch App 696	147
Robinson v Kilvert (1889) 41 Ch D 88	99
Robinson v Preston (1858) 4 K & J 505; 70 ER 211	148, 149
Roe v Siddons (1888) 22 QB D 224	130
Rogers v Rice [1892] 2 Ch 170	108
Rosenberg v Cook (1881) 8 QBD	61
Rudge v Richens (1873) CP 8 LR 358	117, 123
Rukandema-Kamuru v Kabale Town Council CA No MKA 10 of 1985	90, 111, 112
Runda Coffee Estates Ltd v Ujager Singh [1966] EA 564	52, 91, 142, 143
Rundo Coffee v Singh (1966) EA 573	64
Rurangaranga v Mbarara Municipal Council and others CA No 10 of 1996 (unreported)	75, 81
Rwamutatiri v Kamono (1978) HCB 300 (unreported)	77
Said bin Mbarak v Kapacee 10 KLR 100	112
Sajabi v Amreliwalla and Wamala [1956] 22 EACA 71	120, 121, 122
Samuel v Jarrah Timber & Wood Paving Corporation [1904] AC 323	125, 126
Sanders v Sanders (1881) 19 Ch D 373	64, 65
Sandhurst Mutual Permanent Investment Building Society v Gissing (1889) 15 VLR 329	79
Sands v Mutual Benefits Ltd [1971] EA 156 (K)	92
Sarson v Roberts [1895] 2 QB 395	99
Sebuliba v Attorney-General CA No 13 of 1991	99, 100
Sejjaka Nalima v Musoke CA No 12 of 1985 (Supreme Court of Uganda); [1992] 5 KALR 132	69, 82
Sentamu v Nalirya CA No 84 of 1959; High Court Digest 538, unreported	153
Sentongo V Shell (U) Ltd CS No 32 of 1993, unreported	72

Case	Page
Serjeant v Nash Field & Co [1903] 2 KB 304	65
Serunjogi v Katabira CS No 547 of 1987 (unreported); [1988-90] HCB 148	26, 56, 57, 58, 97, 142
Settlement Fund Trustees v Nurani [1970] EA 562	136, 137, 143
Sewanyana v Martin Aliker CA No 4 of 1990 (unreported)	77
Shah Champshi Tejshi and others v The Attorney-General of Kenya [1959] EA 630	98, 132
Shah Karamshi Panachand & Co. Ltd v Velji and another [1969] EA 194	112, 113
Shah v Modern Sweet Mart Ltd (1956-57) 8 ULR 99	76
Shah v Shah Vershi Devshi & Co. 17 KLR 20	53
Shell and BP Uganda Ltd v Sikander Husain Esmail and others CS No 1038 of 1975	106
Shevil v Builders Licensing Board (1982) 149 CLR 620	104
Shiloh Spinners Ltd v Harding [1973] AC 691	109
Shokatali Abdulla Dhalla v Sadrudin Meralli CA No 32 of 1994 (unreported)	75, 86, 87
Singh v Godley (1942) 20 KLR 57	110
Singh v Kaur (1936) 17 (1) KLR 1	155
Smith and Snipes Hall Farm Ltd v River Douglas Catchment Board [1949] 2 All ER 179	138
Smith v Seghill Overseas (1875) 10 QB 422	94
Somali Democratic Republic v Anoop Syndirial Treon CA No 4 of 1988 (unreported)	72, 96
South-Eastern Drainage Board v Savings Bank of South Australia (1939) 62 CLR 603	80, 82
Southern Nigeria v John Holt & Co. Ltd [1915] AC 599	158
Souza Figueiredo & Co. Ltd v George Panagopoulos and others [1959] EA 756	72, 102, 103, 105, 106
Souza Figueiredo & Co. Ltd v Moorings Hotel Co. Ltd [1960] EA 926	73, 83, 84, 95, 96, 97, 100
Squire v Rogers [1979] 39 FLR 106	151, 152
Staffordshire & Worcestershire Canal Navigation v Bradley [1912] 1 Ch 91	136
Standard Chartered Bank (U) Ltd v Grand Hotel (U) Ltd Civil Appeal No. 13 of 1999, Court of Appeal, unreported	167
Stanley and Sons Ltd v Alibhai [1963] EA 594 (T)	110
Street v Mountford [1985] 2 All ER 289	92, 93, 94
Summers v Salford Corporation [1943] AC 283	99
Swain v Ayres (1888) 21 QB D 289	57
Swift and Neale v Roberts (1764) 3 Burr 1488, 97 ER 941	178
Taylor Fashions Ltd v Liverpool Victoria Trustees Co. Ltd [1981] 1 All ER 897	52
Taylor v Stibbert (1803) All E Rep R 432	59
Taylor v Twinberrow [1930] 2 KB 16	65
Tehidy Minerals Ltd v Norman [1971] 1 QB 528	21
Telex (Australasia) Pty Ltd v Thomas Cook & Sons (Australasia) Ltd (1970) 2 NSWLR 257	99
The Administrator General of Zanzibar v Khalfan and others [1963] EA 230	146
The Executrix of the Estate of the late Tebajukira and another v Shalita CA No 02 of 1988 (unreported)	87, 109

The Kampala Cotton Co Ltd v Privinlal Madhvani CC No. 485 of 1952, High Court Digest, p 511 98
The Management Committee of Rushasha Primary School v Francis Nkorenta C.A. MKA 11/93 (unreported) 73, 75
The Progressive Mailing House Pty Ltd U Tabali Propetary Ltd (1954) 157 CLR17 104
The Proprietor of Centre Building Units Plan v Bourne [1984] Qd R 13 150
The Trustee, Executors, And Agency Company Ltd and Templeman v Short [1888] 13 AC 793 63
Thomas v Sorrell (1673) Vaugh 330; 124 ER 1098 11, 91
Thursby and others v Plant (1670) 85 ER 254 102
Toohey and others, Ex Parte Meneling Station Pty Ltd and others (1982) 158 CLR 327 136
Travinto Nominees v Vlattas (1973) 129 CLR 1 82
Tulk v Moxhay (1848) 2 Ph 774; 41 ER 1143 56, 139, 140, 142
Turubai v Venkatrao (1902) 27 Bom. 43 64
Uganda Credit and Savings Bank v Eriyazi Senkuba [1966] EA 500 118
Uganda Motors Ltd v Wavah Holdings Ltd CA No 19 of 1991 105, 106, 155
Uganda Post and Telecommunications v AKM Lutaaya CA No 36 of 1995 (unreported) 59, 76, 79, 80
Uganda Spinning Mills Ltd v Placid Weli Iga CS No 547 of 1987; (1988-90) HCB 66
Uganda Thrift Co. Ltd v J.M. Nnambale CS No 550 of 1970 (unreported); [1971] HCB 326 150
United Assurance Co Ltd v Attorney General Civil Appeal No. 1 of 1986, unreported 160
UTC Ltd (in Liquidation) v NZI Securities Australia Ltd and another [1991] 4 WAR 349 115
Variety Timber Ltd v Musa [1971] EA 398 (K) 106, 110
Victoria Tea Estates Ltd v James Bemba & Anor, Civil Appeal No. 49 of 1996, Supreme Court, unreported 265
Viscount Tredefar v Harwood [1929] AC 72 101
Waimiha Sawmilling Co. Ltd (in liq) v Waione Timber Co. Ltd [1926] AC 101 75
Walker v Linom (1907) 2 Ch 59
Wallis's Cayton Bay Holiday Camp Ltd v Shell-Mex & BP Ltd [1975] QB 94 63
Walsh v Lonsdale (1882) 21 Ch 9 56, 58, 95, 97
Wamala v Musoke (1920-29) 3 ULR 120 3
Wandira v Okeya CA No 209 of 1969; (1970) HCB 67, 68
Warren v Keen [1954] 1 QB 15 100
Waswa v Kikungwe (1952-56) 7 ULR 1 116
Waterloo v Bacon (1866) LR 2 Eq 514 136
Western Australia Fresh Food & Ice Co v Freecorn [1904] 1 WAR 22 96
Western Fish Products Ltd v Penwith District Council [1981] 2 All ER 204 11
Westham Central Charity Board v East London Waterworks Co [1900] 1 Ch 624 100
Wheeldon v Burrows [1874-80] All ER Rep 669 132, 133
Wheeler v Mercer [1957] AC 416 11
White v City of London Brewery Company (1889) 42 Ch D 237 118

White v Metcalf [1903] 2 Ch 567	118
White v Taylor (No 2) [1969] 1 Ch 160	136
White v Williams [1922] KB 727	136
Wickham v Hawker (1840) 7 M&W 63; 151 ER 671	136
Willcox v McLeroth (1988) 3 ALL ER 1058	146
Williams v Hensman (1861) J&H 546; 70 ER 862	152, 154
Williams v Usherwood [1983] 45 P & CR 235	63
Wong v Beaumont Property Trust Ltd [1965] 1 QB 173	134
Wood v Leedbitter (1845) 13 M & W 838	142, 143
Wright v Gibbons (1949) 78 CLR 313	146, 153
Wright v Macadam [1949] 2 KB 744	131
Zafropoulos v Recchi [1978] SASR 5	115

Table of Statutes

Uganda

Access to Roads Act, 1969	82, 135
Acquisition of Ginneries Ordinance, Ordinance 7 of 1952	157
Administrator Act (cap 140)	155
Ankole and Toro Landlord and Tenant Law, 1937	3
Ankole Landlord and Tenant Law, 1937	3
Assets of the Departed Asians (Amendment) Decree No. 12 of 1975	159, 161
Assets of the Departed Asians Decree, No. 27 of 1973	159, 161, 162, 164
Buganda Land Law, 1908	160
Busuulu and Envujjo Law 1928	2, 10, 14
Civil Procedure Rules	66, 75, 111
Companies Act	36
Contract Act cap 75	153
Cooperative Societies Ordinance No. 5 of 1946	156
Crown Lands (Declaration) Ordinance, 1922 (Revised Laws of Uganda 1951, cap 118)	49
Crown Lands Ordinance of 1903	3, 4, 9, 10
Crown Lands Ordinance, 1903	4
Declaration of Assets (Non-Citizen Asians) (Amendment) Decree, 1972	159
Declaration of Assets (Non-Citizen Asians) Decree 29 of 1972	159
Declaration of Assets (Non-Citizen Asians) Decree, No. 27 of 1972; Re-enacted as S.1 of Decree 27 of 1973	72, 132, 158, 159
Electricity Act, 1999	40, 132
Electricity Statute, 1999	159
Equitable Mortgages Ordinance 1912	69
Expropriated Properties (Management) Order S.1 No. 78 of 1998	166
Expropriated Properties (Management) Order S.1 No.57 of 1995	166
Expropriated Properties (Repossession and Disposal) Regulations, No. 6 of 1983	165
Expropriated Properties Act, No. 9 of 1982	82, 160, 161, 162, 163, 165
Finance Act 1982	71
Forest Act (cap 246)	38, 82
Immigration Act, 1969	158
Interpretation Act (cap 16)	50
Judicature Act, 1967	106, 108
Judicature Statute, 1996 (Statute No. 13 of 1996)	1, 56, 83, 108, 109, 155
Land Acquisition Act 1965 (cap 14)	39, 40, 41, 42
Land Act, 1998	1, 6, 12, 25, 26, 27, 32, 44, 69, 80, 116, 152
Land Transfer Act (cap 202)	2
Legal Notice No. 1 of 1971	160
Limitation Act (cap 70)	10, 12, 13, 61, 62, 63, 64, 65, 66, 67, 68, 78
Lint Marketing Board Ordinance No. 33 of 1949; and subsequently Ordinance 16 of 1959 (cap 234, Laws of Uganda, 1964]	156

Statute	Pages
Magistrates Act	44
Mining Act (cap 248)	38, 51
Mortgage Decree 1974	116, 117, 118, 119, 120, 121, 122, 123, 124, 125, 128
Mortgage Decree No 17 of 1974	116, 124
National Environmental Statute, 1995	38, 82
National Trading Corporation Act, No 18 of 1966	157
National Trust Decree, 1971	162
Partnership Act (cap 86)	148
Properties and Business (Acquisition) Decree, 1972	194, 196, 198, 204
Properties and Business (Acquisition) Decree, No. 12 of 1975	159, 161, 162, 167
Public Land (Compensation for Resumption) Act	5
Public Lands Act, 1962 (cap 201)	4
Registration of Titles Act	1, 4, 9, 80, 88, 103, 118, 123, 125, 144, 150, 152, 153
Registration of Titles Ordinance 1908	69, 70, 95
Road Act (cap 345)	80
Sale of Goods Act (cap 79)	137
Statutory Instruments Nos. 169 and 174 of 1972	159
Succession Act (cap 139)	155
The African Loans Fund Act, (cap 164)	157
The Expropriated Properties (Management & Disposal) Order S.1 No.32 of 1996	203
The Expropriated Properties (Reversion) Order S.1 No. 33 of 1996	203
The Immigration (Cancellation of Entry Permits and Certificate of Residence) (Amendment) Decree No. 30 of 1972	158
The Immigration (Cancellation of Entry Permits and Certificates of Residence) Decree No. 17 of 1972	158
The National Housing Corporation Act, (cap 321)	157
The Uganda Development Corporation Act, (cap 319)	157
Trade (Licensing) Act, Act 14 of 1969	157
Trustee and Bankruptcy Act (cap 71)	112
Trustees Act (cap 142)	155
Uganda Citizenship and Immigration Control Act, 1999	36
Uganda Credit and Savings Bank Ordinance 20 of 1950	156
Uganda Order in Council of 1902	82
Uganda Wildlife Statute,1996	38
Water Statute 1995	38, 40, 80, 130, 131, 132

Australia

Statute	Pages
Real Property Act 1900 (New South Wales)	72
Stamp Act, 1894 (Queensland)	74
Transfer of Land Act, 1893 (Western Australia)	88, 136, 141
Transfer of Land Act, 1915 (Victoria)	69
Transfer of Land Act, 1954 (Victoria)	72

Kenya

Registered Land Act (cap 300)	137, 144
Registration of Titles Act (cap 281)	79, 79, 112, 133

Papua New Guinea

Simultaneous Deaths Act (cap 332)	146

United Kingdom

Conveyance and Law of Property Act, 1881	106
Distress Act, 1688	105
Distress Amendment Act, 1888	105
Grantees of Reversion Act, 1540	103
Judicature Act of 1873	56
Law of Property Act, 1925	136, 146, 154
Limitation Act 1939	61
Partition Acts 1539 and 1540	153
Partition Acts of 1868 and 1876	154
Statute of Anne of 1705	152

List of Abbreviations

AC	Appeal Cases (English Law Reports)
All ER	All England Law Reports
ALR	Australian Law Reports
Ch	Law Reports, Chancery Division [1891]-
ChD	Law Reports, Chancery Division (1875-90)
CLR	Commonwealth Law Reports (Australia)
EA	East African Law Reports
EACA	Law Reports of the Court of Appeal for East Africa
ER	English Reports
FLR	Federal Law Reports (Australia)
HCB	High Court of Uganda Bulletin (Digest)
KALR	Kampala Law Reports
KLR	Kenya Law Reports
LA	Land Act, 1998 (U)
MD	Mortgage Decree 1974 (U)
NLR	Nigeria Law Reports
NSWLR	New South Wales Reports (Australia)
NZLR	New Zealand Law Reports
PNGLR	Papua New Guinea Law Reports
QB (KB)	Law Reports, Queen's Bench Division
Qd R	Queensland Reports (Australia)
RTA	Registration of Titles Act (cap 205) (U)
SASR	South Australian State Reports
SR (WA)	State Reports of Western Australia
ULR	Uganda Law Reports
VR	Victorian Reports (Australia)
WLR	Weekly Law Reports (UK) Statutes

1

Introduction and Historical Background

SOURCES OF UGANDAN LAND LAW

The sources of Ugandan land law are the Constitution of the Republic of Uganda, 1995, various statutes, customary law, the common law and principles of equity. The Constitution lays down certain fundamental principles with regard to land ownership.[1] Since the Constitution is the supreme law of the country any other law or custom which is inconsistent with its provisions is void to the extent of the inconsistency.[2] With respect to statutory sources of land law the most important are the *Land Act,* 1998 and the *Registration of Titles Act* (cap 205). The *Land Act* mainly deals with land ownership, land administration, and resolution of land disputes.[3] The *Registration of Titles Act,* as its title suggests, deals with the registration and transfer of titles to land.[4]

Customary law constitutes an important source of land law. Customary land law mainly applies to land owned under customary law. Section 28 of the *Land Act* provides that decisions in respect of land held under customary land tenure shall be determined in accordance with the customary law of the community concerned. However, the section precludes the application of any customary practices that discriminate against children, women, and people with disabilities contrary to articles 33, 34 and 35 of the Constitution. The *Judicature Statute*, 1996 (Statute No. 13 of 1996), also empowers the courts to apply and enforce the observance of customary practice for as long as it is not repugnant to natural justice, equity and good conscience and provided it is not inconsistent with any written or applied law.[5] For example, in *Babiruga v Karegyesa and others,*[6] the High Court declined to enforce an alleged Kikiga custom, which said that land formerly cultivated by a child's mother upon her death automatically passes to the children and does not revert to the husband. Karokora J, as he then was, said that such custom was repugnant to natural justice, equity and good conscience because it deprived the man, as head of the family, of his power to control the family property. Moreover, in his Honour's view, it was tantamount to depriving him of his property without compensation contrary to the Constitution.

Customary law is also not applicable where the parties expressly or by implication from the nature of their transaction agreed that other law should regulate the transaction.[7] For example, in the case of *Waswa v Kikungwe,*[8] the court applied the general law of mortgages to a transaction 'resembling' a mortgage of land owned under customary tenure.

The common law is the residue source of land law. The *Judicature Statute* provides that subject to any written law and in so far as written law does not apply or extend to the matter the courts shall apply the common law and the doctrines of equity. The expression 'common law and the doctrines of equity' refers to the unwritten law of Uganda, other than customary law, administered by the High Court of Uganda.[9] Uganda's common law and equity is essentially the common law and the doctrines of equity as applied by the English courts prior to 1902. However, the common law applies in so far as the circumstances of Uganda and of its people permit and

[1] These principles are discussed below.
[2] Article 2 (2) of the Constitution.
[3] The *Land Act* is discussed in detail in Chapter 2.
[4] Provisions of the Act are discussed in Chapter 5.
[5] Section 17 (1), *Judicature Statute.*
[6] D.R. CA No MKA 13 of 1993 (unreported).
[7] Section 17 (2), *Judicature Statute.*
[8] (1952-56) 7 ULR 1
[9] Section 17(5), *Judicature Statute.*

subject to such qualifications as the circumstances may render necessary.[10] Both the common law and principles of equity are still a very important source of Ugandan land law.

Background to the tenure systems

At the time Uganda became an independent state, on 9 October 1962, there were four land tenure systems operating in the country. These were mailo, freehold, leasehold, and customary tenure.

Mailo tenure

Mailo tenure was a quasi-freehold tenure system, which was unique to the kingdom of Buganda. The tenure had its origins in the *1900 Uganda Agreement* between the British colonial administration and the chiefs of Buganda. Under the agreement, about half of the land in the kingdom of Buganda was allocated to chiefs and notables as their private property in perpetuity and the rest of the land became crown land. The allocations were expressed in multiples or fractions of square miles. Hence, the term 'mailo', which is a Luganda language corruption of the English word 'mile', was adopted to describe this new system of land holding. Although initially only a few privileged people owned mailo land, gradually, through sale, donation and inheritance the land was subdivided and fragmented. As a result, by 1962 there were several thousand mailo landowners mainly owning small parcels. The parcels were registered and certificates of title issued to the owners under the *Registration of Titles Act* (cap 205).

The *Uganda Agreement* did not define the nature of mailo land. In practice, mailo land was regarded as an absolute grant in perpetuity akin to the common law freehold estate in fee simple.[11] The land was granted without any conditions of tenure. However, by subsequent legislation mailo land owners were prohibited from transferring or leasing their land to a non-indigenous Ugandan or to a religious organisation without prior authority of the *Lukiiko* (Buganda Council) and the governor.[12] Moreover, mailo land was made subject to the traditional and customary rights of *kibanja* (plot) holders.

Kibanja holders were peasants who had settled on the land as customary tenants with the consent of the mailo owner. The *Busuulu and Envujjo Law* 1928 regulated the rights and obligations of a *kibanja* owner or mailo holder. Under this law if a mailo owner allowed a person to settle on his or her land as a *kibanja* holder, the latter was deemed to enjoy an inheritable permanent right of occupancy subject to payment of a fixed annual rent. In *Lukwago v Bawa Singh and another,*[13] Bennett J said that 'it was the essence of the relationship between a mailo owner and the holder of a kibanja that the latter's right of occupancy inures for an indeterminate period and is heritable by his heir and successor'. A mailo owner could not evict a *kibanja* holder except where the land was required for a public purpose or for other good and sufficient cause, or if the holder left the land unattended for more than six months, but in all cases the eviction had to be sanctioned by a court.[14] For all purposes, a *kibanja* owner's title was as good as that of an owner under customary

---

10 Section 16 (2) (b) (i) and 16 (4) & (5).

11 In the final certificates issued to the original grantees they were described as 'absolute owners'. In official circles the tenure was commonly referred to as a 'freehold'. See Thomas and Spencer: *A History of Uganda Land and Survey Department* (Entebbe, Government Printer 1938), p. 68. Krishna Maini, *Land Law in East Africa* (Nairobi, OUP, 1967), pp. 73-74, argues that mailo tenure was an actual freehold.

12 *Buganda Land Law*, 1908. Also the *Land Transfer Act* (cap 202) barred non-Africans from acquiring any interest in land owned by an African without consent of the Minister. For discussion of this legislation see the case of *Kawalya-Kagwa v Registrar of Titles* [1974] EA 481.

13 [1959] EA 282 at 284.

14 Clause 11, *Busuulu and Envujjo Law.* See also *Lukwago v Bawa Singh and another* [1959] EA 282.

tenure. He or she could sell, pledge, or even mortgage it at will subject only to the condition that he or she had to introduce any new tenant to the mailo owner to whom he or she owed a duty to pay *busuulu.*[15]

Freehold tenure

At the time Uganda attained its statehood, three types of freeholds operated in the country. These were: freeholds created under the *Crown Lands Ordinance* of 1903, the 'native' freeholds of Ankole and Toro, and the 'adjudicated' freeholds.

With respect to the first mentioned freeholds, the *Uganda Order in Council* of 1902, and the *Crown Lands Ordinance* of 1903, gave the Governor extensive powers to dispose of crown land in freehold.[16] The legislation was enacted almost at the inception of the Protectorate with a view to paving way for European settlement. Until 1915, it was the administration's policy to grant crown land to Europeans in freehold, and the Baganda chiefs were actively lobbied to dispose of their mailo land to Europeans in freehold. However, in 1915 the Colonial Office in London instructed the governor to suspend the grant of crown land in freeholds to non-natives and instead grant leaseholds subject to development conditions. The ban was subsequently made a permanent feature of the colonial administration land policy in Uganda.[17] Therefore, though under the *Crown Lands Ordinance*, the Governor had the power to make grants of land in freehold in practice the power was very rarely used.

Native freeholds

The term 'native' freeholds referred to freehold tenure which was peculiar to the kingdoms of Toro and Ankole. These freeholds were granted by the British colonial administration pursuant to the 1900 *Toro Agreement* and the 1901 *Ankole Agreement* with the British. Under the agreements, approximately 255 square miles in each kingdom were allocated to the king and a few of the most senior chiefs in private ownership and 122 square miles were allocated to them as official estates. Unlike mailo, the freehold grants were made from crown land,[18] and were held subject to the *Crown Lands Ordinance*, 1903.[19] As in Buganda the land was gradually subdivided and fragmented into smallholdings. In addition, native freehold, like mailo land, was subject to the rights of customary tenants. Under the respective Ankole and Toro *Landlord and Tenant Law*, 1937, customary tenants on native freehold enjoyed inheritable permanent rights of occupancy subject to payment of a fixed nominal rent. Like their counterparts on mailo land, they could not be evicted without a court order.

Adjudicated freeholds

The adjudicated freeholds were created under the Kigezi, Bugisu and Ankole land registration pilot schemes. In 1955 the protectorate government announced proposals to encourage individual ownership of land amongst the indigenous people. These proposals were overwhelmingly rejected in most districts, as the indigenous people were suspicious of the administration's motives. However,

---

15 *Wamala v Musoke* (1920-29) 3 ULR 120. See also *Matambulire v Kimera* CA No 37 of 1972.

16 See Article 7 (3). 'Crown Land' included any land acquired by the crown through treaties with native rulers and land under control of the crown by virtue of the protectorate. The Crown Lands Ordinance, 1903 prescribed rules for dealing with crown land.

17 See Thomas and Spencer, *A History of Uganda Land and Surveys and of the Uganda Land and Survey Department* (Entebbe, Government Printer, 1938), pp. 52-55, and 63. See also Morris and Read, *Uganda the Development of its Laws and Constitution* p. 46.

18 Under Article 4 of the two Agreements all waste and uncultivated land in the territory was declared to be crown land.

19 See Morris and Read, *Uganda the Development of its Laws and Constitution*, supra, p. 341.

the proposals were eventually accepted in the district of Kigezi and subsequently in Ankole and Bugisu. The people in these districts accepted registration of individual titles mainly because of population pressure and the multiplicity of boundary disputes.[20] Pilot schemes were set up in the three districts to adjudicate individual title under customary law. Once the land was adjudicated the holders were issued with registerable freehold titles under the *Registration of Titles Act.*[21] The adjudicated freeholds were subject to the same legal regime as other ordinary freeholds.

Customary tenure

In pre-colonial Uganda, there were three broad customary land tenure systems.[22] These were communal or tribal tenure, clan tenure, and nomadic tenure.[23] In communal or tribal tenure systems, ownership of the land was vested in the ruler as owner or trustee of the land for members of the tribe. This tenure system was prevalent in Buganda, Bunyoro, Toro, and Ankole. Under clan tenure, ownership of land was organised according to clans as opposed to tribes. The clan tenure system was common, for example, in Acholi and Kigezi. Within the clan and tribal umbrella, specific individual or family rights were recognised to fields, agricultural products and homesteads.[24] The nomadic land tenure system was prevalent in Karamoja. In this system of tenure, grazing rights were vested in the entire members of the tribe with no specific rights vested in individuals.

Under the British protectorate administration all land in Uganda except mailo land was crown land either by virtue of the protectorate or by treaty[25] with the local rulers.[26] Customary land tenure was recognised but within limits. Under the *Crown Lands Ordinance*, 1903, indigenous Ugandans had a right to occupy any unalienated crown lands[27] outside Buganda and urban areas without prior licence or consent of the government in accordance with their customary law.[28] Nevertheless, legally the land occupied under customary tenure was regarded as unalienated crown land. Hence, under s. 33 of the *Crown Lands Ordinance*, the governor had the power to sell or lease such land to any other person. The only right the customary occupants had was to remain in occupation of the land until arrangements were made to re-allocate them some other land. These provisions were re-enacted in the 1962 *Public Lands Act* (cap 201),[29] which replaced the 1903 ordinance.

Therefore, at the time Uganda became an independent state, customary tenants on public land were tenants at will of the government with no legal protection against eviction. Where the government resumed the land, it had no legal obligation to compensate them for the land except for the loss of improvements made on the land such as buildings and crops.[30] The legal status of customary land tenure remained the same even after Uganda became independent until, in 1969, parliament enacted the *Public Lands* Act, 1969. Under s. 24 of this Act land lawfully occupied by

---

[20] Obol-Ochola, ed, *Land Law Reform in East Africa* (1971, Law Development Centre), p. 270.

[21] See Morris and Read, *Uganda the Development of its Laws and Constitution*, supra, p. 339; Okec, 'Pilot Schemes for the Registration of Land titles in Uganda' in Obol-Ochola ed, *Land Law Reform in East Africa* (Kampala, Milton Obote Foundation, 1969) pp. 255-64.

[22] For a detailed analysis of customary tenure in Uganda, see Obol-Ochola, *Customary Land Law and the Economic Development in Uganda* (LL.M Dissertation, University of Dar es Salaam, 1971). The information below is mainly derived from his study.

[23] Obol-Ochola, *Customary Land Law and the Economic Development in Uganda, supra,* pp. 78 - 79.

[24] Ibid, p. 80.

[25] Treaty refers to the 1900 Buganda Agreement. 1900 Toro Agreement and 1900 Ankole Agreement.

[26] Article 7 (3) *Uganda Order in Council*, 1903. See also the *Crown Lands (Declaration) Ordinance* 1922.

[27] 'Alienated' land was land granted in freehold or leasehold, see s 22, *Public Lands Act*(cap 201).

[28] Section 20 and 24, *Crown Lands Ordinance* 1903. See also *Public Lands Act* (cap 201), s. 22.

[29] See Section 22.

[30] *Public Land (Compensation for Resumption) Act.*

customary tenants could no longer be alienated without the consent of the occupants. Any person applying for grant of public land had to state in the application whether or not the land was partly or wholly occupied by customary tenants and if so whether they had freely consented to the proposed alienation. In addition, the Act gave customary occupants of land a right to apply for a lease over the land they occupied.[31]

THE LAND REFORM DECREE

Under the *Land Reform Decree*, 1975, the military government of Idi Amin attempted to overhaul the country's land tenure system. The Decree declared all land in Uganda to be public land, centrally vested with the Uganda Land Commission. The Decree gave the commission the sole power to manage and allocate the land on behalf of the state.[32] Mailo, native freehold and all other freeholds were abolished and automatically converted into 99 years leaseholds for individual holders and 199 years leaseholds for public bodies.[33] The Decree imposed development conditions against all converted leaseholds including former mailo land. Failure to comply with the development conditions within a period of eight years could result in forfeiture of the land to the government.[34] Sale or sublease of the converted leases was prohibited except with the written consent of the Uganda Land Commission.[35] *Bibanja* holders or customary tenants on former mailo and native freehold became 'tenants at sufferance' on public land.[36] Under s. 3 (3) of the Decree, a lessee-on-conversion was given a right to evict such tenants if the lessee required the land for development purposes and subject to paying the tenants compensation for the improvements.

With respect to customary tenants elsewhere on public land, the Decree removed the legal protection that they previously enjoyed under the *Public Lands Act*, 1969. Like customary tenants of former mailo land, their tenure was reduced to tenancy at sufferance.[37] Henceforth, the Uganda Land Commission could at any time lease to another person any land occupied by a customary tenant without the consent of the occupant.[38] The government's only obligation was to pay compensation for any improvements on the land. The right of Ugandans to occupy unalienated public land by customary tenure without government grant or licence was also abolished by the Decree.[39] The occupation of public land without written permission of the prescribed authority was made an offence punishable by imprisonment of up to one year.[40] Customary tenants retained their right to sell or give away their tenure, provided that the transfer did not vest any title in the transferee except over improvements or developments on the land. Any agreement purporting to transfer customary tenure as if it were an actual title was void and constituted an offence punishable by up to two years imprisonment.[41]

---

31 Section 25, *Public Lands Act*,1969.

32 Section 1(1), *Land Reform Decree.*

33 Section 2, *Land Reform Decree.*

34 Section 8(1), *Land Reform Decree.*

35 Section 10, *Land Reform Decree.*

36 Section 3 (l), *Land Reform Decree.* At common law, the term 'tenant at sufferance' refers to a person who remains on the land without consent and without objection of the landowner. Such a person could be evicted at any time without notice see Megarry and Wade, *Law of Real Property,* supra, pp.42-43.

37 Section 3 (1), *Land Reform Decree*

38 Section 3 (2) *Land Reform Decree.*

39 Section 5 (1) *Land Reform Decree.*

40 Sections 5 and 6, *Land Reform Decree.*

41 Section 4, *Land Reform Decree.*

The object of the *Land Reform Decree* was to give the government greater control over land use and management. The government of the day, in its wisdom, felt that by making security of land tenure dependent upon land use it would promote agricultural development.[42] The immediate consequence of the Decree was confusion and apprehension in the general public.[43] For several reasons such as apathy, lack of funds, manpower and other logistical support, most of the Decree's provisions were never implemented.[44] Though technically for more than twenty years the Decree was the main source of Ugandan land law, in practice the Decree remained a dead letter in the statute books until the *Land Act*, 1998, formally repealed it.[45]

CONSTITUTIONAL REFORM OF LAND TENURE LAW

The 1995 Ugandan Constitution prescribes the underlying land law and tenure policy of the country. Article 237 of the Constitution declares that land in Uganda is vested in the citizens of Uganda, as opposed to the government, to be owned in freehold, mailo, leasehold and customary tenure. Non-citizens of Uganda may own land but only in leasehold. The Constitution reinstates mailo and freehold tenures, which were abolished by the *Land Reform Decree.* With respect to customary tenure, Article 237(4) provides that all Uganda citizens owning former public land under customary tenure have a right to acquire a certificate of ownership of their land and to convert their title to freehold in a manner prescribed by parliament. The Constitution also gave 'lawful' and '*bona fide*' occupants of mailo land, freehold and leasehold a moratorium against eviction until parliament enacted an appropriate law to regulate their relationship with the registered owners of such land.[46] Parliament was required to enact the appropriate legislation within a period of two years of its first session. The legislative provisions are contained in the *Land Act*, 1998, which is considered in the following chapter.

---

42 Parliament of Uganda Parliamentary Debates (hereafter '*Hansard*'), 20 June 1998, p.4048.

43 See generally the Makerere Institute of Social Research and the Land Centre of the University of Wisconsin Report: Land Tenure and Agricultural Development in Uganda (1989).

44 Final Report of the Technical Committee on the Recommendations Relating to Land Tenure Reform, October 1990, p.21.

45 Section 99, *Land Act*

46 Article 237 (8) and (9). The terms 'lawful' and '*bona fide*' occupants were left to be defined by Parliament, see Chapter 2.

2
Land Ownership

The *Land Act*, 1998, provides an institutional framework for the reform of land tenure law in Uganda. The Land Bill, formerly known as the Land Tenure and Control Bill, was debated for over five years before it was finally enacted as the *Land Act*.[1] The debate generated so much controversy throughout the country that the government at one time was fearful that it might lead to civil war. Fortunately, that did not eventuate. The controversy, which still lingers on, is hardly surprising given that in Uganda, as in most other developing countries, land is a very sensitive issue. Added to this the Bill came out at a time when Ugandans were enjoying relative freedom of speech, and many took advantage of it to speak out quite freely about the proposed land tenure reform.

In this chapter provisions of the Act are discussed under the following subheadings:

(i) Government land
(ii) Freehold
(iii) Leasehold
(iv) Mailo land
(v) Customary tenure
(vi) Ownership of land by non-citizens

Government land

Previously, all land in Uganda was public land centrally vested with the Uganda Land Commission.[2] As a result of the land tenure law reform brought about by the Constitution and the *Land Act*, most land in Uganda is now privately owned in mailo, freehold and customary tenure. Government land is limited to the land that was in government use at the time the Constitution came into effect on 22 September 1995. Land in government use would include land on which there are government offices, buildings, schools, hospitals, police and military quarters. If the government wants any other land it has to purchase the land from willing sellers or by compulsory acquisition in accordance with the Constitution.[3] Since it was not a common practice to mark the land that was in government use, the demarcation of government land is likely to generate disputes with adjoining landowners and with district land boards.

Freehold tenure

Section 4(2) of the *Land Act*, defines 'freehold tenure' as a tenure that derives its legality from the Constitution and its incidents[4] from written law. As already seen, the Constitution states that freehold is one of the land tenure systems under which citizens of Uganda may own land.[5] The incidents of freehold tenure mentioned in the *Land Act* are perpetual existence and full ownership.[6]

---

1 The proposal to reform the land tenure system commenced in 1983 as part of the country's overall study of the Agriculture policy undertaken by the Makerere Institute of Social Research, in collaboration with the Land Centre of the University of Wisconsin. See *Hansard*, 20 June 1998, p.4042. Also the Report of the Uganda Constitutional Commission, chaired by Justice Odoki, 1992, was pivotal of the debate and outcome.

2 *Land Reform Decree* 1975, s 1(1).

3 See article 239 of the Constitution and s.43 of the *Land Act*.

4 The expression 'incidents' refers to rights that accrue to a holder of freehold land.

5 Article 237 (3). See also s. 3, *Land Act*.

6 Section 4(2)(a).

Section 4(2)(a) stipulates that freehold tenure may involve either a grant of land in perpetuity or for a lesser period, which may be subject to a stipulated condition. A freehold estate granted in perpetuity at common law is known as a fee simple absolute. It is the largest estate in terms of duration known to the common law. The term 'absolute' is used to distinguish it from modified fees such as a conditional fee simple.[7] The latter is a fee simple estate granted subject to a condition, which may or may not happen. Although such an estate has a potential for perpetual duration it may be terminated if the condition upon which it was granted is breached. For example, a grant of land to X on condition that he or she develops the land is a conditional freehold. If X fails to develop the land the grantor may terminate the estate.[8] The section also envisages grant of a freehold estate for life. A life estate is a freehold that terminates upon the death of the grantee.[9]

At common law, a holder of land in fee simple absolute had almost unlimited rights of ownership. To a certain extent this is also reflected in the *Land Act*. Section 4(2)(b) stipulates that subject to the law, a holder of land in freehold has full power of ownership. This includes the power to use and develop the land for any lawful purpose, to sell, dispose of by will, lease, mortgage and create rights and interests for other people in the land as he or she sees fit.[10] The provision expressly states that this list is not exhaustive of the rights of an owner of land in freehold. Unlike the *Land Reform Decree*, 1975, the Act does not impose any development conditions upon a holder of land in freehold.[11] This is a deliberate government policy. Experience with the *Land Reform Decree* had shown that development conditions were difficult if not impossible to enforce and invariably ineffective in promoting agricultural development of land.[12] The framers of the Act envisaged that the psychological sense of responsibility arising from ownership of freehold land would be strong enough incentive for landowners to develop their land without official coercion. They also expected that landowners who were unable or unwilling to use their land would freely dispose of it in an open market. Time will tell whether or not all this will eventuate.

The apparent underlying policy of the *Land Act* is for citizens of Uganda to own their land as freehold or mailo tenure. As is discussed below, the Act makes provision for the conversion of leases of former public land held by Ugandan citizens to freehold tenure subject to compliance with certain prescribed conditions. [13] The Act also provides for customary land tenure to be converted to freehold.[14]

LEASEHOLD TENURE

Leasehold tenure is a form of tenure whereby one party grants to another a right to exclusive possession of land for a specified period, usually though not necessarily, in return for a periodic payment of money called rent.[15] A lease can be granted for any duration except in case of a lease to a non-Uganda citizen. Section 41(3) of the *Land Act* limits the maximum period for which a lease can be granted to a person who is not a citizen of Uganda to ninety-nine years.

---

7 Gray, *Elements of Land Law* (2nd ed, London, Butterworths, 1993), p.85.

8 For example, under the *Crown Lands Ordinance*, 1903, freeholds were granted subject to development conditions, see s 9 of the Ordinance. See also s 20, *Public Lands Act*, 1969.

9 See Chapter 3.

10 However, see restrictions imposed on dealings affecting family land, Chapter 3. See also Article 242 of the Constitution.

11 However, the Act does not preclude the imposition of conditions on future grants of freeholds. See s. 4(2)(a) and 4(3).

12 See Makerere Institute of Social Research and the Land Tenure Centre, University of Wisconsin-Madison, USA, *Report on Land Tenure and Agricultural Development in Uganda* (June, 1989), pp. 108-111 *et seq*. See also the *Report of the Technical Committee on Land Tenure Reform* (June, 1993).

13 Section 29, *Land Act*. See below.

14 Section 10.

15 Sections 2 and 4(5), *Land Act*. The features of a lease are discussed in detail in Chapter 6.

Any owner of customary land[16], mailo or freehold may grant a lease to another person out of his or her land. The Uganda Land Commission and the district land boards also have the power to grant leases out of the land vested in them.[17] Traditionally, leases in Uganda were granted subject to development conditions and other covenants, which imposed obligations on the tenant to use the land in a particular way.[18] Indeed, this was one of the main reasons for the conversion of mailo and freehold land to leases under the *Land Reform Decree*.[19] However, the *Land Act* does not impose any covenants or conditions in a lease. It is up to the parties to determine the terms of their lease. In practice, it is most unlikely that a landowner, especially the Uganda Land Commission or district land board, would grant a lease without imposing development conditions or some other land use covenants. Subject to the terms of the lease, a lessee is entitled to exercise all the powers of the landowner as are appropriate to the type of lease.[20]

Conversion of leases into freehold

Article 237(5) of the Constitution empowered parliament to enact a law whereby any lease that was granted to a Uganda citizen out of former public lands[21] might be converted into a freehold. The *Land Act* makes provision for the conversion of such leases. Section 29 of the Act prescribes a number of conditions that must be satisfied before a lease is converted to freehold. First, the lease must have been granted to a Uganda citizen[22] and had been current when the *Land Act* came into effect. Secondly, the applicant must satisfy the district board[23] that the lease was validly granted and that there were no customary tenants at the time the lease was granted. If there were such tenants, the board must be satisfied that they were duly compensated as required by the law. In addition, the board must be satisfied that the lessee has complied with all development conditions and other conditions upon which the lease was granted. Thirdly, s. 29(1)(f) prohibits a board from converting any lease to freehold tenure, if the size of the land over which the lease is held exceeds one hundred hectares, unless the board is satisfied that it is in the public interest that such lease should be so converted.

Section 29(2) provides that where a board approves the conversion of a lease held over land which exceeds a hundred hectares, the conversion shall not be effective until the applicant pays the market value as determined by the Chief Government Valuer for the new interest. It follows that, if the land does not exceed one hundred hectares, the board should not charge the lessee for the new interest. The conversion is completed by appropriate registration under the *Registration of Titles Act*. Upon conversion, any sublease over the subject land it is automatically upgraded to a lease.[24]

---

16 See s. 9(2(a), *Land Act.*

17 See ss. 54 (c), 61 (2)(c) and 70, *Land Act.*

18 See for example, ss. 15-16, *Crown Lands Ordinance*, 1903.

19 See above.

20 Section 5 (e), *Land Act.* The general law applicable to all leases is discussed below in chapter 6.

21 These are leases which were granted by a former controlling authority (either the Uganda Land Commission or a statutory body such as an Urban Council) under the *Public Lands Act*, 1969 or its predecessor, see s 2 *Land Act.*

22 It is not very clear whether 'granted' refers to the original grant or includes a situation where the lease was originally granted to a non-citizen but the current lessee is a Ugandan. The use of the term 'granted to' instead of 'held by' a Ugandan suggests that parliament intended the former interpretation rather than the latter.

23 Under s. 60(1)(c) of the *Land Act*, the district land board in which the land is situated is deemed to be the lessor.

24 Section 29(3)

Mailo tenure

Section 4(4) of the *Land Act,* describes 'mailo tenure' as a form of tenure which derives its legality from the Constitution and its incidents from written law. As we have seen, the Constitution declares mailo as one of the four land tenure systems in Uganda. From a legal perspective, mailo tenure is virtually freehold tenure. Mailo tenure, like freehold tenure, entails holding registered land in perpetuity.[25] Section 4(4)(c) provides that subject to the customary and statutory rights of 'lawful' or *'bona fide'* occupants of the land, a mailo owner is entitled to enjoy all powers of ownership of a freehold owner. Mailo land may also be subject to conditions, restrictions and limitations, which may affect its incidents of tenure just like freehold tenure. It is suggested that the only legally significant difference between freehold and mailo tenure is that mailo is subject to customary and statutory rights of lawful or *bona fide* occupants of the land.[26]

'Lawful' and *'bona fide'* occupants

As we have seen, the *Land Reform Decree*, 1975, empowered mailo owners to evict customary tenants from their land if the landowners required the land for economic development. Also, under the general law of torts, subject to the *Limitation Act* (cap 70), a landowner was entitled to evict at any time a person who occupied his or her land without the landowner's consent. Hence, potentially thousands of ordinary people who were in occupation of mailo land as customary tenants or squatters were at a risk of possible eviction by landowners. During the deliberations that led to the promulgation of the 1995 Constitution, many representatives in the Constituent Assembly were apprehensive that landowners might evict these people *en masse,* and this might lead to social unrest. To forestall the problem article 237(8) of the Constitution provides that all persons in 'lawful' or *'bona fide'* occupation of mailo, freehold or leasehold land shall enjoy security of tenure until parliament enacted an appropriate legislation regulating the relationship between such occupants and the registered proprietors. The provision was intended to be a temporary measure pending the enactment of the appropriate legislation within a period of two years of the first session of parliament.[27] Because the debate of this matter was contentious, and threatened the making of the Constitution, the Constituent Assembly left it to parliament to define the terms 'lawful' and *'bona fide'* occupant.[28]

'Lawful' occupant

Under section 30 (1) of the *Land Act*, the term 'lawful occupant' has three meanings. First, it means persons occupying land by virtue of the *Busuulu and Envujjo Law* of 1928, or the respective Toro and Ankole landlord and tenant laws of 1937. Effectively these are customary *bibanja* (plots) owners on mailo land and native freehold land.[29]

Secondly, the term 'lawful occupant' means a person who entered the land with the consent of the registered owner and includes a purchaser. A registered owner is a person who is registered as proprietor of the land under the *Registration of Titles Act*.[30] The latter Act provides for the registration of mailo, freehold and leasehold land, but does not make provision for the registration of customary land or land vested in the government. Therefore, the second limb of the definition refers to a person who entered into occupation of mailo, freehold or leasehold land with the consent of the landowner. The key requirement of the provision is that the person must have entered into

---

[25] Section4(4)(a). It is noteworthy that this provision, unlike s.4 (2) (a), does not include the possibility of mailo tenure being for a period less than perpetuity.

[26] Section 4(4)(b) and (c).

[27] Article 237(9).

[28] *Hansard*, 23 June 1998, p. 4106.

[29] See Chapter 1

[30] Section 2, *Land Act.*

possession with the consent of the registered owner of the land. This obviously excludes a squatter. A licensee is also excluded by s.30(4) of the *Land Act*, which expressly states that a person who is on the land on the basis of a licence from the owner shall not be taken to be a lawful occupant.[31]

A literal interpretation of s. 30(1)(b) could include *any* tenant. For example, suppose that in 1990 Mukasa leased his land to Okello for a period of ten years at an annual rent of twenty thousand shillings. It is arguable that since Okello entered the land with Mukasa's consent, he is a lawful occupant within meaning of s. 30(1)(b). Similarly, it could be argued that all monthly tenants are lawful occupants under the Act. However, in our view, it would be preposterous to suggest that parliament could have intended that all tenants on registered land were lawful occupants and, accordingly, were tenants by occupancy under the *Land Act*.[32] Although the provision is not very clear it is submitted that in the context of the Act and the apparent underlying policy objectives the term lawful occupants was meant to apply only to persons who were in occupation of registered land with the consent of the owner without grant of any specific tenancy but in expectation that they would remain on the land for an indefinite period. A possible example is a licensee protected by the principle of proprietary estoppel.[33] This may arise in a situation, for example, where a landowner knowingly allows or encourages another person to build on the land thereby creating an expectation in the mind of that person that he or she will grant him or her an interest in the land. A court of equity may order the landowner to make good the developer's expectations, for example, by granting him or her an interest in the land as the court deems appropriate.[34] It is submitted that under the Act the person in our example would be a lawful occupant and protected by the provisions of the Act discussed below.

Section 30(1)(b) expressly states that the expression lawful occupant includes a purchaser.[35] Presumably, this refers to a person who had purchased or agreed to purchase certain land from the registered owner but by the time the Act came into effect title had not been transferred to him or her. At common law, if a seller of land allowed a purchaser to enter into possession prior to settlement, in the absence of any agreement to the contrary, the purchaser was presumed to be a tenant at will of the seller.[36] Under the *Land Act*, such a purchaser is deemed a tenant by occupancy.[37] Section 30(1)(b) is silent on whether to qualify as a tenant by occupancy the purchaser must have paid the agreed purchase price. The probable inference is that payment is not a requisite.

The third meaning of 'lawful occupant' is a person who was in occupation of certain land under customary tenure but whose tenancy was not disclosed or compensated for by the registered owner when he or she applied for a public lease over the land.[38] As we have seen, under s. 24 of the *Public Lands Act*, 1969, an applicant for a lease was required to disclose whether or not the land was occupied by customary tenants, and if it were so, whether they had consented to the alienation

---

31 Under the general law, a 'licence' is permission given to a person to enter another's land for some specified purpose which otherwise would be a trespass (*Thomas v Sorrell* (1673) Vaugh 330; 124 ER 1098 at 1109). Unlike a lessee, a licensee has no right to exclusive possession, see *City Council of Kampala v Mukibi* [1967] EA 368.

32 The meaning of tenancy by occupancy is discussed below.

33 Unlike a bare licence, a licence protected by the doctrine of proprietary estoppel creates an entitlement to property rights in or over land, see *Western Fish Products Ltd v Penwith District Council* [1981] 2 All ER 204.

34 See e.g., *Babiruga v Karegyesa and others* D.R CA No MKA 13 of 1993 (unreported).

35 The reason for inclusion of a purchaser in the definition of a lawful occupant is not very clear. If a person had purchased the land why should he or she be a tenant by occupancy and not the actual owner of the land?

36 *Wheeler v Mercer* [1957] AC 416 at 425,435.

37 But it seems that the definition of lawful occupant could include a purchaser who was not in occupation.

38 Section 30(1)(c)*Land Act*.

of the land. In addition, under the *Land Reform Decree,* 1975, where public land occupied by customary tenants was leased to another person, the customary tenants were entitled to compensation for their improvements on the land.[39] Under the *Land Act,* such occupants are deemed tenants of the registered owner by occupancy, and accordingly, are protected by the Act.

***Bona fide* occupant**

The term '*bona fide* occupant' has two meanings. First, it refers to a person who before the coming into effect of the 1995 Constitution had occupied or improved certain land without being challenged by the registered owner of the land or by the agent of the owner.[40] Unlike a 'lawful occupant', a *bona fide* occupant entered the land without the consent of the landowner. So essentially, a *bona fide* occupier is a trespasser or a squatter. Although the words '*bona fide*' are used to describe the occupier there is no requirement in the provision that he or she must have entered the land in good faith.[41] The motive of the person when he or she entered the land is not material.

The period of twelve years of occupation corresponds with the twelve-year limitation period prescribed by the *Limitation Act* (cap 70) for recovery of land.[42] It should be stressed that the provision requires that the person (or his or her predecessor in title)[43] must have been on the land, unchallenged by the registered owner, for a complete period of twelve years. Accordingly, if the landowner establishes that at any time before expiration of the twelve-year period[44] he or she challenged the person claiming to be a *bona fide* occupier, the provision would not apply.[45] What constitutes the requisite challenge for this purpose is not very clear. The term 'challenge' is not defined anywhere in the Act. According to both legal and English language dictionaries, the word has various meanings. They include the following: 'to object or take exception to' 'lay claim to', 'demand as a right', and 'formally question the legality of some act'.[46] It is submitted that if at any time during the twelve-year period the registered owner sued the occupier for trespass that would constitute sufficient challenge for the purposes of the provision. The same would be the case where the landowner physically evicted or attempted to evict the intruder from the land. However, the legal position is less certain in several other situations. For example, suppose the landowner had reported the intruder to the authorities, such as the local council, or warned the intruder verbally or in writing to stay off his or her land, would the courts treat such acts as sufficient assertion of ownership for this purpose?[47] In our view, they should, but it remains to be seen how the courts will interpret the provision. A narrow interpretation would favour the squatters and a wide interpretation would favour the landowners.

---

39 Section 3(3)(b)(iv).

40 Section 30 (2), *Land Act.*

41 In the original bill, a *bona fide* occupier included a person who occupied or developed land genuinely believing that the registered owner was not available. That provision was omitted from the final Bill, see *Hansard*, 20 June 1998, pp. 4052-4053, 4058.

42 Section 6 of the *Limitation Act,* provides that no action to recover land can be instituted after expiration of twelve years from the date the action accrued. This provision is discussed in Chapter 4.

43 The right of a *bona fide* occupant is transferable. See s. 30(5), *Land Act.*

44 It is submitted that a challenge made after twelve years would be ineffective.

45 Mr Mutyaba MP, chairperson, Sessional Committee on Lands, Water and Environment, said that evidence of even a single challenge was enough to re-establish the owner's rights on the land, see *Hansard*, 20 June 1998.

46 *Black's Law Dictionary* (5th ed, New York, West Publishing Co, 1979); *The Oxford English Dictionary*, vol.11 (2nd ed. Oxford, Clarendon Press, 1989).

47 Under the *Limitation Act* , the only way an owner can stop the running of the limitation time is by either suing for recovery of the land or by physically retaking possession. Constant protests not amounting to physical repossession of the land do not suffice to stop the limitation time running against the landowner (*Nambalu Kintu v Efulaimu Kamira* CA No 26 of 1973 (unreported); [1975] HCB 221). See below Chapter 4. It is thought that the expression 'challenge' entails a less stringent requirement.

As we shall presently see,[48] under the *Limitation Act* (cap 70) where a squatter remains in adverse possession of any land for a period of at least twelve years the owner is precluded from evicting him or her. By operation of law, the squatter becomes the owner of the land.[49] There are some similarities between the requirements for a *bona fide* occupant and for acquisition of title by adverse possession. In both instances, the person in occupation must have entered the land without the authority of the owner and remained in occupation unchallenged for at least a period of twelve years. However, they differ in other respects. First, under the *Limitation Act* the twelve-year limitation period may be extended for up to thirty years where the landowner was under disability.[50] There is no provision in the *Land Act* for extension of the twelve- year period. Secondly, a *bona fide* occupant is deemed under the Act to be a tenant – by occupancy of the registered owner.[51] In contrast, under the *Limitation Act* after expiration of the requisite period not only is title of the landowner extinguished but also the intruder becomes the absolute owner of the land by operation of law.[52] Thirdly, the term *bona fide* occupier only applies to a person who had been in occupation for at least twelve years before the coming into effect of the 1995 Constitution. There is no time limit with respect to adverse possession. For example, suppose that Zake is the owner of the subject land. In 1985, Kasoma settled on the land without Zake's consent and has remained there since unchallenged by Zake. Kasoma would not qualify as a *bona fide* occupant because in 1995 he had not been in occupation of the land for twelve years.[53] However, Kasoma could claim ownership of the land by adverse possession under the *Limitation Act*, if by 1997 he were still in occupation of the land.

It is possible for a person to satisfy the requirements for a *bona fide* occupier under the *Land Act* and adverse possessor under the *Limitation Act*. It is submitted that in that event the person has a choice to assert his or her claim to the land either under the *Land Act* or the *Limitation Act*. For example, in our illustration if Kasoma had settled on the land in 1982 he would be entitled to claim the land as a *bona fide* occupier. Alternatively, he would be equally entitled to claim absolute ownership of the land in fee simple on the basis of adverse possession and the operation of the *Limitation Act*.[54] In our opinion, the *Land Act* does not preclude the doctrine of adverse possession. It is further submitted that the provisions of the *Land Act* cannot be construed so as to override a title acquired by adverse possession, because that would be tantamount to deprivation of property without compensation contrary to article 26 (2) of the Constitution.

The second meaning of a '*bona fide* occupant is a person (or a successor in title of such a person)[55] who had been settled on land by the government or its agent including a local authority.[56] Unlike the first definition of a *bona fide* occupant, in this instance there is no requirement that the person must have settled on the land for a particular minimum period. The main object of this provision was to protect from eviction hundreds of landless people, including asylum seekers who had been settled on certain land by the government under the Ranch Restructuring Scheme.[57] Most of the land was former public land owned in leasehold by various individual ranchers. Section 30(3)(a) prescribes that where the government settled people on land belonging to any person it must pay compensation to the registered owner of the land. The reason for this requirement

---

48 See below Chapter 4.

49 See eg *Nambalu Kintu v Efulaimu Kamira* CA No 26 of 1973 (unreported); [1975] HCB 221.

50 Section 22(1)(d), *Limitation Act*.

51 See below Chapter 4.

52 Sections 6 and 17, *Limitation Act*. See further discussion below, Chapter 4.

53 See also below discussion of persons who do not qualify as *bona fide* occupants.

54 See Chapter 4.

55 Section 30(5).

56 Section 30(2)(b), *Land Act*.

57 *Hansard*, 20 June 1998, p.4054.

was to avert possible legal challenge of the provision on the grounds that it deprives the ranchers of their property without compensation contrary to article 26(2) of the Constitution.[58] Compensation must be paid within a period of five years from the date the Act came into effect.[59]

Non-*bona fide* occupant

Section 31(1) of the *Land Act,* imposes an obligation on a person who does not satisfy the requirements of a *bona fide* occupier to initiate negotiations with the registered owner to regularise his or her occupancy. Section 31(2) provides that if the parties fail to reach an agreement within a prescribed time either party may invite a mediator[60] to assist them in their negotiations. The mediator may accept the invitation if he or she is satisfied that there are reasonable prospects that the parties will reach a compromise.[61] The object of the provision for negotiation was to avert possible mass eviction by the landowners of persons who did not qualify as *bona fide* occupants, which could result in social unrest.[62] It should be stressed, however, that there is nothing in the provision to compel a landowner to let such occupants remain on the land. The expectation of the legislature is that the occupier and the landowner would between themselves come to some form of compromise, which may result in a formal contract of sale or lease of the land to the occupier.[63] Therefore, it would seem that where the parties fail to agree, with or without mediation, there is nothing to stop the landowner from evicting the occupier if the former does not vacate the land voluntarily.[64]

It is worth stressing that the above provision only applies to persons who entered the land prior to the coming into effect of the 1995 Constitution. Any person who thereafter occupied or in future occupies another's land without permission of the landowner is not protected by the Act. The landowner may evict such a person at any time without notice.

Tenant by occupancy

The *Land Act* deems a *bona fide* or lawful occupant of land to be a tenant by occupancy of the registered owner of the land.[65] A tenant by occupancy holds the land subject to such terms and conditions as are stated in the Act or may be prescribed by the minister.[66] As is discussed below, for as long as a tenant by occupancy complies with those terms and conditions he or she enjoys a secure tenure.[67]

Rent payment

A tenant by occupancy is required to pay to the registered owner of the land an annual nominal ground rent as determined by the relevant district land board.[68] A tenant or landowner aggrieved by the board's determination is entitled to appeal against the decision to the land tribunal, which

---

58 *Ibid.*

59 Section 30(3)(c).

60 Section 90 of the Act provides for the establishment of the institution of mediator. See Chapter 3.

61 Section 31(3).

62 *Hansard*, 20 June 1998, pp.4053, 4132.

63 *Hansard*, 20 June 1998, p. 4058, per Mr Mutyaba MP.

64 There is nothing in the provision to compel the landowner to negotiate (or negotiate in good faith) with the occupant (compare with s. 39(4)). See *Hansard,* 24 June 1998, p. 4132.

65 Section 32 (1). Also s. 2 (definitions of 'tenant by occupancy').

66 Sections 32(2) and 94(d).

67 Section 32 (1) & (2).

68 Section 32 (3). There was a lot of controversy whether tenants by occupancy should pay ground rent. In parliament, some members wanted payment of rent to be abolished altogether whilst other members wanted to impose an economic rent. Eventually, it was agreed to impose a nominal rental, as was the case under the *Busuulu and Envujjo* law 1928. See generally *Hansard,* 22 June 1998, pp. 4074 - 4976, 4079, 4083 and 4090. See also Hansard 23 June 1998, pp. 4121 and 4125.

may reverse, vary or confirm the decision.[69] However, the Act prescribes that no tenant by occupancy shall be required to pay ground rent in excess of one thousand shillings per annum irrespective of the size of the land or its location.[70] Hence, whether a *kibanja* is in Kampala or in Mubende the maximum ground rent payable by the holder is one thousand shillings. The same is true whether the size of the land is one acre or five acres. Parliament imposed only a nominal rent mainly because it did not want to overburden tenants by occupancy with payment of commercial rent, which the vast majority of them could not afford to pay and would certainly have led to social unrest. It was precisely for the same reason that the colonial administration fixed the *busuulu* at eight shillings per annum in 1928. The busuulu remained the same throughout the colonial period and after Uganda became an independent state. By the time the payment of *busuulu* was abolished by the *Land Reform Decree,* 1975, it had ceased to be an economic rent and most mailo owners had long stopped collecting it.

Although many mailo owners feel that the Land Act unfairly deprived them of their source of income, in our view they are no worse off than they were prior to the Act. The main purpose of rent payment is not to provide income to the mailo owner; but rather, it functions as an acknowledgment by the kibanja holder of the mailo owner's superior title.[71] This recognition, albeit symbolic, is essential for maintaining the fabric of society, especially in a hierarchical society like Buganda.[72] The Act provides that the ground rent may be revised every five years by regulations made under the Act.[73]

Where a tenant by occupancy defaults in payment of ground rent for a period exceeding two years, the registered owner is entitled to serve on him or her notice to show cause why the tenancy should not be terminated. The notice must be in the prescribed form and a copy forwarded to the relevant land committee.[74] If the tenant disputes the notice, he or she may refer the matter to the land tribunal within a period of six months after the date of service.[75] Where the tenant does not challenge the notice within the prescribed period or pay the outstanding rent within a period of one year from the date of the notice, then the landowner may apply to the land tribunal for an order to terminate the tenancy for non-payment of rent.[76] Section 33 prescribes the powers and matters to be taken into account by the tribunal when determining an application for termination of a tenancy for non-payment of rent. The tribunal is required to ascertain that the applicant is the registered owner of the subject land or his or her duly authorised agent.[77] The tribunal must also be satisfied that the registered owner has not himself or herself been in breach of the tenant's rights. In particular, the landowner must not have interfered with the tenant's quiet enjoyment of the land.[78] Moreover, the tribunal must examine the circumstances surrounding the tenant's failure to pay. For example, it should establish whether the tenant had made any efforts to pay, whether the reason for failure to pay is lack of money or he or she has money but simply refuses to pay. The tribunal is also required to examine whether the tenant had abandoned the land leaving behind his or her dependants with no means of support and similar matters. In other words, the tribunal must take into account all relevant surrounding circumstances, which would assist it to come to a fair decision.[79]

---

69 Section 32(4).

70 Section 32(5).

71 *Hansard,* 24 June 1998, p. 4125.

72 *Hansard,* 22 June 1998, p. 4090, per Mrs Bitamazire MP.

73 Section 2 (8). Parliament rejected a proposal for rent to be varied from region to region and for more frequent rent review, see *Hansard*, 20 June 1998, p.4058.

74 Section 32 (6).

75 Section32(7).

76 *Ibid.*

77 Section 33(1)(a).

78 Section 33(1)(b). Compare with the obligations of a landlord under the general law, discussed in Chapter 6.

79 Compare the courts' power to grant relief from forfeiture of a lease for non-payment of rent, see Chapter 6.

After giving both parties a fair opportunity to be heard, the land tribunal may, at its discretion, make any one of the following three orders.[80] First, it may direct the tenant to pay the amount due either in a lump sum by a particular date or in instalments over such a period as it shall set. Secondly, the tribunal may make an order granting the application to terminate the tenancy but suspend the operation of the order to some future date. The object of suspension is to give the tenant an opportunity to pay the outstanding money subject to such terms as the tribunal might stipulate. Thirdly, the tribunal may grant the order for termination of the tenancy. Where the tribunal makes a termination order, it must give the tenant at least six months from the date of the order to vacate the land. The tribunal at its discretion may grant the order subject to any other conditions, such as a requirement for the tenant to pay the landlord's court expenses, damages, and any other compensation it sees fit.

From the foregoing, it is quite clear that the land tribunal has a wide discretion to determine the appropriate remedy where the tenant defaults in payment of the annual ground rent. It is submitted that the underlying legislative policy is for the tribunal not to terminate a tenancy by occupancy for non-payment of rent except in exceptional circumstances. This is also the policy adopted by the courts under the general law with respect to ordinary leaseholds.[81]

Right of a tenant by occupancy to enter into transactions

The right of a tenant by occupancy constitutes a proprietary interest in land. Just like other proprietary interests, a tenancy by occupancy is inheritable[82] and, subject to the provision of the Act, it could be sold, sublet, or pledged[83] by the holder of the right of occupancy.[84] Moreover, a tenant by occupancy may create third party rights in respect of his or her occupancy,[85] sub-divide, and undertake any other lawful transaction in respect of the occupancy.[86] However, the power of a tenant to deal with his or her right of occupancy is subject to the approval of the registered owner of the land. Section 35(3) states that prior to entering into any deals affecting the land the tenant must apply to the landowner in a prescribed form for his or her consent to the transaction.[87] The landowner has up to six weeks from the date of receipt of the application in which to respond.

The landowner may approve the transaction with or without attachment of conditions or refuse outright.[88] Where the landowner refuses or imposes conditions which are unacceptable to the tenant, or fails to communicate his or her decision to the tenant within a period of six weeks the tenant may appeal to the tribunal.[89] The tribunal has a wide range of powers that it may use in this regard. It may dismiss the appeal, allow the transaction without any conditions, or subject it to any conditions, including imposing fresh conditions. The land tribunal may also at its discretion adjourn the proceedings to allcw further negotiations between the parties.

Where the landowner gives his or her consent to a transaction, the consent must be communicated to the tenant in the prescribed form duly signed by the landowner.[90] A copy of the consent signed by the landowner or secretary to the tribunal (if the tribunal gives the consent following an appeal) must be sent to the recorder. Under s. 35(8), the recorder must maintain in the prescribed form a record of consent. Section 35(9) declares that a transaction entered into by a

---

80 Section 33 (2).

81 See Chapter 6.

82 Section 35(2).

83 'Pledge' normally applies to personal property. It is where a debtor hands over goods to a creditor as security for a loan. Probably similar rules would apply by analogy in respect of a tenancy by occupancy.

84 Section 35(1).

85 For example, grant a licence to another person to cultivate part of the land or collect firewood.

86 Lawful transaction would include mortgage of the occupancy.

87 Note that there is no requirement for consent in case of inheritance of the right of occupancy, see s 35(2).

88 Section 35(4).

89 Section 35(5) & (6).

90 Section 35(4).

tenant without the requisite consent shall not be effective to pass any interest in land. The section specifically prohibits the recorder from making any entry of a transaction of which there is no consent in the prescribed manner. The object of this rather elaborate procedure is to eliminate areas of potential disputes between the parties over whether, for example, consent was given or not or the terms under which it was given. It is submitted that where a tenant by occupancy purports to transfer his or her land without prior consent or despite the landowner's refusal to give his or her consent to the transaction, the landowner is entitled to treat the purported transferee as a trespasser and to evict him or her. The legal position is less clear as to whether the breach would entitle the landowner to terminate the tenant's right of occupancy. Under the general law of leases, the landlord may terminate the lease if the tenant in breach of the lease agreement parts with possession without the landlord's consent.[91] It is thought that the legal position is different with respect to termination of a right of occupancy. The *Land Act* stipulates the circumstances in which a tenancy by occupancy may be terminated or terminates. As we have seen, a tenancy by occupancy may be terminated where the tenant defaults in payment of rent.[92] In addition, as we shall presently see, it terminates where the tenant voluntarily abandons the land.[93] The Act does not mention any other ground for termination of a tenancy by occupancy. In our view, parliament intended these to be the only grounds for termination of a tenancy by occupancy. Accordingly, it is submitted that where the tenant purports to transfer his or her occupancy to another without consent, the landlord has no power to terminate the tenant's right of occupancy unless the tenant abandons the land or defaults in payment of rent.[94]

Option to purchase

The *Land Act* gives a tenant by occupancy and the landowner a statutory right of first refusal to purchase each other's interest. Section 36(1) states that where a tenant by occupancy wishes to assign his or her right of occupancy, he or she must give the first option of purchasing it to the landowner. Section 36(2) gives a tenant by occupancy a similar right where the landowner wishes to assign the land.[95] Note that the provision only applies on a willing-seller willing-buyer basis. [96] The object of the provision is to give either party the first opportunity to negotiate to purchase where one of them decides to sell.

To facilitate the negotiations between the parties the person who wishes to sell must communicate the terms of the offer to the other party with sufficient details to be understood by the latter.[97] For example, where a tenant by occupancy wishes to sell his or her plot, he or she should inform the landowner of the terms of the sale such as the asking price, terms of payment, whether the sale excludes all or certain fixtures such as crops, iron-sheets and similar items. Upon receipt of the offer, the offeree has up to three months to reject, accept, or make such a response as would enable the parties to enter into 'meaningful' negotiations.[98] Where the parties enter into negotiations, if

---

[91] *City Council of Kampala v Mukibi* [1967] EA 368.

[92] Section 33.

[93] Section 38.

[94] For example, the tenant may abandon the land where the landowner evicts the person to whom he or she purported to transfer the occupancy.

[95] With respect, it is submitted that the draftsperson used the wrong legal terminology ('option to purchase') to describe the right of the parties. An option to purchase is a right given to a person to compel the owner of the land to sell it to him or her in accordance with the terms of the grant. The landowner has no choice where the holder of the option decides to exercise his or her right to buy. Section 36 does not give either party a right to force the other to sell. Rather, it gives them a right of pre-emption or a right of first refusal to buy, but only if the owner decides to sell. See Megarry and Wade, *Law of Real Property*, supra, pp.604-605.

[96] Section 36(3).

[97] Section 36(4).

[98] Section 36(5). This provision overrides the general law of contract where a counter offer is regarded as an outright rejection unless accepted by the offeror.

after three months they have not reached an agreement, then either party is free to refer the matter to the mediator to assist with the negotiations.[99] If, after three months of negotiations, the mediator is unable to assist the parties to reach an agreement, he or she must make a declaration to that effect. Thereafter, the party that is seeking to sell is free to dispose of the interest as he or she thinks fit.[100]

It is noteworthy that the above section does not expressly provide for the situation where the party to whom the offer is made ignores it or fails to respond within the prescribed three-month period.[101] The question is whether in such a case the person who makes the offer would be entitled to treat the other's silence as a rejection of his or her offer, and if so, whether he or she would be entitled to dispose of the land to any other person. It is suggested that if the landowner is the offeror he or she would be entitled to treat the tenant's silence as a rejection of the offer and, therefore, he or she could sell the land to any other person. The reason is that, apart from this provision, there is no requirement under the Act for the landowner to seek the tenant's consent to dispose of his or her land. The legal position is less clear on whether a tenant by occupancy could do the same. This is because under s. 35, as we have seen, a tenant by occupancy needs the consent of the landowner or of the tribunal prior to undertaking any transaction affecting his or her right of occupancy. Indeed, a transaction entered into without the requisite consent in the prescribed form is not effective to create any interest. It would seem that even if the landowner ignores or rejects the offer, the tenant must obtain the requisite consent prior to selling to another person otherwise the transaction would not be effective to transfer the interest.

Subdivision and/or co-ownership between tenant and registered owner

A registered owner and a tenant by occupancy may by mutual agreement subdivide the land over which the tenant has a right of occupancy so that each acquires exclusive occupancy or ownership of a portion or portions of that land.[102] The provision probably envisages a situation, for example, where a tenant may wish to relinquish part of his or her plot to the landowner in exchange for exclusive ownership over the part retained. Another possible example is where the landowner wishes to build on part of the land occupied by a tenant. He or she may negotiate with the tenant to surrender to him or her that part of the land in exchange for exclusive ownership over the remainder of the plot. The object of the above provisions is to facilitate the parties to negotiate a mutually convenient land settlement.

Instead of subdivision, the tenant and the landowner may agree to become co-owners of the land either in joint tenancy or tenancy in common.[103] Where they decide to become tenants in common they should stipulate in their agreement the shares of each party and any other terms of their agreement. Co-ownership would be the best option for the parties where the plot is too small for subdivision or where the parties wish to conduct a joint venture such as building a house for rent or commercial farming.

Where the parties subdivide the land or agree to become co-owners they must inform the Registrar of Titles accordingly. Section 37(2) of the *Land Act* provides that the parties must submit to the registrar documentary evidence of their agreement and, where applicable, the certified survey plans. Upon satisfaction that the parties have complied with all statutory requirements, the Registrar must make the appropriate entries on the certificate of title and issue to each party a fresh certificate. The registrar must also inform the recorder of the changes that have to be made on the certificate of occupancy or have it cancelled.

---

[99] Section 36(6).

[100] Section 36(7).

[101] Compare with s. 35 (5) and (6), with respect to the requirement for the landowner to give consent to a transaction. Failure to give consent within the prescribed period is regarded as a refusal.

[102] Section 37, *Land Act*.

It is submitted that where a plot is subdivided and each party is issued a certificate of title for its portion of the land, the effect is to extinguish prior existing rights and to create fresh rights. Thus, the former tenant by occupancy becomes an absolute owner in freehold or mailo of the portion of the land he or she retained. Likewise, the portion of the plot allotted to the landowner becomes his or hers absolutely freed from any claim by the previous tenant by occupancy. Where the parties agree to become co-owners of the land over which the tenant has a right of occupancy the nature of their interest depends on their agreement. For example, they may decide to co-own the tenant's plot as a 'plot'. On the other hand, they may agree to co-own the plot in freehold or mailo tenure. It is suggested that in order to avoid future disputes, when the parties submit their documents for registration the registrar should ensure that the documents not only state the nature of co-ownership but also the tenure under which the land is co-owned. Where the agreement is to co-own the plot as a plot, appropriate changes will be made to the certificate of occupancy. If the agreement is to co-own the plot in freehold, they will be registered as such and the certificate of occupancy cancelled accordingly.

Application for a certificate of occupancy

A tenant by occupancy may apply for a certificate of occupancy in respect of his or her plot. The certificate of occupancy is a registerable interest under the *Registration of Titles Act* (cap 205).[104] Section 34 of the *Land Act* provides that where a tenant wishes to acquire a certificate of occupancy he or she must make an application to the registered owner of the land for consent for the certificate to be issued. Upon receipt of the application, the landowner is required to forward it to the land committee[105] in the jurisdiction where the land is located. The committee's function is to determine, verify, and adjudicate any boundary disputes between the parties.[106] Section 34(2) states that the committee must nominate a day when it will meet both parties at the site of the land in question. The date appointed must not be earlier than three weeks and not more than three weeks from the date the landowner received the application. In adjudicating disputes, the land committee must observe the rules of natural justice.[107] That is to say it must not make a determination without first giving an opportunity to both parties to be heard. Secondly, the committee must not be biased or even appear to be biased in favour of or against either party. There is appearance of bias where, for example, a member of the committee is a relative or close friend of one of the parties. To avoid appearance of bias such member should not sit on the committee. Similarly, if a committee member has been involved in serious personal disputes with one of the parties, he or she should excuse himself or herself from the committee's deliberations.

Other than observance of the rules of natural justice, the committee is free to set its own procedure and is not bound by the ordinary rules of evidence. Thus, it could hear evidence that is otherwise inadmissible in court proceedings, call witnesses on its own motion and use evidence contained in official records or adduced in other proceedings.[108]

After the land committee makes its determination, it must inform both parties of the outcome. There is no provision for appeal against the committee's boundary determination. However, it is submitted that the land tribunal has the jurisdiction to review the committee's decision in accordance with the principles of administrative law.[109]

---

[104] See s. 2, *Land Act,* definition of 'registrable interest'. See also s. 34 (9).

[105] Land committees are established under s. 65 of the *Land Act.*

[106] It would seem from the provision that the Committee's power is only to adjudicate disputes over boundaries. It has no jurisdiction to determine other disputes, such as whether the applicant qualifies as a *bona fide* occupier.

[107] Section 34(3).

[108] Section 34.

[109] See the land tribunals' powers, s 77(2)(d).

Consent of the landowner

Section 34(5) provides that an applicant for a certificate of occupancy shall not be entitled to be issued with a certificate of occupancy if his or her rent is in arrears. Subject to this provision, s. 34(6) states that upon receipt of the committee's determination the landowner must immediately give his or her consent to the application. The consent must be given in the prescribed form.[110] If the landowner refuses or neglects to give his or her consent within a period of six months from the date he or she received the committee's determination, the tenant has a right to appeal to the land tribunal.[111] Under s. 34(7) the land tribunal has power to give consent for the grant of a certificate of occupancy.[112] It seems that parliament intends that the landowner shall not reject an application for a certificate of occupancy except on reasonable grounds. Certainly, this was the view of Mutyaba MP, chairperson of the Sessional Committee on Land. In his speech he said that: 'This consent should come as a matter of course, where the landlord withholds consent, he must give very good reasons and the tenant has a right of appeal to the land tribunal.'[113] Once a tenant obtains the requisite consent of the landowner or the land tribunal, as the case may be, he or she is entitled to obtain a certificate of occupancy.

Effect of a certificate

Section 34(8) provides that the recorder must issue a certificate of occupancy to the tenant upon presentation of the requisite consent. Thereafter, the recorder is required to notify the Registrar of Titles of the issue of the certificate. The registrar is required to record the certificate as an encumbrance on the certificate of title of the landowner.[114] The effect of endorsing the certificate of occupancy on the landowner's certificate of title is that the tenant's interest in the land will bind any person who purchases or deals in that land. In other words, the land rights of the holder of a certificate of occupancy would constitute an exception to indefeasibility of title under the *Registration of Titles Act*.[115]

However, it is submitted that even without endorsement a tenancy by occupancy constitutes an exception to indefeasibility of title. In the case of *Lukwago v Bawa Singh and another*,[116] it was held that title of a registered proprietor of mailo land was subject to the interest of any 'tenant' and that a *kibanja* holder was a tenant within meaning of s. 61 of the *Registration of Titles Act*. Moreover, s. 32(9) of the *Land Act* expressly declares that the security of tenure of a lawful or *bona fide* occupant is not to be prejudiced by reason only that he or she does not possess a certificate of occupancy. The latter provision makes it absolutely clear that except as provided by the Act, the security of tenure of lawful and *bona fide* occupants is guaranteed not only against the registered owner but also against subsequent dealers in the land.

Possession of a certificate of occupancy provides documentary evidence that the named person has a right of occupancy over the subject land. This undoubtedly will facilitate land transactions with respect to rights of occupancy. Moreover, since the certificate of occupancy is granted after verification and determination of the boundaries, it is likely to reduce future disputes over landownership and/or boundaries. The *Land Act*, however, does not say whether or not possession

---

[110] Section 34 (6).

[111] Section 34 (7).

[112] There is no particular procedure provided in the Act for the tribunal when dealing with a tenant's appeal in this regard. Compare with the procedure for appeal against a landowner's decision to give consent to a transaction, s. 35(5)-(7).

[113] See *Hansard*, 20 June 1998, p. 4055.

[114] Section 35 (9).

[115] See s. 61, *Registration of Titles Act*. See Chapter 5.

[116] [1959] EA 282 at 285. The principle of indefeasibility of title is discussed in Chapter 5.

of a certificate of occupancy is deemed to be conclusive evidence that the holder is a *bona fide* or lawful occupant of the plot in question or that the requisite consent was properly obtained. It is noteworthy that s. 9(1) of the *Land Act* declares with reference to a certificate of customary ownership that it is conclusive evidence of the customary rights and interests specified in it.[117] If parliament intended the grant of a certificate of occupancy to be similarly conclusive, one would think it would have expressly stated so. Accordingly, in the absence of such provision it is thought that parliament did not intend the grant of a certificate of occupancy to be conclusive evidence of title. It is submitted, however, that as between the immediate landowner and tenant the certificate of occupancy is conclusive. In the absence of fraud, both parties will be estopped from re-opening matters that should have been raised and determined by the tribunal before the certificate was issued.

Termination of tenancy by occupancy

As we have seen, a tenancy by occupancy may be terminated where the tenant defaults in payment of rent.[118] In addition, section 38 provides that a tenancy by occupancy may be terminated where the tenant voluntarily abandons his or her occupancy or is ordered to vacate the land by statutory authority. There is no other provision in the *Land Act* for termination of a tenancy by occupancy. In our view, this means that a tenancy by occupancy cannot be terminated except on the ground of non-payment of rent, voluntary abandonment of the land and forced abandonment by a statutory authority.

Voluntary abandonment

A tenant by occupancy voluntarily abandons or is deemed to have abandoned his or her right of occupancy in the following circumstances. First, a tenant abandons the land where he or she makes his or her intention known to the registered landowner.[119] In law, to abandon land means to give up all claim in relation to it with no intention of ever again asserting, claiming right, or interest over it.[120] Because abandonment entails voluntary relinquishment of one's property, the courts do not lightly infer the intention to abandon.[121] There must be evidence that clearly indicates that the owner freely intended to give up his or her property and never again to assert claim over it.[122] It is thought that in construing the provision the courts would apply an equally strict test. The fact that a tenant by occupancy informed the landowner that he or she intended to abandon the land will not necessarily be treated as conclusive where evidence indicates, for example, that the tenant was acting under some extraneous pressure or mistake. The courts may also investigate any possible motive for the alleged abandonment of the land to ensure that the tenant freely intended to abandon the land. In any case, if the subject land is family land within meaning of s. 40 of the Act, it cannot be abandoned without consent of the family members.[123]

Secondly, a tenant by occupancy is deemed to have abandoned the land where he or she leaves the whole land unattended by himself or herself, or family member or agent for a period of three or more years.[124] We should emphasise that the provision applies only where the tenant leaves unattended the whole land. Therefore, a tenant who attends only to part of his or her land and

---

[117] See s. 61, *Registration of Titles Act*, with respect to a certificate of certificate of title issued under that Act. See Chapter 5.

[118] Sections 32 and 33, see above.

[119] Section 38(2)(a).

[120] *Tehidy Minerals Ltd v Norman* [1971] 1 QB 528 at 553 per Buckley LJ.

[121] *Getobed v Pridmore* (1970) 115 Sol Jo 78 (case of an easement).

[122] *Tehidy Minerals Ltd v Norman* [1971] 1 QB 528 at 553.

[123] The opening sentence of s. 38(1) states that the section is subject to section 28 (which deals with rights of women and children regarding customary land). It is thought that this is a typographical error, as section 38 and s. 28 have nothing to do with each other. The provision should be subject to section 40, which deals with restrictions on transfer of family land.

[124] Section 38(2)(b).

leaves the rest derelict is not deemed to have abandoned the land. Where a tenant was unable to attend to the land due to a disability and had no other family member or any other person to look after the land he or she could apply to the tribunal for an extension of the three-year period.[125] What constitutes disability in this regard is not defined. It is suggested that it would include serious illness and bereavement. It may perhaps also include a situation where a tenant was in exile or prison. In all such cases, the tenant would be entitled to an extension of time, which is equivalent to the period he or she was under disability. It is thought that the extended period of grace would run from the date of the tribunal's judgement rather than the date the person ceased to be under disability.

The effect of voluntary abandonment is that the tenant's right of occupancy ceases to be an encumbrance on the land and the registered owner is free to deal with the land formerly occupied by the tenant as he or she pleases. The Act allows the former tenant to remove any structures, buildings, and other things he or she placed on the land, except dams and trees.[126] The landowner has no obligation to compensate the outgoing tenant for loss of his or her right of occupancy.[127]

Involuntary termination of occupancy in urban areas

Section 38(4) deals with a situation where a person or a body acting under statutory power condemns a tenant by occupancy's building or orders the building to be demolished. The section provides that where the land on which the building is situated is an urban area, the tenant's right of occupancy shall not be deemed to have been extinguished by such order.[128] However, if because of planning or building restrictions imposed under any legislation the tenant is unable to develop the land, he or she may assign his or her right of occupancy provided that the landowner has the first option to purchase.[129] Section 38(4)(iii) empowers the landowner, subject to the approval of the district board, to acquire the right of occupancy upon payment to the tenant for the right of occupancy and for the improvements on the land as determined by a valuer appointed by the government.

Conversion of tenancy by occupancy to a registrable interest

Section 39 of the *Land Act* empowers a tenant by occupancy to convert his or her right of occupancy to any one of the following registrable interests: mailo, freehold, leasehold or sublease.[130] The power to convert the tenancy is subject to the approval of the registered owner of the land. Section 39(2) provides that a tenant by occupancy may apply to the registered landowner for permission to convert his or her tenancy. The landowner may grant his or her consent with or without any conditions,[131]or reject the application outright or invite the tenant to enter into negotiations.[132] Unlike the application for a certificate of occupancy, where the tenant could appeal to the tribunal against the landowner's refusal to give consent, in this case, there is no such right. It would seem it is up to the parties to reach an agreement.[133] Section 39(5) provides that where the parties have agreed to negotiate either of them could invoke the assistance of the mediator to bring them to a settlement. But if after a period of three months of negotiations the parties fail to reach an agreement,

---

[125] Section 38(3).

[126] The provision does not prescribe a time limit within which a former tenant must remove fixtures.

[127] Section 38 (1)(c).

[128] Section 38(4)(i). The provision does not say what happens where the land is rural. Presumably, the effect would be the same.

[129] Section 38(4)(ii).

[130] The expression 'registrable interest' refers to an interest for which provision is made for registration under the *Registration of Titles Acts*: mailo, freehold, leasehold and sub-leasehold, certificate of customary ownership and certificate of occupancy, see s. 2 of the *Land Act*.

[131] Section 39(3).

[132] Section 39(4). The section says that the registered owner must respond within a period of three months from the date of receiving the application. The provision does not say what happens if the owner fails to respond within the prescribed period.

[133] See also *Hansard*, 20 June 1998, pp. 4055, and 27 June 1998, pp. 4269-4270.

the mediator shall make a report to that effect and he or she may withdraw from the negotiations. However, the parties, if they so agree, may continue to negotiate.

CUSTOMARY LAND TENURE

Customary land tenure is a system of land ownership governed and regulated by customary principles and usually sanctioned by customary authority.[134] As we have seen, customary land tenure is one of the four systems of land ownership in Uganda recognised by the Constitution and the *Land Act*. [135] With the exception of land in Buganda and urban areas, most land in Uganda is owned under customary land tenure. The specific tenure varies according to the ethnic group and region of the country.[136] In some parts of the country, ownership of land is mainly communal, based on clans, with individual usufructuary rights over specific plots. But generally there is a steady evolutionary change towards individual ownership. This trend is more pronounced in the densely populated districts in the southern and eastern parts of the country and less so in the northern and north-eastern parts.[137]

From a legal perspective customary land tenure, mailo, and freehold are similar in that ownership of land under all three tenures is in perpetuity.[138] The main legal difference between customary land tenure and the other tenures is that customary law regulates customary land tenure. Section 4(1)(b) of the *Land Act* provides that customary land tenure shall be governed by rules generally accepted as binding by the particular community. Any person acquiring land in that community shall equally be bound by those rules.[139] However, the application of any customary rule is subject to the rule not being repugnant to natural justice, equity, and good conscience, or being incompatible either directly or indirectly with any written law.[140] Also s. 28 of the *Land Act* expressly renders void any customary rule or practice that denies women, children and disabled persons access to ownership, use or occupation of land.[141]

Certificate of customary ownership

Article 237(4)(a) of the Constitution empowers all Ugandan citizens owning land under customary tenure to acquire certificates of ownership in a manner prescribed by parliament. On the basis of this article, s.5(1) of the *Land Act* provided that individuals, families or communities owning land under customary tenure on former public land[142] may acquire a certificate of customary ownership in respect of the land they occupy. The power to issue a certificate of customary ownership is vested with the relevant district land board following an elaborate prescribed procedure.

Procedure for application

Essentially the procedure for application of a certificate of occupancy is as follows. The applicant must submit an application in the prescribed form together with the requisite fee to the land committee in the parish where the land is situated. Upon receipt of the application, the committee is required to advertise the application by posting a notice in a prescribed form in a prominent place

---

134 Section 4 of the *Land Act*.

135 Article 237(3) of the constitution, and s 3, *Land Act*.

136 See Morris and Read, *Uganda: the Development of its Laws and Constitution*, supra, pp.353-359.

137 See generally Obol-Ochola, *Customary Land Law and the Economic Development in Uganda*, supra, pp. 67-116.

138 Sections 4(1)(h); 4(2)(a) and 4(4)(a).

139 Section 4(1)(c).

140 Section 17(1), *Judicature Statute* (No 13 of 1996).

141 See below for discussion of this provision.

142 Former public land means land previously administered under *Public Lands Act*, 1969, prior to the *Land Reform Decree*, 1975.

in the parish and on the subject land. The notice should specify the location of the land and its approximate area. In addition, the notice should contain an invitation to any person with an interest or claim in the subject land, including owners of adjacent land, to attend a meeting of the committee at a specified time to make his or her claim. The meeting should not be scheduled earlier than two weeks from the date of publication of the notice.[143]

The land committee must meet to hear and determine the application on the day advertised in the notice. Section 6(1)(a) states that the committee shall determine, verify and mark the boundaries of all interests to which the land is subject.[144] Claims of other persons over the subject land must also be heard and determined. These may include rights of way or any other easements[145] and 'third party' rights over the land.[146] If in the course of its proceedings the committee deems it necessary it may adjourn its hearing and invite an officer from the district land office or any other person with recognised knowledge of local matters to conduct further investigation of a claim.[147] In making its determination, the committee is obliged to safeguard interests and rights in the land of women, minors, persons with disability and absentees.[148] The committee is also required to take account of any interest in the land in respect of which no claim is made.[149]

In the event of any disputed claims, the committee must use its best endeavours to mediate between the rival parties in order to arrive at an agreed settlement.[150] However, the committee is required to adjudicate in accordance with customary law any dispute referred to it by a person with interest in the subject land or referred to it by an owner of adjoining land.[151] For example, a person may challenge an application on the ground that the customary law of the particular community does not recognise individual ownership or that the applicant's rights over the land do not constitute ownership. When adjudicating over disputes the committee must observe the rules of natural justice.[152] It should be noted that, the committee is not bound by rules of evidence or procedure of an ordinary court. Hence, for example, it can admit evidence, which is otherwise inadmissible in ordinary courts and call witnesses on its own motion.[153] If it so wishes, it may seek advice on any matter before it of a customary institution within the parish which is reputed to deal with land matters. Generally, the committee is free to determine its own procedural rules, including, but not necessarily adopting customary procedures for resolving land disputes.[154]

On the conclusion of its hearing and determination, the committee is required to write its report. The report should include a record of all claims made in relation to the land and whether or not, in its view, any claims have been established and it should give the reasons for its view. In addition, the report must set out the committee's findings and recommendations, with reasons, on the

---

143 Section 7(2)(b).

144 Note that there is no requirement for the land to be surveyed (compare with the requirements for application for freehold title, s. 14(3)).

145 See s. 6(1)(b). At Common law an easement must have certain essential features, see Chapter 8. Probably, in the context of the provision the term would include rights which are not easements at Common law.

146 Third party rights include leases, rights of use, pledges and other encumbrances whether by virtue of customary law or otherwise.

147 Section 7(4).

148 Section 6(1)(g). Also under s. 4(1)(d) any customary practice that tends to discriminate against women and children is rendered void.

149 Section 6(1)(h).

150 Section 7(5).

151 Section 6(1)(c).

152 Section 6(2). See above for meaning.

153 Section 6(2)(a)-(c).

154 Section 6(2)(d) and (e).

application. The report should state whether it recommends that the application be rejected, approved unconditionally, or approved subject to conditions or restrictions[155] to be endorsed on the certificate.[156]

The committee must submit its report to the relevant land board with a copy to the applicant. It must also make a copy of its report available for inspection by all persons who made claims or who were heard by the committee.[157]

The decision whether or not to grant a certificate of customary ownership rests with the land board after considering the committee's report. The board is given wide powers in dealing with the committee's recommendations. It may accept the committee's recommendation to issue or not to issue a certificate of customary ownership or it may reject it outright. It may reject the committee's recommendation to grant a certificate or vary the conditions or restrictions proposed by the committee.[158] Conversely, the board may order a certificate to be issued contrary to the committee's recommendations.[159] It is also within the board's powers to return a report to the committee with instructions for further action that it requires to be taken. Section 8(2) states that where the board rejects or varies a committee's recommendations it must give reasons for its decision.

The board is required to communicate its decision in writing to the Recorder.[160] Where the board decides that a certificate of customary ownership should be issued, the Recorder shall issue the certificate to the applicant with endorsements of conditions, restrictions, or limitations imposed by the board.[161] There is no provision in the Act for any person to be heard or to make a representation to the board. However, under s. 8(6) anv person aggrieved by a decision of the board has a right to appeal to the land tribunal. The tribunal may confirm, vary, reverse or modify the board's decision and may make such other order as it is empowered to make under the Act.

Effect of a certificate

A certificate of customary ownership is deemed by the Act to be conclusive evidence of the customary rights and interests endorsed on the certificate.[162] However, a certificate does not change the tenure system under which the land in question is owned. Section 9 (1) states that the land to which the certificate refers continues to be owned, occupied, and used in accordance with customary law. Land transactions and third party rights affecting the land also continue to be regulated by customary law. Subject to the provisions of the Act,[163] and third party rights endorsed on the certificate, a certificate entitles the holder to deal with the land as any other landowner may. He or she may lease the land, allow others to exercise usufructuary rights over the land [164] or dispose of the land by will.[165] Except where restricted by endorsements on the certificate, a certificate holder may mortgage, pledge, subdivide, or sell the land as he or she wishes.[166]

---

155 Restrictions may include exclusion of a right to sell or mortgage the land, see s. 9(2).

156 Section 7(6)(a). Under s. 6(e), the committee is required to record any third party rights pertaining to the land. Clearly, such rights must be included in its report for endorsement on the certificate. See also s. 8(3).

157 Section 7(6)(b)-(d).

158 The Board cannot alter third party rights recommended by the committee, s. 8(3).

159 Section 8.

160 Section 8(4).

161 Section 8(5). Note that where the committee recorded third party rights, the certificate cannot be issued unless those rights are endorsed on the certificate, s. 8(3).

162 Section 9 (1).

163 Dealings affecting family land are subject to s. 40 of the *Land Act*. See Chapter 3

164 These are rights to use or derive profit from the land, s. 9(6). For example, a right given to a person to cultivate part of the land for one season is a usufructuary right.

165 Section 9(2) (a), (b) and (h).

166 Section 9(2) (c), (d) and (f).

Where a certificate holder enters into any transaction affecting the land, he or she must provide the recorder with a copy or record of the transaction. The recorder is required to keep records of such transactions in the prescribed manner.[167] Section 9(4) provides that a transaction involving a lease, mortgage or sale of the land shall not be effective to pass any interest in the land unless the recorder registers it.[168] This provision is mainly intended to protect third parties dealing in customary land. For example, a person wishing to purchase such land just needs to search the recorder's register for recorded encumbrances. He or she need will not be concerned by unrecorded claims over the land. The requirement to record transactions will also help to minimise disputes between the landowner and persons claiming to have acquired interests in the land. It is submitted, however, that the fact that a transaction is not recorded does not mean it is devoid of legal efficacy. An unrecorded transaction would be effective as a contract between the parties to the agreement, though not binding on third parties.[169] For example, where a landowner mortgages the land the mortgage will bind the land even though it is not recorded, though if the landowner mortgaged the land to another person and the transaction thereof is recorded the latter would prevail.

The government anticipates that the provision of certificates of customary ownership would facilitate dealings in customary land. In particular, it is expected that possession of a certificate of customary ownership would enable holders to obtain credit on security of their land from financial institutions. Section 9(2) of the Act requires financial institutions to accept the certificates as evidence of title.[170] On the other hand, s. 9(5) makes it clear that where a mortgagor of customary land defaults in repayment of the loan, the lender has a right to sell and to execute a transfer of the land, just like any other mortgaged land.

Conversion of customary tenure and grant of freeholds

The *Land Act* makes provision for owners of land under customary tenure to change their tenure to freehold and for the grant of land in freehold out of former public land. Section 10(1) provides that any person, family, community or association[171] holding land under customary tenure on former public land, may convert the tenure into freehold in accordance with the provisions of the Act. It is not necessary for a landowner to apply for a certificate of title prior to applying for conversion of his or her customary tenure to freehold.[172] In other words, an owner of customary land could directly apply to convert his or her tenure to freehold instead of applying for a certificate of customary ownership.

Applicant without a certificate of customary ownership

The procedure for tenure conversion where the applicant has no certificate of customary ownership, is similar to that followed for application of a certificate of customary ownership discussed above. The application must be made to the land board in the prescribed format. The form together with the prescribed fee must be submitted to the committee of the parish in which the subject land is situated.[173] Upon receipt of the application, the committee shall exercise with respect to the application all its functions specified in s 6 and follow the same procedure as it follows for the application of a certificate of customary ownership.[174] Section 12(2) specifically requires the

---

[167] Section 9(3).

[168] This provision has some similarities with s. 51, *Registration of Titles Act* (cap 205).

[169] Similar principles will apply as with unregistered transactions under the *Registration of Titles* Act. See for example, *Serunjogi v Katabira* CS No 547 of 1987 (unreported); [1988-90] HCB 148. See Chapter 5.

[170] The provision was added, according to one member of parliament, to re-assure banks that the certificates will be recognised by the courts, see *Hansard*, supra, p. 4169-70.

[171] 'Association' means a Communal Land Association established under s. 16 of the *Land Act*.

[172] This is implied in s. 12(4) and 13(2).

[173] Section 10 (3) and 11 (2).

[174] Section 12 (1) and 13 (1).

committee, in considering any application, to take into account whether customary law applicable to the subject land recognises or provides for individual ownership. As with an application for certificate of customary ownership, the committee is required to submit its report and recommendations to the land board, which is responsible for the final decision.[175]

Applicant with a certificate of customary ownership

Where a holder of a certificate of customary ownership seeks a tenure conversion he or she must submit an application together with the prescribed fee to the relevant land committee for assessment of the application and recommendation. Since by virtue of the certificate of occupancy the applicant is the confirmed owner of the land described in the certificate of occupancy, the committee is required to accept the content of the certificate without fresh scrutiny.[176] However, in making its report and recommendation, the committee is required to take into account whether customary law applicable to the subject land recognises or provides for individual ownership of land.[177] The committee may also take into account any new or additional matters, which were not dealt with in the original report on the application for a certificate of customary ownership.[178]

Application for grant of freehold

The above refers to application by customary owners to convert their tenure to freehold. The Act prescribes a similar procedure to be followed by a person applying for a freehold over unowned former public land.[179] Under Article 241(1)(a) of the Constitution, one of the functions of a district land board is to hold and allocate any land in the district that is not owned by any person or authority.[180] The land envisaged would include land in the district which no individual group or other identified entity owns. In most districts it is unlikely that there is such an unowned land.[181] The board may also allocate in freehold any land it holds after expiration of a lease granted by a former controlling authority.[182]

Power of the board

The board is required to consider the application for conversion of customary tenure to freehold or for grant of a freehold in light of the committee's report and recommendation.[183] But in the end the decision rests with the board. Thus, it may accept the recommendation with or without conditions or restrictions proposed by the committee or subject it to additional conditions, restrictions or third party rights.[184] It may return the report to the committee with instructions for further investigation and or hearing.[185] It may, on the other hand, approve an application for conversion that the committee recommended should be rejected.[186] The board is not required to give any reasons for its decision except where it rejects the committee's recommendation or varies any conditions or restrictions it recommended.[187]

---

175 Section 10 (4) and 14 (1).

176 Section 12(4) and 13(2).

177 Section 12(2).

178 Additional matters may include third party rights, see s. 14(2).

179 Section 11(1)

180 See also s. 60(1)(a) of the *Land Act.*

181 See *Hansard*, supra, pp. 4183 – 4185.

182 See definition of 'former controlling authority': s. 2. The district land boards hold reversionary interests in such leaseholds, see s. 60(1(c).

183 Section 14(1).

184 Section 14 (1)(a) & (b); Also s. 10(2).

185 Section 14(1)(c).

186 Section 14(1)(d).

187 Section 14(1)(d).

Section 10(4) stipulates that upon receipt of the committee's report and recommendation, the board shall cause the land, in respect of which the application is made, to be surveyed.[188] This provision seems to suggest that the land must be surveyed before the board considers the application, whereas s. 14(3) says that the board shall cause the land to be surveyed before approval of the report and recommendation. The implication of the latter provision is that the survey should only be required where the application is to be approved. In other words, there must be a provisional decision to approve, which is pivotal upon the land being surveyed. So if, for example, the board decides that it would not approve a recommendation for tenure conversion, the applicant should not incur unnecessary expenses in survey fees. It is submitted that this interpretation reflects the legislative intention. In any event, it is suggested that in practice a board should not require an applicant to have his/her land surveyed except after a preliminary examination of the application reveals that the application is likely to be approved.

The decision of the board approving the conversion to freehold must be in the prescribed form.[189] The board is required to communicate its decision to the Registrar of Titles with instructions to issue the applicants with the appropriate certificate of title.[190] Where the board has determined under s.14 (2) that other persons are entitled to the benefit of 'third party rights' in respect of the land, it may direct that the converted freehold shall be subject to such conditions or restrictions as the board considers desirable for the efficient and equitable land management or to give full protection to those rights.[191] Third party rights may include, for example, public right of way, right of access to a well on the land, a right to graze animals, to hunt and other customary rights commonly exercisable over other people's land in the area.

There is no provision in the *Land Act* empowering the board or the registrar to impose fees or any other charges on successful applicants for conversion of their customary land tenure to freehold or for the registration of converted titles. Presumably this means that the legislature intended that no fees should be charged for the service. With respect to an application for a freehold over land owned by the board, the Act expressly provides that the board shall charge a prescribed fee for the freehold title. Section 14(5) requires the board to set a fee at a fair market valuation as approved by the Chief Government Valuer.[192]

Issuing a certificate

Once the board approves an application for conversion of customary tenure or grant of a freehold title, it must send a copy of its decision in a prescribed form to the Registrar of Titles with instructions to issue a certificate of freehold title to the applicant.[193] The board's decision must be accompanied by a certified survey plan of the land to which it relates. Upon receipt of the documents, the registrar is obliged to register the land and issue a certificate of title as instructed by the board.[194] Where the board's decision contains a request to the registrar to endorse on the certificate certain restrictions or conditions as encumbrances[195] against the freehold, the registrar must endorse the same on the certificate of title.[196]

---

[188] The applicant is responsible for the costs involved in the survey, see *Hansard*, supra, p. 4182.
[189] Section 10(2).
[190] Section 14(1)(a) and s. 14(6).
[191] Section 14(4).
[192] Section 14(5).
[193] Section 14(6).
[194] Section 15(1)
[195] See s. 14 (6)(b).
[196] Section 15(3). For example, the board may impose a restriction against sale or subdivision of the land. The reason for the endorsement is to preserve the restrictions against the principle of indefeasibility of title. See discussion of this principle in Chapter 5.

Section 15(2) empowers the registrar, acting on the advice of the Commissioner for Surveys and Mapping, to issue to an applicant a certificate of title endorsed with the words 'Limited as to Parcels'. Under s. 39A of the *Registration of Titles Act*, such a certificate is issued in respect of land for which no certificate has been previously issued and no survey plan has been deposited. The registrar may remove the limitation as to parcel subject to certain conditions being fulfilled. First, the Registrar must be satisfied by deposit of a survey plan that there is no person in possession of the land adversely to the title of the applicant. Secondly, the registrar must have given notice to the apparent owners of adjoining land of his or her intention to remove the limitation and the notice must have expired.[197]

The land comprised in a limited certificate is subject to all provisions of the *Registration of Titles Act* just like any other land registered under the Act.[198] It seems that the only purpose of issuing a limited certificate is to protect claims of persons in adverse possession of the land.[199] If that is so, in our view it is unnecessary because an adverse possessor is already protected under s. 61 of the *Registration of Titles Act*.[200] Moreover, considering the fact that approval of an application for tenure conversion or grant of land in freehold is given after the committee and the board have examined the application, s.15(2) seems to be unnecessary. Furthermore, s. 15(1) states that the registrar shall issue a certificate where the board's approval is accompanied with a certified survey plan. Since a limited certificate is issued only where there is no certified survey plan,[201] s.15(2) seems to be superfluous.

Is the certificate conclusive?

Under the *Registration of Titles Act*, once a certificate of title is issued it cannot be impugned, except as provided by s. 61. That section guarantees the registered owner an indefeasible title apart from the exceptions mentioned therein.[202] However, as is discussed below, there are other exceptions to the principle of indefeasibility, which operate outside the Act.[203] An issue that is likely to arise in this regard is whether title of a registered proprietor can be impugned on the ground that the land committee or board did not follow the prescribed procedure for the grant of a certificate of freehold, and as a result, certain claims or interests were not endorsed on the certificate. It is submitted that if the registered owner had knowledge of other people's claims over the land or of improper procedure, then his or her title could be impugned on ground of fraud.[204]

The case is more complex where the registered owner had no such knowledge prior to registration or is a bona fide purchaser from a registered proprietor. Section 56 of the *Registration of Titles Act* provides that:

> No certificate of title issued upon application to bring land under this Act shall be impeached or defeasible by reason or on account of any informality or irregularity in the application or in the proceedings previous to the registration of the certificate, and every certificate of title issued under any of the provisions herein contained shall be received in all courts as evidence of particulars

---

197 Section 39B, *Registration of Titles Act*.

198 Section 39D, *Registration of Titles Act*.

199 Section 6 of the *Limitation Act* prohibits a landowner from evicting or bringing an action for recovery of land against a person who has been in adverse possession of the land for more than twelve years. This law applies to all land, including land owned under customary tenure, see *Citamong v Olinga* [1988] HCB 86. For further discussion see Chapter 4.

200 Adverse possession constitutes an exception to indefeasibility of title. See Chapter 5. Also see Chapter 4.

201 See s. 39A of the *Registration of Titles Act*.

202 See Chapter 5.

203 See Chapter 5.

204 See *In the Matter of Ruzhwengyibwa* and *In the Matter of Ruzigana* Misc. C No 48 of 1976 (unreported); *Katarikawe v Katwiremu and another* CS No 2 of 1973; [1977] HCB 187.

> therein set forth and of the entry thereof in the Register Book, and shall be conclusive evidence that the person named in such certificate as the proprietor of or having any estate or interest in or power to appoint or dispose of the land therein described is seized or possessed of such estate or interest or has such power.

On the surface, this provision seems to preclude impeachment of a certificate of title on any ground of irregular procedure.[205] However, in the case of *Matovu and others v Sseviri and another*,[206] the Court of Appeal held that the provision did not apply where land was granted in violation of the principles of natural justice. In that case, the appellants applied to the Uganda Land Commission for a lease over certain public land, which they claimed to occupy under customary tenure. The local land committee inspected the land and recommended that the lease be granted to the appellant. On going to survey the land, they found that the first respondent had already surveyed the land and had obtained a certificate of title. The respondent claimed that the commission gave him an offer of a lease over the disputed land which he accepted, had the land surveyed and obtained a certificate of title. (Under the *Land Reform Decree*, 1975, (repealed by s 99 of the *Land Act*, 1998), the Uganda Land Commission had the power to grant land in leasehold including land occupied under customary tenure.) The appellants sought an order for cancellation of the certificate on grounds, inter alia, that the commission did not give them a hearing prior to granting the lease to the respondent. The trial judge held that s 56 of the *Registration of Titles Act* precluded impeachment of a certificate of title on the ground of irregularity in the procedure prior to registration. In allowing the appeal, the court observed that:

> Since the courts will assume that Parliament intended an administrative agency to make decisions in accordance with natural justice, it follows that in interpreting s 56 *REGISTRATION OF TITLES ACT*, which provides that a certificate of title shall not be impeached or defeasible on account of any informality or irregularity, this court would attach such meaning on the words 'informality or irregularity' as would not include a breach of natural justice.

Accordingly, the court ordered the respondent's certificate cancelled.[207]

On the basis of the above decision, it is arguable that a certificate issued in breach of the statutory procedure might be cancelled, at any rate if as a result of the breach other claimants were denied natural justice, notwithstanding the principle of indefeasibility of title. In our view, the district land tribunals should trade with caution when dealing with such cases otherwise the main objective of registration of titles, certainty of title, would be undermined.

Communal land associations

Section 16 of the *Land Act* provides for the formation of communal land associations for the purpose of ownership and management of land under customary law or other law. A communal land association may own the land under a certificate of customary ownership, or leasehold or freehold.[208] The principle objective of such an association is to protect and regulate the rights of joint land users.[209] The government envisages that formation of land associations is likely to appeal to traditional joint users of land for pastoral farming such as the Karimojong. However, there is nothing in the Act to prevent any other land users from forming a communal land association, for example, to protect family or clan land from outside pressure or to provide for sound management of such land.

---

[205] See also ss. 61, 184, and 186, *RTA*. See 'Indefeasibility of title' in Chapter 5.

[206] CA No 7 of 1978 (unreported); [1979] HCB 174.

[207] The court also found that title was obtained through fraud.

[208] Section 23.

[209] See Hunt and Eturu, 'Land Act Implementation Study Economic Appraisal Draft Report', 6 August 1999.

Any number of people may form a communal land association. There is no prescribed minimum or maximum number of members. Section 17 (1) stipulates that where a group of persons wishes to form a land association they may apply to the District Registrar of Titles to become an association under the Act. The Act stipulates that upon receipt of an application, the District Registrar of Titles shall convene a meeting of the persons seeking to form an association. The Registrar or nominee must chair the meeting. If at that meeting at least 60 per cent of the members vote for the association to be incorporated under the *Land Act*, they will elect office bearers of their association. At least one third of those elected must be women.[210] The officials shall be responsible for drafting the association's Constitution with the assistance of the District Registrar of Titles. Before the association applies for incorporation the Registrar must certify that its Constitution complies with the provisions of the *Land Act*.

Once satisfied that all the statutory requirements are complied with, the District Registrar of Titles must incorporate the association. An incorporated association is a body corporate.[211] Its officers can sue or be sued in its name, and may enter into contracts binding the association and all its members.[212] The managing committee of the association is charged with the responsibility to hold and manage the land on behalf of all members. However, the power of the committee to enter into land transactions is limited. Section 20(3) prohibits the management committee from entering into any binding land transactions on behalf of the association unless and until the members, by majority vote (at a meeting convened for the purpose), approve the transaction. Any transaction that is not approved by the members is deemed to be void and shall not give rise to any interest or right in the association's land.[213]

Individual member holdings

Although land held by the association is communally owned, members may own part or all of the land in their individual capacity. Section 23 (1) stipulates that where customary law of the area provides for individual or family ownership, the association must recognise and give effect to such ownership. Under s. 23(3), members are given power to apply to the association for a certificate of customary ownership or freehold title of the portion of the land they own individually or as a family. If the association approves the application, a certificate or freehold title shall be granted following the prescribed procedure. There is a right of appeal to the land tribunal by any person aggrieved by the association's decision.[214] The Act is silent as to whether or not the land of a member who is granted a certificate of customary ownership or freehold title would still be subject to the association's rules. It is suggested that the association could give its approval to grant a certificate of customary ownership or freehold title to a member subject to any restrictions, for example as regards use of the land, in its constitution. These could be endorsed on the applicant's certificate.[215] It is submitted that where a certificate is issued without restrictions the owner would be entitled to deal with the land as he or she pleases. Certainly this would be the case where a freehold title is granted.

Areas of common land use

The management of the association may, and must where members demand it, set aside land for common use. For example, it may set aside land for grazing or watering of livestock. The association is required by law to set up a scheme, approved by the members, for the management of such land.[216] Members of the association have a right to use the common land in accordance with the

---

210 Section 17(4)(b).

211 Section 19(3).

212 Section 20(1).

213 *Ibid.*

214 Section 23(4). It is suggested that the expression 'any person' would include members of the association.

215 See s.9.

216 Section 25. For the content of the management scheme, see s.26.

management scheme. Members of the community who are not members of the association may use such land only with the approval of the association. However, the association must not unreasonably withhold its consent.[217]

Discriminatory customary practices

Section 28 of the Act renders void any customary practices affecting customary land that deny women, children or persons with disabilities access to ownership, occupation or use of customary land. For example, a customary rule that prohibits a married woman from inheriting her father's land is likely to be void under the Act. This provision was enacted in response to complaints especially by women parliamentarians and women's organisations that historically some customary practices have been responsible for the marginalisation of women.[218] It is rather surprising that the scope of the provision is limited to decisions affecting customary land and not across the board to all land. In any case, it is thought that Article 33 of the Constitution, which prohibits laws, cultures and customs that are discriminatory, renders void such practices irrespective of the tenure under which the land is held.

Restrictions on ownership of land by non-Ugandans

Non-citizens of Uganda are prohibited from owning land in freehold or mailo tenure.[219] They can only lease land for a period that must not exceed 99 years.[220] The statutory restrictions imposed on non-citizens are discussed in more details in Chapter 3.

---

[217] Section 25 (4) See s. 27 for rights and obligations of community members using common land.

[218] See *Hansard*, supra, pp. 4114, 4097 and 4201.

[219] Section 41(1), *Land Act*.

[220] Section 41(2), *Land Act*.

3

Land Administration Control and Dispute Settlement

The Ugandan Constitution incorporates the policy of decentralisation of governance. One of the main aims of this policy is to involve local people in the decision-making process in matters affecting them. This objective is clearly reflected in the *Land Act* with regard to land management and dispute settlement. This chapter deals with the machinery for land administration, control imposed on landowners and provision for resolving land disputes under the Act.

LAND ADMINISTRATION

The main bodies responsible for land management are the Uganda Land Commission, district boards, and land committees.

The Uganda Land Commission

Previously, all land in Uganda was public land centrally vested in the Uganda Land Commission, which had the sole power of management and allocation of the land on behalf of the state.[1] The Uganda Land Commission's powers are now limited to managing land vested in or acquired by the government in accordance with the Constitution.[2] The commission is also charged with the responsibility of managing land acquired abroad by the government. However, it may delegate its powers of management of government land in a foreign country to a Uganda mission.[3]

For exercising its powers under the Constitution and the *Land Act*, the Uganda Land Commission is given extensive auxiliary powers. For example, it has power to purchase land or other interests in land, erect or demolish buildings, sell or lease land held by it, cause survey of government land and do other things, as may be necessary or incidental to the exercise of those powers.[4] In the exercise of its powers, the commission is required to abide by government policy. Section 56(2) specifically empowers the minister responsible for land to give the commission policy directives as are necessary to ensure compliance with government policy.

Land Fund

In addition to management of government land, the Uganda Land Commission is vested with the duty to administer the Land Fund established under the *Land Act*.[5] The Fund's financial sources include monies appropriated by parliament for this purpose, loans, grants from donors, money paid into the fund under the Act and from any other source approved by the minister.[6]

The original object of setting up a Land Fund was to provide a source of revenue to be used to buy out 'absentee' mailo landowners in the former 'lost' counties of Buyaga and Bugangaizi in Kibaale district. This was to resolve a longstanding historical political dispute between the kingdoms of Buganda and Bunyoro.[7] However, the issue was so controversial that in the end parliament decided that the Land Fund should not be restricted to a particular area but rather be used nationwide

---

1 *Land Reform Decree* 1975, s. 1(1).

2 See article 239 of the Constitution and s.50 of the *Land Act*. See also Chapter 2.

3 Section 50 (b), *Land Act*.

4 Section 54, *Land Act*.

5 Section 42(1) & (2).

6 Section 42(3).

7 See *Hansard*, supra, p. 4056: The dispute originated in the 1890s when the British colonial administration confiscated two counties of Bunyoro and annexed them to Buganda as a punishment for Bunyoro's insurgency against the British. The annexed land was subsequently allocated to Baganda notables as mailo land under the 1900 Buganda Agreement.

to assist disadvantaged people to acquire land.[8] Accordingly, s. 42(4) prescribes that monies from the fund shall be utilised for the following purposes: to give loans to tenants by occupancy to enable them to acquire registrable interests,[9] to re-settle persons rendered landless by government action or other activities and to assist other persons to acquire titles.[10] In addition, the money could be used by the government to purchase or acquire registered land to enable tenants by occupancy to acquire registrable interests pursuant to the Constitution.[11] The commission is required to submit a written report to the minister every six months on its operation and management of the Fund giving such information as the minister may specify. The minister in turn must submit an annual report to parliament on the performance of the fund.[12]

District land boards

The Constitution provides for the establishment of a district land board for each district.[13] Section 57(1) of the *Land Act* puts into operation this provision. The Act provides that membership of the district land board shall consist of a chairperson, one member representing urban councils and one member from each county in the district. To ensure gender balance in land administration, s. 58(3) prescribes that at least one third of the board members must be women. The Act also requires that at least one of the members of the board must have qualifications and experience in matters relating to land.[14] The Act disqualifies from nomination as a board member a person who is less than eighteen years old, of unsound mind, bankrupt, a member of parliament, or a person convicted of a criminal offence that involves moral turpitude.[15] Members of a district land board hold office for a period of five years and they are eligible for re-appointment for a further one term.[16] A member may be removed from office by the district council but only if he or she is unable to conduct his or her duties, for misconduct, incompetence or failure to attend board meetings for six consecutive times without reasonable cause.[17]

Functions of the board

The Constitution states that the district land board shall own land within the district which is not owned by any person or authority.[18] This provision is re-enacted in s 60(1)(a) of the *Land Act*. The land envisaged is that which does not belong to an individual, family, clan, or other identifiable entity. A possible example of such land is communal grazing land over which no particular person or body claims ownership. During the parliamentary debate of the provision, several members claimed that there was no land in their constituencies that was not owned by a person or authority.[19] Nevertheless, the provision was incorporated in the Act as a residue in the event that there was such land in a particular district.[20] The Act gives the district land board the sole power to sell, lease, or otherwise deal with this land, if any, within the district.[21] The Act also vests with the board the

---

8 See *Hansard*, 20 June 1998, p. 4056, 23 June 1998, pp 4099,4101,4112, 24 June 1998, p. 4127-28 June 1998, pp. 4291-98.

9 See also s. 42(5).

10 For example, a loan could be given to a landowner to assist him or her with the costs of surveying his or her land for the purpose of acquiring a certificate of title, see s. 42(5)(e).

11 Section 42(4)(b). See also A|rticle 237(9)(b) of the Constitution and s. 32 of the *Land Act*.

12 Section 42(14) & (15).

13 Article 240(1).

14 Section 58(4). It should be noted that this does not necessarily entail legal qualifications (compare s. 75(2) with respect to qualifications of the chairperson of the district land tribunal).

15 Section 58(2), *Land Act*.

16 Section 59(1), *Land Act*.

17 Section 59(2).

18 Article 241(1)(a).

19 *Hansard*, 25 June 1998, pp. 4183-85

20 *Hansard*, 25 June 1998, p. 4185, per Minister of Lands.

21 Section 60(1).

reversionary interest in any leasehold land in the district granted by a former designated authority.[22] Accordingly, the board takes over the role and powers of the lessor under the lease agreement and the *Public Lands Act.*[23]

As already seen, the district land board is charged with a duty to facilitate the registration and transfer of interests in land, approve applications for the grant of certificates of customary ownership of land and for conversion of customary tenure to freehold.[24] Other functions of the board include causing maps and surveys to be made, compiled and maintained; reviewing the list of rates of compensation payable in respect of improvements on the land and; dealing with any other matter that is incidental or connected to its functions.[25] In carrying out its powers and functions, the district land board is required to take into account national and district council land policies, as well as circumstances of different customary land tenure systems in the district. Otherwise, it must exercise its powers independently of any other body including the district council and the Uganda Land Commission.[26]

Land committees

The Land Act provides for the appointment at each parish level of a land committee. The district council, on the recommendation of a sub-county council, appoints the committee consisting of four members.[27] Provision is also made for the appointment of a similar committee for each gazetted urban area and city division. The district council appoints the latter committees on the recommendation of the relevant urban or city division council.[28] Section 66(2) prescribes that at least one of the land committee members must be a woman. As we have seen, the object of this requirement is to maintain a gender balance in land administration. The Act also requires that at least one of the members must be conversant with land matters. The object is to guard against appointing a committee where none of the members has any knowledge of matters pertinent to landownership. As we shall presently see, the committee has very important functions under the Act that require sound knowledge of local land matters. If at least one of the members is knowledgeable, he or she may guide the others in their deliberation.

The main function of the committee is to determine, verify, and mark boundaries of customary land situated in the parish which is the subject of an application for a certificate of customary ownership and to recommend to the board whether to grant the certificate.[29] The committee exercises a similar function with respect to application for conversion of customary tenure to freehold.[30] Another function of the land committee is to advise the district land board on matters of customary land law applicable in its parish.[31] The land committee also functions as guardian of the interests of minor children with respect to transactions affecting family land.[32] In carrying out its functions, the committee is expected to act in collaboration with traditional institutions.

---

22 These are leases granted by urban authorities over former public land, see S 2, definition 'former designated authority'.

23 Section 60(8), *Land Act.*

24 Section 60(1). See also sections 8 and 10.

25 Section 60 (1).

26 Section 61(1).

27 Section 65(1).

28 Section 65 (2).

29 Sections 6,7 and 8. See also Chapter 2.

30 Section 10-18. See also Chapter 2.

31 Section 6 (1) (f).

32 Section 40(1)(iii). See below.

CONTROL OVER LAND

There is very little control over landowners under the *Land Act*. Generally, landowners are free to deal with their land as they so wish. In this part we shall consider statutory control under the following subheadings: restriction on ownership of land by non-citizens; protection of family land; control over land use and compulsory acquisition of land.

Ownership of land by non-citizens
As already seen, article 237(1) of the Constitution declares that land in Uganda belongs to its citizens and shall be vested in them in freehold, mailo, leasehold and customary tenure. Article 237(2)(c) states that a non-citizen may acquire a lease in land in accordance with the laws prescribed by parliament. Likewise, the *Land Act* provides that a non-citizen of Uganda may acquire a lease for a maximum period of 99 years.[33]

The *Land Act* expressly prohibits a non-citizen of Uganda from acquiring or owning mailo or freehold land.[34] The ban on non-citizens owning freehold and mailo land is not new in Uganda. It goes back to 1916, when the Secretary of State for the British Colonies prohibited the governor from alienating freehold land to non-Africans.[35] The ban was reinforced in 1921 by a Buganda *Lukiiko* resolution, which prohibited the Baganda from selling outright their mailo to non-natives. The policy against the granting of freeholds to non-Africans was maintained throughout the colonial period and after Uganda became an independent state. The difference between the previous and current ban is that the former applied to 'non-Africans' who included Uganda citizens of non-African origin. Neither the Constitution nor the *Land Act* makes any reference to the race of citizens or non-citizens. Hence, ownership of land in freehold or mailo land is open to all citizens of Uganda regardless of race.

For purposes of land ownership, a person is deemed not to be a citizen of Uganda if the person is not a citizen of Uganda as defined by the Constitution and the *Uganda Citizenship and Immigration Control Act*, 1999.[36] With respect to a corporate body, a company limited by shares is deemed not to be a citizen of Uganda if the majority of its shareholders are non-citizens. If the company has no shares, it is deemed not to be a citizen of Uganda where non-citizens hold the majority vote. Where a company is incorporated in Uganda it is deemed to be a non-citizen unless its articles of association contain a provision that restrict transfer or issue of shares to persons who are not citizens of Uganda.[37] If for any reason an owner of freehold or mailo land loses his or her Uganda citizenship, the tenure automatically converts to leasehold for a period of ninety-nine years from the date of loss of citizenship.[38] In that case, the district land board in which the land is situated becomes the lessor.[39] The Act does not expressly imply any terms in the converted lease nor does it include a requirement to pay ground rent. The absence of any such a provision suggests that parliament had no intention to impose any covenants in the leasehold. It should also be noted that the Act does not make provision for payment of compensation to the landowners for conversion of their freehold or mailo tenure to leasehold. Since a lease is a smaller estate than mailo and freehold, it is arguable that the conversion to leasehold constitutes deprivation of property

---

33 Section 41(1) & (2).

34 Section 41(4). Interestingly, the provision does not mention ownership or acquisition of land under customary tenure. This may raise the issue whether, for example, a Muganda who becomes an Australian citizen may inherit customary land.

35 H.F. Morris and James S. Read, *Uganda, The Development of its Laws and Constitution*, supra, 337.

36 Section 41(7)(a) of the *Land Act*. For the definition of a 'Uganda citizen' see generally articles 9 – 13 of the Constitution and the *Uganda Citizenship and Immigration Control Act*, 1999, Part III.

37 Section 7(e) of the *Companies Act*.

38 Section 41(6) of the *Land Act*..

39 There is no provision in the Act that expressly says so, but this power may be implied in s.60(1)(a).

without compensation contrary to Article 26 (2) of the Constitution. If that is true, s. 41(6) of the *Land Act* might be challenged on constitutional grounds.[40]

Protection of family land

The Uganda Constitutional Commission reported that throughout the country many people had expressed concern about the right of family members to own land and have a say in its management. The commission observed that there were elements of injustices in this regard, which could be eliminated only by clearly defined rights.[41]

The recommendations of the constitutional commission report are reflected in the *Land Act*. Section 40 of the Act prohibits a landowner from selling, mortgaging, leasing, donating (except in a will), or entering into any other transaction in respect of land the family resides on and earns a livelihood from (herein referred to as 'family land') without prior written consent of the landowner's spouse.[42] This provision applies to any land irrespective of the system of tenure under which the land is owned. The section stipulates that the landowner's spouse must personally communicate his or her consent to the parish committee in the area where the land is situated.[43] This is to ensure that the consent is freely given without coercion or intimidation by the landowner. Where the landowner resides on the land with dependent children who have attained the age of majority,[44] they too must give their consent prior to the transaction taking effect. If the children are minors, the parish committee must give consent to the transaction.[45] In all cases, the Act requires that the consent should not be unreasonably withheld. A person aggrieved by a denial of consent may appeal to the Land Tribunal. In an appropriate case, the tribunal may dispense with the requirement for consent.[46]

Under the general principles of the law of contract, where the making of a contract is prohibited by statute, not only is the purported contract void but also any consideration transferred pursuant to such contract normally is not recoverable.[47] It is thought that this is the intended legal consequence under the Act. This view is partly based on s. 40(4) of the Act. The section states that if a purchaser[48] is a *bona fide* purchaser for value and had no notice that consent was not given, that purchaser shall be entitled to recover from the landowner any consideration paid even though the transaction is void. The converse is that where the purchaser is not a *bona fide* purchaser or had notice of the absence of consent the money is not recoverable. Thus, for example, where a bank lends money to a landowner on security of family land without his or her family's consent, the mortgage would be void. The bank would not be entitled to recover the money advanced unless it satisfied the requirements of a *bona fide* purchaser for value without notice.[49]

---

40 For detailed discussion see John Mugambwa, 'Examining Land Law and Tenure issues arising under the new Uganda Constitution', in Pal Ahluwalia and Paul Nursey-Bray (ed).), *The Post-Colonial Condition – Contemporary Politics in Africa* (Nora Science Publishers, New York, 1997) p. 67.

41 The Uganda Constitutional Commission (chaired by Justice Odoki), Government Printer, 1992.

42 The use of the conjunction 'and' suggests that the consent provision does not apply where both or one of the elements is missing. For example, if the landowner has an investment house he or she does not require his or her spouse's consent to dispose of it.

43 Section 40 (3)

44 The provision envisages mature age children who for some reason, such as physical disability are dependent on the landowner for sustenance. See *Hansard* pp. 4114 and 4097.

45 Section 40(1)(ii) and (iii).

46 Section 40(5) & (6).

47 *Kulubya v Singh* [1963] EA 408. In that case it was held that where prohibition was intended to protect a particular class of people, any member of that class is entitled to recover consideration he or she paid under the illegal contract

48 The term 'purchaser' includes a buyer, mortgagee, lessee and grantee, s. 40 (4).

49 An example would be where the bank in good faith was not aware that the mortgaged land is family land.

The spouse and or dependent children of the landowner have a right to lodge a caveat on the certificate of title or the certificate of customary ownership of the land in question. The object of a caveat is to give notice to any potential dealer in the land that the land is subject to the requirement of consent.[50] However, it is submitted that in view of s. 40(4), whether or not a caveat is lodged a transaction affecting the land would still be void without the requisite consent. The significance of a caveat is that where it is lodged a person who enters into a transaction affecting the land without the prescribed consent, when he or she attempts to recover the consideration will have a heavy onus to prove that he or she was a *bona fide* purchaser without notice.

It should be noted that when a landowner mortgages the land with the appropriate consent, and he or she defaults in payment of the mortgage debt, the mortgagee does not require consent of the landowner's family to sell the land.[51] The reason for this is obvious. By consenting to the transaction the family members are deemed to accept the risk involved in the event of default. Indeed, that is why the section requires consent of the family. It would be unfair to require a mortgagee to seek family consent again before exercising the power of sell. Interestingly, it would seem that s. 40 does not apply where it is sought to sell family land in execution of a judgement debt against the landowner, including, ironically, to recover consideration paid by a *bona fide* purchaser under a void transaction. In our view, s. 40 needs amendment to strengthen the protection of family land.

Control over land use

Whilst the Constitution vests ownership of land in the citizens of Uganda, it gives the government power to regulate land use under laws made by parliament and policies made from time to time.[52] Examples of such laws include: the *Forest Act* (cap 246),[53] the *National Environmental Statute*, 1995,[54] the *Water Statute* 1995 and the *Mining Act*. Section 44 of the *Land Act* provides that a landowner or occupier of land must use and manage the land in accordance with the aforementioned statutes and any other law.[55]

Under article 237(2) of the Constitution, the government has power to take over the management of environmentally sensitive areas for the benefit of society as a whole. Such land includes forests, water systems, swamps, national parks, and gazetted areas. Section 45(1) of the *Land Act* enacts a similar provision. The Act provides that the government shall be the trustee of such land or, if requested, it may allow a local government to be the trustee of the land for the benefit of society as a whole.[56] Section 45(4) prohibits the government, central or local, from leasing or alienating any land it holds in trust. However, subject to other specific legislation, which deals with the subject land, it may grant concessions, licences and permits in respect of such land.[57] Parliament may review any land held in trust by the government or a local government, if the people who reside in the area where the land is situated request it.

Compulsory acquisition of land

The Constitution of Uganda protects individual rights to property. Article 26(2) of the Constitution prohibits the government from compulsorily depriving any person of his or her property or right to possession unless three conditions are satisfied. First, the taking of possession or acquisition of

---

50 Section 40(7).

51 Section 40(2).

52 Article 242.

53 See s 14(2) of the *Forest Act*, for example, prohibits clearance, use or occupation of land in a forest reserve for grazing, camping etc without licence.

54 For example, the Statute (ss.35 and 37) imposes restrictions on the use of lakes, rivers and wetlands.

55 For example, s.26(4) of the *Uganda Wildlife Statute*, 1996, provides that historical land use rights of individuals may be limited within a wildlife conservation area..

56 Section 45(2).

57 Section 45(5). See for example, the *Uganda Wildlife Statute*, 1996, *National Environmental Statute*, 1995, and the *Forest Act* (cap 246).

property must be necessary for public use, interest of defence, public safety, public order, public morality, or public health. Secondly, it must be made under a law which provides for prompt payment of fair and adequate compensation. Thirdly, the law must provide for a right of access to the courts to interested persons aggrieved by the decision.

The power of the government to acquire private property compulsorily is not unique. All governments irrespective of their political persuasion reserve to themselves this power. It is based on the philosophy that in certain circumstances individual rights may be sacrificed for the general good.[58] Provided the individual is adequately compensated and the power otherwise used fairly, compulsory acquisition of property is not objectionable on human rights grounds. For example, under s. 2(1) of the *Land Acquisition Act* 1965 (cap 14), the minister is empowered to acquire any land if he or she is satisfied that the land is required for a 'public purpose'. The Act makes provision for payment of compensation to any person whose estate or interest in the land is extinguished as a result.[59] Any interested person aggrieved by the minister's decision or by the compensation paid may appeal to the High Court.[60]

Prima facie, the minister decides whether acquisition of particular land is 'required' (or 'necessary')[61] for a public purpose or one of the several purposes mentioned in article 26(2) of the Constitution. However, if an aggrieved interested person appeals, the court determines whether the acquisition is indeed necessary for the particular purpose. It is submitted that the expression 'necessary for public use' entails two separate requirements. First, acquisition of the land must be justified as necessary, not absolutely, but in a sense that it is reasonably requisite for or conducive to achieving a specified purpose.[62] Secondly, the purpose must be for public use or other purpose specified in article 26(2) of the Constitution. Both of these requirements must be satisfied for the acquisition of a particular parcel of land to be lawful. For example, acquisition of certain land may be necessary in order to achieve a particular objective. Nevertheless, if that objective were not a public purpose the acquisition would be unlawful.

Conversely, if land is ostensibly acquired for public use but its acquisition is not actually necessary to accomplish that purpose the acquisition would be contrary to the Constitution and therefore void. Whether or not the acquisition of a particular piece of land is required for public use would depend on the circumstances of each individual case. It is suggested that the courts are not likely to interfere with the minister's decision to acquire particular land upon allegation that acquisition of the land is not necessary because, for example, the government has some other land, which it could use. The reason is that the decision whether acquisition of particular land is necessary for public use is mainly one of policy which the minister is in the best position to make. However, where there is evidence of impropriety or ulterior motive against the minister the courts could question his or her decision under the usual rules of administrative law.[63] Ulterior motive and impropriety are serious allegations, which must be strictly proved.

The issue that is more likely to cause legal controversy is whether the purpose for which the minister purported to acquire particular land is a public purpose or one of the several purposes mentioned in article 26(2) of the Constitution. Certain situations are straightforward. For example, where land is acquired by the government for its own or local authority use, in the absence of proof of an ulterior motive it would be scarcely arguable that the land is not required for public purpose whatever actual use it puts it to. This is because the public interest is directly concerned with the government action and undertaking. Sometimes a statute may expressly state that land acquired

---

58 For detailed discussion see John Mugambwa 'Article 26(2) of the 1995 Constitution of Uganda and the Protection of Private Property,' (1998) vol 4.1 *East African Journal of Peace and Human Rights* (70).

59 Sections 5 and 6, *Land Acquisition Act*.

60 Sections 12-13.

61 The terms 'required' and 'necessary' mean the same thing.

62 See definition of 'necessary' in *Black's Law Dictionary* (6th, edn).

63 See for example, *In re (An Application by) Bukoba Gymkhana Club* (1963) EA 478.

for a particular purpose is a public purpose. For example, s. 84(2)(b) of the *Water Statute*, 1995, provides that acquisition of land for purposes of the statute shall be deemed to be for a public purpose within meaning of article 26 of the Constitution. Another example, s. 72(4) of the *Electricity Act*, 1999, provides that where the minister is satisfied that certain land is required for providing or maintaining electricity service to the public, the land may be acquired under the *Land Acquisition Act* and the *Land Act*. The section declares that the acquisition of such land shall be deemed to be in the public interest whether the beneficiary is a public entity or a private person. It is submitted that, unless there is proof of ulterior motive, the minister's decision to acquire land compulsorily for any purpose mentioned in the *Water Statute* or the *Electricity Act*, cannot be overturned by the land tribunal on an allegation that it is not a public purpose.

The legal position is less clear where, for example, in the absence of a statutory provision such as above, the minister seeks to acquire land in order to re-grant it to a private person or body. It is submitted that expropriation of land for private use may legitimately qualify as public use within the meaning of article 26(2) of the Constitution where there appears to be substantial public gain. For instance, where the government expropriates customary land for a private developer to construct a factory this would constitute a public purpose notwithstanding that the developer also stands to benefit.[64] It would be different if, for example, the minister expropriates land to sell to another for his or her private use.

Compulsory acquisition under the *Land Act*

In addition to its powers under the *Land Acquisition Act*, the government may acquire land by compulsory process under the *Land Act*. Section 43 of the Act provides that the government or local government may acquire land in accordance with the provisions of articles 26 and 237(2) of the Constitution.[65] The Act gives the district land tribunal jurisdiction to determine any disputes relating to the amount of compensation to be paid for land acquired under this provision.[66] In determining the amount of compensation, the tribunal must take into account certain prescribed factors.[67] For example, if the land acquired is customary land its value is determined by reference to the open market value of the land, without taking into account the improvements.[68] In the case of a building, the method of assessment varies depending on whether the land is urban or rural. If it is urban land, the value of the building is its open market value and if rural, it is the depreciated replacement cost of the building. Where there are standing crops on the land, their value must be included except annual crops that could be harvested during the period of notice given to the landowner.[69] The value of the crops must be assessed in accordance with a list of rates compiled and kept by the district land board.[70]

---

64 For detailed discussion see Mugambwa 'Article 26(2) and the Protection of Private Property' *supra* pp. 88-89.

65 This provision appears to be redundant in view of the minister's powers under the *Land Acquisition Act*, 1965. Interestingly, there is no provision in the *Land Act* that expressly requires the government to make prompt and adequate payment to persons whose land is compulsorily acquired. (Section 42(7)(b), which provides for fair compensation and a right to remain on the land until paid, applies only where land is acquired under s. 42(4)(b) utilising the Land Fund). However, it is arguable that the constitutional requirement is implied in section 43 by the expression 'in accordance with the provisions of article 26 and clause (2) of article 237(2) of the Constitution'.

66 Section 77(1)(b). The implication is that the district land tribunal has no jurisdiction to determine disputes relating to, for example, whether the purpose for which the land is purportedly acquired is necessary for a public purpose.

67 Section 78(1), *Land Act.*.

68 Section 78 (1)(a).

69 Section 78 (1) (c).

70 Section 78(3). Under s. 60(1)(e), the district land boards must compile and maintain a list of rates of compensation payable in respect of crops and buildings of a non-permanent nature.

The Act also requires the government to pay a 'disturbance allowance' to the persons whose land it acquires under s. 43. This is an additional compensation over and above the compensation assessed. The allowance is fifteen per centum (or thirty per centum if less than six month's notice is given for vacant possession) of the overall assessment of the land.[71] This allowance is for the inevitable inconvenience a person suffers because of being forced to leave his or her home.

Compensation from the Land Fund

The Act provides that the Land Fund shall be utilised, inter alia, by the government to acquire registered land to enable tenants by occupancy to acquire registrable interests pursuant to the Constitution and to resettle persons rendered landless by government action or natural disaster.[72] The landowners may of course voluntarily sell or make their land available for this purpose. The section does not expressly give the government power to acquire the land compulsorily if the landowner refuses to sell or give up land required for this purpose. However, it would seem under s. 42(7) that parliament intended that the minister, if necessary, could acquire the land by compulsory process under the provisions of the *Land Acquisition Act*.[73] Section 42(7) prescribes special rules (which override inconsistent provisions of the *Land Acquisition Act*) for compensation of persons whose land is compulsorily acquired. First, it states that compensation must be paid to the landowners at 'a fair market valuation assessed on a willing seller willing buyer basis'. This probably means that compensation must be assessed at the market value. If this is right then it is suggested that the provision is unnecessary because essentially that is what article 26(2)(6)(b) of the Constitution says and there is nothing in the *Land Acquisition Act* to suggest otherwise. The provision most likely was inserted in order to re-assure landowners, especially mailo landowners, that adequate compensation would be paid in the event of compulsory acquisition of their land to enable tenants by occupancy to obtain registrable interests.

Secondly, s. 42(7)(b) provides that a person whose land is acquired shall not be evicted until he or she receives the compensation awarded or agreed upon. This provision overrides s 6 of the *Land Acquisition Act*. The latter section provides that, if the minister certifies that it is in the public interest, the assessment officer may take possession of any land acquired under the Act at any time after publication of the declaration of acquisition. Thirdly, s. 42(7)(c) provides that the assessment of compensation must include losses caused by severance or injurious affection. It is noteworthy that under the *Land Acquisition Act*, there is no provision for compensation for injurious affection. Nor does the general law normally take into account injurious affection when assessing compensation.

Fourthly, s. 42(7)(d) provides that compensation must include all reasonable costs of disturbance of the person from whom the land is acquired.[74] Such costs would most likely include expenses incurred to transport the landowner and his or her family and personal effects to the new place of abode. Presumably, it could also include any increase in transport costs incurred by the landowner to travel to and from his or her place of work. Finally, s. 42(7)(e) provides that where customary land is acquired, a person who was using the land as his or her home shall be paid an additional 'disturbance' allowance. The allowance must not exceed fifteen per centum of the total sum awarded. Presumably, the Uganda Land Commission (or, in case of dispute, the district land tribunal) shall determine the amount of compensation to be paid in accordance with the circumstances of each case, if the amount shall not exceed fifteen per centum of the total sum awarded.

---

[71] Section 78(2).

[72] Section 42 (4)(b) and (c).

[73] It is implied in the provision that the acquisition of such land is in the public interest within the meaning of article 26 (2)(a) and 237(2)(a) of the Constitution. In the end it will be for the courts to decide whether or not that is the case.

[74] Section 42(7)(d).

It should be pointed out that the provisions for compulsory acquisition of land are confusing and, in our view, need re-drafting. For example, as we have pointed out above, it is not clear what purpose s.43 serves in view of the powers already possessed by the minister under the *Land Acquisition Act*.[75] The two provisions need to be reconciled or one of them should be deleted. Secondly, if the minister acquires land under the *Land Acquisition Act*, it is not clear whether the tribunal in assessing the compensation must take into account the requirements of s. 78 of the *Land Act*. A strict interpretation of this section suggests that it only applies where the government acquires land under s. 43 of the *Land Act*.[76] Yet, in our view, there is no logical reason why it should make a difference whether the land is acquired under the *Land Act* or the *Land Acquisition Act*. Finally, we have assumed that parliament intended that s. 42(7), which overrides contrary provisions of the *Land Acquisition Act*, applies only where the government uses the Land Fund to acquire land for the purpose of enabling tenants by occupancy to obtain registrable interests or to resettling people rendered landless. The reason for the assumption is that s. 42 deals exclusively with the Land Fund. Again, there appears to be no logical reason why the same rule should not apply in other cases of compulsory land acquisition.

LAND DISPUTES SETTLEMENT

Under the *Land Act*, all courts below the High Court ceased to have jurisdiction to deal with land disputes.[77] The powers originally exercised by magistrate's courts are now vested with land tribunals created under the Act. As we shall presently see, under the tribunal system for the first time in Uganda's legal history non-lawyers will play a greater role in formal land disputes settlements than hitherto. Indeed, potentially the majority of the people involved in land dispute settlements will be non-lawyers. The involvement of non-lawyers, with diverse backgrounds and knowledge, is likely to have substantial impact on the development of land tenure law in this country. The nature and extent of the non-lawyer influence on land law remains to be seen. Nevertheless, lawyers will undoubtedly continue to play a very important role representing their clients before the tribunals and, of course, in the event of an appeal against a tribunal's decision the High Court will check and balance the tribunals' interpretation of the law. We shall consider each of the institutions established under the Act and their jurisdiction.

Land tribunals

The establishment of Land Tribunals is a constitutional requirement. Article 243 of the Constitution requires parliament to enact a law for the establishment of land tribunals, which shall be vested with the power, *inter alia,* to determine disputes relating to landownership, transactions and the assessment of compensation for compulsory acquisition of land. That law is the *Land Act*, 1998. The Act provides for the creation of land tribunals at district, sub-county, city division and urban areas levels.

District land tribunals

Section 75(1) of the Act provides that a tribunal, known as the district land tribunal, shall be established in each and every district in the country. A district land tribunal is the highest tribunal

---

[75] It has been suggested that the *Land Acquisition Act*, 1965, violates articles 26 and 42 of the Constitution. It conflicts with article 26 because it allows the taking of possession before compensation is paid and does not provide for prompt payment of fair and adequate compensation. It conflicts with article 42 (which provides for a fair hearing before an administrative body and a right to apply to court against an administrative decision) in that it has no provision for any hearing or challenge to the minister's decision that land is required for a public purpose. See McAuslan and Mwebaza, 'Legal Appraisal', Annex 6, Vol.2, p. 14, Government of Uganda Report on the Land Act Implementation Study, 9 September 1999:

[76] See also s. 77(1)(b).

[77] Section 98(7). See provision for transitional jurisdiction below.

in the district. Its membership shall consist of a chairperson and two other members all appointed by the Chief Justice, acting on the advice of the Judicial Service Commission.[78]

Section 75(2) stipulates that the chairperson of the district land tribunal must be a lawyer who is qualified to be a Magistrate Grade 1. There are no formal educational requirements for tribunal members.[79] However, s.75(3) prescribes that only persons with knowledge and experience in land matters shall be eligible for appointment as members of the tribunal. The Act does not give any guidance as to what constitutes the requisite knowledge and experience for this purpose. Most lawyers because of their training would qualify for appointment as tribunal members. Nevertheless, in our view, knowledge and experience in land matters does not necessarily mean that members have to be lawyers, because, if that were the legislative intention, it would have said so, as it did with respect to the qualifications of the chairperson. It will be up to the Chief Justice to determine in each case whether a particular candidate satisfies the statutory requirements. Potential candidates would include former civil servants, chiefs, former local council officials, and any other person who worked in an environment that enabled him or her to acquire knowledge and experience in relation to land matters. Besides knowledge and experience in land matters, the person to be appointed must be at least thirty years old, of sound mind, character and proven integrity, have no criminal record involving moral turpitude and have never been declared bankrupt. Unlike membership of the land boards and committees, which must consist of at least one-woman member, there is no statutory requirement for gender balance on a district land tribunal.[80] However, in this era of 'political correctness' it is thought that when making appointments the Chief Justice will be mindful of the need for gender balance wherever possible.

Terms of service

Article 243(4) of the Constitution provides that a member of a land tribunal shall hold office on terms and conditions determined by a law made by parliament. Section 76 of the *Land Act* stipulates that a member of a district land tribunal shall hold office for a period of five years and may be eligible for re-appointment. To foster their independence the Act protects members from arbitrary termination of their appointment. Section 76(2) empowers the Chief Justice to remove a member from office but only on the grounds stated therein. The grounds are: inability to perform his or her functions due to infirmity of mind or body, misconduct, incompetence, absence from at least five consecutive sittings without lawful excuse, conviction of a criminal offence involving moral turpitude, or if declared bankrupt. Members of the tribunal shall receive a salary and allowances as determined by the Public Service Commission on the recommendation of the Judicial Service Commission. Their salary and allowances shall be charged on the Consolidated Fund.[81]

Jurisdiction of district land tribunals

District Land Tribunals have jurisdiction to deal with, virtually, any disputes over land within their geographical jurisdiction. Section 77(1)(a) provides that a district land tribunal shall determine land disputes relating to the grant, lease, repossession, transfer or acquisition of land whether arising under the Act or otherwise and whether between individuals or involving the Uganda Land

---

78 Section 75(5). Article 243(3) of the Constitution, requires that the chairperson of a land tribunal shall be appointed on the advice of the Judicial Service Commission.

79 In view of the requirements that members of the lower tribunals must have completed a minimum formal education of Ordinary Level or its equivalent for sub-county tribunals, s. 81(3)(b), and a Diploma level for the urban land tribunals, s. 82(3)(b), high education qualifications will be expected of members of the district land tribunals.

80 A proposal to insert a similar requirement as for land boards and committees was rejected by parliament because it may in some instances complicate recruitment of tribunal members with the requisite qualifications. See *Hansard*

81 Section 75(6)

Commission or other authorities with responsibility over land.[82] The district land tribunal has also jurisdiction to determine disputes over the amount of compensation payable for land acquired by compulsory process.[83] As we shall presently see, lower tribunals have a financial jurisdiction limitation. Section 77(1)(c) expressly gives the district land tribunal the jurisdiction to deal with land disputes beyond the financial jurisdiction of lower tribunals. Moreover, it has the power to make consequential orders relating to cancellation of entries and or vesting of title in respect of cases handled by the lower tribunals.[84]

Section 77(2) provides that in exercising its jurisdiction under the Act, the district land tribunal shall have all the powers of a Magistrate Grade 1 under the *Magistrates Act*. Additionally, the tribunal has the power to grant orders of specific performance, injunctions, declarations, and such other relief and orders as the circumstances of the case may require. Specific powers of the tribunal include the following: power to cancel, vary, or postpone the operation of any action, notice, order, decree, or declaration. Moreover, it may substitute a different decision for the one determined by any official, board, committee, association, or the commission. Furthermore, the tribunal may confirm a decision or order made by any official, board, association, or the commission, notwithstanding any procedural error, if it is satisfied that no injustice will be caused by such confirmation.

Rules of procedure

It is envisaged under the Act that the rules of procedure of the district land tribunal will not necessarily be the same as those followed by the ordinary courts. Section 79(1) provides that the land tribunals shall follow rules of procedure made by the Chief Justice. In formulating the rules, the Chief Justice is enjoined to make such necessary modifications to the rules of evidence as would facilitate the expeditious disposal of land disputes. Moreover, since the same rules will apply in the lower tribunals, they must be made in such a way that lower tribunals constituted by non-lawyers can apply them.[85]

Appeal

The district land tribunal shall hear appeals from lower land tribunals within its jurisdiction established under sections 81 and 82 of the Act.[86] An appeal against a decision of the District Land Tribunal in exercise of its original or appellate jurisdiction lies to the High Court.[87]

Sub-county, urban district and city division tribunals

The *Land Act* provides for the establishment of a land tribunal in each sub-county, gazetted urban area and division in a city.[88] A sub-county tribunal shall consist of a chairperson and two other members. At least one of the members must be a woman.[89] The Judicial Service Commission appoints members of the tribunal.[90] Section 81(3) provides that a person shall not be appointed to the tribunal unless he or she is at least thirty years old,[91] has completed a minimum formal education of Ordinary Level or its equivalent, has not been declared bankrupt or convicted of a criminal offence involving moral turpitude.[92]

---

82 See also Chapter 2.

83 Section 77(1)(b). See also 'Compulsory acquisition of land', above.

84 Section 77(1)(d).

85 Section 79(2).

86 Section 88(2).

87 Section 88(1) and (3).

88 Sections 81(1) 82(1) and (4).

89 Section 81(2). It seems that this requirement must be satisfied even if the chairperson is a woman.

90 Section 83.

91 The age requirement does not apply where a person holds a diploma or higher degree, s. 81(4).

92 Section 81(3).

Urban and city division land tribunals consist of a chairperson and two members[93] appointed by the Judicial Service Commission.[94] In this instance there is no statutory requirement for at least one of the members to be a woman. However, as earlier suggested, most likely the Judicial Service Commission will, wherever possible, be sensitive to gender bias when making appointments. For a person to be eligible for appointment he or she must be at least thirty years old,[95] have completed a minimum formal education of at least Diploma level from a recognised institution, and have not been declared bankrupt nor convicted of a criminal offence involving moral turpitude.[96]

Terms of service

Members of the land tribunals shall hold office for a period of five years and are eligible for re-appointment. A member may be removed from office only on grounds specified under the *Land Act.* Section 84(2) provides that a member may be removed from office for inability to perform duties due to infirmity of mind or body, misbehaviour, incompetence or abandonment of duties. Members of the land tribunal shall be paid such salaries and allowances as specified in their letters of appointment, and the money drawn from the Consolidated Fund.[97]

Jurisdiction of land tribunals

Land tribunals have the power to determine any land disputes within their respective jurisdictions. However, there is a financial limit to their jurisdiction. A sub-county land tribunal's jurisdiction is limited to determining land disputes whose value does not exceed two thousand five hundred currency points (fifty million shillings).[98] The pecuniary jurisdiction of urban district land tribunals and city division tribunals is limited to five thousand currency points (one hundred million shillings) and twelve thousand five hundred currency points (two hundred and fifty million shillings), respectively. Besides the financial limitation, sub-county, urban and city division tribunals have no power to order for the cancellation of entries on a certificate of title, cancel a certificate of title or make a vesting order. The tribunals have to refer such cases to the relevant district land tribunal.[99]

Rules of procedure

The rules of procedure made by the Chief Justice under s. 79(1) for the district land tribunals, shall equally apply in the lower tribunals.[100]

Appeals

An appeal shall lie from sub-county, urban, and city division tribunals to the district land tribunal.[101]

Alternative dispute resolution

In addition to the tribunals, the *Land Act* provides two alternative mechanisms for resolving land disputes. First, there is the customary dispute settlement and mediation, and secondly, the mediator. We shall consider each of these institutions separately.

Customary dispute settlement and mediation

All societies in Uganda have had and continue to have their own traditional ways of resolving disputes, including land disputes, outside the formal court system. In some communities, traditional

---

93 Sections 82(3) and (5).

94 Section 83.

95 This requirement does not apply to a person who holds a University degree in 'land matters', s 82(7). There is no definition in the Act of the expression 'land matters'.

96 Section 82(3).

97 Section 87.

98 'A currency point' represents twenty thousand Uganda shillings, see Schedule, *Land Act.*

99 Section 85(2). See also s. 77(2).

100 Section 86.

101 Section 88(2).

institutions still play a very important role in settling disputes even though their role has not hitherto been officially recognised. The *Land Act* for the first time gives a legal recognition to the role of traditional institutions as a possible avenue for resolving land disputes. This is an avenue which ought to be encouraged. Section 89(1) expressly declares that the provision for land tribunals shall not be construed as intended to undermine or limit the functions of traditional authorities in determining disputes over customary land or acting as mediators over disputes involving such land. The provision gives parties to a dispute over customary land an opportunity, if they feel more comfortable, to refer the matter to a customary institution that is more familiar to them. Section 89(2) provides that at the commencement of a case or at any time during the hearing, if the land tribunal is of the view that because of the nature of the dispute, it ought to be dealt with by traditional mediation rather than by litigation, the tribunal may advise the parties to refer their dispute to such institution. For example, in a land dispute between members of the same family, if the tribunal thought that the parties' elders should resolve the dispute through mediation it might advise them accordingly. In that case, the tribunal should adjourn the proceedings for a period of up to three months to allow the traditional dispute process to proceed. However, if at the end of the period specified by the tribunal the matter is still unresolved, the parties are free to resume proceedings before the land tribunal.[102] It is important to note that this provision only applies to disputes involving customary tenure.

Mediator

The *Land Act* makes provision for the appointment and use of a mediator to resolve land disputes. The use of mediation to settle disputes is, of course, not new. As we have stated above, mediation has always been the most common way of resolving disputes in all communities in Uganda. The Act simply gives it official recognition. Section 90(1) provides that the land tribunal shall appoint a mediator on an ad hoc basis. There are no required formal qualifications for a mediator. However, s. 90(2) prescribes certain qualities that a person must have to be eligible for appointment as a mediator. These include a requirement that the person must be of high moral character and proved integrity; and, by virtue of his or her knowledge, work, reputation or standing in society, must be capable of assisting or likely to assist parties to a land dispute to reach an amicable settlement.

The *Land* Act specifies two situations where a mediator appointed under s. 90 should be used. First, a mediator may be used in negotiations to regularise the relationship between a registered owner and persons on his or her land who do not qualify to be *bona fide* occupants.[103] Secondly, a mediator may be used to help a tenant by occupancy and the registered landowner enter into a negotiated settlement where either wishes to assign his or her interest.[104] It should be stressed that a mediator has no power to coerce the parties into agreement. The mediator's role, as described by the minister of Lands during the parliamentary debate of the Land Bill, is 'to narrow down any disagreement between the parties'.[105] To do this a mediator needs to demonstrate skills of persuasion and conciliation. But in the end it is up to the parties to make up their minds. For example, in the negotiations between a landowner and a non-*bona fide* occupant to regularise their relationship, if, in spite of the mediator's efforts, the parties fail to agree it would seem that the landowner may evict the occupant.[106] With respect to negotiations between a tenant by occupancy and a registered owner, if after three months of negotiations the mediator is unable to assist the parties to reach an agreement, the party wishing to assign may proceed to dispose of his or her interest as he or she wishes.

---

[102] The right to resume proceedings where mediation fails is implied. See *Hansard*, 29 June 1998, p. 4352.

[103] Section 31(2) and (3). See also Chapter 2.

[104] Section 36(6) and (7).

[105] *Hansard*, 28 June 1998, p 4299. See also p. 4300.

[106] See Chapter 2.

Mediation as opposed to litigation is encouraged in other situations under the *Land Act*. For example, in the case of an application for a certificate of occupancy, the land committee is required to use its best endeavours to resolve conflicting claims by mediation.[107] Similarly, under section 21(1)(b), if disputes arise between members of a land association, the District Registrar of Titles is required to refer the matter to the land board or some other person to act as a mediator. It is important to note that a mediator in this instance need not be a person formally appointed as a mediator by the land tribunal under s. 90 of the Act.

Transitional jurisdiction

Section 98(5) of the *Land Act*, provides that the High Court shall continue to hear any land dispute cases pending before it prior to the commencement of the Act: 2 July 1998.[108] Section 98(6) gives similar powers to magistrates' courts and local council courts to complete any such cases pending before them prior to the commencement of the Act. The magistrates' and local council courts must complete all pending cases within a period of two years from the date the Act came into effect.

When that period expired on 2 July 2000, the magistrates' courts and local council courts ceased to have the jurisdiction to continue hearing land cases they were yet to dispose of.[109] A subsequent amendment of s 98, Land (Amendment) Act 2000, authorises these courts to complete such cases.

It should be emphasised that this is just a temporary measure to enable these courts to finish the cases filed before the *Land Act* came into effect, but it does not otherwise restore their jurisdiction over land disputes.

---

[107] Section 7(5). See also Chapter 2.

[108] This provision is probably unnecessary in view of the fact that the High Court has unlimited original jurisdiction in all matters, see article 139(1) of the Constitution.

[109] By the time the two-year period expired many of such cases had not yet been disposed of.

4
General Principles of Land Law

This chapter deals with some of the most important general principles of land law. They are considered under the following subheadings:

1. The doctrine of tenure and estates
2. Meaning of land
3. Equitable and legal interests in land
4. Adverse possession

THE DOCTRINE OF TENURE AND ESTATES

There are two basic tenets of the English law of real property. They are the doctrine of tenure and the doctrine of estates.

Doctrine of tenure

The doctrine of tenure states that the crown, who is the Lord Paramount, owns all land in England.[1] There is no land which is allodial or owned by a subject and not held either directly or indirectly of the crown. The crown's title is variously described as the 'radical' or 'absolute' or 'ultimate' title.[2] The origin of the doctrine of tenure is founded in the traditional belief that some time after the Norman conquest of England in 1066, William I declared all lands in England to be his by conquest and surrender.[3] The king rewarded his followers with grants of land, not absolutely but conditionally on performance of various services. The term 'tenure' signifies holding land from a superior lord in return for services.[4]

Doctrine of estates

The doctrine of estates refers to the interest that the subjects own in land. According to English land law, a subject does not own land but holds an estate of the crown. An estate is an abstract entity which authorises a person to remain in possession of the land for a period, subject to the performance of tenurial duties.[5] The estate itself is property, which is the subject of ownership both at law and in equity.

Estates are classified into two broad groups: estates of freehold and estates less than freehold. The term 'estate of freehold' refers to estates that are of uncertain duration: fee simple, fee tail, and life estates. A fee simple estate is the largest estate in terms of duration that can exist at common law. The term 'fee' designates that it is inheritable and 'simple' indicates that it is inheritable by the general heirs[6] of the holder for the time being.[7] A fee simple estate only determines when the holder of the estate dies intestate and without any relatives whatsoever capable of inheriting it under intestate succession.[8] Since it is virtually impossible that a person could die intestate and without any relatives, a fee simple is capable of enduring indefinitely. For all practical purposes, an estate

---

1 *Attorney-General of Ontario v Mercer* (1883) LR 8 App Cas 767.

2 *Amodu Tijani v Southern Nigeria* [1921] 2 AC 399.

3 Megarry and Wade, *The Law of Real Property*, supra, 12.

4 *Ibid.*

5 *Ibid*, p. 38 *et seq.*

6 The expression 'general heirs' means relatives of any sort.

7 Burn, *Cheshire and Burn's Modern Law of Real property*, (14th ed, London, Butterworths, 1988), pp.149-50.

8 *Ibid.*

in fee simple is equivalent to full ownership of the land itself. Nevertheless, the basic thesis of English land law is that the radical title to all land remains with the crown.

A fee tail was a freehold estate that, unlike a fee simple estate, was inheritable by a limited class of relatives. Normally, its inheritance was limited to lineal descendants of the original grantor. For example a grant 'to A and heirs male of his body' meant that the estate was inheritable only by A's male descendants. If there were no male descendants, the land reverted to the original grantor or his successor in title.[9] The object of entailing was to ensure that the land remained to benefit a closed family. Fee tail estate is obsolete.

A life estate is an estate that endures for the life of the grantee or some other person's life. For example, where in a will a testator grants his house to 'A for life' it means that A has a freehold estate for as long as he or she is alive. After A's death the house will pass on to some other person named by the testator. A life estate is a freehold estate because its duration is uncertain, as it is not known when the holder will die and the estate terminate. However, a life estate cannot be inherited as it determines upon the death of the holder.

The expression 'estate less than freehold' refers to an estate whose date of termination is certain or fixed. The only such estate is a lease. A lease is a grant of land for a definite period. A lease, even if it is for 1000 years is not a freehold estate because the date of its termination is certain.[10]

Relevance of the doctrines of tenure and estates

According to *Salmond's Jurisprudence*,[11] upon the introduction of the common law in a colonial protectorate (as Uganda was), all land in the territory was vested in the crown. In other words, the radical or allodial title was vested in the crown in the same way as it did when William 1 conquered England in 1066.[12] With respect to Uganda, by virtue of the *Crown Lands (Declaration) Ordinance*, 1922,[13] it was affirmed that all land and any rights therein in the protectorate 'shall be presumed to be the property of the crown unless they have been or are thereafter recognised by the government by document to be the property of a person or until the contrary thereof be proved'. The effect was that, until the termination of the protectorate all land in Uganda not held under title (apart from mailo very little was so held), was deemed crown land, which legally was at the absolute disposal of the crown.[14] Arguably, mailo was allodial land or vested in individual holders and not held by the crown.[15]

Whether the doctrines of tenure and estates were introduced in Uganda by virtue of the protectorate and/or legislation is purely of academic interest. Under article 237(1) of the Constitution, the ultimate title to the land in Uganda is vested in the citizens of Uganda in accordance with the land tenure systems provided by the Constitution.[16]

---

9 Burn, *Cheshire and Burn's Modern Law of Real property*, supra, p. 149.

10 *Ibid*, p. 34.

11 10th ed, Appendix V, pp. 520 - 21(cited Roberts-Wray, *Commonwealth and Colonial Law* (London, Stevens & sons, 1966, pp. 625-26). See also Morris and Read, *Uganda: The Development of its Laws and Constitution* (London, Stevens, 1966): p. 44.

12 For criticism of Salmond's thesis, see Roberts-Wray, *Commonwealth and Colonial Law* (London, Stevens & sons, 1966), pp. 626-27.

13 *Revised Laws of Uganda* 1951, cap 118.

14 Morris and Read, *Uganda: The Development of its Laws and Constitution* (London, Stevens, 1966), p.45.

15 Obol-Ochola, *Customary Land Law and the Economic Development in Uganda*, supra, pp. 24 - 26.

16 See Chapter 2.

MEANING OF LAND

To lay people land is the solid portion of the earth's surface. But in law the term 'land' means more than that. The common law conception of land is summed up in the Latin maxim: *cuius est solum eius est usque ad coeolum et ad inferos*. Translated literally, the maxim means that the person to whom the soil belongs also owns the heavens above and everything below it.[17] The statutory definition of land also indicates that the concept of land covers much more than the physical portion of the earth's surface. For example, s. 2 of the *Registration of Titles Act* (cap 205) defines land as including 'messuages,[18] resources, tenements and hereditaments corporeal or incorporeal'.[19] Other statutory definitions may be wider or narrower depending on the object of the particular legislation. The definition of land is important because it determines the nature and extent of the rights of a landowner against the rest of the community. We shall examine some of these rights and their limitations.

Rights above the surface

The airspace above the surface belongs to the owner of the surface land. Any intrusion in the airspace by another is trespass. The fact that the intrusion is insignificant or that it causes no damage to the surface owner is not a defence. For example, in *Kelson v Imperial Tobacco Co. of Great Britain and Ireland*[20], the defendants fixed an advertising sign on their building projecting eight inches over the plaintiffs' building. It was held that the intrusion in the plaintiffs's airspace constituted trespass to land. The defendants were ordered to remove the offending object.

The question is, to what height does ownership of airspace extend? Is it to the 'heavens above' as the above maxim states? Some of the older cases suggest a positive response.[21] But modern cases have adopted a common sense approach and imposed a limit on the airspace above the surface. The authority commonly cited in this regard is the case of *Bernstein of Leigh (Baron) v Skyviews and General Ltd.*[22] In that case, the defendants without prior authority of the plaintiff took a single aerial photograph of the plaintiff's house from a height of one hundred metres. The plaintiff instituted proceedings alleging that the defendants had wrongfully entered the airspace above his house to take the photograph. He claimed damages for trespass. Griffiths J whilst admitting the maxim that a surface owner was entitled to the airspace above his or her land rejected the proposition that the landowner's rights extend to an unlimited height. His Honour emphasised the importance of balancing the rights of a landowner to enjoy the use of his or her land against the rights of the general public to take advantage of technology in the use of airspace, such as flying a plane. In his Honour's judgement the appropriate balance is best struck by restricting the landowner's right to such height as is necessary for the ordinary use and enjoyment of his or her land and the structures on it. Above that height, in his Honour's view the landowner had no greater rights in the airspace than any other member of the public.[23] In the instant case, Griffiths J found that the plane was flying one hundred metres above the ground and that there was no evidence to show that its mere presence in the plaintiff's airspace caused any interference with any use to which the plaintiff put or might put his land. He held that there was no infringement of the plaintiff's airspace and thus no trespass was committed.

The case of *Bernstein of Leigh (Baron) v Skyviews and General Ltd* stands for the proposition that land includes the airspace above the surface to a height the owner might conceivably use. The

---

17 Gray K, *Elements of Land Law* (2nd ed, London, Butterworths, 1993), p. 6.

18 'Messuage' means a house or similar structure and garden.

19 'Corporeal' refers to the physical soil and structures thereon, and 'incorporeal' are legal rights over land such as easements. See also definition of land in s. 3 *Interpretation Act* (cap 16).

20 [1957] 2 QB 334.

21 See authorities cited in *Bernstein of Leigh (Baron) v Skyviews and General Ltd* [1978] QB 479

22 [1978] QB 479.

23 *Ibid*, p. 488.

court did not quantify the height which is necessary for ordinary use. Clearly, each case depends on its own facts. It is important to note that the test is not whether the incursion interferes with the landowner's actual use of the airspace. Rather, it is whether the incursion is of such a nature and at such a height as may interfere with the ordinary use of the land by the owner.

There is no Ugandan case law to date which deals with this issue. It is thought that the test in *Bernstein of Leigh (Baron) v Skyviews and General Ltd* is of general application and likely to be followed.

Rights below the surface

At common law, the landowner is entitled to everything below the surface. On the analogy of *Berstein of Leigh (Baron) v Skyviews and General Ltd*, the surface owner's rights are probably limited to such depth as is necessary for his or her ordinary use and enjoyment of the structures thereon. Below that depth the landowner has no greater rights than members of the public.

The landowner's rights do not include minerals. Section 3 of the *Mining Act* (cap 248), states that the entire property in and control of all minerals and mineral oils in, under or upon any lands or waters in Uganda are and shall be vested in the government.

Fixtures

The common law definition of land includes everything that attaches to it. This proposition is summed up in yet another Latin maxim: *quic quid plantatur solo, solo cedit.* Literally translated it means that which attaches to the land goes with it. The maxim is primarily used to determine the rights of a landowner over things attached to or embedded in the land. The classical rule is that where a person fixes a thing (or chattel) on another's land or building on the land in such a way that in law it is a fixture, it becomes the property of the landowner.[24] The landowner has no legal obligation to compensate the person who attached the thing to the land.[25]

The rule is illustrated by a Nigerian case of *Francis v Ibitoye*.[26] In that case, the plaintiff was negotiating with the defendant to purchase the latter's land. Before the negotiations were concluded the plaintiff without the knowledge or consent of the defendant proceeded to construct a house on the land. Unfortunately, the negotiations for the sale of the land fell through. The plaintiff sued the defendant for compensation for the building he had erected on the land. It was held that the defendant was not under any legal obligation to compensate him. The judge said:

> I know of no authority for such a claim... It is trite law that a building erected in [such] circumstances... becomes the property of the landowner without any obligation to re-compensate the builder.[27]

However, in equity, the court may intervene in a case where the landowner's assertion of his or her strict legal rights is unconscionable. Lord Cranworth in the famous case of *Ramsden v Dyson* espoused the circumstance which would give rise to equitable jurisdiction to intervene.[28] His Lordship said that:

> If a stranger begins to build on my land supposing it to be his own, and I, perceiving his mistake, abstain from setting him right, and leave him to persevere in his error, a court of equity will not allow me afterwards to assert my title to the land on which he had expended money on the supposition that the land is his own. It considers that, when I saw the mistake... it was my duty to be active and to state my adverse title; and it would be dishonest in me ...afterwards to profit by the mistake which I might have prevented.

---

24 *Francis v Ibitoye* (1936) NLR 1.

25 *Lomolo v Kilembe Mines Ltd* CS No 395 of 1976; (1978) HCB 157; *Francis v Ibitoye* (1936) NLR 1.

26 (1936) NLR 1.

27 *Ibid*, 12. See also *Lomolo v Kilembe Mines Ltd* CS No 395 of 1976; (1978) HCB 157 (trespasser carrying out improvements on the land).

28 (1866) LR 1,HL 129:140-41.

Equity's intervention is based on the principle variously known as the doctrine of 'proprietary estoppel' or 'estoppel by acquiescence' or 'estoppel by encouragement'.[29] Lord Cranworth in his judgement stressed that for the equity to arise the person must expend money or do some act mistakenly believing that the subject land belongs to him or her, or that he or she is authorised by the landowner. Secondly, that the true owner must be aware at the material time that the land belongs to him or her and that the other person is mistaken.[30] Once the equity is established, the court has a wide discretion to determine the most appropriate remedy to satisfy the equity. For example, the court may order the landowner to compensate the other person for the improvements,[31] or grant the improver a right to remain on the land subject to any terms determined by the court.[32]

The High Court, in *Babiruga v Karegyesa and others*[33], applied the principle of *Ramsden v Dyson*. In that case, the respondents constructed a number of houses on the appellant's (their father's) land without his consent. The court found that the appellant was aware and acquiesced in the respondents' building on his land. Accordingly, it held that the respondents had an equitable right to be on the land. Their right was subject to termination on the appellant paying them compensation for the buildings they had constructed on the land.

Similarly, in the case of *Musoke Bafirawala v Jogga*,[34] the High Court ordered the landowner to pay compensation to the defendant for improvements he had made on the land. The facts of the case were as follows. In 1960, the plaintiff went abroad leaving the defendant as caretaker of his land with authority to collect rent and send the money over to the plaintiff. For some years the defendant managed the land on the plaintiff's behalf. Subsequently, he abandoned his caretaker role and instead assumed ownership of the land. He carried out improvements on the land including construction of other buildings. Ten years later, when the plaintiff returned, he instituted these proceedings for vacant possession. The court granted the order but ordered the plaintiff to compensate the defendant for the improvements on the land. Interestingly, in this case the court ordered the plaintiff to pay compensation even though from the facts of the case, the plaintiff was not aware of the defendant's activities until he returned to Uganda. The case does not disclose the legal basis upon which the order for compensation was made. If it was made simply on the ground that the plaintiff benefited then it does not accord with established legal authorities.[35]

Test for a fixture

A fixture is a thing attached to the land in such a way that in law it becomes part of the land. Generally, two broad tests are employed to determine whether an item has lost its character as a

---

29 In *Taylor Fashions Ltd v Liverpool Victoria Trustees Co. Ltd* [1981] 1 All ER 897, 915, Oliver J, said that whatever one calls it is really immaterial.

30 (1866) LR 1, HL 129, pp.140-41. More recent English cases have stated that the principle of proprietary estoppel entails a broader approach directed at ascertaining whether in a particular case it would be unconscionable for a party to deny that which he or she allowed or encouraged another to assume to his or her detriment. See *Taylor Fashions Ltd v Liverpool Victoria Trustees Co Ltd* [1981] 1 All ER 897, pp. 911-12, 915-16.

31 See e.g. *Musoke Bafirawala v Jogga* CS No 33 of 1973; (1976) HCB 26 (unreported); *Crabb v Arun DC* [1976] Ch 179.

32 *Babiruga v Karegyesa and others* DR CA No MKA 13 of 1993 (unreported); *Inwards v Baker* [1965] 2 QB 29.

33 CA No MKA 13 of 1993 (unreported). See also *Runda Coffee Estate Ltd v Jager Singh* (1966) EA 564..

34 CS No 33 of 1973; (1976) HCB 26 (unreported).

35 Writers, Goff and Jones, *The Law of Restitution* (4th ed; 1993), pp.166-67, state that English law has not yet quite accepted a general principle that a person who improves another's land is entitled to compensation even if it is proved that it has benefited the landowner. Curiously, in the case of mistaken improvement of a chattel the courts may award compensation, see e.g., *Greenwood v Bennett* [1973] 1 QB 195.

chattel and become a fixture. They are the degree of annexation and the object of annexation.

The degree of annexation is determined by the means by which the thing is attached to the land, for example, by nails, bolts, mortar or its own weight. As a general proposition, an item that is attached to the land by any means other than by its own weight *prima facie* is deemed to be a fixture.[36] For example, a building, a notice board screwed onto the wall, electricity cables, a rainwater tank standing on a plinth held by mortar or cement, are all *prima facie* fixtures. The slightest fixing to the land is sufficient to raise the presumption that an item is a fixture.[37] Where this is the case, the person who asserts that it is not a fixture has the onus of proving it.[38] Conversely, if a thing is resting on the ground by its own weight, *prima facie* it is not a fixture and the onus of proof is on the person who says that it is a fixture.[39] Examples of such items include chairs in a building without any attachment, a carpet and a pile of bricks lying on the ground without any mortar.

The burden of proof is discharged by employing the second test: the object of annexation. The object of annexation refers to the intention of the person who affixed the thing to the land. If his or her intention was to make a permanent and substantial improvement to the land or building then the item is part of the land. If, on the other hand, his or her objective was for a temporary purpose, for more complete enjoyment of the thing as a chattel, then it remains a chattel.[40]

The classical illustration of the two tests is the case of *Holland v Hodgson.*[41] In that case, Mason was the owner of certain land on which he carried on the business of a textile manufacturer. He mortgaged the land and all fixtures thereon to the plaintiff. Subsequently, Mason, in bankruptcy, assigned all his property to the defendants in trust for the benefit of Mason's unsecured creditors. The defendants seized 436 looms in the factory and sold them. The looms were attached to the floor of the factory by means of nails driven through holes in the feet of the looms, or into beams specially built for the purpose. In some cases, they were attached to the floor by plugs of wood driven into holes drilled in the floor. It was impossible to remove the looms without drawing out the nails, but this could easily be done without causing any serious damage to the floor. The plaintiff claimed that the looms were fixtures and, therefore, they were part of their mortgage. The issue was whether the looms had become fixtures and therefore part of the plaintiff's mortgage. The court found that *prima facie* the looms were fixtures since they were not resting on the land by their own weight alone but were attached by nails and bolts. The court also found that the object of annexation was to carry out a permanent improvement to the land. The court rejected the defendant's argument that the looms were attached to the floor merely to make them steadier and more capable for their convenient use as chattels but not to make a permanent improvement to the land. The court held that though the looms were slightly attached and could easily be removed, the object of the owner in setting them up was to enhance the value of the factory premises to which they were attached. Accordingly, it was held that the looms were fixtures and part of the plaintiff's mortgaged land.

The principle espoused in *Holland v Hodgson* is more easily stated than applied to concrete factual situations. The most difficult task is to determine the intention of the person who fixed the thing. The courts have laid down certain guidelines for determining the intention of the parties. For example, where a thing is firmly held and its removal would entail destruction or serious damage to

---

36 *Holland v Hodgson* (1872) LR 7 CP 328.

37 *Ibid.*

38 *Ibid.*

39 *Ibid.*

40 *Shah v Shah Vershi Devshi & Co.* 17 KLR 20; *Holland v Hodgson*, Ibid.

41 (1872) LR 7 CP 328.

the thing itself or to the building, most likely it was intended to be a fixture. If it could easily be removed, then it is unlikely to be a fixture.[42] The purpose for which the subject matter is used in relation to the main use of the land is another important guideline. Where there is a strong linkage then it is more likely to be held to be a fixture.[43] The capacity in which the fixer attached the thing could [44] also provide a guideline as to the intention of the person. If the person was the landowner at the time, most likely he or she intended the thing to be permanently on the land. The converse is likely to be the case if the person who attached the thing to the land was a tenant, especially on a short term lease. It should be stressed, however, that none of these guidelines is conclusive. All facts and circumstances of the case have to be taken into account, and each case depends on its own facts.

Right to remove fixtures

In certain circumstances, the person who attached a fixture is entitled to remove it. First, the fixer may of course remove his or her fixtures where both parties expressly agree. Secondly, even in the absence of an agreement at common law it is implied that certain fixtures installed by a tenant belong to the tenant who attached them and that he or she has a right to remove them from the land.[45] The fixtures a tenant can remove from the land are trade fixtures, ornamental fixtures and fixtures for household purposes. These fixtures are collectively known as 'tenant's fixtures'.[46]

Trade fixtures are fixtures attached to the land by a tenant for purposes of trade or in connection with the business he or she conducts on the land. Examples of trade fixtures include machines, petrol pumps, shelves in a shop and shop counters. Ornamental fixtures are those fixtures which a tenant attaches to the land for decoration. These include tapestries,[47] statues and pictures. Fixtures used for domestic purposes include cookers, water pumps,[48] curtains and blinds.[49] It is important to note that doors and windows installed by a tenant are not 'tenant's fixtures'. Hence in the absence of express agreement the tenant who attached them cannot remove them when the lease expires.[50] Also, fixtures attached by the tenant for use in connection with agriculture are not treated as trade fixtures. Therefore, a tenant who attached such fixtures is not entitled to remove them.[51] Examples of agricultural fixtures include a fence or shed erected by a farmer to enclose animals. Ironically, fixtures erected in connection with market gardening[52] are not treated as agricultural fixtures, but as trade fixtures. Consequently, the tenant who attached them may remove them.[53]

As a general rule, unless otherwise agreed a tenant must remove the fixtures from the land before the lease expires and whilst he or she is in possession. Fixtures that are not removed in time by the tenant are deemed forfeited to the landlord and become his or her property absolutely.[54] As

42 *Berkley v Poulett* (1976) 241 EG 911. Compare with *Holland v Hodgson*

43 For example, in *Holland v Hodgson* the looms were part of the factory.

44 *Reynolds v Ashby & Sons* [1904] AC 466; *Hulme v Brigham* [1943] KB 152; *Berkley v Poulett* (1976) 241 EG 911

45 Megarry and Wade, *The Law of Real Property*, supra, p. 736

46 *New Zealand Government Property Corp v HM & S Ltd* [1982] 1 QB 1145.

47 *Re: De Falbe; Ward v Taylor* [1901] 1 Ch 523.

48 *Grymes v Boweren* 130 ER 1349.

49 G *Colegrave v Dias Santos* 107 ER 311

50 *New Zealand Government Property Corp v HM & S Ltd* [1982] 1 QB 1145, p. 1157.

51 *Elwes v Maw* (1802) 3 East 38; 102 ER 510. The common law rule is illogical and unfair. In some jurisdictions, for example, England and Australia, it has been replaced by statutory provision which entitle tenants to remove agriculture fixtures.

52 These are small holding farms where vegetables and fruits are grown for sale.

53 See Megarry and Wade, *The Law of Real Property*, supra, p. 736

54 *Poole's Case* (1703) 1 Salk 368; 91 ER 320. For exception to the rule see generally the Privy Council judgement in *New Zealand Government Property Corp v HM & S Ltd* [1982] 1 QB 1145.

a condition for the removal of tenant's fixtures, the person who removes the fixtures must make good any damage caused in the course of removal.[55]

EQUITABLE AND LEGAL INTERESTS IN LAND

An interest in land can be legal or equitable. A legal interest is an interest in land that was recognised and protected by the common law courts. In contrast, an equitable interest was recognised and protected by the Court of Equity even though at law the interest was not recognised.[56] This is what is known as 'duality of ownership'.[57] The legal equitable dichotomy is rooted in English history.

Origin of the dual system

Until the nineteenth century, the English legal system was divided into two separate jurisdictions: courts of the common law and the Court of Equity or Chancery. The Court of Equity evolved mainly because of dissatisfaction with the common law. In the beginning, the courts of the common law were very formalistic and operated on the writ system, which was very rigid. The choice of a wrong writ resulted in loss of a case irrespective of its merits. If no writ provided a formula to fit a litigant's case, there was no remedy.[58] A classical illustration of the rigidity of the common law courts, was the claim of a beneficiary under a trust. The institution of a trust (or uses) was employed to transfer property to a trusted person (hence, 'trustee') who was to hold the property not for his or her own benefit but for the purposes of carrying out instructions given to him or her by the transferor.[59] For example, where A, owner of Blackacre in fee simple, wished to benefit his minor children (X and Y) after his death, he would convey his estate to B for the use of X and Y. The effect was that B became the owner of Blackacre but held in trust for the benefit of the children. By the fourteenth century fraud was rampant amongst trustees, who, in breach of trust failed to honour their promises to hold the land for the benefit of the beneficiaries. The common law courts provided no redress to the beneficiaries because the common law only recognised the trustee's legal title. They had no appropriate form of action to protect a beneficiary divorced from the legal title.

Litigants who could not find the current writs began to address their grievances to the king 'the fountain of justice' to grant them a remedy. The king came to refer such petitions to the Lord Chancellor, who might order the trustees to carry out their trust. Later petitions were directly referred to the King's Council presided over by the Chancellor, Keeper of the King's conscience. Gradually, the Chancellor developed a court system parallel to that of the courts of the common law. This court came to be known as the Chancery or Court of Equity.

The Chancellor mainly applied the principles of reason and conscience as appeared appropriate to him[60] and not black-letter rules of law.[61] But by the nineteenth century the rules of equity had settled into a consistent and systematic body of law. These rules run side by side with the common

---

55 *Mancetter Developments Ltd v Garmanson Ltd* [1986] QB 1212. The obligation not to commit waste applies not only to the tenant but also to whomsoever he or she assigned the right to remove a fixture (1219 per Dillon CJ,).

56 Megarry and Wade, *The Law of Real Property*, supra, p. 110.

57 E.H. Burn, *Cheshire and Burn's Modern Law of Real Property* (14th ed. London Butterworths, 1988), p. 43.

58 Megarry and Wade, *The Law of Real Property*, supra, p. 110.

59 For example, a trustee could be instructed to use the proceeds of the land for the welfare of the grantor's young children after the grantor's death. Such an arrangement had a further advantage of avoidance of feudal dues on inheritance. See generally E.H.Burn, *Cheshire & Burn's Modern Law of Real Property*, supra, pp. 38-42.

60 Thus, the adage that equity varies as the Chancellor's foot, see Megarry and Wade, *The Law of Real Property*, supra, pp. 111-12.

61 Megarry and Wade, *The Law of Real Property*, supra, p. 112.

law. Thus, in our example above where A conveyed Blackacre in fee simple to B to the use of X and Y, at law A was recognised as the legal owner of Blackacre. Equity did not deny that B was the legal owner of Blackacre, but prevailed upon B to carry out the trust in accordance with A's instructions. Hence, there was a duality of ownership with B owning a legal fee simple estate in Blackacre, and X and Y an equitable estate in fee simple.[62]

Fusion of the courts of law and equity

Prior to the *Judicature Act* of 1873 (UK), a litigant seeking a legal remedy, for example damages, had to go to the common law courts. One seeking an equitable remedy, such as an order for specific performance, had to go to the Chancery. The *Judicature Act* of 1873 rendered forum hunting unnecessary. The Act fused the administration of law and equity [63] by giving the Supreme Court the jurisdiction to administer both principles of law and equity as is appropriate in the circumstances of each case. Where the two principles were in conflict, equity prevailed.[64]

In Uganda, the High Court has full jurisdiction to apply law and equity as appropriate. Section 16(4) of the *Judicature Statute, 1996,* provides that, '... in every cause or matter before the High Court, the rules of equity and the rules of the common law shall be administered concurrently'. The subsection goes on to say that if there is any variance between these rules with reference to the same subject matter, the rules of equity shall prevail.

Nature of equitable interest

Most interests in land exist both at law and in equity. Thus, a fee simple,[65] lease[66] and mortgage[67] could be an equitable or a legal interest. One exception to this general proposition is a restrictive covenant, which only exists in equity.[68]

In the eyes of equity, an equitable interest in many respects is as good as a legal interest. An equitable interest is as much a proprietary interest as a legal interest. It can be disposed of *inter vivos* or by will or intestate succession, just like a legal interest.[69] Remedies that accrue to a holder of a legal interest are available to a holder of a similar interest in equity. Indeed, the courts treat a holder of an equitable interest as if his or her interest were a legal interest. This is because equity regards as done that which ought to be done.[70] The classical illustration of this principle is the case of *Walsh v Lonsdale.*[71] In that case, the defendant entered into a contract to lease certain premises to the plaintiff for a period of seven years. Although the lease was in writing it was not executed by deed as required by law. Nevertheless, the plaintiff went into possession. Under the terms of the lease agreement rent was supposed to be paid in advance. When the plaintiff defaulted in payment of rent in advance the defendant distrained his goods as he was entitled to do at common law.[72] The plaintiff sued the defendant for trespass to goods. He argued that the defendant had no right to levy a distress for rent because distress is a legal remedy, which is only available where there was a legal lease. In this case, there was no legal lease, as the purported lease was not created by deed. The court dismissed the plaintiff's argument holding that in the eyes of equity a tenant in possession

---

62 Effectively B was a manager whilst X and Y enjoyed the benefits.

63 Note that this does not mean that the principles of common law and equity were fused, it just fused their administration.

64 *Judicature Act,* s. 25(11).

65 See e.g., *Serunjogi v Katabira* CS No 547 of 1987 (unreported); [1988-90] HCB 148.

66 See e.g., *Walsh v Lonsdale* (1882) 21 Ch 9.

67 See e.g., *Barclays Bank D.C.O. v Gulu Millers Limited* (1959) EA 540.

68 *Tulk v Moxhay* (1848) 2 Ph 774; 41 ER 1143

69 See Megarry and Wade, *The Law of Real Property*, supra, p. 114.

70 See eg *Walsh v Lonsdale* (1882) 21 Ch 9.

71 (1882) 21 Ch 9.

72 Distress is a self-help remedy involving the right of a landlord to seize and detain a tenant's chattels to force the latter to pay outstanding rent.

under a specifically enforceable contract for a lease was in the same position as if a lease had been executed. Accordingly, as far as equity was concerned the plaintiff was already a lessee for seven years and subject to all the terms of the agreement and all rights and remedies available at law. Hence, the defendant was entitled to exercise his common law remedy of distress as if a legal lease for seven years had been granted.

A holder of an equitable interest is not in exactly the same position as a holder of a similar interest at law. The reason is that a legal interest is a right *in rem* whilst an equitable interest is a right *in personam*. A right *in rem* is a right which is good against the whole world. The right is in the land itself and whoever acquires that land is bound by that right whether or not he or she was aware of it.[73] On the other hand, a right *in personam* is a right against a person or persons who in the eyes of equity ought to be bound. For example, a right *in personam* binds a trustee, a volunteer (or someone who acquires property by way of gift) and a purchaser with notice. But it does not bind a *bona fide* purchaser for value of the legal estate without notice of an earlier equitable claim over the subject land.[74] For example, suppose A conveys Blackacre to X to hold in trust for Y. As we have seen, X will have a legal estate in Blackacre and Y an equitable interest. In addition to X, the trustee, Y's equitable interest is enforceable against any person who acquires the land from X by way of a gift or inheritance or purchase with knowledge of Y's equitable interest.[75] But suppose X conveys the legal estate in Blackacre to Z. If Z is a *bona fide* purchaser for value without notice of Y's equitable interest, he or she will not be bound by Y's beneficial claim over the land.[76] The distinction between legal and equitable interests in this regard is more pronounced under the *Registration of Titles Act* (cap 205). Section 61 of the Act provides that a registered proprietor holds the land free from any unregistered interest except as provided in the Act.[77]

Another major distinction between legal and equitable interests is that the enforcement of equitable interests depends on the willingness of the court to grant specific performance of the contract according to its terms.[78] Thus, no equitable interest would arise where for any reason the court would not grant the remedy of specific performance.[79] A court may, for example, decline to award specific performance where in its view the plaintiff's claim could be adequately satisfied by the payment of damages.[80] Likewise, the court may refuse to grant specific performance if the person seeking the order does not come to court with 'clean hands'. For example, in *Swain v Ayres*[81] the court refused to grant an order of specific performance in favour of a tenant because he was in breach of several terms of his agreement with the landowner.

Creation of equitable interests

An equitable interest may be formally created by written agreement of the parties. But more often, an equitable interest is created by operation of law where the parties enter into a specifically enforceable contract to convey or create a legal interest in land. This is because of the equity maxim: 'equity looks on that as done which ought to be done'. In other words, equity treats the legal interest as if it were already conveyed. The classical exposition of this rule is the case of *Lysaght v Edwards*.[82] In that case, E entered into a written contract to sell certain land to the

---

73 Megarry and Wade, *The Law of Real Property*, supra, p. 113.

74 *Pilcher v Rawlins* (1872) 7 Ch App 259.

75 *Ibid.*

76 *Ibid.* See further discussion below 'priorities'.

77 In practice a registered interest is equated to a legal interest and an unregistered interest to equitable interest. For further discussion see Chapter 5.

78 *Serunjogi v Katabira* CS No.547 of 1987 (unreported); (1988-90) HCB 148.

79 *Swain v Ayres* (1888) 21 QB D 289.

80 *Lutakome v Sentongo* (1988-90) HCB 95.

81 (1888)21 QB D 289.

82 (1876) 2 Ch D 499.

plaintiff. On signing the contract, the plaintiff made a down payment and promised to pay the balance upon execution of a deed of conveyance. Unfortunately, E died before he signed the deed. The plaintiff sued the executor of E's estate for an order of specific performance, and the court obliged. It ordered the executors to convey the legal title to the plaintiff as promised by E upon payment of the purchase price. Sir George Jessel MR, in delivering his judgement, said: [83]

> The... moment you have a valid contract for sale the vendor becomes in equity a trustee for the purchaser of the estate sold, and the beneficial ownership passes to the purchaser, the vendor having a right to the purchase-money, a charge or lien on the estate for the security of the purchase-money, and a right to retain possession of the estate until the purchase-money is paid, in the absence of express contract as to the time of delivering possession.

The principle of *Lysaght v Edwards* was followed in the case of *Serunjogi v Katabira.*[84] In that case, by a memorandum of agreement which was duly signed by both parties, the defendant sold to the plaintiff a piece of land and a house situated thereon. The plaintiff paid the full purchase price, but the defendant failed or neglected to transfer title and deliver up possession to the plaintiff. The plaintiff sued for specific performance of the agreement. Byamugisha J, after citing the above mentioned principle in *Lysaght v Edwards,* held that, 'I am satisfied on the facts and circumstances before me that this is a case, in which the court will exercise its discretionary powers and grant the remedy of specific performance'. Her Honour ordered the defendant to deliver up vacant possession of the suit property to the plaintiff within thirty days from the date of the judgement.

The principle of *Lysaght v Edwards* is equally applicable to contracts to create other interests in land such as a lease,[85] mortgage,[86] and easement.[87]

Priorities

It may so happen that two or more people assert rival claims over the same land. For example, suppose that Nabakooza sells her land to Nansubuga. Later, Nabakooza purports to sell the same land to Nalumaga. Both Nansubuga and Nalumaga claim title over the land. The question is: which of these interests should take precedence over the other? The answer to this question will depend on how their interests are ranked against each other in accordance with certain prescribed rules.

The rules for ranking competing interests over the same land envisage four possible situations:

(i) claim to legal right followed by claim to legal right;
(ii) claim to equitable right followed by claim to legal right;
(iii) claim to legal right followed by claim to equitable right; and
(iv) claim to equitable right.

Competing legal interests

As a general rule an earlier created legal interest prevails over any subsequently created legal interest.[88] Thus, in our example above if Nabakooza conveyed the legal title to Nansubuga her interest would prevail over Nalumaga's claim.

Equitable interest followed by legal interest

As a general rule, a legal claim prevails over an earlier created equitable interest unless there are equitable grounds for its postponement. The rule is where equities are equal one with a legal

---

[83] Ibid, p. 506.
[84] CS No.547 of 1987 (unreported); (1988-90) HCB 148.
[85] See e.g., *Walsh v Lonsdale* (1882) 21 Ch D 9.
[86] *Barclays Bank D.C.O. v Gulu Millers* [1959] EA 540.
[87] *McManus v Cooke* (1887) 35 Ch D 681.
[88] *Northern Counties of England Fire Insurance Co v Whipp* (1884) 26 Ch D 482.

interest prevails.[89] Equities are equal where the claimant of a legal interest is a *bona fide* purchaser of a legal estate for value without notice of the earlier equitable interest.[90] The term 'purchaser' technically denotes a person to whom land is expressly transferred by action of the parties rather than by operation of law.[91] Thus, a buyer, donee (by will or *inter vivos*), mortgagee or lessee is a purchaser.[92] But a person who acquires land by intestate succession is not a purchaser because he or she acquires title by operation of law. The expression 'value' means that the purchaser must have given sufficient consideration in money or money's worth such as some other land or provision of service.[93] Promise of marriage is also considered as valuable consideration.[94] *Bona fide* implies that the purchaser must be acting in good faith or honestly.

The purchaser must not have had notice of a rival equitable claim to the land at the time of purchase. Notice need not be actual notice; it may be constructive or imputed notice. Constructive notice is knowledge of facts which, if the purchaser had acted prudently, he or she would have known. For example, in *Uganda Post and Telecommunications v AKM Lutaaya*,[95] the respondent leased a large piece of land from the mailo owner, second respondent. Unknown to him part of the land was occupied by the first appellant with the consent of the mailo owner. The respondent successfully sued the first appellant in the High Court for trespass. On appeal, the decision was reversed. In delivering the judgement of the court, Karokora JSC, with the concurrence of the other members of the Court, said that:

> [T]he law is very clear that if a person purchases an estate which he knows to be in the occupation of another other than the vendor, he is bound by all the equities which the parties in such occupation may have in the land....

Karokora, JSC, cited several English cases to support the proposition that occupation of land by a third party constitutes constructive notice to the purchaser of any equitable rights that the occupier might have in the land.[96] If a purchaser employs an agent, such as a lawyer, to act on his or her behalf, any actual or constructive notice that the agent receives is imputed to the purchaser.[97]

Legal interest created prior to equitable interest

As a general rule, where a legal interest is created first it will not be affected by subsequent equitable claims. As we have seen in our example, where Nabakooza sells and conveys the legal title to Nansubuga and later she purports to sell the same house to Nalumaga, Nansubuga's legal title will not be affected by the subsequent sale. However, in certain circumstances a prior legal claim may be displaced by a subsequent equitable claim under the principle of equitable estoppel. Under this principle, a holder of a prior legal interest may be estopped from denying that the vendor had title to convey to a subsequent purchaser. For example, the principle would be invoked where Nansubuga conspired with Nabakooza in order to defraud Nalumaga or where she was guilty of gross negligence that enabled Nabakooza to enter into the transaction with Nalumaga to the latter's detriment. A good illustration is the case of *Walker v Linom*.[98] In that case, a purchaser of a legal estate left the title deeds with the vendor after he had paid the purchase price. The vendor

---

89 Burn, *Counties of England Fire Insurance Co v Whipp* (1884) 26 Ch D 482.

90 *Pilcher v Rawlins* (1872) 7 Ch 250.

91 *In Re: Ivan Mutaka* Misc C No 81 of 1976 (unreported); [1980] HCB 27.

92 *Caunce v Caunce* [1969] 1 ALL ER 722.

93 *In Re: Ivan Mutaka* Misc C No 81 of 1976 (unreported); [1980] HCB 27.

94 *A-G v Jacobs Smith* [1895] 2 QB 341.

95 CA No 36 of 1996 (unreported).

96 See for example, *Jones v Smith* (1841) 1 Hare 43; 66 ER 943; *Taylor v Stibbert* (1803) All E Rep R 432; *Hodgson v Marks* [1971] Ch 892.

97 *Pilcher v Rawlins* (1871) 7 Ch 250.

98 (1907) 2 Ch 104.

which enabled the vendor to defraud the defendant. In the circumstances, it was held that the purchaser's legal estate must be postponed to the defendant's equitable mortgage though it was created later.[99]

Competing equitable claims
In a situation where all rival claims are equitable interests, the rule, variously stated, is that where equities are equal in all respects priority of time gives a better equity.[100] In other words, it is first in time first in right. Equities are unequal where a holder of a subsequent equitable interest was guilty of fraud or negligent conduct that enabled the vendor to deceive the latter that there were no other equitable claims to the land. A good illustration of the rule is the case of *Rice v Rice*.[101] The plaintiff sold land to P and he signed a document indicating that P had paid him the full purchase price. As it turned out there was still outstanding money. Later, P created an equitable mortgage in favour of TP. When P defaulted in paying the mortgage debt, the land was sold but the proceeds were not enough to pay the mortgage debt and the balance of the purchase price to the plaintiff. The plaintiff claimed that he had priority over the proceeds since his equitable lien[102] was earlier than the equitable mortgage. The court held that the first in time rule applies only where equities are equal. In determining the merits of each case, the court will look at all circumstances and the conduct of the parties. In this case, by signing the receipt acknowledging full payment the plaintiff armed the purchaser with false colours, which enabled him to present himself as owner of an unencumbered fee simple. Therefore, the plaintiff's first in time equity had to be displaced.

It should be noted that in determining priorities between competing equitable interests the doctrine of notice does not apply. Hence, the fact that the subsequent claimant had no notice of an earlier equitable interest is of no consequence.[103]

Priorities over registered land
The general law rules for determining priorities do not apply to land registered under the *Registration of Titles Act* (cap 205).[104] As is explained more fully below,[105] under the Act priority of competing interests is determined in accordance with the date of registration and not the date of the transaction.[106] In the absence of fraud on the part of the first person to be registered, he or she takes a better title than that of a person who purchased the same land earlier but did not register his or her interest.[107] The Act also modifies the doctrine of notice. Section 145 of *Registration of Titles Act* expressly states that in the absence of fraud a purchaser shall not be 'affected by notice actual or constructive of any trust or unregistered interest, any rule of law or equity to the contrary notwithstanding'. In other words, unlike the general law, under the Act the fact that a proprietor prior to purchase had actual or constructive notice of an unregistered (or equitable) claim over the land does not by itself constitute fraud.[108]

---

99 Mere carelessness is not a sufficient ground for displacement of an earlier equitable legal interest, see *Northern Counties of England Fire Insurance Co v Whipp* (1884) 26 Ch D 482

100 *Rice v Rice* (1854) 2 Drew 73; 61 ER 646.

101 *Ibid.*

102 An unpaid seller has a lien over the land sold for the balance of the purchase price, which constitutes an equitable interest.

103 *Rice v Rice* (1853) 2 Drew 73; 61 ER 646.

104 All land that is owned under mailo, freehold and leasehold tenure is subject to the Act. The only land to which the Act does not apply is customary tenure.

105 See Chapter 5.

106 Section 44, *RTA*. For illustration see e.g., *Kazzora v Rukuba* CA No 13 of 1992 (unreported).

107 See *Kazzora v Rukuba* CA No 13 of 1992 (unreported).

108 For detailed discussion of this provision see chapter 5.

However, where neither competing interest is registered then priority is determined by reference to the general law principles which apply to competing equitable interests. The case of *Ndigejjerawa v Kizito and Kubulwamwana*[109] illustrates this point. In that case, Kizito was the registered proprietor of the subject land. By a written contract Kizito agreed to sell the subject land to Kubulwamwana. Four days later by another written agreement he purportedly sold the same land to Ndigejjerawa. The latter lodged with the Registrar of Titles certain documents for the purpose of transfer of his title. But the transfer was not registered because the documents were not in order. Consequently, at the time of trial neither Ndigejjerawa nor Kubulwamwana had a registered title. Under the *Registration of Titles Act,* an unregistered interest constitutes an equitable interest.[110] The issue was who between Ndigejjerawa and Kubulwamwana had a better equitable claim to the land. Ndigejjerawa argued that since he lodged his documents for registration his claim should have priority over Kubulwamwana's claim. It was held that Kubulwamwana's equitable interest had priority because it was created earlier than Ndigejjerawa's interest. The court said that a prior lodgment for registration of an instrument of transfer, which was not in a registrable form, could not give Ndigejjerawa a better claim to the land than Kubulwamwana. It might have been different if Ndigejjerawa's document were in a registrable form.

ADVERSE POSSESSION AND LIMITATION

The concept of possession

At common law, possession of land is the root of title.[111] A person who is in possession has a title, which is good against the whole world except a person with a better claim.[112] If any person who is not the owner or his or her duly authorised agent, interferes with the land the possessor may bring an action in trespass against him or her. The fact that the person in possession is a squatter is irrelevant, for as far as the common law is concerned a wrongful possession is effective against everyone else except one with a better title.[113] So long as it is enjoyed, possession gives rise to rights, including the right to defend possession against third parties, to sell or devise the interest.[114]

Power to evict squatters

The risk for a person in wrongful possession is that the true owner might at any time evict him or her without prior notice or compensation for the improvements on the land.[115] However, the power of a landowner to evict a squatter is limited by the *Land Act*, 1998 and the *Limitation Act* (cap 70).[116] We have already seen that under the *Land Act* a landowner is prohibited from evicting a person who qualifies as a *bona fide* occupant except in the very limited circumstances described in the

---

[109] (1952-6) 7 ULR 31.

[110] *Katarikawe v Katwiremu and another* CS No 8 of 1972; (1977) HCB 187. For more discussion see Chapter 5.

[111] *Asher v Whitlock* (1865) LR 1 QB I.

[112] *Asher v Whitlock* (1865) LR 1 QB I. A possessor is deemed to have a fee simple estate unless a lesser estate is proved, see Pollock and Wright, *An Essay on Possession in the Common Law,* supra, pp. 93-94.

[113] Pollock and Wright, *An Essay on Possession in the Common Law*, supra, pp. 94-95. At common law title is relative. In order to defeat a possessor's title the person challenging it must rely on the superiority of his or her own title and not the weakness of the possessor's title, see *Perry v Clissold* [1907] AC 73.

[114] *Asher v Whitlock* (1865) LR 1 QB I; *Rosenberg v Cook* (1881) 8 QBD 162. In *Lomolo v Kilembe Mines Ltd* CS No 395 of 1976; (1978) HCB 157, Ssekandi J, held that since a squatter had no title to land she or he could not transfer any. It is respectfully submitted that His Honour erred unless he meant that a squatter could not confer a better title than a possessory title.

[115] *Lomolo v Kilembe Mines Ltd* CS No 395 of 1976; (1978) HCB 157; *City Council of Kampala v Odido* CS No 232 of 1969; *Babiruga v Karegyesa and others* D R CA No MKA 13 of 1993 (unreported).

[116] The *Limitation Act* is based on the 1939 English *Limitation Act.*

Act.[117] The Act applies to any action to recover land registered under the *Registration of Titles Act* (cap 205)[118] as well as land owned under customary tenure.[119] However, the Act does not preclude the Uganda Land Commission from recovering possession of land vested in it by the Constitution or any other law.[120]

Limitation period

The *Limitation Act* limits the period within which an action can be brought to recover land. Beyond that time, an action is statute barred. Section 6 of the Act provides that no person shall make an entry or bring an action to recover land after the expiration of twelve years from the date the cause of action accrued to him or her or to a person through whom he or she claims.[121] The right of action is deemed to accrue to a landowner when a stranger enters into adverse possession of his or her land.[122] This may happen by the stranger dispossessing the rightful owner or by entering into possession following abandonment of possession or death of the rightful owner.[123] Either way possession must be acquired without permission or licence of the owner.[124] Thus, where a person occupies land as a servant or caretaker of the landowner, the limitation time does not run in that person's favour irrespective of the period he or she remains in possession.[125] Similarly, time does not run in favour of a tenant for the duration of the lease.[126] However, possession gained by permission becomes 'adverse possession' if a person remains in possession after the permission is withdrawn or expires.[127] For example, a tenant becomes an adverse possessor if after the lease expires he or she remains in possession without the landlord's consent.[128] Also, if a person collects rent under a lease wrongfully claiming ownership of the land he or she is deemed to be in adverse possession of the subject land from the date rent is paid to him or her.[129]

Proving adverse possession

In the absence of contrary evidence, the owner of land with a paper title is deemed to be in possession of the land. Hence, where a person without documentary title claims ownership of land on the basis of adverse possession, he or she must prove to have both factual possession and the intention to possess.[130] Factual possession entails exercise of sufficient physical control over the entire land. This can be established by proof, for example, of use of the land for accommodation, cultivation or grazing animals, or generally dealing with the land as an owner might be expected to

---

117 See Chapter 2.

118 See s. 30, *Limitation Act.*

119 *Citamong v Olinga* CA No 104 of 1982; (1985) HCB 86 (unreported); *Mbazira v Abasagi Nansubuga* CA No 14B of 1992; (1992-93) HCB 241; *Nambalu Kintu v Efulaimu Kamira* CA No 26 of 1973 (unreported); [1975] HCB 221.

120 Section 32 (1), (a), *Limitation Act.*

121 If on the date the right of action accrued the plaintiff was under disability the period of limitation is extended to a maximum of six years from the date the person ceased to be under disability or died, whichever is the earlier, notwithstanding that the twelve year period had expired.

122 Section 12(1), *Limitation Act.*

123 *Rains v Buxton* (1880) 14 Ch D 537:539.

124 *E.R Ives Investment Ltd v High* [1967] 2 QB 379. At p. 396, Denning MR, said that a licence from the owner negates the otherwise adverse quality of possession enjoyed by a claimant.

125 *Cobb & another v Lane* [1952] 1 All E R 1199.

126 *Hayward v Chaloner* [1968] 1 QB 107. Special rules apply in case of a tenancy at will and a year to year tenancy, see *Limitation Act,* s. 11.

127 *Colchester Borough Council v Smith* [1991] Ch 448

128 *Hayward v Chaloner* [1968] 1 QB 107.

129 Section 12(3) (b), *Limitation Act.*

130 *Powell v McFarlane* (1977) 38 P& CR 452, pp. 470-72.

deal with it.[131] Whether a particular act or acts constitute sufficient control varies depending on the nature of the land, its size and the manner in which land of that nature is normally enjoyed.[132]

Factual possession must be accompanied with an intention to possess (*animus possidendi*). This means that the person claiming title by adverse possession must have an intention to possess the land to the exclusion of everyone else including the landowner.[133] The intention to exclude must be plain for all to see. Where there are other people using the land it must be apparent that they are doing so with his or her permission.[134] Just like factual possession, the degree of the requisite intention varies depending on the circumstances of each case. However, it is not required to prove that the squatter consciously intended to exclude the true owner. Rather, what is required is proof of intention to exercise exclusive control.[135] For example, a person who encloses land, which is adjacent to his or her plot under a mistaken belief that it is part of his or her land, satisfies this requirement even though he or she had no conscious intention to exclude the true owner.[136]

Running of time

The limitation time begins to run against the owner from the time the right of entry or the right to bring an action to recover the land first accrues to him or her or to the person through whom he or she claims.[137] The *Limitation Act* prescribes specific rules for determining when the right of action is deemed to accrue in various circumstances.[138] Generally, time starts to run against the true owner from the day a squatter enters into adverse possession.[139] The Act does not specifically state whether the landowner must have knowledge of the adverse possession before time starts to run against him or her. According to English authorities, as long as the squatter's possession is open for all to see and not clandestine, time begins to run against the owner from the date of entry even if the owner is unaware of it. For example, in *Rains v Buxton*,[140] for many years an intruder occupied a cellar in the plaintiff's house without knowledge of the plaintiff. It was held that, in the absence of fraud, the limitation period commenced to run from the date the intruder entered into adverse possession and not when the owner found out.

However, judicial authorities in Uganda suggest that time does not start to run against a landowner until he or she become aware of the intrusion. For example, in *Musoke Bafirawala v Jogga*,[141] the plaintiff in 1960 went abroad and lived there for many years. He left the defendant in charge of his house with instructions to collect rent and send the proceeds to him. For some time, the defendant collected the rent on the plaintiff's account. Subsequently, he stopped sending money that he collected to the plaintiff and, without the plaintiff's knowledge, carried out structural improvements to the land. The plaintiff found out only when he returned from overseas. In an action for eviction the defendant pleaded that the action was time barred because he had been in adverse possession for the requisite limitation period. The issue was whether the time started to run against the plaintiff from the date that the defendant asserted ownership of the house or from when the plaintiff became aware of it on his return to Uganda. Manyindo J held that time began to run at the later date.

---

131 *Ibid.*

132 *Ibid.*

133 *Buckingham City Council v Moran* [1969] 2 All ER 225.

134 *Wallis's Cayton Bay Holiday Camp Ltd v Shell-Mex & BP Ltd* [1975] QB 94.

135 *Bligh v Martin* [1968] 1 WLR 804.

136 *Williams v Usherwood* [1983] 45 P & CR 235.

137 Section 6, *Limitation Act*.

138 Sections 7-11.

139 Section 7. It should be noted that time does not start to run merely because the owner has abandoned possession. It only starts to run when a squatter actually enters, see s. 12 (1). See also *The Trustee, Executors, And Agency Company Ltd and Templeman v Short* [1888] 13 AC 793.

140 (1880) 14 Ch D 537.

141 CS No 32 of 1973; (1976) HCB26 (unreported).

Ssekandi Ag. .J expressed a similar view in the case of *Nambalu Kintu v Efulaimu Kamira.*[142] In that case, as in *Musoke v Jogga,* the defendant originally entered the land with the consent of the landowner. When the plaintiff sued for possession the defendant sought to argue that the action was time barred as he had been in adverse possession of the land for more than twelve years. The issue was, when did the cause of action accrue to the plaintiff for the purposes of determining the limitation period? His Honour held that the cause of action did not accrue until the plaintiff discovered the challenge to his interest.

Neither Manyindo J, in *Musoke v Jogga*, nor Ssekandi Ag J, in *Nambalu Kintu v Efulaimu Kamira,* cited any authority for the legal proposition that time does not begin to run against the landowner until he or she has knowledge of the adverse claim to his or her land. It is suggested that the authority of the two cases should be limited to situations where the intruder originally entered with the consent of the landowner. This is because in such situations the owner assumes, justifiably, that the 'intruder' is in possession pursuant to the original consent. The following passage from the judgement of the High Court of India in *Turubai v Venkatrao,*[143] supports this proposition:

> [It] is fully established that when there is no act of taking possession, something more than a mere adverse claim is necessary to make possession adverse. Thus 'one who holds possession on behalf of another does not, by a mere denial of that other's title, make his possession adverse, so as to give himself the benefit of the Statute of Limitations': *Bejoy Chundra v. Kally Prosonno* (1878),4 Cal. 327. There must be some 'adverse act', so that if the possession has commenced and continued in accordance with 'any contract, express or implied, between the parties in and out of possession, to which the possession may be referred as legal and proper, it cannot be presumed adverse.... That is to say, if there be no adverse act, nothing overt and no unmistakable ouster, or taking of possession, and all that is done is referable to, or consistent with and susceptible of explanation by, some title which does not impugn but recognise the right of the person seeking to recover possession, then there can be no possession adverse to that person without notice or intimation to him of some kind, that an adverse claim has been set up in opposition to his right theretofore recognised: *Ittappan v. Manavikrama* (1897), 21 Mad. 153, p. 159

It is submitted that the legal position is different where the person entered the land as a trespasser. In that case, as long as the trespasser's occupation is open and not clandestine, the limitation time will immediately start running against the owner whether or not he or she is aware of the intrusion.[144] A landowner who for more than twelve years is unaware of intruders on his or her land does not deserve legal protection.

Stopping time running

The possession of a squatter must be continuous for a total period of twelve years or any extended period that may be required by the operation of the Act.[145] If before the limitation time runs out[146] the squatter abandons possession the land ceases to be in adverse possession and time stops running against the owner.[147] Where subsequently the squatter (or another intruder) re-enters a fresh limitation period will begin to run calculated from the date of re-entry. However, where a squatter does not abandon possession but instead purports to transfer the land to another person, the latter may add the grantor's period of adverse possession to his or her own to make up the necessary limitation period.[148] For example, if A was in adverse possession for ten years and sold

---

142 CA No 26 of 1973; (1975) *HCB* 221 (unreported).

143 (1902), 27 Bom. 43 at 52-4, cited with approval in *Jandu v Kirpal and another* [1975] EA 225 (K) at 234.

144 *Rains v Buxton* (1890) 14 Ch D 537.

145 Sections 7 and 22.

146 Once time has run out, title is extinguished and cannot be revived by subsequent events, see *Sanders v Sanders* (1881) 19 Ch D 373.

147 Section 12 (21), *Limitation Act*. See also *Allen v Roughley* (1955) 94 CLR 98.

148 *Hasanali Manuji v Dar & Sons* (1935) 32 EACA 111.

or devised his interest to B, the latter would be credited with the ten years of adverse possession of his predecessor. The owner can stop time running if before the period expires he or she brings an action of ejectment[149] or asserts ownership of the land under possession. The assertion of ownership must be accompanied by effective and physical resumption of possession of the land.[150] Once the owner resumes possession it effectively interrupts the running of the limitation period even if he or she remains in possession for a brief period.[151]

The limitation time also stops running when a squatter acknowledges the owner's right to the land. Section 23(1) of the *Limitation Act* provides that whenever a squatter in a signed written document[152] addressed to the owner[153] acknowledges the superiority of the owner's title to the land, or makes any payment to the owner on account of that title, the limitation time begins to run afresh as from that date. For example, suppose that Okello has been in adverse possession of Opio's land for five years. If Okello in writing admits to Opio that he (Opio) is the owner of that land or pays him for use of the land, the five years Okello was in adverse possession will cease to count in reckoning the limitation period. The acknowledgment need not be express or take any particular form, as long as on the true construction of the document it is an admission of the owner's superior title.[154] It is important that the acknowledgment or payment be made before expiration of the limitation period. The reason is that once time lapses title of the owner is extinguished by operation of the Act and cannot be revived by subsequent activities.[155]

Consequences of lapse of time

At the expiration of the limitation period the dispossessed owner loses his or her right to re-enter or sue to recover the land.[156] Moreover, unless the title is registered under the *Registration of Titles Act,* it is deemed to be extinguished.[157] For example, if the dispossessed owner holds his or her title under customary tenure or tenancy by occupancy, upon expiration of the limitation period his or her title is automatically extinguished by operation of the *Limitation Act.* Legally, the squatter does not succeed to the title of the person he or she dispossessed. Rather, he or she is left in occupation of the land with a title gained by possession 'resting on the infirmity of the right of others to eject him.'[158] The title so acquired by the squatter is a freehold in fee simple estate because the largest estate known to the common law is presumed unless a lesser estate is proved.[159] The presumption could be rebutted, for example, where a squatter dispossesses a lessee. Upon expiration of the lease the landlord could re-enter since the limitation period does not run against a landlord until the lease expires.[160]

---

149 The issuing and serving of summons for possession suffices for this purpose, see *Serjeant v Nash Field & Co* [1903] 2 KB 304.

150 *Nambalu Kintu v Efulainu Kamira* CA No 26 of 1973; (1975) HCB 221 (unreported). Mere protests against the squatter's possession held not to be effective to constitute re-entry.

151 *Randall v Stevens* 118 ER 907.

152 See also s. 24.

153 An admission made to a third party, for example, in an affidavit to the government, is not effective, see *Re: Beavan* [1912] 1 Ch 196.

154 *Ediginton v Clark* [1964] 1 QB 367.

155 *Sanders v Sanders* (1881) 19 Ch D 373. Compare with *Colchester Borough Council v Smith* [1992] 2 WLR 728.

156 Section 6.

157 See ss. 17 and 30 of the *Limitation Act*. See also *Nambalu Kintu v Efulainu Kamira* CA No 26 of 1973; (1975) HCB 221 (unreported). The consequence of expiration of the limitation time upon a title registered under the *Registration of Titles* Act, is discussed below.

158 *Taylor v Twinberrow* [1930] 2 KB 16, at 23 per Scrutton LJ.

159 *Perry v Clissold* [1907] AC 73.

160 See s. 8(1) of the *Limitation Act*. See also *Fairweather v St Marylebone Property Co. Ltd* [1963] AC 510.

It is submitted that where a squatter dispossesses an owner of land under customary tenure. the presumption is that the squatter's title is a freehold rather than a customary title. Part of the reason for this is that the title acquired by a squatter is not the same as that of the person he or she dispossessed. Moreover, although the *Limitation Act* applies to customary land,[161] the doctrine of adverse possession is alien to customary land tenure.[162] Therefore, the courts have to refer to the common law to determine the nature of title acquired by adverse possession.

Special provision applies with respect to land registered under the *Registration of Titles Act.* Section 30 of the *Limitation Act* provides that although upon expiration of the limitation period a registered proprietor is barred from evicting or suing for recovery of land, the proprietor's title is not thereby extinguished. However, the section deems the proprietor to hold his or her title for the benefit of the person who dispossessed him or her. For example, suppose that Rashida is the registered proprietor of certain mailo land and Isanga is in adverse possession of the land. After the expiration of the twelve years limitation period, though Rashida remains as the registered proprietor of the land, she is deemed to hold the title in trust for Isanga.[163]

The *Registration of Titles Act* makes provision for the adverse possessor to make an application to the registrar of Titles for an order vesting in him or her as estate in fee simple or other estate claimed.[164] Section 86 states that upon satisfaction that the applicant has complied with the appropriate procedure and with all the legal requirements, the registrar 'may' grant the order sought and cause the land to be registered in the name of the applicant. The process is completed when the registrar cancels the existing title (and any claims registered against it) and issues a fresh certificate of title to the applicant.[165] Although s. 86 appears to give the registrar unfettered discretion to register an applicant as proprietor, it is submitted that he or she cannot refuse to do so if an applicant satisfies the statutory requirements, except on reasonable grounds.[166] A responsible ground for refusal would include where, for example, the registrar believes that the registered proprietor whose action is time barred might be granted leave by a court to file his or her action out of time under the *Civil Procedure Rules.*[167] The registrar may also decline to register a title acquired by adverse possession if there is a possibility that the registered proprietor was under disability and would be entitled to extension of the limitation period.[168]

Where a person has been in adverse possession for the requisite statutory period, it is submitted that even if his or her title were unregistered it would defeat that of the proprietor he or she dispossessed. The reason is that, as we have seen, under s. 30 of the *Limitation Act*, after expiration of the limitation time the proprietor is not only precluded from evicting the squatter but also he or she is deemed to hold title on the squatter's behalf. Effectively the proprietor is left with a title, which is like an eggshell whilst the squatter enjoys the benefits thereof. This view is further strengthened by s. 61 of the *Registration of Titles Act.* Under that section, title of a registered proprietor is not indefeasible as regards 'any rights subsisting under any adverse possession of such land'. In *Lake v Jones*,[169] the Supreme Court of the Australian State of Victoria, interpreting

---

161 See below.

162 *Muwereza v Mbusye* CA No 118 of 1975 (unreported); *Nambalu Kintu v Efulaimu Kamira* CA No 26 of 1973; (1975) HCB 221 (unreported).

163 However, see ss. 30 and 32 of the *Land Act*, 1998, above.

164 Sections 77-84 of the *Registration of Titles Act.*

165 Section 86 (b).

166 It is established law that discretionary powers, however wide they are drawn are not absolute, see *In Re: (An Application by) Bukoba Gymkhana Club* [1963] EA 478

167 *Uganda Spinning Mills Ltd v Placid Weli Iga* CS No 547 of 1987; (1988-90) HCB 148.

168 See s. 22 of the *Limitation Act.*

169 (1889) 15 VLR 728

a similar provision, held that its effect was to give persons in adverse possession of registered land the same rights, as they would have against a title holder under the common law.[170]

Adverse possession, prescription and acquiescence
It is important to distinguish adverse possession from the doctrines of prescription and acquiescence. Though the three have certain similarities they are conceptually different.[171]

PRESCRIPTION

Prescription is primarily a common law doctrine extended by statute by which an intruder after a long period of uninterrupted use and occupation may acquire a proprietary interest over another's land.[172] Unlike adverse possession, the doctrine of prescription is confined to acquisition of interests in land that do not carry a right to exclusive possession.[173] For example, a person may by prescription acquire an easement, such as a right of way, over neighbouring land.[174] But a person cannot acquire a fee simple estate by prescription. In the case of *Lomolo v Kilembe Mines Ltd*,[175] Ssekandi Ag J, said that a squatter by lapse of time extinguishes the owner's title by 'prescription'. With due respect to the learned judge, it is submitted that his Honour's statement is conceptually wrong. A squatter extinguishes another's title by adverse possession and not by prescription.

Another major difference between adverse possession and prescription is that prescription operates positively as it leads to acquisition of a previously non-existing interest. For example, acquisition of an easement under the doctrine of lost modern grant is based on a legal fiction that the easement had its origin in a grant to the person enjoying it or to his or her predecessor in title but the grant was lost.[176] In contrast, adverse possession, as we have seen, operates negatively. The intruder enters and remains on the land without the permission, pretended or otherwise, of the landowner. After the time expires, the former owner's right to recover possession is extinguished, leaving the intruder in possession with a title based on his or her own actual possession.[177]

ACQUIESCENCE

The doctrine of acquiescence or laches entails unreasonable delay in enforcing or asserting a legal right.[178] It is based on the maxim that equity aids the active and not the indolent. Thus, where a landowner knows that his or her rights are being violated and he or she chooses to sit idly by, he or she is taken to have acquiesced in the violation and will be estopped from arguing otherwise.[179] The courts' equitable jurisdiction to refuse to grant relief on the ground of acquiescence is expressly saved by s. 29 of the *Limitation Act*.[180] Unlike adverse possession, the doctrine of acquiescence can only be used as a defence against an action and not as a basis for establishment of a cause of

---

[170] See also *Kisee Maweu and others v Kiu Ranching and Co-operative Society* (1982-88) 1 KAR 746. Adverse possession as an exception to indefeasibility in discussed in chapter 'Registration of Titles'.
[171] *Nambalu Kintu v Efulaimu Kamira* CA no 26 of 1973; (1975) HCB 221.
[172] *Dalton v Angus* (1881) 6 App. Cas 740.
[173] James P.S., *Introduction to English Law* (5th ed; London, Stevens, 1984), p. 1030. Compare *Uganda Spinning Mills Ltd v Placid Weli Iga* CS No 29 of 1989; (1988-90) HCB 144.
[174] See for example, *Dalton v Angus* (1881) 6 App Cas 740.
[175] *Lomolo v Kilembe Mines Ltd* CS No 395 of 1976; (1978) HCB 157.
[176] *Nambalu Kintu v Efulaimu Kamira* CA No 26 of 1973; (1975) HCB 221; *Dalton v Angus* (1881) 6 App. Cas 740. For further discussion see Chapter 8.
[177] *Nambalu Kintu v Efulaimu Kamira*, ibid.
[178] *Citamong v Olinga* CA No 104 of 1982; (1985) HCB 86.
[179] *Citamong v Olinga*, ibid.
[180] *Wandira v Okeya* CA No 209 of 1969; (1970) HCB 60.

action.[181] But to raise this defence two things must be satisfied. Firstly, the defendant must have dealt with the land under an honest but a mistaken impression that it is his or her land. Secondly, the true owner must have been aware of the defendant's activities on his land and chose to do nothing.[182] For example, in *Citamong v Olinga*,[183] the appellant, for a period of thirty years, occupied and cultivated the respondent's land. Although the latter was aware of the intrusion he made no attempt to stop it or recover the land. In an action to evict the appellant the High Court held that the respondent had taken too long to assert his rights. In equity he was deemed to have acquiesced in the appellant's long and uninterrupted occupation.[184] Unlike adverse possession where the timeframe within which to institute eviction proceedings is strictly fixed by the *Limitation Act*, there is no fixed time for the doctrine of acquiescence to operate. It is up to the court to decide whether or not in the circumstances of a particular case it considers that the delay to bring action was unreasonable. For example, in *Citamong v Olinga*, the delay was for a period of thirty years, in *Wandira v Okeya* ten years,[185] and in *Lomolo v Kilembe Mines* [186], it was only seven years.

---

[181] *Citamong v Olinga, ibid.*

[182] *Ramsden v Dyson* [1886] LR 1 HL. 129. Compare with adverse possession where the owner's knowledge is irrelevant.

[183] *Ibid.*

[184] See also *Wandira v Okeya* CA No 100 of 1969; (1970) HCB 60.

[185] CA No 100 of 1969; (1970) HCB 60.

[186] CS No 395 of 1976; (1978) HCB 157.

5

Registration of Titles

INTRODUCTION

The system of registration of titles which operates in Uganda, is commonly known as the 'Torrens System'. It takes its name from Sir Robert Torrens, an Australian who played a leading role in its development and implementation in Australia in the 1850s.[1] Torrens, who was not a lawyer, aimed to set up a system of conveyance which was simple to operate, secure and fair. The system was first introduced in Sir Robert's own State of South Australia in 1858, and subsequently it spread to other Australian states, New Zealand, Malaysia, Papua New Guinea, some states in the USA and some Canadian provinces.[2] The Torrens system was introduced in Uganda by the *Registration of Titles Act* (cap 205), which was enacted in 1922 by Ordinance No. 22 of 1922 and came into effect on 1 May 1924.[3] It repealed the *Registration of Titles Ordinance* 1908 and the *Equitable Mortgages Ordinance* 1912.[4] The Act is based on the *Transfer of Land Act,* 1915, of the Australian State of Victoria.

The *Registration of Titles Act* automatically applies to all mailo land included in any final mailo certificate and all lands alienated in freehold or leasehold and any transaction relating to such land.[5] By s. 3 of the Act it is provided that provisions of this Act shall prevail over any other inconsistent law dealing with registered land.[6]

Customary land tenure is not registrable under the Act.[7] Owners of land under customary tenure who wish to bring their land under the Act must convert their tenure to freehold as provided under the *Land Act.*[8]

SCHEME OF THE ACT

The system of title registration under the *Registration of Titles Act* revolves around a centralised 'Register Book'. The book embodies certificates of title kept in a running form each representing a separate parcel of land described therein and registered under the Act. If land is brought under the Act for the first time (for example, a fresh grant of freehold or leasehold, or where part of mailo land is sold and a fresh certificate is issued), the registrar is required to prepare a certificate in duplicate.[9] One copy is retained by the registrar and kept in the register book, the other is issued to the person (or his or her nominee) who is registered as 'proprietor' of the land or interest.[10] The duplicate issued to the proprietor is referred to throughout the Act as the 'duplicate certificate' of title.[11]

---

1 See generally Douglas J Whalan, *The Torrens System in Australia* (Sydney, Law Book Company, 1982), p. 5-12.

2 See Rowton Simpson, *Land Law and Registration* (Cambridge, Cambridge University Press, 1976).

3 For background reading see H.M. West, *Land Policy in Buganda* (Nairobi, East African Publishing House, 1975), pp. 163-87.

4 *Barclays Bank D.C.O. v Gulu Millers* (1959) EA 540 p. 549.

5 Section 9(1), *RTA*.

6 This provision is discussed in *Sejjaka Nalima v Musoke* CA No 12 of 1985 (Supreme Court of Uganda); [1992] 5 KALR 132.

7 Certificates of customary ownership of land are 'recorded' by a recorder established under s. 69 the *Land Act*, 1998. See Chapter 2.

8 See Chapter 2.

9 Sections 38, *RTA*.

10 See ss. 38 and 39(2) *RTA*. See also s. 2 definition of 'proprietor'. Note that there may be more than one separate and distinct proprietor over the same piece of land. For example, if a mailo owner mortgages his land he will remain as the proprietor of mailo land and the mortgagee will be proprietor of a mortgage over the same land.

11 Section 39 (1), *RTA*.

Any transaction affecting registered land, such as a mortgage or lease, must be endorsed on the register book and the certificate of title.[12] For this reason, the duplicate certificate must be produced whenever any dealing concerning the parcel of land is lodged for registration.[13] Section 38(1) of *Registration of Titles Act* requires the registrar to record transactions in such a manner as to preserve their order of priority, which, generally, is the order of presentation for registration and not the order of the date the transactions were entered into.[14]

ESSENTIAL FEATURES

The Torrens system has two essential features that distinguish it from other systems of conveyance: title by registration and the principle of indefeasibility of title. The two features are inter-dependent and they are both essential to the Torrens system.

Title by registration

Under the Torrens system, interests in land are created or transferred not by execution of documents as under the common law, but by registration in the manner prescribed by the *Registration of Titles Act*. The key provision is s. 51. It stipulates that an instrument purporting to confer an interest in land is not effective to pass any estate or interest in land or bind the land by way of mortgage until the instrument is registered as provided under the Act. The case of *Ndigejjerawa v Isaka Kizito and Sabane Kubulwamwana* illustrates the application of this provision.[15] In that case, Kizito under a written agreement sold his land to the second respondent and the latter paid the purchase price. Four days later, Kizito purported to sell the same land to the appellant and the latter paid the purchase price. The appellant immediately lodged with the Registrar of Titles a certain document executed by Kizito for the transfer to be registered. Later the second respondent also lodged with the registrar a document of transfer signed by Kizito. However, neither document was registered, because they were not in a registrable form. In court, the appellant contended that he was the owner of the land, because he lodged his document of transfer with the registrar before the second respondent lodged his. In response to this argument, Ainsley J said that:[16]

> It must be remembered that mailo land (and any land which is subject to the *Registration of Titles Ordinance*) can be transferred only by the execution of an instrument which fulfils certain statutory requirements and by the registration of that instrument. No document or instrument can be registered unless it fulfils certain requirements, and no instrument (however perfectly it fulfils the statutory requirements) is effectual to transfer any interest in land until it is registered

Accordingly, his Honour held that neither the appellant nor the second respondent achieved a transfer of the land to himself by the execution of his document or by paying the purchase price.

However, once the instrument is registered, the estate or interest in the land passes and the land become liable and subject to the covenants and conditions set forth in the instrument. It is partly for this reason that a title under the Torrens system is described as a title conferred by registration because without registration no title is transferred.

---

12 See ss. 38 (1), 49 & 42 (2) *RTA*.

13 Section 66, *RTA*. The registrar may at his or her discretion dispense with this requirement, see s. 49, *RTA*.

14 See s. 44, *RTA*. In the absence of fraud on the part of the first person to be registered, he or she takes a better title than that of a person to whom the same land was sold first but did not register his or her interest, see *Kazzora v Rukuba* CA No 13 of 1992 (unreported); *Hotel International Ltd v The Administrator of the Estate of the Late Robert Kavuma* CA No 37 of 1995.

15 (1953) 7 ULR 31. See also *Kazzora v Rukuba* CA No 13 of 1992 (unreported).

16 Ibid, p. 32.

The Act provides that a registered proprietor of any estate or interest in land wishing to transfer, create an easement, lease or mortgage, may do so by completion of the relevant prescribed form.[17] The instrument, signed by the proprietor and witnessed, is presented to the registrar together with the duplicate certificate of title, and such other documents or consents as may be necessary or required by any law.[18] If the instruments and accompanying documents are in order and subject to payment of any prescribed fees, registration will proceed. The registration is brought about when the registrar enters the instrument purporting to affect the subject estate or interest in the Register Book upon the file constituted by the certificate of title.[19] Thereafter, whoever is named in the certificate as the grantee or proprietor or having an estate or interest in the subject land is deemed to be the duly registered proprietor thereof.[20]

Unregistered instruments

Though s. 51 of the *Registration of Titles Act* states that no estate or interest can be created or transferred until the instrument purporting to create or transfer the same is registered, the section does not thereby deny unregistered instruments any legal efficacy.[21] The Court of Appeal for Eastern Africa in *Souza Figueiredo & Co Ltd* v *Moorings Hotel Co Ltd* [22] discussed the nature and effect of unregistered instruments under the Act. In that case the respondent (registered proprietor) entered into a contract to lease the suit properties to the appellant for a period in excess of three years. The appellant entered into possession though the lease was not registered. Before the three years expired the appellant vacated the premises with rent in arrears. When sued for the arrears the appellant contended that since the agreement for the lease was not registered as required by s. 51, the lease had no effect and, hence, the appellant was not liable to pay rent. In response to the respondent's argument that there was an equitable lease, the appellant submitted that the principles of equity could not override the provisions of the *Registration of Titles Act*. Sir Kenneth O'Connor P, with the concurrence of the other judges, held that though s. 51 says that no estate or interest in land can be created or transferred by an unregistered instrument:

> [T]here is nothing in the ... [Act] which renders such instruments ineffectual as contracts between the parties to them: there is nothing in the ... [Act] to say that an unregistered document purporting to be a lease of, or an agreement to lease, land which is subject to the operation of the [*Registration of Titles Act*] for more than three years is void. In my view it can operate as a contract *inter parte* and can confer on the party in the position of intending lessee a right to enforce the contract specifically and to obtain from the intending lessor a registrable lease.[23]

---

17 See ss. 82, 98, 100 and 114, respectively. Instruments not in appropriate form may be rejected (s. 181), though alterations which do not affect the substance of the instrument, are permissible (s. 209) and the registrar may permit instruments presented in vernacular.

18 For example, it is required, under s.43C of the *Finance Act* 1982, that no transfer purporting to transfer an interest in land shall be registered without production by both the transferor and transferee of their respective income tax clearance certificates from the Commissioner of Income Tax.

19 Section 42 (2), *RTA*.

20 Section 42 (4), *RTA*.

21 *Berry v Heider and another* (1914) 19 CLR 197.

22 [1960] EA926

23 *Ibid*, p. 931.

Applying this principle to the facts of the case, His Honour held that the respondent was entitled to the payment of the sums due under a contract to pay rent for the period during which the appellant enjoyed possession.[24]

Although Sir Kenneth O'Connor P. held that an unregistered lease constitutes a contract *inter parte*, he denied that it operates to create an equitable lease. His Honour reasoned that because of s.51, *Registration of Titles Act,* in Uganda no estate (whether legal or equitable) could derive from an unregistered instrument.[25] His Honour refused to follow Australian case law that the corresponding provision does not prevent the creation of an equitable estate where an instrument of transfer is not registered.[26]

The decision of *Souza Figueiredo & Co Ltd v Moorings Hotel Co Ltd* that s. 51, *Registration of Titles Act,* precludes the creation of equitable interests has never been questioned by the courts.[27] However, there are several cases where the courts have held that an equitable interest is created by virtue of the contract between the parties. For example, in *Katarikawe* v *Katwiremu and another,*[28] Ssekandi J, held that though in a contract of sale of land an unregistered instrument of transfer is not effective to transfer title, the purchaser acquires an equitable interest in the land, which is enforceable against the vendor.[29] Similar views were expressed by Oder JSC in *Alibhai and another v Karia and another.*[30] In that case the first respondent entered into a contract to purchase the suit property from the appellants. Before he paid the purchase price the appellants fled the country following the expulsion of Asians from Uganda by the military government. The Departed Asians Property Custodian Board took over the suit property by virtue of Decree No. 27 of 1972. Subsequently, the Board transferred the land to the first respondent and he was registered as proprietor. The appellant sought an order for the transfer to be set aside. One of the issues was whether property passed to the respondent before the transfer was registered and, if so, when. Oder JSC, with the concurrence of Manyindo DCJ and Karokora JSC, held that:

> After the contract of sale, property in the suit property passed to the first respondent, who obtained the equitable estate thereto and retained it after the appellants left Uganda. The appellants in whom the legal estate remained became trustees of the first respondent and were under a duty as such ...to transfer the legal estate in the suit property to the respondent on completion of the contract. It is that legal estate, in my view, which vested in the [Board].

Oder JSC's interpretation of s. 51 of the *Registration of Titles Act,*[31] mirrors the view generally regarded as authoritative in Australia with respect to interpretation of analogous provisions. In Australia the legal position is that the counterpart of s.51 renders an instrument ineffectual to create a legal or equitable interest or estate in the land, before registration.[32] But the provision does not avoid the contract behind the instrument or render it inoperative. That contract, and not the instrument, is regarded as effective, in accordance with the principles of equity, to bring into

---

[24] In any event it was held that the appellant having gone into possession was a tenant at will and as such was bound to pay rent for the period he was in possession, p. 937.

[25] [1960] EA 926 p. 931.

[26] *Ibid,* pp. 933-34.

[27] This case is cited in several cases as authority for the proposition that an unregistered lease constitutes a contract *inter parte*. See, for example, *City Council of Kampala v Mukibi* [1967] EA 368 (U); *Somali Democratic Republic v Anoop Syndirial Treon* CA No 4 of 1988 (unreported).

[28] CS No 2 of 1973; (1977) HCB 187 (unreported).

[29] See also *Popatlar Hirji* v *I.H. Lakhani & Co* (EA) Ltd [1960] EA 437 (U); *Sentongo v Shell (U) Ltd CS No 32 of 1993, unreported.*

[30] CA No 53 of 1995 (unreported).

[31] See, for example, s. 41 of the *Real Property Act* 1900 (New South Wales); s.43 of the *Real Property Act* 1861 (Queensland); and s 40(1) of the *Transfer of Land Act,* 1954 (Victoria).

[32] *Barry v Heider* (1914) 19 CLR 197; *Chan and another v Cresdon Properties Limited* [1989] 168 CLR 242.

existence an equitable estate or interest in the land.[33] In our view, Oder JSC's interpretation is preferred over that of Sir Kenneth O'Connor P in *Souza Figueiredo & Co Ltd v Moorings Hotel Co Ltd.*

Indefeasibility of title

The second essential feature of the Torrens system is the 'principle of indefeasibility of title'. Basically this means that once a person is registered as proprietor of an estate or interest in land, the government guarantees that his or her title cannot be divested or attacked by rival claims to the land except as prescribed under the *Registration of Titles Act*. Interestingly, the expression 'indefeasibility' though widely used in judgments and scholarly work does not appear anywhere in the *Registration of Titles Act*. Its meaning and scope is, nevertheless, extracted from what Professor Whalan describes as a 'mosaic of sections'.[34] They include s. 56, which declares that the certificate of title shall be conclusive evidence of all particulars and endorsements thereon, and that the person named in the certificate as the proprietor is possessed of the estate or interest described. The courts are required under the section to receive and treat the certificate of title as conclusive evidence of its particulars. Section 61 declares that, subject to the exceptions stated therein, the estate or interest of a proprietor registered under the Act prevails over any other unregistered interest or claim over the land. Sections 184 and 186 protect a registered proprietor against any action for ejectment or damages. Except as stated in these provisions, production by a person of a certificate of title in his or her name is deemed to be an absolute bar and estoppel against any legal action.[35]

The indefeasibility principle was designed to achieve two main objectives. First, it was designed to protect title of the registered proprietor from unregistered interests. Secondly, to save persons dealing with registered land from the trouble and expense of going behind the register book in order to investigate the validity of title or possible rival claims to the land, and thus simplify and expedite the process of transfer.

The application of the principle of indefeasibility is illustrated by the case of *Lwanga v The Registrar of Titles*.[36] The facts of the case were as follows. In 1920, the applicant's late father bought the suit property, but title to the land was never transferred into the deceased's name. After the deceased's death, one Katamba fraudulently caused the land to be transferred and registered in his name. Later Katamba sold the subject land to one Salongo, an innocent purchaser, who was registered as proprietor of the land. A Magistrates' Court convicted Katamba of forgery and ordered that the suit property be transferred to the applicant. When the applicant attempted to enforce the order, the registrar refused to comply. The applicant instituted these proceedings in the High Court against the registrar. Odoki Ag J, as he then was, upheld the registrar's grounds for refusing to transfer title into the applicant's name. He held that Salongo was a *bona fide* purchaser for value, therefore, under s. 189 of the *Registration of Titles Act*, his title could not be impeached or cancelled notwithstanding that he acquired his title from a forger. His Honour observed that one of the paradoxes of registered conveyance is that though registration obtained by fraud is void, it is capable of becoming a good root of title to a *bona fide* purchaser for value.[37]

The Australian case of *Breskvar and another v Wall and others* also provides a good illustration of the operation of the principle of indefeasibility.[38] In that case, Mr and Mrs Breskvar borrowed money from one Petrie. As security for the loan they handed over to him the certificate of title of

---

33 *Chan and another v Cresdon Properties Limited* [1989] 168 CLR 242 at 257.

34 *The Torrens System in Australia*, supra, at 293.

35 *Kampala Bottlers Ltd v Damanico (U) Ltd* CA No 22 of 1992 (unreported).

36 Misc. Cause No 7A of 1977; (1980) HCB 24 (unreported).

37 See also *The Management Committee of Rushasha Primary School* v *Francis Nkorenta* C.A. MKA 11/93 (unreported). *Olinda De Souza v Kassamali Namji* [1962] EA 756; *Nazarali Hassanali Sayani v Edward Mperese Nsubuga* CS No 364 of 1993 (unreported).

38 (1971) 126 CLR 376.

their land and a memorandum of transfer which, at Petrie's insistence, they signed in blank (ie signed the transfer forms without inserting the name of the transferee). Under the Queensland Stamp Act, 1894 a blank instrument of transfer was declared to be 'absolutely void and inoperative' both at law and in equity. Petrie without the authority and knowledge of the Breskvars inserted in the instrument of transfer the name of Wall, an accomplice, as the transferee and had the land registered in Wall's name. Wall then sold the land to A Pty Ltd, which bought it in good faith without knowledge of the fraud. But before A Pty Ltd could register its transfer, the Breskvars lodged a caveat to prevent registration and commenced these proceedings to have Wall's registration cancelled and the register book rectified to restore their names as proprietors. On their behalf it was argued that since the instrument of transfer was executed by way of security only, it was ineffective to transfer the fee simple estate to Wall. Moreover, the transfer form having been signed in blank was void under the provisions of the Stamp Act.

The High Court of Australia unanimously dismissed the Breskvars' argument. It held that, except as provided by the Act, the conclusiveness of the certificate of title is definitive of the title of the registered proprietor. Berwick CJ in his judgement observed that:[39]

> The Torrens System of registered title ... is not a system of registration of title but a system of title by registration. That which the certificate of title describes is not the title which the registered proprietor had, or which but for registration he would have had. It is title which registration itself has vested in the proprietor. Consequently, a registration from a void instrument is effective according to the terms of the registration. It matters not what the cause or reasons for which the instrument is void.

The effect of the judgement was that, notwithstanding Petrie's fraud, Wall by virtue of registration became the proprietor of the suit land. Because he was a party to Petrie's fraud his title was defeasible. But by the time the Breskvars attempted to set aside Wall's title it was too late as Wall had already transferred an equitable title to A Pty Ltd, which title the court ruled prevailed over the Breskvars' equitable claim.[40]

Exceptions to indefeasibility

The principle of indefeasibility of title though central to the Torrens system is not absolute. It is subject to several exceptions, some of which are expressed within the *Registration of Titles Act*. Others are created by overriding statutes and by the courts in the exercise of their inherent jurisdiction.

(a) Exceptions within the Act

Section 61 of the Act guarantees the indefeasibility of a registered title subject to the following exceptions stated in the section.

(i) Encumbrances notified on the folium

A registered proprietor takes his or her title subject to estates or interests which are endorsed on the register book and certificate of title at the time of purchase. This is self-explanatory. The register book is like a mirror: what you see is what is there and what you do not see is not there.[41] Where there is a notification of an encumbrance a person searching the register book should pay attention to the contents of any document relating to the encumbrance. For example, if the land is subject to a mortgage he or she should ascertain the amount that is outstanding for obviously it would affect the value of the land.

---

39 *Ibid*, pp. 385 - 86.

40 The court found that on a balance of equities the Breskvars were more to blame because they were grossly negligent in signing the instrument of transfer in blank.

41 However, see exceptions to indefeasibility below.

(ii) Fraud

Section 61 of the *Registration of Titles Act* stipulates that the title of a registered proprietor is indefeasible except in case of fraud. It should be stressed that the fraud, which must be proved to invalidate a registered title, must be the fraud of the person whose title it is designed to impeach. Thus, the fact that the registered proprietor bought the land from a rogue or a person who acted fraudulently in transferring the land does not mean that the transferee's title was acquired through fraud.[42] In *Musisi v Grindlays Bank (U) Ltd and others,*[43] Masika CJ said that a person registered through fraud is one 'who becomes a registered [proprietor] through a fraudulent act by him or to which he is a party or with full knowledge of the fraud'. Similarly, in *Kampala Bottlers Ltd* v *Damanico (U) Ltd,* Wambuzi CJ said, 'the transferee must be guilty of some fraudulent act or must have known of such act by somebody else and taken advantage of such act.'[44] In other words, it must be established that the proprietor gained registration through participation in fraud.

The term 'fraud' is not defined in the Act. In *Assets Company Ltd* v *Mere Roihi,*[45] a New Zealand case on appeal to the Privy Council, Lindley LJ said that fraud in the Torrens system meant 'actual fraud, ie. dishonesty of some sort, not what is called constructive or equitable fraud'.[46] A useful description of what constitutes fraud within the Torrens system is also found in a passage in another Privy Council judgement in *Waimiha Sawmilling Co Ltd (in liq)* v *Waione Timber Co Ltd*:[47]

> If the designed object of a transfer be to cheat a man of a known existing right, that is fraudulent, and so also fraud may be established by a deliberate and dishonest trick causing an interest not to be registered and thus fraudulently keeping the register clear.

A common element of both definitions is 'dishonesty' or desire to 'cheat' on the part of the proprietor whose title is being challenged.

Fraud is a very serious allegation to make against another person. Where a person accuses another of fraud, it must be pleaded in accordance with the *Civil Procedure Rules,* Order VI Rule 2, and particulars of the fraud must be given and proved strictly by the person alleging it.[48] In *Alibhai and another v Karia and another,* Oder JSC said that although the standard of proof for fraud may not be as heavy as to require proof beyond reasonable doubt, something more than a mere balance of probability (which is generally applied in civil matters) is required.[49]

The case of *Lusweswe v Kasule and Coulibally*[50] illustrates a fraudulent transaction. The plaintiff was the original registered proprietor of two adjacent plots of land, which we shall refer to

---

42 *Lusweswe v Kasule and Coulibally* CS No 1010 of 1983 (unreported); *Hotel International Ltd v The Administrator of the Estate of the late Robert Kavuma* CA No 37 of 1995 (unreported).

43 CS No 869 of 1981 (unreported);[1983] HCB 39.

44 CA No 22/92 (unreported). In *Rurangaranga v Mbarara Municipal Council and others* CA No 10 of 1996 (unreported), Wambuzi CJ, held that a proprietor who purchased land knowing that the grant to the vendor was not authorised, acted fraudulently.

45 [1905] AC 176.

46 *Ibid*, p. 210. For discussion of equitable fraud see Chapter 4.

47 [1926] AC 101 pp. 106-07.

48 *Kampala Bottlers Ltd* v *Damanico (U) Ltd*, C A No 22 of 1992, per Platt JSC. Although it is not necessary that the word 'fraud' should be used, the facts must be so stated as to show that fraud is charged. It is not allowed to leave fraud to be inferred from facts pleaded. See *Kazzora v Rukuba* CA No 13 of 1992 (unreported).

49 CA No 52 of 1995. See also *Kampala Bottlers Ltd* v *Damanico (U) Ltd*, CA No 22 of 1992; *Patel v Lalji Makanji* [1954] EA 314; *Kazzora v Rukuba* CA No 13 of 1992 (unreported); *Shokatali Abdulla Dhalla v Sadrudin Meralli* CA No 32 of 1994 (unreported).

50 C S No 1010/83. For other cases see *Management Committee of Rushasha Primary School v Nkorenta* C.A. MKA 11/1993 (unreported); *Matovu and othersl v Sseviri and another CA No 7 of 1978 (unreported);* [1979] HCB 174; *Loke Yew v Port Swettenham Rubber Co Ltd* [1913] AC 491.

as plot A and B respectively. The plaintiff had built a house on plot A and there was a driveway to the house that passed through plot B to the public road. There was no building on plot B. During the political turmoil in the late 1970s, the plaintiff was detained in prison, and in his absence his property, including his certificates of title for the two plots, was looted. Eventually, when the plaintiff applied for a replacement certificate he discovered that the title to plot B had been transferred and registered in the name of Coulibally, the second defendant. The latter alleged that he had bought the plot from one Kasule, first defendant, who allegedly bought it from the plaintiff. The plaintiff denied ever selling the land to anyone. The plaintiff sought an order under s.185 for the registrar to cancel registration of the second defendant on ground of fraud and restore the plaintiff's name as proprietor.

The issue was whether Coulibally was involved in fraud. It was held that there was sufficient circumstantial evidence to establish fraud against him. Firstly, all records of the alleged instruments of transfer from the plaintiff to the first defendant, and from first defendant to the second were missing from the registrar's office. Secondly, there was no evidence to show that the second defendant searched the register book or investigated the ownership of the house on plot A, the driveway of which passed through plot B. Thirdly, even though Coulibally had allegedly bought plot B he occupied the house on plot A, which he knew he had no right to occupy. Finally, the fact that neither defendant appeared in court to defend the case raised a strong suspicion against their innocence. The court ordered the registrar to cancel the second defendant's registration and restore the plaintiff as proprietor of the suit property.

Notice of unregistered interest is not fraud

In equity a purchaser of a legal estate is bound by any prior equitable interest over the land of which he or she had notice prior to purchase.[51] Notice in this context is of two types: actual notice and constructive notice. Actual notice is where the purchaser was actually aware of the existence of the equitable interest. Constructive notice is knowledge the purchaser would have acquired if he or she had taken reasonable steps to investigate title. For example, if at the time of purchase of the land, a third party was in possession of the land, the purchaser is deemed to have constructive notice of whatever claim the person in possession might have over the land.[52] Though the purchaser in such a situation may be innocent of actual fraud, in equity constructive knowledge is deemed to constitute fraud.[53]

In contrast, under the Torrens system notice by itself is not fraud. Section 145 of the *Registration of Titles Act* provides that except in the case of fraud, a dealer is not required to inquire or investigate the antecedents of the title he or she seeks to purchase or be concerned with unregistered interests. The section goes on to say that mere notice of unregistered interests, whether actual or constructive, notwithstanding any rule of law or equity to the contrary, does not impute fraud. For example, in *Shah* v *Modern Sweet Mart Ltd,*[54] the plaintiff purchased and was registered as the proprietor of the suit property. It was not disputed that at the time of registration he was fully aware that the defendants claimed an unregistered lease for a term of seven years over the property. In an application for vacant possession, the defendants in their defence argued that since the plaintiff had notice of their unregistered lease agreement he was bound by it in equity. It was held that s.145 specifically prohibits the application of the rules of equity; consequently, though at the time of purchase the plaintiff was aware of the unregistered lease agreement, he was not bound by it.[55]

---

51 *Uganda Post and Telecommunications v AKM Lutaaya* CA No 36 of 1995 (unreported).

52 Megarry and Wade, *The Law of Real Property* (5th ed, Stevens & Sons. London, 1984), pp. 148-49.

53 The expression 'equitable fraud' or 'constructive fraud' is sometimes used to describe fraud imputed merely on the basis of notice, see *Assets Company Ltd v Mere Roihi* [1905] AC 176, p. 210.

54 (1956-57) 8 ULR 99.

55 See also *Kyazze v Eunice Busingye* CA No 13 of 1990 (unreported). Compare this case with *Uganda Post and Telecommunications v AKM Lutaaya* CA No 36 of 1995 (unreported); *Management Committee of Rushasha Primary School v Nkorenta* C.A. MKA 11/1993 (unreported).

In *Katarikawe* v *Katwiremu & another*,[56] Justice Ssekandi said that although mere knowledge of unregistered interests cannot be imputed as fraud, where knowledge was accompanied by a 'wrongful'[57] intention to defeat such interest it would amount to fraud. In that case, the plaintiff alleged that in 1971 he purchased the suit property from the first defendant. Before the title was transferred to the plaintiff he entered into possession and carried out various improvements including building a house on the suit land. On several occasions he reminded the first defendant to affect the transfer but the latter did not, claiming that he had misplaced the certificate and that he was in the process of getting a replacement copy. Meanwhile, on 4 May 1972, the suit land was registered in the name of the second defendant, who happened to be the brother-in-law of the first defendant.

The plaintiff instituted these proceedings against both defendants. The second defendant alleged that he purchased the disputed land from the first defendant in 1968 but did not pay the purchase price because he had no money. He denied that he was registered through fraud merely because at the time his title was registered he was aware of the plaintiff's unregistered claim over the disputed land. Accordingly, he submitted that his title was indefeasible. Ssekandi J held that there was sufficient circumstantial evidence from which it could be inferred that he was registered in consequence of fraud. Firstly, the plaintiff had been in possession of the disputed land for over a year and had openly carried out improvements on the land before the second defendant's title was registered. Secondly, the fact that the defendants were relatives raised strong suspicion of a conspiracy to defraud the plaintiff. Thirdly, the second defendant's claim that he purchased the land in 1968 though he never paid the purchase price was implausible.[58]

(iii) The estate of a proprietor claiming under a prior instrument of title

The title of a registered proprietor is not indefeasible as against the interest of another proprietor claiming the same land under a prior registered title (s. 61). The provision envisages a situation where the same land is erroneously included in two or more certificates of title. The error may be committed by the registrar's office, District Land Board or by the parties.[59] For example, suppose that Mukasa subdivides his land into two plots: A and B. He sells plot A to Okello and the latter is registered as proprietor of the land. Then he sells plot B to Amooti. By mistake the certificate of title issued to Amooti includes both plots A and B. Two years later Amooti purports to sell both plots to Kato and he is registered as proprietor of both plots. Even though Kato purchases in good faith his title is not indefeasible to the extent that it includes plot A, which is comprised in Okello's prior certificate. Thus, Okello may eject Kato from plot A.[60]

(iv) Land included by wrong description

Section 61 *Registration of Titles Act* stipulates that the title of a registered proprietor is not absolute as regards any portion of land that may have been included in his or her certificate of title by wrong description of parcels or boundaries. The effect of the exception is that title to such land remains in the true owner and he or she can bring an action for ejectment under s. 184(d) or have the mistake rectified. The case of *Rwamutatiri* v *Kamono*[61] provides a good illustration of a situation

---

56 CS No 2 of 1973; [1977] HCB 187 (unreported).

57 His Honour borrowed this term from the Kenya *Registration of Titles Act* (cap 281), definition of fraud in s. 2 thereof.

58 See also *Management Committee of Rushasha Primary School v Nkorenta* CA MKA 11 of 1993 (unreported); *In the Matter of JP Ruzigana* MSC No 48 of 1976; (1977) HCB 93 (unreported).

59 See, for example, *Sewanyana v Martin Aliker* CA No 4 of 1990 (unreported); *Makerere University v St Mark Education Centre and another* CS No 378 of 1996. Compare with *Hotel International Ltd v The Administrator of the Estate of the late Robert Kavuma* CA No 37 of 1995 (unreported).

60 See also s. 184 (e), *RTA*. In *Sewanyana v Martin Aliker* CA No 4 of 1990 (unreported), the plaintiff's action failed on technical grounds.

61 (1978) HCB 300 (unreported).

contemplated by the provision. In that case, the defendant and the plaintiff owned adjoining pieces of land under customary tenure. The defendant, with a view to bringing his land under the Act, had it surveyed, but in the process the surveyors inadvertently included land that belonged to the plaintiff. The facts are not very clear, but it appears that before the defendant's land was registered the plaintiff successfully sued the defendant for encroachment. However, when the certificate of title was issued to the defendant it included the land claimed by the plaintiff. The latter commenced these proceedings under s. 185 seeking an order from the registrar to cancel the defendant's certificate in so far as it affected the plaintiff's land. The plaintiff based his claim on the earlier encroachment judgement in his favour against the defendant. The application was dismissed on technical grounds. It is submitted that the appropriate course of action would have been for the plaintiff to institute fresh proceedings for ejectment under s. 184(d) *Registration of Titles Act* on the ground of wrong description of boundaries or parcel of land, coupled with an application for cancellation under s. 185.

It should be noted that the scope of this exception to indefeasibility is limited. Section 61 states that the exception does not apply if the land is transferred to a *bona fide* purchaser for value. Thus, if by the time the action is brought, the land is already transferred and registered in the name of an innocent purchaser for value, the latter acquires an indefeasible title.[62]

(v) Public rights of way and easements

Public rights of way and easements acquired by enjoyment or user or subsisting over or upon or affecting registered land constitute an exception to indefeasibility under s. 61, *Registration of Titles Act*. A public right of way is a dedication to the public of the occupation of the surface land for the purpose of passing and re-passing.[63] An easement, on the other hand, is a right over another's land for the benefit of some other land.[64] An easement may be acquired by express or implied grant or by prescription. Under s. 62 of the *Registration of Titles Act*, the registrar is obliged to endorse on the certificate any subsisting easement which appears to have been created by deed or writing, but there is no obligation to endorse on the certificate an easement acquired by prescription or by implied grant or reservation. It is thought that the effect of the exception is that a registered proprietor takes title subject to any easement and public right of way,[65] which has not been otherwise extinguished even though the same is not endorsed on the certificate of title.[66]

(vi) Adverse possession

Under the *Limitation Act* (cap 70) if a landowner does not eject or commence proceedings against an intruder in adverse possession within a period of twelve years, the landowner effectively loses his or her land to the intruder.[67] By operation of law the latter becomes the owner of the land. The doctrine of adverse possession applies to land registered under the *Registration of Titles Act*.[68] Section 61 provides that title acquired by adverse possession prevails over the title of the registered proprietor. A good illustration is provided by a Kenyan case of *Kisee Maweu and others*

---

62 For a good illustration see *Western Australia Fresh Food & Ice Co* v *Freecorn* [1904] 1 WAR 22.

63 *Makumbi (Mrs E) & another* v *Puran Singh Ghana & another* [1962] EA 331.

64 For detailed discussion of easements, see Chapter 8.

65 *Makumbi (Mrs E) & another* v *Puran Singh Ghana & another* [1962] EA 331. See also s. 72(1) of the *Land Act*, 1998, which states that all land shall be subject to public rights of way that were in existence at the time the Act came into effect. All public rights of way are vested in the government on behalf of the public.

66 This view is based on Australian authorities, see eg *James* v *Stevenson* [1893] AC 162; *Nelson v Hughes* [1947] VLR 227; *Di Masi* v *Piromalli* [1980] WAR 57 (cf *Australian Hi-Fi Publications Pty Ltd* v *Gehl* [1979] 2 NSWLR 619).

67 Sections 6 and 17. See e.g., *Nambalu Kintu v Efulainnu Kamira* CA No 26 of 1973; (1975) HCB 221.

68 Section 70 stipulates the procedure for registration of a title acquired by adverse possession, see generally Part 7, *RTA*.

v Kiu Ranching and Co-operative Society Ltd.[69] The facts of the case were as follows. The appellants were among a number of people who settled on the suit land in 1933. In 1961 the respondents were registered as proprietors of the subject land under the *Kenya Registration of Titles Act* (cap 281). Soon after their registration, they commenced ejection proceedings against the appellants. The appellants claimed title over the land on the basis of adverse possession. The trial judge struck out their defence on the ground that the certificate of title was conclusive evidence of the respondents' title. In any case, according to the trial judge, the period of adverse possession against the respondents should be calculated from 1961 when they were registered as proprietors. On appeal to the Kenyan Court of Appeal, it was held that the limitation period began to run against the respondents from the date that the appellants began to squat on the land and not the date of registration of the respondents' title. Accordingly, the appellants had been in adverse possession for more than the requisite limitation period. Platt AJA said that, in his view:

> [T]he owner of registered land acquires an absolute and indefeasible title, to such an extent that he can immediately put any squatter or trespasser off the land ... The adverse possessor stoutly possesses the land, but he has not the slightest interest until the twelfth year has been completed. Now he emerges as the owner, and however absolute and indefeasible the title is, it is lost forever.[70]

This exception to indefeasibility makes it imperative for potential dealers in land in their own interests to physically inspect the land for possible squatters. As the above case indicates, if the squatters have been in possession for more than twelve years, title of the proprietor would be extinguished. In other words, the land would not be worth buying. If the period is less than twelve years the proprietor or his or her successor in title has the balance of the period within which to eject them otherwise the title would be extinguished.

(vii) Interest of any tenant of land

Section 61 states that the interest of any tenant whose possession is not adverse prevails over the title of a registered proprietor even though his or her interest is not entered as an encumbrance on the Register Book. The effect of the exception is that the possessor's claim under the tenancy agreement prevails over whomsoever is the registered proprietor even though the tenancy is not registered. For example, the interest of a 'lawful' or *'bona fide'* occupant would prevail over the title of the registered proprietor under this provision.[71] Also in *Uganda Post and Telecommunications v AKM Lutaaya* it was held that the respondent's registered leasehold was subject to the appellant's title acquired by possession with the consent of the landlord prior to the leasehold.[72]

In the Australian State of Victoria earlier cases interpreting an identical provision construed 'tenant in possession' as limited to a tenant who was in possession for a term not exceeding three years. The reason was that the courts felt that the object of the provision was to protect interests arising from short-term tenancies, which were not registrable under the Act.[73] Later cases, however, gave a wider interpretation of the proviso. For example, in *Sandhurst Mutual Permanent Investment Building Society* v *Gissing*[74] a registered proprietor sought to eject the defendant who had been let in possession by the previous registered proprietor under a contract of sale. It was held that the defendant's possession of the land as a 'tenant' together with an option to purchase the land

---

69 (1982) 1 KLR 746.

70 *Ibid*, p. 752.

71 See definition of the term 'lawful occupant' and 'bona fide occupant', s. 30, *Land Act* 1998. In any case, as discussed below, such tenancy constitutes an exception to indefeasibility by virtue of the *Land Act*.

72 CA No 36 of 1995 (unreported). This case was, in our view, wrongly decided on the basis of general law principles.

73 See, e.g., *Calvert v Tate* Argus 8 August 1867, cited *Sandhurst Mutual Permanent Investment Building Society* v *Gissing* (1889) 15 VLR 329, p. 330.

74 (1889) 15 VLR 329

constituted an interest, which prevailed against the claim of indefeasibility of title of the proprietor, notwithstanding that the encumbrance was not recorded on the register book. Highnboth CJ said that:[75]

> [T]enant must be deemed to include at least every tenant who is in actual occupation, and holds under some landlord, and that every interest in the land of such a tenant which grows out of, and is not discoverable from, his right to continue in occupation as a tenant, is protected by the terms of this provision against the claims of a proprietor under a certificate of title.

Because of this exception a person who deals in land without physical inspection of the land to ascertain whether another person is in possession does so at his or her own peril.[76] It should be stressed that for this exception to apply the person must be lawfully in possession as a tenant and not as a squatter.[77]

(viii) Lease, licence or other authority granted by the minister

A lease, licence or other authority granted by the minister or a government department or office or public authority in *respect of which no provision for registration is made*, constitutes an overriding right over the land affected. For example, under the *Road Act* (cap 345), the minister is given power to declare any land a road reserve, and, where land is so reserved, construction of buildings and other structures in or within a prescribed distance thereof is prohibited.[78] Under the same Act, power is given to the Road Authority to dig and take away materials required for the construction of roads from any part of a road reserve without payment to anyone.[79] Since there is no provision for the registration of road reserves under the *Registration of Titles Act*, the ministerial power overrides a registered title.

(ix) Unpaid rates, taxes and charges

Section 61 of the *Registration of Titles Act* states that a registered proprietor takes the land subject to any outstanding rates or charges which, without reference to the provisions of the *Registration of Titles Act*, are declared under a written law to be chargeable on the land in favour of the government or a public body. For example, s. 95(1) of the *Water Statute*, 1995, provides that rates, charges or fees levied under the Act and any interest and penalty payable thereon, is a charge against the land in respect of which the rates, charges or fees are levied. Thus, where after buying a house the new owner discovers that there are outstanding water charges incurred by the previous owner, the new owner should ensure that the charges are paid, otherwise the water authority might cause the land to be sold in order to recover the moneys due to it. Obviously, the owner could recover the money from the person who was primarily responsible, but as far as the National Water and Sewerage Corporation is concerned the charges are attached to the land. Searching the register book will not of course reveal outstanding debts to the corporation.[80]

(x) Registrar's powers as an exception to indefeasibility

The registrar is given certain powers, which within limits constitute further exception to the principle of indefeasibility of title. The powers are granted under s. 92 of the *Land Act* 1998.[81] Under this

---

75 *Ibid*, p. 331.

76 See, e.g., *Uganda Post and Telecommunications v AKM Lutaaya*, supra.

77 For rights of squatters see 'adverse possession' in Chapter 4.

78 See ss. 3 and 6.

79 Section 7. It is possible that this provision violates article 26 of the constitution, which prohibit taking of private property without compensation.

80 For a good illustration see *South-Eastern Drainage Board* v *Savings Bank of South Australia* (1939) 62 CLR 603.

81 Originally, the powers were granted under ss. 69 and 178 (a), *RTA*. Both these provisions were repealed by s. 97 of the *Land Act*, 1998.

provision, the registrar is empowered to correct errors and supply omissions in the register book and the certificate of title. The section provides that where a certificate of title contains a misdescription of land or boundary or if it was wrongly or illegally obtained or retained, the registrar is empowered to demand whomever has it to return it for correction or cancellation. If a person ordered to deliver up a certificate refuses or ignores the order, the registrar may dispense with its production and amend the registry and, where necessary, issue a special certificate without reference to the district land tribunal or court.[82] However, the registrar is required to give a fair hearing to any party likely to be affected by his or her decision. A person aggrieved by the registrar's decision is entitled to appeal to the district land tribunal within a period of sixty days. Where a certificate of title is cancelled the person in whose favour it is cancelled is prohibited from transferring the land until the appeal period expires or pending the results of the appeal against the registrar's decision.[83]

The foregoing provision appears to give the registrar extensive powers. The powers are not identical with the situations excepted from indefeasibility in ss. 61 and 184 of the *Registration of Titles Act.* They are distinct from the power of the courts to cancel entries under s. 185 of the *Registration of Titles Act*. The registrar exercises his or her powers under ss. 92 of the *Land Act* on his or her own account without resort to the court. For example, where the registrar erroneously issues a certificate of title to another, he or she could recall and cancel the certificate following the procedure prescribed in the section.[84] However, it is not clear whether the registrar is entitled to exercise these powers against a registered proprietor who is a bona fide purchaser for value. For example, suppose X illegally obtains a certificate of title of certain land. Before the registrar recalls the certificate X transfers the land to Y, an innocent purchaser for value, and Y is registered as proprietor of the subject land. Can the registrar cancel Y's certificate under s. 92 of the *Land Act*? On the face of the provision, it would seem that the registrar could do so. The onus would then be on Y to appeal to the district land tribunal against the decision on the ground of the principle of indefeasibility.

If the above interpretation is right, then section 92 makes drastic changes to the operation of the Torrens system in Uganda.[85] The provision may be justified on the ground that it enables the registrar to correct promptly errors in the register and to deal with cases where he or she considers that title was wrongfully obtained. This may be particularly important, for example, in the case of fraud where the rightful owner is unable, due to financial reasons, to protect his or her interest. On the other hand, the power to correct or cancel entries in the register could undermine the principle of indefeasibility. Moreover, the exercise of this power may expose the registrar's office to frequent challenge in the courts by aggrieved interested persons. Unless the registrar exercises the powers in only the most obvious cases of fraud or wrongdoing the registrar will find himself or herself constantly dragged to court at the taxpayer's expense.

(b) Overriding statutory exceptions to indefeasibility

Statutory provisions operating outside the *Registration of Titles Act* may supersede the principle of indefeasibility. This may be done by the creation of rights that are enforceable against a

---

82 Previously, where the person with the certificate of title refused or neglected to surrender it, the registrar could not cancel the certificate without a court order, s. 69, *RTA*. See also *Gatare v Parkash Kaur and others* HCCS 106 of 1995 (unreported).

83 Section 92(11), *Land Act*, 1998

84 In *Rurangaranga v Mbarara Municipal Council and others* CA No 10 of 1996 (unreported), Wambuzi CJ, and Karokora JSC, expressed a view, *obiter dictum*, that under sr 69, *RTA*, the Registrar had power to cancel a certificate of title, which was fraudulently or wrongly obtained or retained.

85 In *Assets Company Ltd v Mere Roihi* [1905] AC 176 at 194-195, the Privy Council observed that the powers of the Registrar under the New Zealand provision analogous to s. 61, *RTA*, were 'significant and extensive'. Nevertheless, the Board held that those powers could not be exercised to the prejudice of a bona fide purchaser for value. See also *Fraser v Walker* [1967] AC 569, pp. 585-86.

registered proprietor or by destruction of existing registered interests. Whether or not a particular statutory provision overrides the principle of indefeasibility is a matter of statutory interpretation. Some statutes contain express overriding provisions. For example, the *Access to Roads* Act, 1969, s. 3 thereof empowers a landowner who has no access to a public road, to apply for a court order for a right of way over another's land. If the application is granted, the right of way is registrable in the register book against the land affected notwithstanding any inconsistence with the provisions of the *Registration of Titles Act*.[86]

In other statutes the legislative intention to override the provisions of the *Registration of Titles Act* is implied by application of ordinary principles of statutory interpretation.[87] One of these principles is that where provisions of a later statute are inconsistent with those of an earlier Act, the former prevails.[88] If the later Act contains plain language that indicates that it was intended to apply to registered land, then it must be given its plain meaning.[89] The *Land Act,* 1998, is a typical example of such legislation. For example, s. 32(2) provides that a tenant by occupancy is deemed to be a tenant of the registered proprietor. Section 34(9) provides that where a tenant by occupancy is granted a certificate of occupancy the registrar is required to notify it as an encumbrance on the relevant certificate of title of the mailo owner. But s. 32(9) states that for 'the avoidance of doubt' lack of a certificate of occupancy does not prejudice the security of tenure of a tenant by occupancy under the Act. In our view the latter provision means that a proprietor's title remains subject to the rights of a tenant by occupancy whether or not those rights are endorsed on the certificate of title. Clearly the intention of the provision is to override the principle of indefeasibility. Similarly, it is thought that the provisions of s. 40 of the *Land Act*, which prohibit transactions affecting family land except with the consent of relevant family members, constitute an exception to indefeasibility. The provision renders any transaction entered into without the requisite consent null and void.[90] The intention of the legislature to protect family land would be defeated if transactions entered into without the requisite consent were held valid under the principle of indefeasibility of title.[91]

Other examples of overriding statutory provisions are found in statutes that control land use to protect environmentally sensitive areas. The statutes include the *Forest Act* (cap 246), *National Environmental Statute*, 1995; and the *Uganda Wildlife Statute*, 1996. Section 44 of the *Land Act* imposes an obligation on any landowner or occupier of land to manage and utilise the land in accordance with these statutes and any other written law.

Judicial inroads - *rights in personam*

If s. 61 of the *Registration of Titles Act* were construed literally, there would be no room for further exceptions to the principle of indefeasibility except as provided therein. However, the courts have not been deterred by the section from making additional inroads to the principle of indefeasibility

---

86 Section 6, *Access to Roads Act*. See also s. 1(2) of the *Expropriated Properties Act,* No 9 of 1982, which nullifies any title to land to which the Act applies 'notwithstanding the provisions of any written law governing the conferring of title to land'. For discussion of this provision see *Gokaldas Laximidas Tanna v SR Rosemary Munyinza* Civil Appeal No. 12 of 1992, Supreme Court [1994-5]; HCB 53; *Makerere Properties Ltd v Attorney General* CA No 36 of 1996. See also Chapter 10.

87 In *Miller v Minister of Mines and another* [1963] 1 All ER 109 at 113, the Privy Council held with reference to the New Zealand Torrens Act, that it was not necessary that there should be a direct provision overriding the provisions of the Act. 'It is sufficient if this is proper implication from the terms of the relative statute'.

88 *Sejjaka Nalima v Musoke* CA No 12 of 1985.

89 *South-Eastern Drainage Board v Savings Bank of South Australia* (1939) 62 CLR 603; *Travinto Nominees v Vlattas* (1973) 129 CLR 1. See also *Sejjaka Nalima v Musoke* CA No 12 of 1985.

90 Section 40(4) of the *Land Act.*

91 The same argument applies to s. 41 of the *Land Act,* which prohibits non-citizens of Uganda from holding land other than leasehold.

on the basis of their inherent equitable jurisdiction.[92] The judicial power to intervene without statutory sanction was espoused by the Privy Council in *Fraser* v *Walker*:[93]

> Their lordships have accepted the general principle that registration under the ... [Torrens Acts] confers upon a registered proprietor a title to the interest in respect of which he is registered which is also immune from adverse claims, other than those specifically excepted. In doing so they wish to make it clear that this principle in no way denies the right of a plaintiff to bring against a registered proprietor a claim *in personam* founded in law or in equity, for such relief as a court acting *in personam* may grant.

Spry JA, in the East African Court of Appeal, expressed similar views in *Adonia* v *Mutekanga*:[94]

> Although the concept of the sanctity of the register runs through the Act, it is clear that the legislature intended to reserve to the High Court the power to enforce fiduciary obligations ...

A claim *in personam* is a personal obligation of legal or equitable nature assumed by a registered proprietor before or after registration of his or her title. Unlike a right *in rem,* which is enforceable against the whole world, a right *in personam* is only enforceable against a person who was a party to the obligation.[95] For example, if a proprietor enters into an enforceable contract to sell his or her land, the purchaser by virtue of the contract acquires an equitable interest in the land.[96] That interest is a right in *personam* as against the proprietor. If the proprietor refuses to transfer the title to the purchaser, the court by order of specific performance can force him or her to transfer it in accordance with the contract.[97] The courts pierce the veil of indefeasibility to prevent the proprietor from avoiding the consequences of his or her own act.[98]

Protection of unregistered interests by caveat

The registration of an interest provides the best security against the principle of indefeasibility. However, there may be circumstances where a person claiming title is unable to register it, for example, because the proprietor has refused to sign the appropriate instrument of transfer or to hand over the certificate of title to enable registration. The *Registration of Titles Act* makes provision for lodging a caveat for protection of unregistered claims to land. A caveat operates as a statutory injunction to the registrar to prevent registration of any dealings which might affect the interest, the subject of the caveat. Lodging a caveat serves as an interim measure, usually, pending judicial determination of the caveator's claim over the land. In *Kazzora v Rukuba*, the Supreme Court held that the doctrine of *lis pendens* (whereby a pending suit affecting land and registered in the register of pending actions acts as a bar to the registration of dealings affecting that land until the action is disposed of) does not apply in Uganda.[99] Accordingly, the only way to protect an

---

92 The High Court is entitled and bound to apply the doctrines of equity where not inconsistent with written law and as far as the circumstances of the country allow, see s. 16 (2)(c)(i), *Judicature Statute*, 1996.

93 [1967] 1 AC 569 at 585.

94 [1970] EA 429 at 433.

95 Megarry & Wade, *Modern Law of Real Property*, p. 113.

96 *Katarikawe* v *Katwiremu and another* CS No 2 of 1973; (1977) HCB 187; *Ismail Jaffer Alibhai and others v Nandala Harjivan Karia and another* CA No 53 of 1995 (unreported).

97 *Souza Figueiredo & Co Ltd v Moorings Hotel Co Ltd* [1960] EA 926; *Ismail Jaffer Alibhai and others v Nandala Harjivan Karia and another* CA No 53 of 1995 (unreported).

98 See for example, *Bahr and another* v *Nicolay and others* (1988) 164 CLR 604.

99 CA No 13 of 1992 (unreported). See also *Njuki v Musisi Nyanzi* HCCS No 0434 of 1996 (unreported).

unregistered claim over registered land is either to lodge a caveat or seek a court injunction.[100] A caveat may also serve as notice to the caveatee[101] and the public of the nature of the claim the caveator has over the land.[102]

A caveat may be lodged by the registrar or by a private person. Section 178 (b) of the *Registration of Titles Act* empowers the registrar to lodge a caveat, on behalf of the government or a person who is under disability or absent from the country, to prohibit registration of any transaction affecting land that belongs to or appears to belong to the government or such person. The provision also empowers the registrar to lodge a caveat to prevent registration of any dealings in any land where there appears to be a misdescription of land or boundary or fraud. A private person may lodge a caveat against bringing land under the Act (s. 22); against granting an application to rectify a boundary or area of land (s. 169); against registering a title based on adverse possession (s 85); and against registration of any dealing or transfer of an estate or interest in land in which he or she has an interest (s. 148).

To lodge a caveat a person must have a caveatable interest over the land.[103] A caveatable interest has been defined in several Australian cases to mean a claim of a proprietary or quasi-proprietary nature in the particular land.[104] An example of a caveatable interest includes a claim of a grantee under a will; a claim under a contract of sale,[105] lease,[106] mortgage;[107] option to purchase;[108] and a claim based on adverse possession. Claims that have been held not to be caveatable include a deserted wife's claim over the matrimonial home based on occupation,[109] a claim by a mere licensee;[110] a claim by a shareholder in land owned by a company under liquidation;[111] and a claim based on an inconclusive contract of sale.[112] A common factor running through all the examples of non-caveatable claims is that, under the general law, none of the claims, even if proven, would constitute a proprietary interest in land.

Once a caveat is in place, the registrar is prohibited from registering any transaction affecting the land except as expressed in the caveat or with the consent of the person who lodged the caveat.[113] It should be stressed that lodging a caveat does not validate or prove the caveator's title. It simply maintains a status quo by preventing registration of rival claims (which otherwise would defeat the caveator's claim under the principle of indefeasibility) until the courts determine the caveator's claim. For example, the fact that a transfer is registered subject to a caveator's claim

---

[100] In *Katarikawe v Katwiremu and another* CS No 2 of 1973; [1977] HCB 187, Ssekandi J, held that taking possession of title deeds by a purchaser is insufficient to protect an unregistered interest unless a caveat is lodged.

[101] A 'caveator' is the person who lodges the caveat, and a 'caveatee' is the person against whom a caveat is lodged. Usually the registered proprietor is the caveatee, but the term could also be used to refer to a rival claimant against whom a caveat is lodged.

[102] *Boyes* v *Gathure* [1969] EA 385, per Spry JA, at 388.

[103] *Namusisi and others v Ntabazi* CS No 887 of 1988.

[104] See, e.g., *Municipal District of Concord* v *Coles* (1906) 3 CLR 96. In *Kuper & Kuper* v *Keywest Construction Pty Ltd* [1990] 3 WAR 419 it was held that a person has a caveatable interest in all cases where an injunction could be issued to prevent the proprietor from meanwhile dealing with the land.

[105] *Fernandes* v *Houstein* (1963) 4 FLR 355.

[106] *Souza Figueiredo & Co Ltd* v *Moorings Hotel Co Ltd* [1960] EA 926.

[107] See s. 138, *RTA*.

[108] *Ramji v Rattansi* [1969] EA 309

[109] *Dickson v McWhinnie* [1958] SR (NSW) 179. However, under s. 40(7) of the *Land Act*, a spouse and dependent children of a landowner have a right to lodge a caveat against the family land.

[110] *La Martina* v *Penny* [1968] SASR 41.

[111] In *Re a Caveat; Ex P The Canowie Pastoral Co Ltd* [1931] SASR 502.

[112] *Genrich* v *Maitland Holding Pty Ltd* [1982] Qd R 58.

[113] Section 150, *RTA*, but this provision does not apply to a caveat lodged by a beneficiary under a will or settlement, s. 153.

of an option to purchase the land does not mean that the registered proprietor admits that the caveator has the option, which binds his or her title. It simply means that the proprietor's title is subject to the caveator's interest specified in the caveat *provided that the claim is proved.*[114]

Duration of a caveat

In *Olojo* v *Rajab*,[115] Tsekooko J was critical of a caveat that was lodged for twenty years. His Honour observed that the caveat scheme under sections 148-150, *Registration of Titles Act,* was meant as a temporary measure and not 'to provide caveators with everlasting protection in the sense that once a caveat is lodged, the caveator should be lulled into sleeping over his protected interests perpetually.' To use a caveat in that manner was, in his view, an abuse of the caveat scheme. With respect, his Honour's criticism was justified. The caveat scheme is not supposed to be a cheap substitute for registration of titles. Unfortunately, however, there is not a provision in the Act that prescribes a time limit after which a caveat ceases to be valid. Under the Act, a caveat ceases to be effective only where it is withdrawn by the caveator,[116] lapses in certain situations or is revoked by a court.

Section 149(2) of the *Registration of Titles Act* provides that a caveat lodged against a *proprietor*[117] automatically lapses if the proprietor applies for its removal,[118] unless the caveator commences legal proceedings within sixty days of notification of the application or applies to court for extension of the caveat before expiration of the sixty days.[119] Where the caveator seeks extension, the court at its discretion may extend the caveat for any duration as it sees fit on condition that the caveator undertakes to pay damages suffered by any person as a result of delay in registering their interest.[120] Once a caveat lapses it cannot be renewed by a person or on behalf of a person who lodged it in respect of the same estate or interest.[121]

Section 149(1)of the *Registration of Titles Act* empowers a court at any time to revoke a caveat at the instance of a caveatee. The section provides that a proprietor or any person prejudicially affected by a caveat[122] may cause the caveator to be summoned before a court to show cause why the caveat should not be removed. If the caveator fails to show reasonable cause the court will revoke the caveat. For example, in *Boyes* v *Gathure*,[123] the court revoked a caveat because it did not properly identify the interest claimed as prescribed by the relevant statutory provisions. In the same case, Newbold P expressed a view that the courts would revoke a caveat if it includes land over which the caveator had no claim. His Honour reasoned that such a caveat is fundamentally irregular to the whole basis on which caveats are entered and the defect cannot be cured by amendment of the caveat.[124] A caveat will also be removed if the caveator has no caveatable claim.[125] In Australia, if a caveat is properly lodged and the caveator has a caveatable interest, the

---

[114] *Leros Pty Ltd* v *Terara Pty Ltd & another* (1992) 106 ALR 595.

[115] CS No 1241/86 (unreported).

[116] Section 148, *RTA*.

[117] The provision appears to be limited to a proprietor and not apply to other caveatees, e.g. a person wishing to register a mortgage. Also provision does not apply to caveats lodged by beneficiaries under a will or by the registrar.

[118] In *Njuki v Musisi Nyanzi* HCCS No 0434 of 1996, Sebutinde J held that where the registered proprietor was dead the administrator of the deceased's estate or a person who had purchased the land during his or her lifetime could apply under s. 149(2) for removal of a caveat.

[119] See s. 149 (3).

[120] In *Khadir Juma et al* v *Abdul Juma Martin* CS No 951 of 1990; (1988-90) HCB 154 (unreported) an application to extend a caveat was rejected because there was no evidence that the proprietor (trustee) was about to deal with the land.

[121] Section 149 (3). See, e.g., *Kazzora v Rukuba* CA No 13 of 1992.

[122] Compare with s. 149(2), above.

[123] [1969] EA 385.

[124] *Ibid* at 389-90.

[125] *Municipal District of Concord* v *Coles* (1906) 3 CLR 96.

courts would be reluctant to revoke it. It has been held, in several cases, that the courts will not order the removal of a caveat in summary proceedings, under provisions corresponding with s. 149 of the *Registration of Titles Act*, unless the caveator's claim to the estate or interest appears to be without any foundation.[126]

Under s. 151A of the *Registration of Titles Act*, the registrar is required to remove from the register book a caveat which has been withdrawn or has lapsed under sections 148 and 149 respectively, or where he or she is satisfied that the nature of the interest or estate claimed has ceased to exist. It is submitted that the provision does not give the registrar independent powers to remove caveats; it merely obliges him or her to 'clean up' the register.

Liability for wrongful lodgement of a caveat

A caveat lodged against dealing in land may cause financial loss to the proprietor and other persons. This is particularly so where the proprietor seeks to sell the land. Potential buyers might be discouraged from dealing in the land because they interpret, with some justification, the caveat as a warning to stay away from the land. To deter abuse of the caveat scheme, the Act empowers the courts to order compensation to be paid to the proprietor or any other person who suffers loss by any person who enters a caveat without a reasonable excuse. Whether or not in a particular case a caveat was lodged without a reasonable cause is a question of fact to be determined in the circumstances of each case. The fact that the caveator had no caveatable interest does not necessarily mean that he or she had no reasonable grounds to enter the caveat.[127] Conversely, the fact that the caveator has a caveatable interest does not by itself mean that he or she had a reasonable cause to lodge a caveat.[128]

Remedies for deprivation of land

Under the *Registration of Titles Act*, a person wrongfully deprived of his or her land may bring an action of ejectment and or for damages against the person responsible. In an appropriate case, they may also be entitled to compensation from the government.

Ejectment

At common law ejectment is the primary remedy available to a person who is wrongfully dispossessed of his or her land.[129] Under the *Registration of Titles Act*, the remedy of ejectment is limited by the principle of indefeasibility. Consistent with this principle s. 184 of the *Registration of Titles Act* protects a registered proprietor against any action of ejectment except in circumstances stated in the section.[130] The circumstances include action by a mortgagee to eject a mortgagor in event of default in payment of the mortgage debt. Similarly, a lessor may sue a lessee for ejectment in default of payment of rent. The action of ejectment in these two cases is based on breach of contract. Action of ejectment may also be brought against any proprietor whose title was acquired in any circumstances which fall within any one of the exceptions to the principle of indefeasibility.[131] Apart from these situations, s. 184 states that the production of a certificate of title shall be held in every court to be an absolute bar and estoppel to any action of ejectment 'any rule of law or equity to the contrary notwithstanding.'[132]

---

[126] Whalan, *The Torrens System in Australia*, pp. 251 - 53.

[127] *Kuper & Kuper* v *Keywest Construction Pty Ltd* [1990] 3 WAR 419.

[128] *Hooke v Holland* [1984] WAR 16.

[129] Megarry and Wade, *The Law of Real Property*, p. 105.

[130] Action for ejection or recovery of land in this context includes cancellation of any interest entered on the register book, e.g., a mortgage, lease etc. see *Fraser v Walker* [1967] 1 AC 569 at 583.

[131] Section 184 (c) (d) and (e). For example, a person registered through fraud may be ejected under s. 184(c), see *Nazarali Hassanali Sayani v Edward Mperese Nsubuga* CS No 364 of 1993; *Shokatali Abdulla Dhalla v Sadrudin Meralli* CA No 32 of 1994 (unreported). See also discussion of exceptions to indefeasibility above.

[132] However, see above judicial inroads on the concept of indefeasibility.

The effect of s. 184 was considered by the Supreme Court in *The Executrix of the Estate of the late Tebajukira and another* v *Shalita*.[133] In that case, a lease was terminated by forfeiture and a re-entry was noted on the register book. Subsequently, the lessee (appellant) sought judicial relief against forfeiture. The Supreme Court dismissed the application as misconceived because the *Registration of Titles Act* made no provision for a lessee to eject a lessor. In delivering his judgement, Chief Justice Wambuzi observed that:

> It seems to me that para (b) of ... [s 184] simply means that a lessor may bring an action of ejectment or recovery of land against a lessee who is in default notwithstanding that the lessee is registered as proprietor of the lease. There is no provision for the converse.... Accordingly, in my judgement the case of a lessee purporting to bring an action in ejectment or recovery of land against his lessor falls under 'any case other than as aforesaid' in s 184 in respect of which the production of a certificate is an absolute bar and estoppel to any such action. The expression 'any rule of law or equity to the contrary notwithstanding' must have been designed to rule out relief against forfeiture when a registered proprietor has re-entered.[134]

Where an application is made for ejectment in a case not expressly barred by s. 184, the court is empowered to direct the registrar to cancel a certificate or an entry and to substitute another for it.[135] In *Lwanga v The Registrar of Titles*,[136] it was held that a person who obtains a judgement for recovery of land must seek a court order, under s. 185 of the *Registration of Titles Act*, for the registrar to enter his or her name as proprietor of the suit property instead of the other person. This order is known as a 'consequential order' because it is made consequent upon recovery of land.[137]

Compensation

Section 186 of the *Registration of Titles Act* provides that a person deprived of an estate or interest in land in consequence of fraud, error, omission or misdescription in the certificate of title or entry or in bringing land under the Act may bring an action for compensation. The action for compensation may be brought against a person responsible for the loss and or against the registrar. The action in section 186 is a special action, which is separate and different from any action the victim may have at common law.

The term 'deprived' is not defined anywhere in the Act. In the case of *Breskvar and another v Wall and others*,[138] the High Court of Australia defined the term with reference to the equivalent statutory provisions that it meant 'irrevocable' loss or loss by a superior title. According to this definition a person is deprived of his or her land only if he or she is no longer in a position to recover the interest by appropriate legal action. For example, in that case, the appellants were not deprived of their land when it was registered in the name of a rogue because by appropriate legal action they could have recovered the land from him. However, the appellants irrevocably lost their land once the rogue sold it to an innocent person who acquired a title superior to theirs.

Deprivation, for purposes of s. 186, need not be a total or complete loss of an estate or interest in land. A proprietor whose land is encumbered with a mortgage without his or her authority is 'deprived' of land within the meaning of the section. For example, in *Registrar of Titles* v *Franzon*,[139]

---

[133] CA No 02 of 1988 (unreported).

[134] See also *Ahmed Farah and another* v *Kiwanuka* CS No 687of 1993 (unreported). Also *Assets Company Ltd* v *Mere Roihi* [1905] AC 176 at 195.

[135] Section 185. Also *Re: Habib Lubwama* (1991) HCB 74 (unreported); *Shokatali Abdulla Dhalla v Sadrudin Meralli* CA No 32 of 1994 (unreported).

[136] Misc. C No 7A of 1977; (1980) HCB 24. See also *In Re: Ivan Mutaka* Misc C No 81 of 1976 (unreported); (1980) HCB 27.

[137] *Ibid.*

[138] [1971) 126 CLR 376. The detailed facts of this are stated above.

[139] (1975) 132 CLR 611.

a rogue solicitor fraudulently mortgaged his clients' land to a bank, and the mortgage was registered. The solicitor absconded with the money. It was held by the High Court of Australia that where a mortgage is registered against a proprietor's land it constitutes deprivation of land because the title is less by the amount of the mortgage than it was before. Similarly, a mortgagee is deprived of his or her interest in land where the mortgage is unlawfully cancelled or where order of priority of the mortgage is reversed without his or her consent.

The action for compensation under s.186 must be brought against the 'wrongdoer' or the person who is primarily responsible for the loss. If a person is deprived of land as a result of bringing the land under the *Registration of Titles Act*, the wrongdoer is the person who made the application to bring the land under the Act or a person through whose error such land was registered.[140] Where the deprivation is in consequence of fraud, error or misdescription, the wrongdoer is the person who acquired title through such fraud, error or misdescription. For example, if X fraudulently transfers P's land to himself and he is the registered proprietor, X is the wrongdoer and P is entitled to sue him for compensation under s. 186 (a). X would still be liable even where he transfers the land to TP. But no action for compensation can be brought against TP or any other person who is a *bona fide* purchaser for value. This is because of the principle of indefeasibility under s. 61 and s. 181 of the *Registration of Titles Act.* The latter provision expressly absolves a *bona fide* proprietor for value from any liability for damages suffered by a person ('P') deprived of an estate or interest in consequence of fraud, error or misdescription.[141] Under s.186(a), a person deprived of his or her estate or interest in land may claim compensation from the government but only if X, the wrongdoer, is dead, bankrupt or has absconded from the court's jurisdiction.[142] Where the government pays compensation under this provision, it is empowered to recover the money from the wrongdoer, or his or her estate, as a state debt.[143]

Action for compensation may also be brought against the government under s.191 of the *Registration of Titles Act*. There are two types of actions that may be brought under the section.

Firstly, an action may be instituted where a person suffers loss through any omission, mistake or misfeasance of the registrar. In that case, the Registrar is the real defendant because it was through his or her mistake that the loss was sustained. For example, if the registrar omits to enter a caveat that is properly lodged as a result of which a rival interest is registered, a claim for compensation may be made under s. 191. Unlike s. 186, the person who suffers loss need not be deprived of an estate or interest in land to be eligible to claim under s.191. For instance, a guarantor of a mortgage who suffers loss due to the registrar's negligence in registering a mortgage, may sue for compensation under s. 191 even though he or she is not deprived of an interest in land.[144]

Secondly, a person who suffers loss as a result of the registration of another as proprietor may bring an action for damages against the registrar if the person is barred by the Act from suing for ejectment and where the remedy for recovery of damages 'as herein provided' is inapplicable. In *Registrar of Titles* v *Franzon*,[145] the High Court of Australia liberally interpreted a similar provision[146] as giving a person deprived of land in consequence of fraud a right to seek compensation from the government wherever s. 186 of the *Registration of Titles Act* is inapplicable. For example, in that case, action against the bank was barred by the Act because of the principle of indefeasibility. No action could be brought against the rogue solicitor under the section since he never acquired title.[147] Accordingly, the High Court held that the plaintiff was entitled to claim compensation from

140 Section 186 (a).

141 For a good illustration see *Registrar of Titles* v *Franzon* (1975) 132 CLR 611.

142 See eg *Armour* v *Penrith Projects Pty Ltd* [1979] 1 NSWLR 98.

143 Section 187, *RTA*.

144 See Whalan, *Torren System in Australia*, supra, p. 356.

145 (1975) 132 CLR 611.

146 Section 205, *Transfer of Titles Act*, 1894, Western Australia.

147 The rogue solicitor encumbered the land with a mortgage by forging the signatures of the proprietors.

the registrar under the equivalent of s. 191of the *Registration of Titles Act.* The court reasoned that a wide interpretation of the provision was consistent with the Torrens system's dual objectives to provide a title that was secure and to compensate proprietors who suffer loss due to the operation of the Act.

There are two other provisions in the Act under which claims for damages may be made against the registrar. First, s. 192 provides that a person may seek compensation from the government where he or she suffers loss as a result of rectification of a certificate of title or the bringing of land under the *Registration of Titles Act* in consequence of inaccuracy in government survey. Secondly, under s.193 a person who suffers loss or damage arising from the exercise or supposed exercise of the registrar's powers under the Act, and provided he or she is not a party to the application or dealing in connection with which such power was exercised, notwithstanding s.186 and 191, may sue the government for compensation. It is thought that the situation contemplated by the section would include the exercise of the registrar's powers under s. 92 of the *Land Act.*

The procedure for making claims for compensation against the government is stipulated in s. 194. The section provides that the claimant may, in the first instance, submit a written application accompanied by an affidavit to the registrar. If liability is admitted, the registrar will issue a certificate to that effect to the Attorney General. But the authority to make payment remains with the minister responsible. Where it is necessary to sue the government for compensation, action must commence within a period of six years from the date of deprivation of the estate or interest.[148]

[148] Section 196 (1). The limitation period is 30 years in case of disability.

6
Leases

Introduction

Under s. 4(5) of the *Land Act*, 1998, a leasehold tenure is defined as a form of tenure whereby one party grants to another exclusive possession of land for a period usually, but not necessarily, in return for a monetary consideration called rent. The term 'lease' or 'tenancy' refers to the estate granted[1] and the 'reversion' is the interest retained by the grantor during the currency of the lease. The party leasing is known as the lessor or landlord and the other party is the lessee or tenant. In practice, the expression tenant and landlord, respectively, are normally used to refer to a lessee and lessor of residential premises and a short-term lease; whilst lessee and lessor are used for other leases. But this distinction has no legal significance. In this chapter the terms are used interchangeably.

Leases may be classified into fixed term and periodic leases. A fixed term lease is a lease whose duration is fixed by the parties at the onset so that once the term expires the lease comes to an end. For example, a lease for twelve months or forty-nine years is a fixed term lease and it expires at the end of the term. A periodic lease is a lease which continuously renews from one term to another until terminated by proper notice served by either party.[2] Periodic leases may run on a weekly, fortnightly, monthly, quarterly or yearly basis. The type of periodic tenancy depends on the agreement of the parties. In the absence of an express agreement the mode by which rent is paid determines the nature of the tenancy. Thus, where rent is payable on a weekly, monthly or yearly basis, it is implied that the parties intended to create a weekly, monthly or yearly tenancy, respectively.[3] The significance of this classification is discussed below.

There are other types of tenancies which do not fall in either of the above classifications: tenancy at will and tenancy at sufferance. At common law, a tenancy at will is implied when a landowner allows another person to enter into possession as a tenant without specification of the terms of the tenancy agreement.[4] Either party may terminate such a tenancy at any time. But if a tenant at will begins to pay rent calculated on a regular periodic basis, a yearly, monthly, weekly or other periodic tenancy will be implied.[5] In contrast to a tenancy at will, a tenancy at sufferance is implied where a former tenant remains in possession after the expiration of a fixed term without the consent and without objection of the landowner.[6] Like a tenancy at will, a tenancy at sufferance is terminable at any time without notice.[7]

The *Land Act*, 1998, creates a new type of tenancy known as 'tenancy by occupancy'. This is a unique tenancy, which is subject to statutory rules and customary law. Tenancy by occupancy is discussed elsewhere.[8]

---

1 The words 'demise' and 'term' also mean the same thing.

2 *Prudential Assurance Co Ltd v London Residuary* [1992] 3 All ER 504

3 *Rukandema-Kamuru v Kabale Town Council* CA No MKA 10 of 1985; *Bweya Steel Works Ltd v National Insurance Corporation* CS No 63 of 1985; [1985] HCB 58.

4 *Bweya Steel Works Ltd v National Insurance Corporation* CS No 63 of 1985 (unreported); [1985] HCB 58.

5 *Ibid.*

6 *Noor Hassan v Mukiibi* CA No. 103 of 1977; [1978] HCB 162. In *Bweya Steel Works Ltd v National Insurance Corporation*, supra, Odoki J said that a tenancy at will is implied where a former tenant remains in possession after his or her lease expires. With due respect, it is submitted that in such a situation a tenancy at sufferance is implied and not a tenancy at will.

7 For further discussion see below in this chapter.

8 See Chapter 2.

LEASES AND LICENCES DISTINGUISHED

A licence is permission to enter another's land for some specified purpose which otherwise would be trespass.[9] The main distinguishing feature between a lease and a licence is that a lease creates an interest in land while a licence does not.[10] One of the legal consequences of this distinction is that a licence unlike a lease only binds the licensee and the licensor, but not other persons dealing with the land.[11] Moreover, as a licensee has no interest in the land, he or she cannot sue in trespass or nuisance persons interfering with his or her occupation of the land.[12]

ESSENTIAL FEATURES OF A LEASE

At common law, a lease has two essential features: certain duration and exclusive possession. Though a lease is normally granted for monetary consideration, this is not an essential feature. Section 5(d) of the *Land Act* expressly states that a lease may be created even where there is no requirement for rent payment.[13]

Duration

At common law, a lease can be of any duration, but it must have a certain or ascertainable beginning and ending before it takes effect; otherwise it is void as a lease. The classical example of the application of this rule is the case of *Lace v Chantler.*[14] In that case, the plaintiffs during the Second World War sub-let a house to the defendant for the duration of the war. It was held that the lease was void for uncertainty of duration because at the time the purported lease agreement took effect it was neither certain nor ascertainable when the war would end.

The requirement for certainty of duration has been criticised in several English cases and academic writings as unnecessary.[15] Indeed, in some cases judges have attempted to undermine the rule by giving it a broad interpretation or creating artificial exceptions. An example of such cases is *Ashburn Anstalt v Arnold and another.*[16] The respondents granted the appellant a right to occupy their premises rent-free for an indefinite period. The agreement was subject to a proviso that the respondents could terminate the arrangement, if they required the land for re-development, by giving three months notice. The notice had to be accompanied by a certificate from a reputable developer stating that the respondents were ready to develop the land. It was argued that the lease was void for uncertainty of duration. The Court of Appeal held that the duration of the lease was not uncertain because the circumstances under which the lease could be determined were objectively ascertainable: three months notice of termination and the certification of a developer. However, the House of Lords in *Prudential Assurance Co Ltd v London Residuary* brought the attempt to reform the rule to an abrupt end.[17] There, Lord Templeman affirmed the classical common law rule that duration of a lease must be certain or ascertainable at the time the purported lease is supposed to take effect. His lordship was emphatic that at common law the landlord and tenant have no power to create a term which is uncertain.[18]

---

9 *Goldsack v Shore* [1950] KB 708 at 714. Licences are discussed in Chapter 8.

10 *Thomas v Sorrell* (1673) Vaugh 330; 124 ER 1098 at 1109.

11 *Runda Coffee Estates Ltd v Ujager Singh* [1966] EA 564.

12 *Hill v Tupper* (1863) 2 H & C 121; 159 ER 51;

13 See also *Ashburn Anstalt v Arnold and another* [1988] 2 All ER 147 at 154.

14 [1944] 1 All ER 305.

15 See Gray, *Elements of Land Law* (2nd ed, Butterworths, London, 1993), pp. 687-93

16 [1988] 2 All ER 147.

17 [1992] 3 All ER 504

18 3 All ER 504 at 510. At 512, Lord Browne-Wilkinson accepted the archaic common law rule,but suggested that the Law Commission should examine the need for its continued retention.

In Uganda, the definition of a lease under the *Land Act* seems to override the common law definition. Section 4(5)(c) states that the duration of a leasehold tenure is usually but not necessarily defined by reference to a specific date of commencement and to a specific date of ending. It is submitted that the phrase 'usually but not necessarily' indicates that parliament intended to dispense with the common law requirement that the beginning and ending of a lease must be certain. Hence, a lease agreement such as that granted in *Lace v Chantler*, would not be void for uncertainty under the *Land Act*. Of course, where the terms of a lease agreement, including its duration, are so uncertain that the court cannot objectively determine the obligation of the parties, the agreement would be void in accordance with the general law of contract.[19]

Exclusive possession

Section 5(c) of the *Land Act* defines a lease as a form of tenure under which the landlord grants, or is deemed to grant, the tenant exclusive possession of land. Thus, exclusive possession is the linchpin of a lease and is what distinguishes a lease from a mere licence.[20] A grant of exclusive possession is a right to use land to the exclusion of everyone else including the landowner for the duration of the grant.[21] Whether an occupier has exclusive possession depends on the intention of the parties, objectively determined from all the terms of their agreement and the surrounding circumstances.[22] An express statement purporting to grant exclusive possession is neither necessary nor conclusive of the occupier's legal status.[23] The extent of the control over the land retained by the landowner determines whether the occupier has exclusive possession.[24] If the landowner retains general control over the premises, it is a strong indication that the occupier has no exclusive possession and, therefore, he or she is a mere licensee. For example, in *City Council of Kampala v Mukibi*,[25] the plaintiffs leased certain premises to the defendant subject to a covenant that the tenant should not part with possession or sublet without their consent. The defendant allowed hairdressers to use the premises, paying him a daily fee. The plaintiffs sought to terminate the lease on the ground that the defendant parted with possession in breach of the tenancy agreement. The court held that a tenant is not in breach of a covenant not to part with possession or sublet unless he or she gives exclusive possession to another person. In this case, the court found that although the defendant allowed hairdressers to use the premises subject to payment of a daily fee, he did not give them exclusive possession. Sir Udo Udoma CJ observed that:[26]

> A point of great importance which supports the case of the defendant that he never at any time parted with possession of the premises is the fact that he was always in charge of the key. It was his practice always to open the premises in the morning and to admit the hairdressers and at the close of the business in the evening after collecting his own dues to lock up the premises and retain the key with him. ... It is clear from the evidence that the hairdresser could only make use and occupy the premises with the leave and licence of the defendant, who could turn them out at any time.

This case should be compared with that of *City Council of Kampala v Mukubira and another*.[27] The facts of the two cases were similar, however, in the latter case Goudie J, held that the defendant had parted with possession. His honour distinguished the two cases on the grounds that the

---

[19] *Bweya Steel Works Ltd v National Insurance Corporation* CS No 63 of 1985; [1985] HCB 58; *Sands v Mutual Benefits Ltd* [1971] EA 156 (K).

[20] *Street v Mountford* [1985] 2 All ER 289 at 292.

[21] *Street v Mountford* [1985] 2 All ER 289 at 292

[22] *Appah v Parncliffe Investments* [1964] 1 WLR 1064; *Radaich v Smith* (1959) 101 CLR 209

[23] *Ibid*. See also *Karamat Ali v Champion Shoe Company* (1949) 16 EACA 15.

[24] *Desai v Cooper* (1950) KLR 32.

[25] [1967] EA 368 (U).

[26] *Ibid*, at 376-77.

[27] [1968] EA 497 (U).

defendant tenant in the instant case only paid infrequent visits to the premises and took no personal part in the business carried on by the persons he allowed on the premises, nor did he exert any form of supervision.[28]

It should be emphasised that the fact that the owner retains a right of access for certain purposes or occasions does not necessarily mean that the occupier does not have exclusive possession.[29] For example, it is common practice for landlords to retain a right to enter at certain times for purposes of inspection of the premises.[30]

The issue that has generated much controversy in legal circles, especially in England, is whether a grant of exclusive possession is conclusive of a lease. According to some English authorities, unless the parties intended to create a lease, a mere grant of exclusive possession, though strong evidence of a lease, does not necessarily mean that the grantee is a lessee as opposed to a licensee. For example, in *Errington v Errington and another,* [31] a father allowed his son and daughter-in-law to reside in his house. He promised them that if they paid off the outstanding mortgage debt he would transfer title to them. They had only paid off part of the mortgage debt when the father died. In his will, he left the house to his widow. In an action for eviction, one of the issues was whether the defendants were tenants or licensees. The court held that, though the defendants were granted exclusive possession, they were mere licensees because the parties had no intention to create a tenancy.[32]

In contrast, other authorities support the proposition that a grant of exclusive possession for a term is conclusive evidence that the grantee is a lessee irrespective of the subjective intention of the parties. According to these authorities, the intention of the parties is relevant but only for the purpose of determining whether they intended the grantee to exercise exclusive possession.[33] The authority often cited for this proposition is the judgement of Windeyer J in the High Court of Australia case of *Radaich v Smith.*[34] In that case, Windeyer J stated categorically that exclusive possession was the litmus test for a lease. His Honour dismissed the authorities that hold that a person with a right of exclusive possession can be a licensee. He observed:

> To say that a man who has, by agreement with a landlord, a right of exclusive possession of land for a term is not a tenant is simply to contradict the first proposition by the second.[35]

The House of Lords, in *Street v Mountford,*[36] endorsed Windeyer J's judgement in *Radaich v Smith.* Lord Templeman, with the concurrence of the other judges, echoed Windeyer J's statement that a grant of exclusive possession was the determinant whether an occupant was a licensee or a lessee.[37] Notwithstanding this judgement, in England the issue whether exclusive possession is conclusive of a lease is still troublesome.[38] Indeed, in *Street v Mountford,* in his judgement Templeman

---

28 See also *Appah v Parncliffe Investments* [1964] 1 WLR 1064. See also *Desai v Cooper* (1950) KLR 32.

29 *Street v Mountford* [1985] 2 All ER 289 at 289

30 Under s. 102(a) of the *Registration of Titles Act,* it is implied that the landlord has a right to enter once in every year to inspect the premises.

31 [1950] 1 KB 290

32 See also *Crane v Morris* [1965] 1 WLR 1104 at 1107-1108 per Lord Denning MR

33 *Radaich v Smith* (1959) 101 CLR 209; *Street v Mountford* [1985] 2 All ER 289 at 289

34 (1959) 101 CLR 209

35 *Ibid*, at 222

36 [1985] 2 All ER 289.

37 *Ibid*, at 300.

38 For a very good discussion of the English position, see Kevin Gray, *Elements of Land Law* (2nd ed, Butterworths, London, 1993), pp. 708-28

LJ conceded that there could be exceptional circumstances in which a person with exclusive possession could be a licensee. Those special circumstances include occupation by a service occupier[39] and family arrangements where the parties had no intention to contract.[40]

Whether a grant of exclusive possession is conclusive of a lease is yet to be considered by the courts in Uganda. The courts have a choice of authorities to follow either way.[41] It is submitted that the rule that the existence of exclusive possession is conclusive of a lease is preferred, as it is a general principle not limited to its particular facts.[42] The English precedents, which hold to the contrary, could be distinguished on the ground of the peculiar circumstances under which those cases were decided.[43] Moreover, the definition of 'leasehold' in s. 4(5)(c) of the *Land Act*, as a tenure under which a landowner 'granted another person... exclusive possession', seems to support the proposition that exclusive possession is conclusive of a lease. Of course, where exclusive possession is granted without an intention to enter into a contract, neither party would be contractually bound by the arrangement.[44]

CREATION OF A LEASE

Contract

A lease is created either by agreement of the parties or by operation of law.[45] In Uganda, unlike other common law countries, there is no legal requirement that an agreement for a lease must be in writing.[46] Thus, a contract to grant a lease may be oral or in writing or both. The agreement may also be inferred from the conduct of the parties. For example, a lease may result without express agreement where a person enters into possession of land and pays rent, which is accepted by the landowner.[47]

Tenancy by estoppel

The relationship of landlord and tenant may be created by estoppel. There is a well established common law principle that where a person enters onto land as a tenant of another both parties are estopped from denying that a lease exists.[48] It is important that there must be sufficient evidence of the parties' conduct from which it could be established that the parties recognised each other as landlord and tenant. For example, in *Pardhan Jivraj v Dudley-Whelpadale*,[49] it was held that

---

39 A service occupier is an employee who occupies his or her employer's premises in order to perform his or her duties. See *Smith v Seghill Overseas* (1875) 10 QB 422. See also James, 'Some Problems Concerning Leases and Licences' (1967) 3 *East African Law Journal* 218 pp. 244-49.

40 *Street v Mountford* [1985] 2 All ER 289 at 294.

41 See also the Kenyan case of *Hatim v Mohsin Bin Saleh* [1957] EA 486, where the Court of Appeal for East Africa followed *Errington v Errington and another* [1950] 1 KB 29. But see *Desai v Cooper* (1950) 24 KLR 32.

42 For a contrary view see James, 'Some Problems Concerning Leases and Licences' (1967) 3 *East African Law Journal* 218 at 239 *et seq*.

43 The English position is peculiar because of the ongoing controversy over that country's *Rent Restriction Acts*, which apply to leases and not licences.

44 *Street v Mountford* [1985] 2 All ER 289.

45 Section 5(a), *Land Act*, 1998.

46 *Jama Noor Shakiya v Hassanali Ahmed Jusub* (1965) EA 241 (U); *Mayanja-Nkangi v National Housing Corporation* [1972] 1 ULR 37.

47 *Mayanja-Nkangi v National Housing Corporation* [1972] 1 ULR 37.

48 *Pardhan Jivraj v Dudley-Whelpadale* (1920-29) 3 ULR 193; *Kanjee Naranjee Ltd v Tulsidas Dharamshi Ghadialy* [1965] EA 171; *Industrial Properties (Barton Hill) and others v Associated Electrical Industries Ltd* [1977] 1 QB 580.

49 (1920-29) 3 ULR 193.

payment and acceptance of rent provided the requisite evidence that the defendant and plaintiff regarded each other as landlord and tenant. Similarly, in *Kanjee Naranjee Ltd v Tulsidas Dharamshi Ghadialy,*[50] the court found from the parties' correspondence that there was sufficient evidence to establish that the defendant implicitly acknowledged the plaintiff as his landlord from the date he entered into possession.

The effect of a tenancy by estoppel is that neither the tenant nor the landlord can set up lack of title in the other as a defence to an action for breach of covenant or for rent due.[51] For example, in *Pardhan Jivraj v Dudley-Whelpadale*, the defendant was in possession under a lease which was not registered as required by the *Registration of Titles Ordinance*, 1908. Under s. 6 of the Ordinance, unregistered leases were inadmissible in evidence. Notwithstanding, it was held that as between the parties, the defendant was estopped from pleading that the lease was defective. In *Industrial Properties (Barton Hill) and others v Associated Electrical Industries Ltd*, the defendants refused to pay the agreed rent to the plaintiffs when later it transpired that the plaintiffs had only an equitable title and not a legal title in the land. It was held that the defendants were estopped from challenging the plaintiffs' title as long as no other person with a superior title interrupted their possession.

Registration requirement

Leases over land registered under the *Registration of Titles Act* (cap 205) are created subject to the provisions of that Act. Sections 100 and 108, respectively, provide that a proprietor wishing to lease or sublease his or her land for a term in excess of three years should execute the prescribed forms. A lease or sublease exceeds three years not only where the agreement stipulates a fixed period in excess of three years, but also where a shorter term is granted with a perpetual option to review.[52] For example, in *Popatlal Hirji v L.H. Lakhai & Co (EA) Ltd*,[53] it was held that a sublease for one year, which was renewable annually at the option of the tenant, was a lease in excess of three years and therefore subject to the statutory form. Under s. 51, until such a lease is registered pursuant to the provisions of the Act, it is not effective to create an estate in the land.[54] But upon registration a lease is created and the land become subject to the covenants of the lease.

Unregistered lease

At common law, a purported lease that does not comply with formalities merely operates as a contract whereby the proposed lessor promises to lease and the proposed lessee to take the land subject to the terms of their agreement.[55] Failure by either party to comply with the agreement could result in an action for damages.[56] Moreover, where a purported lessee enters into possession under the agreement he or she becomes a common law tenant at will,[57] and upon payment of rent the tenancy at will becomes a yearly tenancy.[58]

In equity, on the other hand, failure to follow legal formalities to create a lease does not necessarily render the lease void. Because equity treats as done what ought to be done, an agreement for a lease capable of enforcement by specific performance creates a lease. Such a lease is variously referred to as an 'equitable' or 'informal' lease. This principle was laid down in the famous case of *Walsh v Lonsdale*.[59] The facts of that case were as follows. The appellant and respondent entered

---

[50] [1965] EA 171.

[51] *Industrial Properties (Barton Hill) and others v Associated Electrical Industries Ltd* [1977] 1 QB 580.

[52] *Popatlal Hirji v L.H. Lakhai & Co* (EA) Ltd [1960] EA 437 (U).

[53] *Ibid.*

[54] See *Souza Figueiredo & Co Ltd v Moorings Hotel Co Ltd* [1960] EA 926.

[55] *Walsh v Lonsdale* (1882) 21 Ch D 9.

[56] *Ibid.*

[57] *Souza Figueiredo & Co Ltd v Moorings Hotel Co Ltd* [1960] EA 926.

[58] *Walsh v Lonsdale* (1882) 21 Ch D 9.

[59] *Ibid.*

into a written lease agreement for a term of seven years subject to a periodic payment of rent, in advance. Though the agreement was not by deed, as required by law, the appellant entered into possession. When the appellant defaulted in payment of rent the respondent distrained on his goods.[60] The appellant sued the respondent for conversion on the ground that since the lease was not under deed it was void and, therefore, the respondent was not entitled to distrain on his goods. It was held that, though the agreement was ineffective to create a legal lease, it was effective to bring into existence an equitable lease for a term of seven years. Therefore, in the eyes of equity, the parties were already landlord and tenant subject to the same terms and remedies they would have had if their lease had been created by deed. Accordingly, the respondent was entitled to distrain upon the appellant's goods.

The application of the foregoing principles of the general law, to unregistered leases under the *Registration of Titles Act,* was considered in *Souza Figueiredo & Co Ltd v Moorings Hotel Co Ltd.*[61] In that case, Moorings Hotel Co Ltd (the respondent) entered into an agreement to sublet to Souza Figueiredo & Co Ltd (the appellant) premises for a period in excess of three years. Though the sublease was not registered as required by s. 51, the appellants went into possession. Before the purported sublease expired the appellant vacated the premises owing arrears of rent. In an action for the outstanding rent, the appellants contended that it was not liable, as the agreement had not been registered as required by s. 51 of the *Registration of Titles Act*. The trial judge held for the respondent. On appeal to the East African Court of Appeal, counsel for the appellant argued that a covenant to pay rent contained in an agreement, which operates as a present demise of land in excess of three years, was unenforceable if unregistered. He submitted that a covenant to pay rent is so bound up with the land that it cannot have effect unless it is part of a registered lease. Furthermore, he contended that rent issues out of the land and is bound up with the estate, which the lease creates. Sir Kenneth O'Connor P. with the concurrence of the other members of the Court, agreed with the appellant's counsel that s. 51 avoids the creation of an estate or interest in land by unregistered instruments. However, his Honour rejected the appellant's argument that the agreement was thereby void. He said:

> [T]here is nothing in the [Act] which renders such instruments ineffectual in contracts between the parties to them: there is nothing in the [Act] to say that an unregistered document purporting to be a lease of, or an agreement to lease, land which is subject to the operation of the [Act] for more than three years is void. In my view it can operate as a contract *inter partes* and can confer on the party in the position of intending lessee a right to enforce the contract specifically and to obtain from the intending lessor a registrable lease. That is not to override the provisions of the Act but to act in conformity with them.[62]

On the basis of this principle, his Honour held that the respondent was liable to pay rent for the period during which he was in possession.[63] In addition, his Honour held that the appellant was in any event liable to pay rent because at common law entry into possession under an unregistered lease for more than three years creates a tenancy at will for which rent can be reserved. Hence, whether the term to pay rent was regarded as a contractual stipulation in a document for which specific performance could be obtained in equity or as a term in a common law tenancy at will, it was enforceable.[64]

However, although the learned president of the court held that an unregistered lease constitutes a contract *inter partes*, he denied that it operates to create an equitable lease under the principle of

---

60 Distress (or distrain) is a common law remedy which entitles the landlord to confiscate a tenant's goods if he or she defaults in rent payments.

61 [1960] EA 926.

62 [1960] EA 926 at 931.

63 See also *City Council of Kampala v Mukibi* [1967] EA 368 (U); *Somali Democratic Republic v Anoop Syndirial Treon* CA No 4 of 1988.

64 *Souza Figueiredo & Co Ltd v Moorings Hotel Co Ltd* [1960] EA 926 at 937.

Walsh v Lonsdale. His Honour reasoned that because of s. 51 of the *Registration of Titles Act* in Uganda, an intending lessee cannot derive any estate (whether legal or equitable) from an unregistered instrument. He declined to follow several Australian authorities that held that the provision similar to s. 51 does not preclude the creation, under an unregistered instrument, of an equitable lease for a term.[65]

It is submitted that if s. 51 prevents the creation of an equitable lease, as held by Sir Kenneth O'Connor P, it means that until a lease is registered there is no relationship of landlord and tenant between the proprietor and the intending lessee. Therefore, neither party would be entitled to statutory or common law remedies which arise by virtue of the relationship of landlord and tenant. For example, suppose L enters into an agreement to lease her land to T for a period of 5 years subject to payment of rent of 1 million shillings per annum in advance. T enters into possession even though the lease is not registered. It is submitted that if T defaults in payment of rent in advance, L cannot distrain on her goods unless the right to do so is expressed or implied in their contract.[66] On the other hand, since there is no relationship of landlord and tenant the courts cannot grant T relief against forfeiture for non-payment of rent.[67]

The decision of *Souza Figueiredo & Co Ltd v Moorings Hotel Co Ltd* that s. 51, *Registration of Titles Act,* excludes the principle of *Walsh v Lonsdale,* has never been directly questioned by the courts.[68] In our view, Sir Kenneth O'Connor P was right in his holding that because of s. 51 an unregistered instrument is ineffective to create a legal or equitable lease until it is registered. However, with due respect it is submitted that his Honour erred in his interpretation of the effect of the provision over equitable claims. In our opinion, the section does not affect an equitable lease or other equitable claims arising by virtue of the parties' agreement that precedes the instrument.[69]

RIGHTS AND OBLIGATIONS OF A LANDLORD AND TENANT

Conditions and covenants

The terms of a lease may be expressed as conditions or covenants. A 'condition' is a term which is the essence of the lease agreement and its breach entitles the innocent party to terminate the lease.[70] A 'covenant' is a term of a lease agreement whose breach does not warrant the innocent party terminating the lease unless the agreement expressly gives that right.[71] For example, a landlord cannot terminate a lease for breach of covenant to pay rent unless the right to terminate is expressly reserved in the lease agreement. In practice, most formal leases reserve a right to terminate for breach of any term of the agreement including non-payment of rent. Moreover, for leases registered under the *Registration of Titles Act,* s. 102(b) of that Act implies in the lessor power to re-enter and take possession if breach of any express or implied term continues for more than thirty days.[72]

---

65 *Ibid*, at 933-34. See also further discussion of this case in Chapter 5.

66 See *Souza Figueiredo & Co Ltd v George Panagopoulos and others* [1959] EA 756 (cf *Walsh v Lonsdale,* supra). A landlord cannot distrain upon goods of a tenant at will for rent payable in advance, *see Walsh v Lonsdale* (1882) 21 Ch D 9

67 See below.

68 It has been held in several cases that an equitable interest is created immediately the parties enter into a contract of sale of land. See for example, *Alibhai and others v Karia and another* CA No 53 of 1995 (unreported); *Katarikawe v Katwiremu and another* CS No 2 of 1973; [1977] HCB 187; *Serunjogi v Katabira* CS No 547 of 1987 (unreported); [1988-90] HCB 148. For further discussion, see Chapter 5.

69 *Chan and another v Cresdon Properties Limited* [1989] 168 CLR 242. See also our discussion of s. 51,*RTA,* in Chapter 5.

70 *Lugogo Coffee Co (U) Ltd v Singo Combined Coffee Growers Ltd* CS No. 554 of 1973; [1976] HCB 92.

71 Megarry and Wade, *The Law of Real Property*, supra, pp. 670-71.

72 Terms implied by the Act may be excluded or modified by express agreement, s. 142, *RTA*.

Express covenants

Terms in a lease may be expressed or implied in the lease agreement. Express terms are those which are stipulated in writing or orally in the agreement. Parties to a lease are free to incorporate any terms in the lease provided that the terms are not contrary to any rule of law. Certain terms which are commonly found in formal lease agreements, are set out in the Ninth Schedule of the *Registration of Titles Act.* The parties may adopt these terms or any of them in their lease agreement if they so wish. The terms are set out in two columns. In Column 1 the terms are expressed in a short form of words, and in Column 2 in detailed form of words. Section 103 of the *Registration of Titles Act* provides that where the shorter form of words is used in a lease agreement it is implied that the parties intended the detailed meaning ascribed to that term in the schedule. For example, where the lease states that the lessee shall transfer or sublet the premises the extent of the lessee's obligation is determined by reference to Column 2 opposite the term 'transfer or sublet'. The object of the provision is to avoid prolixity in the drafting of leases.

Covenants implied under the general law against the landlord

In the absence of any express agreement of the parties, the common law implies certain covenants against the landlord and tenant. The covenants implied against the landlord include: covenant for quiet enjoyment, not to derogate from the grant, and to provide premises that are fit for habitation.

Quiet enjoyment

The covenant of quiet enjoyment implies that the landlord, and those claiming through him or her, will not interfere with the tenant's possession.[73] The basis of this covenant is that by letting the premises the landlord gives the tenant the right of possession and he or she thereby guarantees not to interfere with the tenant's exercise of that right or use of the premises.[74] The breach of covenant for quiet enjoyment takes various forms. For example, in *Opinya v Mukasa,*[75] the landlord sought to forcibly evict his tenant by removing the roof from the premises. The court found the landlord liable for breach of covenant of quiet enjoyment. The court awarded punitive damages because of the high-handed manner of the landlord's interference with the tenant's possession. In the case of *The Kampala Cotton Co Ltd v Privinlal Madhvani,*[76] the landlord blocked the tenant's right of way. It was held that the landlord's act constituted a breach of the covenant of quiet enjoyment and damages were awarded to the tenant.[77]

The landlord is not liable for the breach of covenant of quiet enjoyment where the interference with the tenant's possession is due to unlawful activities of other persons. For example, in *Shah Champshi Tejshi and others v The Attorney-General of Kenya,*[78] the government granted a lease to the plaintiffs. The plaintiffs claimed that under the lease they had an implied right of access to a certain road. Later, the government leased the adjoining land to another person and the latter blocked the plaintiffs' alleged access road. The plaintiffs sued the government for breach of the covenant of quiet enjoyment. It was held that the government was not responsible because it had not been established that the interference was lawful or that, if unlawful, it had permitted it.[79] The landlord would be liable if he or she authorised another person to interfere with the tenant's possession or if his or her interference is an inevitable consequence of a purpose the landlord authorised.[80]

---

73 *A.M. Dharas and Sons Ltd v Elys Ltd* [1963] EA 573.

74 *Kenny v Preen* [1963] 1 QB 499.

75 CC No 167 of 1964, High Court Digest, p. 514.

76 CC No. 485 of 1952, High Court Digest, p. 511.

77 See also *A.M. Dharas & Sons Ltd v Elys Ltd* [1963] EA 573 (U) (failure by the landlord to deliver up possession of part of the demised land constitutes breach of covenant of quiet enjoyment).

78 [1959] EA 630.

79 See also *Malzy v Eicholz* [1916] 2 QB 308.

80 *Ibid.* See *Shah Champshi Tejshi and others v The Attorney-General of Kenya.*

No derogation from grant

The implied covenant not to derogate from the grant means that the landlord will not frustrate the use of the land for the purposes that, in the contemplation of both parties, it was let.[81] The covenant is normally implied in a situation where a landlord leases part of his or her land and retains the other part. The effect of the covenant is that the landlord must desist from carrying on activities on the land retained that renders the part leased materially less fit for the purposes for which it was leased. For example, in the Australian case of *Telex (Australasia) Pty Ltd v Thomas Cook & Sons (Australasia) Ltd,*[82] the plaintiffs were the proprietors of a building complex. They leased part of the building to the defendant for business purposes which involved the use of highly sensitive equipment. Later, the plaintiffs installed a cooling system in the building, which interfered with the defendant's equipment. The defendants terminated the lease and vacated the premises. In an action for breach of contract the defendants counterclaimed breach of covenant not to derogate from the grant. It was held that the interference was substantial and constituted a breach of covenant, which entitled the defendants to terminate the lease.[83]

The covenant not to derogate from the grant is implied only where the tenant uses the land for a purpose that was within the contemplation of both parties at the time the lease was entered into. The reason is that the tenant cannot extend the landlord's obligation beyond what was contemplated by both parties.[84] For example, in *Robinson v Kilvert,*[85] the landlord leased the upper floor of his building to the plaintiff for business purposes. The landlord employed a heater in the ground floor, which caused the temperature to rise slightly in the premises leased to the plaintiff. The plaintiff claimed that the rise in temperature damaged the special paper he was drying in his room and rendered it less valuable. It was held that the landlord was not liable for breach of covenant not to derogate from the grant because the plaintiff was using the premises for a special purpose that was not contemplated by both parties.[86]

Fitness for human habitation

At common law, apart from express agreement, the landlord has no obligation to provide premises that are fit for human habitation.[87] But where premises are rented fully furnished,[88] the common law implies against the landlord that the premises are fit for human habitation.[89] Even then, the covenant is only implied at the beginning of the lease and not throughout the term. So, if the premises are fit for human habitation at the commencement of the lease but became unfit during the term, the landlord is not liable.[90] Premises are unfit for human habitation if they are in such a state that they pose a risk of personal injury or to hygiene.[91]

Covenant implied against a tenant

At common law, it is implied against a tenant that he or she will pay rent as it falls due and all rates and taxes except those for which the landlord is by law responsible. Unless otherwise agreed, rent is payable in arrears.[92] In practice, payment of rent is invariably expressed in the parties' lease

---

81 *Aldin v Latimer Clark Muirhead & Co. Ltd* [1894] 2 Ch 437.

82 (1970) 2 NSWLR 257.

83 See also *Aldin v Latimer Clark Muirhead & Co. Ltd* [1894] 2 Ch 437; *Harmer v Jumbi (Nigeria) Tin Areas Ltd* [1921] 1 Ch 200.

84 *Telex (Australasia) Pty Ltd v Thomas Cook & Sons (Australasia)* (1970) 2 NSWLR 257.

85 (1889) 41 Ch D 88.

86 Compare with *Telex (Australasia) Pty Ltd v Thomas Cook & Sons (Australasia) Ltd* (1970) 2 NSWLR 257.

87 *Cruse v Mount* (1932) All ER 781.

88 See *Sands v Mutual Benefits Ltd* [1971] All ER 781.

89 *Cruse v Mount* (1932) All ER 781.

90 *Sarson v Roberts* [1895] 2 QB 395.

91 *Summers v Salford Corporation* [1943] AC 283.

92 Megarry & Wade, *The Law of Real Property*, supra, p. 706.

agreement. It is also implied that at the determination of the lease the tenant will deliver up vacant possession.[93] This obligation not only entails the tenant vacating the entire premises, but also removing all persons on the premises with his or her consent before handing the premises over to the landlord.[94] If the tenant or a person who originally entered with his or her permission remains in possession after termination of the lease, the tenant will be held accountable to the landlord for rent for use and occupation. In addition, the tenant will be liable for the costs incurred by the landlord in ejecting whoever remains in possession.[95]

Finally, the common law implies against the tenant that he or she shall use the premises in a 'tenant-like' manner. This obligation means that the tenant should take proper care of the premises by doing 'the little jobs around the house which a reasonable tenant would do'.[96] For example, the tenant should keep the premises tidy, fix windows when broken by a family member or guest and mend electric lights when they fuse. In addition, a tenant must not commit 'voluntary' or 'permissive' waste. Voluntary waste refers to damage that is committed deliberately or through negligence. It is also voluntary waste for a tenant to alter the premises in some way without consent of the landlord. For example, pulling down a building or changing its structure is voluntary waste.[97] Permissive waste implies an omission that results in the dilapidation of the property, such as where the property is allowed to decay by inaction.[98] According to some authorities, short-term and periodic tenants are not liable for permissive waste.[99]

Covenants implied under the *Registration of Titles Act*
In every lease registered under the Act, certain powers and covenants are implied in favour of the lessor. Section 101 implies against the lessee that he or she will pay rent reserved by the lease and all other dues that are payable under the demised property. The section, in addition, implies that the lessee shall 'keep and yield up the demised property in good and tenantable repair', reasonable wear and tear excepted. Premises are in 'good and tenantable repair' where they are in such a state of repair as would make them 'reasonably fit for the occupation of a reasonably minded tenant of the class who would be likely to take it'.[100] In determining whether the premises are in tenantable repair, regard must be taken of several factors including the age and location of the premises. The obligation of a tenant is not only to maintain the premises in tenantable repair during the term, but also to deliver them up in that order at the end of the lease. Therefore, unless otherwise agreed, where at the commencement of a lease the premises are in disrepair, it is the lessor's obligation to put and keep them in tenantable repair at his or her expense.[101]

By s. 102 it is implied that the lessor has the power to enter the premises at all reasonable times for specific purposes, such as inspection of the premises and repair. The section also implies a power in the lessor to re-enter where rent is in arrears for a period of thirty days or if the lessee is in breach of any express or implied term that continues for thirty days. The parties to a lease agreement may by express declaration in the lease exclude or modify any or all covenants implied under the *Registration of Titles Act*.[102]

---

93 *Kamanyire v Standard Bank* (U) Ltd [1977] HCB 82.

94 *Sebuliba v Attorney-General* CA No 13 of 1991; *Harding v Crethorn* 170 ER 278

95 *Sebuliba v Attorney-General*, ibid. See also *Kamanyire v Standard Bank* (U) Ltd [1977] HCB 82; *Henderson v Squires* (1869) LR 4 QB 170;

96 *Warren v Keen* [1954] 1 QB 15 at 20, per Lord Denning MR

97 *Westham Central Charity Board v East London Waterworks Co* [1900] 1 Ch 624.

98 Megarry and Wade, *The Law of Real Property*, supra p. 95.

99 See Megarry and Wade, *The Law of Real Property*, supra, p. 702

100 *Proudfoot v Hart* (1890) 25 QBD 42.

101 *Proudfoot v Hart, ibid.* Cited with approval in *National and Grindley's Bank (K) Ltd v P.T. Punater* [1965] EA 648 (K).

102 See s 142, *RTA*. See for example, *National and Grindley's Bank (K) Ltd v P.T. Punater* [1965] EA 648 (K).

SUBLEASE AND ASSIGNMENT

A sublease is a transaction whereby a lessee creates a lease that is less than the term that the lessee has.[103] Suppose that Kato is the owner of certain mailo land called '*Mailoacre*'. He leases *Mailoacre* to Nakato for a period of 21 years. Two years later, Nakato leases the land to Waswa for a term of 5 years. Nakato's lease is the 'headlease' and Waswa's is a 'sublease'. Kato is the headlessor and Nakato is the headlessee. As between Nakato and Waswa, the former is the sublessor and the latter is her sublessee.[104] In other words, Kato is Nakato's landlord, whereas Nakato is Waswa's landlady.

An assignment of a lease is a transaction whereby the lessee transfers absolutely the remainder of a term to another person.[105] Thus, in our example above if Nakato, instead of subleasing *Mailoacre* to Kato sold to him the residue of her leasehold the transaction would be an assignment of the lease. The person who assigns is the assignor and the person to whom the lease is assigned is the assignee.[106]

In *Milmo v Carreras,*[107] Lord Greene MR described the distinction between a sublease and an assignment as follows:

> [I]n accordance with a very ancient and established rule, where a lessee, by a document in the form of a sub-lease, divests himself of everything that he has got (which he must necessarily do if he is transferring to his so-called sub-lessee an estate as great as, or purporting to be greater than, his own) he from that moment is a stranger to the land, in the sense that the relationship of landlord and tenant, in respect of tenure, cannot any longer exist between him and the so-called sub-lessee. The relationship must depend on privity of estate. I myself find it impossible to conceive of a relationship of landlord and tenant which has not got that essential element of tenure in it, and that implies that the tenant holds of his landlord, and he can only do that if the landlord has a reversion. You cannot have a purely contractual tenancy. Tenure exists by reason of privity of estate.

At common law, the power to sublease or assign is incidental to all types of leases, including periodic tenancies, unless such power is expressly excluded in the lease agreement.[108] This is also the position under the *Registration of Titles Act.*[109] However, in practice, most formal leases exclude the power to assign or sub-lease. The exclusion may be absolute or qualified by a requirement of the landlord's prior consent. Where the power is excluded the landlord may, at his or her discretion, waive the exclusion with or without any conditions.[110] If the landlord refuses to waive the exclusion, the courts cannot compel him or her to give his or her consent however unreasonable the ground of refusal may be.[111] A total exclusion of a lessee's power to assign or sub-lease though beneficial from the landlord's viewpoint is uncommon because it reduces the value of the lease. Instead, most leases restrict the power to assign or sublease subject to the consent of the lessor.[112] At common law, where the power to assign or sublease is so qualified it is implied that the lessor shall not

---

103 A sub-sub lease is a sublease see *Souza Figueiredo & Co Ltd v Moorings Hotel Co Ltd* [1960] EA 926 at 937.

104 During the currency of the sublease Waswa has possession, which is exclusive of both Kato and Nakato.

105 If a lessee purports to sublease for a period equal to or greater than his or her lease, the transaction is an assignment irrespective of what the parties call the transaction, see *Milmo v Carreras* [1947] KB 306 at 310.

106 See for example, *Souza Figueiredo & Co Ltd v George Panagopoulos and others* [1959] EA 756.

107 [1947] KB 306 at 310.

108 *Keeves v Dean* [1924] 1 KB 685. Courts strictly construe a provision in a lease which restricts the right to sublease or assign, especially, if the restriction is absolute. See *City Council of Kampala v Mukibi* [1967] EA 368 (U) at 377-378.

109 See s 108, *RTA*

110 Waiver may be express or implied from the landlord's conduct.

111 *Viscount Tredefar v Harwood* [1929] AC 72.

112 See for example, *RTA*, Schedule Nine, term no. 1.

withhold the consent except on reasonable grounds.[113] The test for determining whether the grounds for refusal are 'unreasonable' is controversial. Generally, where the grounds have nothing to do with the prospective assignee or sublessee or the purposes for which they intend to use the premises, then the grounds are unreasonable.[114] Both sublease and assignment entail the creation or transfer of an interest in land. Therefore, the formal requirements for the creation of interests in land, and the consequences of non-compliance, discussed above, would equally apply to them.[115]

Enforcement of covenants in a lease

The enforcement of covenants in a lease partly depends on whether there is privity of contract or privity of estate between the parties. Privity of contract means direct contractual relationship, while privity of estate means the existence of tenure or relationship of landlord and tenant.[116] Where there is privity of contract between the parties then all the terms of the lease are enforceable in accordance with the general principles of the law of contract. For example, where Kato leases *Mailoacre* to Nakato, there is privity of contract (and privity of estate) between the two of them. Therefore, they can enforce against each other all the terms of their lease agreement. Indeed, unless otherwise agreed, liability to each other under their contract continues for the duration of the lease even if Nakato subleases or assigns her interest.[117]

Assignment

Where in our previous example Nakato assigns her leasehold to Waswa, then there is no privity of contract between Waswa and Kato. However, since Waswa steps in the shoes of Nakato as tenant of *Mailoacre* for the remainder of the lease, there is privity of estate between him and Kato.[118] At common law, where there is no privity of contract between the parties, but there is privity of estate, only covenants that touch and concern the land are enforceable.[119] Generally, a covenant touches and concerns the land if it affects the nature, quality, use or value of the land.[120] Examples of such covenants include covenant to pay rent, to repair and to use the premises only for specified purposes. Thus, where in our example Waswa defaults in payments of rent, Kato can sue him and or levy a distress over his personal property.[121] However, as already noted, unless Kato expressly agrees to release Nakato she remains liable to Kato under the original contract for the rest of the term even if he consented to the assignment.

Sublease

Where there is neither privity of contract nor privity of estate between the parties they cannot directly sue each other to enforce covenants in the lease. This would be the situation if in our example Nakato subleases *Mailoacre* to Waswa. During the currency of the sublease Waswa will

---

113 *In Re: Gibbs & Holder Brothers & Co Ltd* [1925] Ch 198.

114 *In Re: Gibbs & Holder Brothers & Co Ltd*, ibid. For a useful summary of the relevant tests applied by the courts, see *International Drilling Fluids Ltd v Louisville Investments (Uxbridge) Ltd* [1986] 1 All ER 3210 pp. 325-26, per Balcomb LJ.

115 See for example, *City Council of Kampala v Mukibi* [1967] EA 368; *Souza Figueiredo & Co Ltd v George Panagopoulos and others* [1959] EA 756.

116 Megarry and Wade, *The Law of Real Property*, supra, p. 740.

117 *Thursby and others v Plant* (1670) 85 ER 254.

118 The transfer must comply with legal formalities, see *Souza Figueiredo & Co Ltd v George Panagopoulos and others.*

119 *P&A Swift Investments (a firm) v Combined English Stores Group PLC* [1988] 3 WLR 313.

120 *Ibid.*

121 *Souza Figueiredo & Co Ltd v George Panagopoulos and others* [1959] EA 756.

be in possession as Nakato's tenant and not as Kato's tenant. Accordingly, if, for example, Waswa defaults in payment of rent Kato cannot sue him. However, Kato could indirectly enforce the covenant by suing Nakato for breach of contract. Nakato could then similarly sue Waswa.[122]

Registration of transfer

Section 104 of the *Registration of Titles Act* provides that upon registration of a transfer of a lease a covenant is implied between the transferor and the transferee that the latter shall pay rent reserved in the original lease and be bound by all covenants expressed therein or implied by law against the lessee. The section also implies that the transferee binds himself or herself (and his or her successors in title) to indemnify the transferor against any suits or claims for breach of such covenants. On a literal reading of this provision, it appears that the assignee is liable for all covenants in the original lease whether or not they touch and concern the land. Whether this is a correct interpretation is not settled. However, it is thought that the courts will require more explicit language to accept that the provision was intended to override the common law.[123] With respect to subleases, s. 112 of the *Registration of Titles Act* implies a term that the sublessee and his or her successors in title, in addition to the terms expressed in the sublease, shall be bound by all terms in the headlease (including terms implied in a lease by s. 101). A literal interpretation of the provision might suggest that the headlessor could directly enforce the covenants in the original lease against the sublessee even though there is neither privity of contract nor privity of estate between the two. However, for a similar reason as above, the preferred view is that the courts would not construe the provision as intended to override the common law.

Assignment of a reversion

At common law, apart from covenants that are inherent in the relationship of landlord and tenant (for example, a covenant to pay rent), neither the benefit nor the burden of a covenant runs with the reversion.[124] Thus, suppose in our example above Kato sells *Mailoacre* to Salongo during the currency of Nakato's lease. Salongo and Nakato cannot sue each other for the enforcement of terms in the original lease except as stated above.[125] In England, the *Grantees of Reversion Act*, 1540, replaced the common law. In essence, this Act provides that an assignee of a reversion has the same rights of enforcing covenants as the original landlord.[126] This statute does not apply to Uganda and there is no equivalent statutory provision. Therefore, unless the courts decline to follow the common law rule on the grounds that it is not suitable for Uganda's circumstances, it seems that an assignee of the landlord cannot directly enforce covenants in the original lease against a tenant who entered into possession prior to the assignment.

The assignee of the landlord can overcome the problem indirectly by instituting a chain of actions. For example, where Nakato is in breach of a covenant in the original lease, Salongo cannot sue her but he can sue Kato for breach of contract. Then Kato can sue Nakato for breach of contract or for reimbursement.[127] A more direct way of avoiding the problem is for Salongo to enter into a fresh contract with Nakato on the assignment of the reversion so that privity of contract is established. Another option is for Kato to assign his rights (including a right to sue) and obligations to Salongo with the express or implied consent of Nakato.[128]

---

122 *Moule v Garrett* (1872) LR 7 Ex 101.

123 See Whalan, *The Torrens System in Australia*, supra, p. 163.

124 Megarry and Wade, *The Law of Real Property*, supra, p. 752.

125 Megarry and Wade, *The Law of Real Property*, supra, 357.

126 *Ibid.* Several other common law jurisdictions have similar statutory provisions.

127 See *City & Metropolitan Properties v Greycroft* [1937] 1 WLR 1085.

128 *Souza Figueiredo & Co Ltd v George Panagopoulos and others* [1959] EA 756.

REMEDIES FOR BREACH OF COVENANT

Tenant's remedies

Where the landlord is in breach of any term of the lease agreement, the tenant may seek any appropriate remedies under the general law of contract or tort. For example, if the landlord breaches a covenant of quiet enjoyment the tenant could sue for damages and or an injunction to prevent future breach.[129] The tenant may also terminate the lease where the agreement expressly provides such power. In the absence of such provision, the tenant cannot terminate a lease for breach of a lease agreement unless it is a fundamental breach or a repudiation of the agreement.[130] The test for repudiation is whether it is reasonable for the tenant to infer, from the landlord's conduct an intention no longer to be bound by the lease agreement.[131] The repudiation of a contract is a serious matter and is not lightly drawn.[132]

In practice, mainly for financial reasons, it is rare for tenants to sue their landlord for breach of covenant. Tenants sometimes resort to a self-help remedy of withholding rent to force the landlord to perform his or her obligation under the lease. The risk of such action is that the landlord may turn around and sue the tenant for breach of covenant to pay rent, which may result in forfeiture of the lease. However, in that event, the tenant might set-off the landlord's breach against the claim for rent. A set-off claim, if successful, could reduce or even wipe out the landlord's claim.[133]

Landlord's remedies

There are several remedies available to a landlord where a tenant is in breach of the lease agreement.

Damages

The landlord may bring the usual action for damages for breach of covenant and for other remedies under the general law of contract.[134] For example, in *National and Grindley's Bank (K) Ltd v P.T. Punater,*[135] the tenant breached a covenant to deliver up the premises in good order and condition on termination of the lease. It was held that the landlord was entitled to damages equal to the amount in money by which the premises had been depreciated by the breach. If the breach is for non-payment of rent, the landlord may sue to recover the outstanding rent. Where a tenant breaches a term that entitles the landlord to terminate the lease,[136] the landlord may at his or her option elect to keep the lease on foot.[137] If the landlord opts to terminate the lease for breach of covenant, he or she is entitled to recover outstanding rent up to the date of termination.[138] However, the landlord is not entitled to sue for substantial damages for loss of a bargain or future rent unless the breach is fundamental or constitutes a repudiation of contract.[139] Where the landlord elects not

---

129 See eg. *Opinya v Mukasa* CC No. 167 of 1964; High Court Digest p 514; *A.M. Dharas and Sons Ltd v Elys Ltd* [1963] EA 573.

130 Ordinary principles of contract law including termination for repudiation apply to leases. See *National Carriers Ltd v Panelpina (Northern) Ltd* [1981] AC 675.

131 *Rashad Moledina Co (Mombasa) Ltd and others v Hoima Ginners Ltd* [1967] EA 645 CA (K); *Freeth v Burr* (1874) LR 9 CP 208.

132 *Progressive Mailing House Pty Ltd v Tabali Pty Ltd* (1985) 157 CLR 17 at 32.

133 *Hanak v Green* [1958] 2 QB 9; *British Anzani (Felixstone) Ltd v International Marine Management (UK) Ltd* [1980] QB 137.

134 *Kamanyire v Standard Bank (U) Ltd* [1977] HCB 82.

135 [1965] EA 648 (K)

136 See, e.g., s. 102, *RTA*

137 *Boyer v Warby* [1953] 1 QB 234.

138 *Shevil v Builders Licensing Board* (1982) 149 CLR 620.

139 For example, abandonment of the premises constitutes repudiation, while mere non-payment of rent does not, see generally the High Court of Australia judgement in *The Progressive Mailing House Pty Ltd v Tabali Proprietary Ltd* (1984) 157 CLR 17.

to terminate the lease, he or she may sue for rent as it falls due. At common law, there is no obligation on the landlord to mitigate his or her loss, for example, by re-letting, even in a situation where the tenant has clearly abandoned the premises.[140]

Mesne profits

Where the lease is determined and the tenant remains in possession contrary to the landlord's wishes, the landlord may claim damages for loss of '*mesne profits*'.[141] The action for *mesne profits* is a specie of the law of trespass and it lies to recover damages suffered by the landlord for being kept out of possession.[142] The right to *mesne profits* accrues from the date the tenant was supposed to deliver vacant possession to the time when vacant possession was actually given and the premises made habitable.[143]

Distress for rent

Distress or distrain is an ancient common law remedy of self-help by which the landlord may enter the leased premises if rent is in arrears[144] and confiscate any goods found on the premises of the value of the outstanding rent.[145] The remedy depends on the existence of a relationship of landlord and tenant at the time it is exercised. For example, in *Souza Figueiredo v Panogopaulos,*[146] K, the registered proprietor of the subject land, entered into a contract to sell the land to X. Before the transfer was registered X agreed in writing to lease the land to E for a period of ten years. E duly entered into possession and paid two months rent in advance even though the lease was not registered. Meanwhile, X sold their interest in the land to the respondents. X gave instructions to E to pay rent to the respondents. E did not respond to the letter and did not pay rent to the respondents as told. Before the transfer to the respondents was registered, the respondents instructed a court broker to levy a distress upon E's chattels and sell them. In an action for unlawful distress, it was held that as between the respondents and E there was neither privity of contract nor privity of estate. Accordingly, they were not her landlords and were not entitled to distrain upon the premises.[147] The respondents and the court brokers they employed were found to be jointly and severally liable for trespass and conversion. Similarly, in *Eastern Radio Service and another v R.J. Patel t/a Tiny Tots and another*, it was held that once the landlord determines the lease he or she cannot levy a distress on the former tenant's personal effects.

At common law, the landlord had no right to sell distrained goods without leave of court. He or she could only retain the goods as a coercive measure until paid or authorised by court. The right to sell was introduced in England by the *Distress Act,* 1688[148] and the *Distress Amendment Act*, 1888.[149] Since these statutes are not of general application in Uganda,[150] it is submitted that the

---

140 *Boyer v Warby* [1953] 1 QB 234.

141 *Norman Godhino v Virani* CC 224 of 1938, High Court Digest, p. 256; *Kamanyire v Standard Bank (U) Ltd* [1977] HCB 82.

142 *Anderson v Bowles* (1951) 84 CLR 310 at 325.

143 *Kamanyire v Standard Bank (U) Ltd* [1977] HCB 82. The tenant is liable for mesne profits if a person he or she allowed into possession holds over after the lease expires.

144 Right only arises where rent is in arrears, see *Musumba v Haji Kasaka and Mbarara Auction Mart* (1971) 1 ULR 222.

145 Megarry and Wade, *The Law of Real Property*, supra, pp. 709-12.

146 [1959] EA 756.

147 *Ibid,* at 762. To establish the relationship of landlord and tenant E had to consent to X's assignment of their rights to the respondents, at 761 per Windham JA.

148 [1962] EA 818.

149 Megarry and Wade, *The Law of Real Property*, supra p. 710.

150 See *Uganda Motors Ltd v Wavah Holdings Ltd* CA No 19 of 1991.

landlord has no power to sell without a judicial order. Distress must be carried out by the landlord in person, by a lawyer attorney or by a duly licensed bailiff. Distress by any unlicensed agent is illegal.[151]

Forfeiture

Forfeiture (or re-entry) is the termination of a lease by the lessor before the term expires. As already seen, at common law, in the absence of an express provision for forfeiture, only breach of a condition entitles the landlord to enforce forfeiture of a lease. For example, it is established law that failure to pay rent is a breach of a covenant, which does not entitle the landlord to terminate the lease. On the other hand, parting with possession in breach of the lease agreement is generally regarded as a serious breach, which entitles the landlord to terminate the lease.[152] In practice, most formal leases reserve a right of forfeiture for breach of any term of the lease agreement. Moreover, where a lease is registered under the *Registration of Titles Act,* s.102(5) implies in the lessor power of re-entry after breach of any covenant (including non-payment of rent) expressed in the lease has continued for thirty days.[153] Section 111 extends these provisions to subleases.[154] The implied powers of re-entry can be modified or excluded by express agreement of the parties.[155] Moreover, as we shall presently see, the lessor may waive his or her right of forfeiture.

Prior to the *Judicature Act,* 1967,[156] a lessor seeking to enforce forfeiture had to follow the procedure prescribed by the English *Conveyancing and Law of Property Act*, 1881, which was of general application to Uganda.[157] Section 14 of the Act relevantly provided that a right of re-entry could not be enforced by action or otherwise unless notice in writing had been served to the lessee specifying the breach and requiring a remedy. The right of re-entry could be enforced only if after lapse of a reasonable time the lessee failed to comply with the notice. Since the *Judicature Act* precluded the application of English statutes of general application, the Act no longer applies to Uganda.[158] There is no provision in the *Registration of Titles Act* or any other legislation in Uganda corresponding to s. 14 of the *Conveyancing Act*, which regulates when and how the power of re-entry can be exercised. Accordingly, it is submitted that unless the parties' agreement expressly says so, there is no legal requirement for the landlord to serve notice of forfeiture prior to re-entry.

At common law, once a right of re-entry accrues, the landlord is entitled to enforce it without resort to the courts. The landlord affects a re-entry by physically entering the premises with the intention of determining the tenancy. Forfeiture cannot be effected by written notice unaccompanied by actual physical re-entry.[159] If necessary, reasonable force may be used to eject the tenant. Provided that no more than reasonable force is used the landlord cannot be liable for civil or criminal assault.[160] Upon a successful re-entry the lease is effectively determined.[161] Under s.113 of the *Registration of Titles Act*, the lessor may apply to the registrar to register the re-entry. Upon proof of satisfactory re-entry, the registrar may make the appropriate entry in the register book.[162]

---

151 See *Souza Figueiredo & Co Ltd v George Panagopoulos and others* [1959] EA 756 was decided before the 1967 Judicature Act, which disposed of the application to Uganda statutes of general application.

152 Section 3, *Distress For Rent (Bailiffs)* Act (cap 68).

153 *Variety Timber Ltd v Musa* [1971] EA 398 (K). Denial of the landlord's title is also regarded as a substantial breach, see *Nsubuga and another v Mutawe* [1974] EA 487 (CA).

154 See, for example, *Kiwanuka-Musisi v Seggane* [1973] EA 561.

155 See, for example, *Shell and BP Uganda Ltd v Sikander Husain Esmail and others* CS No 1038 of 1975.

156 Section 142, *RTA*.

157 Repealed by the *Judicature Statute*, 1996.

158 See *Khoja Shia Jamat v Norman Godhino* (1936-51) 6 ULR 47.

159 *Uganda Motors Ltd v Wavah Holdings Ltd* CA No 19 of 1991. The *Judicature Statute*, 1996, does not alter the legal position.

160 See *Kassaja v Registrar of Titles* Misc. Appn. No. 51 of 1993.

161 *Hemming v Stone Poges Golf Club* [1920] 1 KB 720.

162 *Lugogo Coffee Co (U) Ltd v Singo Combined Coffee Growers Ltd* CS No. 554 of 1973; [1976] HCB 92.

Whether or not the re-entry is registered, as between the parties, the lease is terminated for all intents and purposes.[163]

Where the tenant refuses to vacate the leased premises peaceably, it is advisable for the lessor to seek a judicial order for re-entry rather than forcefully eject him or her.[164] The law treats the commencement of proceedings for recovery of the premises as an irrevocable and irretrievable election by the lessor to determine the lease.[165] The filing of a writ is equivalent to actual re-entry from the date of service of the writ to the lessee.[166] To determine a lease effectively, the writ must unequivocally demand possession. If the demand for possession is equivocal, that is to say, accompanied by alternative remedies which are consistent with the continuation of the lease, it does not determine the lease. For example, in *Moore v Ullcoats Mining Co Ltd,*[167] the lessor issued a writ demanding recovery of possession and in the alternative sought an order that the lessee let him inspect the premises in accordance with the lease agreement. It was held that the writ was equivocal since the alternative remedy could only be granted on the footing that the lease was in existence. In contrast, in *Eastern Radio Service and another v R.J. Patel t/a Tiny Tots and another*, it was held that inclusion in the plaint a claim for outstanding rent up to the date of the suit does not render the claim for possession equivocal.[168]

It is important to remember that the fact that the lessor files a suit for possession does not necessarily mean that he or she is entitled to determine the lease. He or she must prove the breach relied upon. Moreover, even if there are sufficient grounds for forfeiture of the lease the court may in an appropriate case grant the lessee relief from forfeiture.[169] Nevertheless, while the suit is pending as between the parties the lease is irretrievably revoked.[170] As a consequence both parties are discharged from the covenants under the lease.[171] Thus, the lessor cannot sue the lessee for rent falling due after the commencement of the proceedings.[172] Moreover, since the power to distrain is dependent on the existence of a relationship of landlord and tenant, the landlord cannot levy distress upon the tenant's goods for rent even though it fell due prior to the proceedings.[173]

If the lessor's action for re-entry is successful, the lessee will be liable to pay damages or *mesne profits* for trespass. Damages are calculated from the date that the writ was served up to the time the lessee delivers vacant possession.[174] If the lease is registered under the *Registration of Titles Act*, the lessor may apply to the registrar, under s. 105, for the re-entry to be endorsed in the register. The section states that the lessor must satisfy the registrar that he or she has recovered possession

---

163 In *Naluswa v Luswabi* Misc. C No. 5 of 1974, it was held, *obiter dictum*, that where the registrar refuses to register a re-entry, the lessor may seek an order of mandamus.

164 *Lugogo Coffee Co (U) Ltd v Singo Combined Coffee Growers Ltd* supra, it was held that the refusal of the registrar to register a re-entry does not keep the lease subsisting.

165 In *Capelinha v Marchese Holdings* (1995) 3 SR (WA) 261, the District Court of Western Australia held that where there was any prospect of physical opposition on the part of the tenant, justified or not, the lessor should not use force.

166 *Eastern Radio Service and another v R.J. Patel t/a Tiny Tots and another* [1962] EA 818. Newbold JA at 835, said that even if the plaint is subsequently amended it could not reverse the effect of the original plaints. But see Sir Trevor Gould JA, at 825.

167 *Ibid.* See also *City Council of Kampala v Mukubira and another* [1968] EA 497 (U).

168 [1908] 1 Ch 575.

169 *Eastern Radio Service and another v R.J. Patel t/a Tiny Tots and another* [1962] EA 818.

170 See below.

171 *Eastern Radio Service and another v R.J. Patel t/a Tiny Tots and another*, supra. See also *City Council of Kampala v Mukubira and another* [1968] EA 497.

172 *Jones v Carter* (1846) 15 M&W 718; 153 ER 1040.

173 *Ibid.*

174 *Eastern Radio Service and another v R.J. Patel t/a Tiny Tots and another*, supra

by 'any proceedings'.[175] Where the lessor's action for possession is unsuccessful, the parties' relationship as landlord and tenant will be restored as before. The lessee will be liable to pay rent reserved under the lease agreement for the period of suspension.[176] Usually, rent is much lower than *mesne profits*.

Relief from forfeiture

Forfeiture of a lease may entail loss to the lessee of a substantial proprietary interest in land. The court of equity, being a court of justice, always regarded the proviso for re-entry for non-payment of rent as merely security for rent. Accordingly, if a lease was terminated for non-payment of rent, the court, at its discretion, granted the tenant relief from forfeiture provided he or she was ready and willing to pay the outstanding rent and all relevant expenses incurred by the lessor.[177] The object of equity's intervention was to prevent the lessor from taking advantage of a breach from which he or she was not proportionately and irreparably damaged.

The equitable power to grant relief from forfeiture for non-payment of rent is enacted in s. 27 of the *Judicature Statute,* 1996. Section 27(1) provides that where the lessor is 'proceeding, by action or otherwise' to enforce a forfeiture for non-payment of rent, the lessee may apply for relief against forfeiture. The lessee's application for relief may be made either in the lessor's action for ejectment,[178] or by his or her own action.[179] If it is the latter, the application must be made before the court makes the order for forfeiture.[180] Where a court has already made an order for forfeiture, the application for relief should be made under s. 27(4) of the *Judicature Statute*.[181] The application must be brought within a period of six months after the date of the judgement.[182]

A lessee can also apply for relief from forfeiture under s. 27(1) of the *Judicature Statute* where the lessor is proceeding to forfeit the lease *otherwise than by action.* The italicised words necessarily refer to forfeiture by taking physical possession.[183] The expression 'proceeding' seems to suggest that the application for relief should be made whilst the lessor is in the process of re-entering. If the process is complete, namely, the lessor obtains possession by peaceable re-entry he or she is no longer 'proceeding' to re-enter, hence, the right to apply for relief from forfeiture is lost. However, English judicial authority suggests that this is not necessarily the case. For example, in *Billson and others v Residential Apartments Ltd*,[184] the House of Lords held, with reference to a similar provision, that the provision does not preclude the lessee from applying for relief even where the lessor has re-entered peaceably.[185]

---

175 *Driscoll v Church Commission for England* [1957] 1 QB 330.

176 See *Naluswa v Luswabi* Misc. C No. 5 of 1974. In the case of *Alibhai and others v The Chief Registrar of Titles*, Misc. Appn. No. 60 of 1992, it was held with reference to s. 185, *RTA*, that the expression 'any proceedings' was not limited to court proceedings. Kalanda J said that the expression applies to other proceedings by any other law 'in which a matter can be solved', per Kalanda J.

177 *Canas Property Co Ltd v Television Service Ltd* [1970] 2 QB 433.

178 *Kiwanuka-Musisi v Seggane* [1973] EA 561 (U); *Haji Musa Magala v Ondowa* HCCC 360 of 1971; *Butagira v Namukasa* CA No. 69 of 1989.

179 See, for example, *Lugogo Coffee Co (U) Ltd v Singo Combined Coffee Growers Ltd* CS No. 554 of 1973; [1976] HCB 92.

180 *Butagira v Namukasa* CA No 69 of 1989.

181 *Rogers v Rice* [1892] 2 Ch 170; *Billson and others v Residential Apartments Ltd* [1992] 1 All ER 141.

182 In *Gomba Marines & Contractors (Ltd) v Kiwana* Misc. Appn. No. 131B/93, Byamugisha J held that an application for relief from forfiture made under s. 24(4) of the *Judicature Act,* 1967 (which is identical with s. 27(4)), where there was no judgment in existence, was misconceived.

183 *Gomba Marines & Contractors (Ltd) v Kiwana*, supra.

184 Forfeiture is effected either by court order or by physical re-entry, see *Kassaja v Registrar of Titles*, Misc. Appn. No. 51 of 1993.

185 [1992] 1 All ER 141.

The power of the courts to grant relief from forfeiture is extensive, but can only be exercised where the breach is for non-payment of rent. The courts have no power under the *Judicature Statute* to grant relief from forfeiture for breach of other covenants.[186] In deciding whether to grant relief the courts take into account all circumstances of the case.[187] These include the period of non-payment of rent, the conduct of the lessee,[188] and delaying to apply for relief,[189] and the disparity between the value of the property forfeited as compared with the loss likely to be suffered by the lessor as a result of the breach.[190]

However, except in exceptional circumstances, the courts almost as a matter of course grant relief from forfeiture of a lease for non-payment of rent if the lessee pays into court all arrears and expenses incurred by the lessor.[191] Such circumstances include where the lessor has already leased or sold the land to an innocent third party. For example, in the case of *Kiwanuka-Musisi v Seggane*,[192] the court declined to grant the lessee relief from forfeiture because by the time he applied for relief the lessor had let the premises to another tenant.[193] The court reasoned that granting the lessee relief from forfeiture in the circumstances would inflict injustice upon the lessor and his new tenant.

In *The Executrix of the Estate of the late Tebajukira and another v Shalita,*[194] a lease was terminated by forfeiture and a re-entry was noted in the register under s. 105 of the *Registration of Titles Act*. Subsequently, the former lessee sought judicial relief against forfeiture and applied for the former lessor to be ejected under s. 184 of the *Registration of Titles Act*. The Supreme Court dismissed the application as misconceived because that section does not make provision for a lessee to eject a lessor. Wambuzi CJ held that the effect of s. 184 in this regard was that, once the landlord re-enters and the re-entry is registered the courts could no longer grant relief from forfeiture.[195] In the case of *Ahmed Farah and another v Kiwanuka,*[196] Byamugisha J cites this case for the proposition that registration of a re-entry was a bar to an application for relief from forfeiture in as much as such application seeks to recover land from the landlord.

With due respect, it is submitted that s. 184 of the *Registration of Titles Act* does not override the courts' jurisdiction to grant relief against forfeiture under the *Judicature Statute*. If it does, then, in our view, the *Judicature Statute,* being a later enactment, should be construed as overriding s. 184 of the *Registration of Titles Act* to the extent of the inconsistency.[197] It is suggested that registration of a re-entry should not be treated as an absolute bar to the exercise of the court's discretion, but as one of the factors to be considered in determining whether to grant relief.

---

[186] In *Butagira v Namukasa* CA No. 69 of 1989, the fact that the application for relief from forfeiture was made more than a year after the landlord had physically re-entered, was not raised as an issue.

[187] *Butagira v Namukasa* CA No. 69 of 1989. It is a moot point whether the courts retain their inherent equitable jurisdiction to grant relief from forfeiture. In *Shiloh Spinners Ltd v Harding* [1973] AC 691 at 723-24, Lord Wilberforce said, *obiter dicta*, that the courts' inherent equitable jurisdiction to grant relief from forfeiture could be exercised in any case where justice demands that relief ought to be granted.

[188] *Ibid.* See also *Lugogo Coffee Co (U) Ltd v Singo Combined Coffee Growers Ltd* CS No. 554 of 1973; [1976] HCB 92.

[189] In *Butagira v Namukasa* CA No 69 of 1989, Odoki JSC said that high handed conduct of a tenant may not be sufficient to deprive him or her of relief from forfeiture (cf Wambuzi CJ).

[190] *Lugogo Coffee Co (U) Ltd v Singo Combined Coffee Growers Ltd*, supra; *Gomba Marines & Contractors (Ltd) v Kiwana*, supra.

[191] *Shiloh Spinners Ltd v Harding* [1973] AC 691.

[192] *Gill v Lewis* (1956) 1 All ER 844 at 85, per Jenkins LJ. The Supreme Court in *Butagira v Namukasa* CA No 69 of 1989, extensively cited this case with approval, supra. See also *Haji Musa Magala v Ondowa* CS No. 360 of 1971.

[193] [1973] EA 561.

[194] See also *Gomba Marines & Contractors (Ltd) v Kiwana*, supra.

[195] CA No. 2 of 1988.

[196] *Ibid.*

[197] Civil Suit No. 687 of 1993 (unreported).

Waiver of right to enforce forfeiture

Where a breach occurs, which entitles the lessor to re-enter, the lessor may at his or her option decide not to enforce forfeiture of the lease.[198] This is known as 'waiver' of the right of forfeiture. Waiver may be express or implied from the lessor's conduct. In the English case of *Matthews v Smallwood*, Parker J said that:[199]

> Waiver of a right of re-entry can only occur where the lessor, with knowledge of the facts upon which his right to re-enter arises, does some unequivocal act recognising the continued existence of the lease. It is not enough that he should do the act which recognises, or appears to recognise, the continued existence of the lease, unless, at the time when the act is done, he has knowledge of the facts under which, or from which, his right of entry arose. Therefore, we get the principle that, though an act of waiver operates with regard to all known breaches, it does not operate with regard to breaches which were unknown to the lessor at the time when the act took place.

In *Kalsi v Commissioner of Lands*,[200] O'Connor P held that if the lessor, with knowledge of the breach, does an act which unequivocally recognises the continuation of the lease, the law presumes an intention to waive the forfeiture, even if that was not the lessor's actual intention. For example, where the lessor, with knowledge of a breach entitling forfeiture, demands rent which is payable in advance he or she is deemed to affirm the continuance of the tenancy.[201] However, the demand and acceptance of rent due before the date of forfeiture does not waive the forfeiture.[202] Similarly, where the covenant is a continuing covenant and is broken from day to day, its breach is not waived by acceptance of rent.[203] It has also been held that since the filing of a suit for re-entry is an irrevocable election to determine the lease, no subsequent action of the lessor can operate as a waiver whilst the suit is pending.[204]

Termination of leases other than by forfeiture

Leases may be terminated by forfeiture, effluxion of time, notice, surrender and merger. Forfeiture is discussed above. The other modes of termination are considered below.

Effluxion of time

At common law, a lease for a fixed term automatically terminates when the period expires. There is no requirement for either party to serve notice of termination unless their lease agreement expressly says so.[205] If the tenant remains in possession without consent or dissent of the landlord he or she becomes a tenant at sufferance.[206] Where the tenant remains in possession with the consent of the landowner, a tenancy at will is implied unless or until some other interest is created.[207] Both tenancies at will and at sufferance become periodic tenancies once the tenant pays rent and the landlord, on a regular basis, accepts it.[208] The nature of the periodic tenancy depends on the mode

---

198 See 'overriding statutory exceptions to indefeasibility' in Chapter 5.

199 *Dr Nur Illahi s/o Nur Mohamed v Patel and others* 1956 [EACA] 80; *Variety Timber Ltd v Musa* [1971] EA 398 (K).

200 [1910] 1 Ch 777 at 786.

201 [1958] EA 367 at 371.

202 *Dr Nur Illahi s/o Dr Nur Muhamed v Patel and others* 1956 [EACA] 80; *Kalsi v Commissioner of Lands* [1958] EA 367; *Stanley and Sons Ltd v Alibhai* [1963] EA 594 (T)

203 *Eastern Radio Service and another v R.J. Patel t/a Tiny Tots and another* [1962] EA 818.

204 *Variety Timber Ltd v Musa* [1971] EA 398 (K). Cf *Kalsi v Commissioner of Lands* [1958] EA 367.

205 *City Council of Kampala v Mukubira and another* [1968] EA 497.

206 *Singh v Godley* (1942) 20 KLR 57.

207 *Noor Hassan v Mukiibi* CA No. 103 of 1977; [1978] HCB 162.

208 *Bweya Steel Works Ltd v National Insurance Corporation* CS No 63 of 1985; [1985] HCB 58. In *Stanley and Sons Ltd v Alibhai* [1963] EA 594 (T), it was held that a demand for rent after expiration of the lease implies a tenancy at will.

of rent payment. If it is paid weekly, it is a weekly tenancy, monthly is a monthly tenancy and yearly is a yearly tenancy.[209]

A tenant who remains in possession without consent of the landowner after expiration of the lease is liable for the costs incurred for his or her eviction and for *mesne profits*.[210] *Mesne profits*[211] are calculated from the date that the lessee was supposed to deliver vacant possession to the date that he or she (and all persons on the land on his or her account)[212] actually vacated the premises.[213] The damages awarded are not necessarily limited to the rent reserved under the expired lease, though such rent is a *prima facie* guide to their calculation.[214]

Notice to quit

A lease for a fixed period cannot be terminated by notice by either party unless the right to terminate is expressly reserved in the lease or in the event of breach of a term, which entitles either party to terminate the lease.[215] Periodic tenancies, on the other hand, are by nature terminable by either party giving an appropriate notice. In the absence of any express agreement between the parties a weekly tenancy is terminable by one week's notice,[216] a monthly tenancy by one month's notice,[217] and a quarterly tenancy by three months notice.[218] The exception to this rule is a yearly tenancy, which is terminable by six months notice.[219]

Subject to the agreement of the parties, a notice to terminate a lease need not take any form. An oral notice is as effective as a written notice.[220] Unless otherwise agreed, the notice must be made to expire at the end of a complete period of the tenancy and should be equal in length to that period.[221] Otherwise, the notice is invalid and ineffectual to terminate the lease.[222] For example, to terminate a monthly tenancy, which commenced on the 1st of the month, the notice must be made to expire on the last day of the month at the end of a full month.[223] Thus, where the landlord wants the tenancy to terminate on 31 December of a particular year the notice must be served not later than 30 November of that year. Where the person seeking to terminate the tenancy is doubtful as to the date on which the period expires, it is customary to add in the notice words to the effect that if the date mentioned is not the correct date on which the period expires, then the notice to quit is to expire on the next proper date of expiry at the end of the current period.[224]

---

209 *Bweya Steel Works Ltd v National Insurance Corporation*, Ibid.

210 *Rukandema-Kamuru v Kabale Town Council* CA No MKA 10 of 1985.

211 *Mayanja-Nkangi v National Housing Corporation* (1972) 1 ULR 371; *Kamanyire v Standard Bank (U) Ltd* [1977] HCB 82.

212 See the definition in s. 2 of the *Civil Procedure Act*.

213 *Sebuliba v Attorney-General* CA No. 13 of 1991.

214 *Mayanja-Nkangi v National Housing Corporation* (1972) 1 ULR 371. In *Kamanyire v Standard Bank (U) Ltd* [1977] HCB 82, where the lessee delivered the premises in an uninhabitable state, mesne profits were calculated till the house was made fit for human habitation.

215 *Clifton Securities v Huntley* [1948] 2 All ER 283.

216 Cheshire and Burns, *Modern Law of Real Property*, supra, p. 435.

217 *Queen's Club Gardens Estate Ltd v Bignell* [1924] 1 KB 117.

218 *Musumba v Haji Kasaka and Mbarara Auction Mart* (1971) 1 ULR 222.

219 *Bweya Steel Works Ltd v National Insurance Corporation* CS No. 63 of 1985; [1985] HCB 58.

220 *Rukandema-Kamuru v Kabale Town Council* CA No. MKA 10 of 1985. See also *Chhagan v Manani* [1964] EA 71.

221 *Musumba v Haji Kasaka and Mbarara Auction Mart* (1971) 1 ULR 22.

222 *Bweya Steel Works Ltd v National Insurance Corporation* CS No. 63 of 1985; [1985] HCB 58.

223 *Ibid.*

224 *Musumba v Haji Kasaka and Mbarara Auction Mart* (1971) 1 ULR 222.

The notice terminating a lease should be reasonably clear to the person to whom it is given that the lease is terminated.[225] If the notice is ambiguous, it is not effective. For example, in *Rajan Nanji v Jadowji Dewji,*[226] the notice to a tenant read that if the tenant did not vacate the premises by a certain date his rent might be increased. It was held that the notice was not effective to terminate the lease. The fact that the tenant remained in possession did not mean he had consented to the new terms. In contrast, in *Balbir v Panesar,* it was held that liberal interpretation should be given to a notice of termination. So that, even if a notice contains some inaccurate statements, effect should be given to it as long as the court is satisfied that the recipient was left in no reasonable doubt as to its meaning.[227]

An action for eviction cannot be brought on the basis of a defective notice.[228] If a landlord purports to re-enter following such a notice he or she will be held liable for damages for breach of contract and the covenant of quiet enjoyment. For example, in *Rukandema-Kamuru v Kabale Town Council,*[229] the court awarded general and aggravated damages against a landlord who evicted a yearly tenant after serving him with only a one-month termination notice.

Surrender

Surrender occurs where, before expiration of a lease, the lessee gives up possession of the land to the lessor. Once the lessor accepts possession the lease merges with the reversion and is thereby terminated.[230] Surrender may be by express agreement of the parties,[231] operation of law or statutory provision.[232] A lease is surrendered by operation of law if the lessor grants, and the lessee accepts, a fresh lease commencing before the current lease expires.[233] A lease is also surrendered by operation of law where the tenant abandons the premises and the landlord re-enters.[234] The subjective intention of the parties is irrelevant in determining whether the lease was surrendered by operation of law.[235] For example, in *Shah Karamshi Panachand & Co Ltd v Velji and another,*[236] the plaintiff leased the suit property to the first defendant for a period of ten years and the lease was registered under the Kenya *Registration of Titles Act* (cap 281). In 1963, the first defendant formed a company (the second defendant) to which he transferred his business. To the plaintiff's knowledge the second defendant continued to carry on business in the same premises.

For three years the plaintiff accepted rent from the second defendant and issued receipts in its name. In 1967, the plaintiff instituted these proceedings for possession against the first defendant on the ground that the lease had expired by effluxion of time and against the second defendant for trespass. The defendants claimed that the original lease had been surrendered in 1963 and fresh lease arrangements were entered into with the second defendant. The court found that there was

---

225 *Ibid.*

226 *Queen's Club Gardens Estate Ltd v Bignell* [1924] 1 KB 117 at 126. This case was cited with approval in *Kikabhai N Mistry v Abdulla Mohamed* (1956) 23 EACA 192; and *Balbir v Panesar* [1972] EA 94.

227 *Kikabhai N Mistry v Abdulla Mohamed, Ibid.*

228 1 EALR 91.

229 [1972] EA 94. See also *Said bin Mbarak v Kapacee* 10 KLR 100. Cf *Bweya Steel Works Ltd v National Insurance Corporation* CS No 63 of 1983; [1985] HCB 58, Odoki J, said that since a notice of termination is a unilateral act it should be construed strictly against the party giving it.

230 *Bweya Steel Works Ltd v National Insurance Corporation, Ibid.*

231 CA No. MKA 10 of 1985.

232 *Kalani v Kaur* CA No. 22 of 1995. See also Megarry and Wade, *The Law of Real Property*, supra, p.684.

233 See for example *Kalani v Kaur* CA No. 22 of 1995.

234 For example, under s.57 of the *Trustee and Bankruptcy Act* (cap 71), the trustee in bankruptcy may, with leave of court, surrender by discharge the bankrupt's lease he considers onerous.

235 Megarry and Wade, *The Law of Real Property*, supra, p. 685.

236 Note that abandonment by itself does not constitute surrender unless the landlord accepts possession, for example by entering into possession or leasing the land to another.

no evidence of express agreement to surrender, but there was surrender by operation of law. In delivering his judgement, Madan J said:[237]

> When the [first defendant] unquestionably abandoned and ceased to occupy the premises as lessee the company... immediately went into possession of them, and thereafter in every manner it acted and was treated and accepted as tenant by the landlord.

His Honour said that even though the plaintiff did not actually re-enter, his acceptance of rent and treatment of the second defendant as his tenant sufficed in law as symbolic resumption of possession. There was surrender by operation of law when the plaintiff went into possession, and created a new monthly tenancy with the second defendant.

Where the surrendered lease is registered under the *Registration of Titles Act,* surrender is effected following the procedure stipulated in sections 56 and 107 of the Act. Upon registration, the interest of the lessee is extinguished and the land freed from the leasehold.[238] There is no time limitation within which to register surrender of a lease.[239] However, as between the lessee and the lessor, surrender of the lease is effective even if it is not entered in the register book.[240]

Merger

Merger is the opposite of surrender. Where the lessee acquires the reversion from the lessor, the lease merges with the reversion and is thereby terminated. The merger is completed by appropriate entry in the register book.

Lessor's rights to fixtures[241]

At common law, unless otherwise agreed, the lessor has no obligation to compensate the lessee for improvements carried out during the term. However, subject to any contrary agreement of the parties, the lessee is entitled to remove certain fixtures installed by the lessee known as 'tenant's fixtures'. The tenant's fixtures are fixtures which the tenant uses for trade, domestic or ornamental purposes. Other fixtures, including tenant's fixtures that cannot be removed without destruction, become a free gift to the landowner.

---

237 *Shah Karamshi Panachand & Co Ltd v Velji and another* [1969] EA 194 at 196.

238 *Ibid.*

239 Section 107 *RTA*. See, for example, *Kalani v Kaur* CA No. 22 of 1995. Note that a lease subject to a registered mortgage cannot be surrendered without the mortgagee's consent.

240 *Kalani v Kaur* CA No. 22 of 1995

241 Fixtures are discussed above in Chapter 4.

7

Mortgages

Introduction

A mortgage is a transaction whereby an interest in land is given as security for the repayment of a loan.[1] The debtor/proprietor of the mortgaged land is called the 'mortgagor' and the creditor is the 'mortgagee'. The secured sum with interest is the mortgage debt.[2]

At common law a mortgage took the nature of a conveyance of the debtor's title to the creditor on condition that upon repayment or performance of some other obligation the creditor should re-convey the title to the mortgagor.[3] For example, if X wished to borrow money from Y on security of his house he would transfer his legal title to Y, subject to the condition that upon repayment of the mortgage debt Y would re-convey the title to the debtor. While Y held the legal title to the land X retained the 'equity of redemption'. The equity of redemption is an equitable interest, which, like other equitable interests, was enforceable against the creditor and any purchaser of the legal title with notice.[4]

The nature of a mortgage under the *Registration of Titles Act* (cap 205) differs from the common law mortgage. Section 115 of the *Registration of Titles Act* expressly provides that a mortgage created under the Act takes effect as a security over the mortgaged land 'but shall not operate as a transfer of the land thereby mortgaged'. In *Re: Forrest Trust Trustee's Executors & Agency Co Ltd* v *Anson,*[5] Herring CJ, described the effect of a mortgage created under the corresponding provision of the *Transfer of Land Act* (Victoria), that 'it confers on the creditor merely a group of powers to secure the money lent'. The debtor (mortgagor) remains the owner of the land subject to fulfilment of his or her obligations under the mortgage agreement.

Although a mortgage created under the *Registration of Titles Act* does not transfer ownership of the land to the mortgagee, it creates in the mortgagee's favour a separate and distinct interest in the mortgaged land. Thus, a registered mortgagee is a 'proprietor' within the meaning of the *Registration of Titles Act.*[6] He or she is a proprietor of a mortgage while the mortgagor is the proprietor of the mortgaged land. In the case of *English, Scottish & Australian Bank Ltd* v *Phillips,*[7] the High Court of Australia compared a Torrens system mortgage to a lease. Like a lease it is a distinct interest, which may be dealt with separately from the fee simple or other estate of the mortgagor.

---

1 *Matambulire v Kimera* CA No 37 of 1972 (unreported).

2 Other securities include pledge, debenture, and floating charge. In Uganda a mortgage of land is the most common form of security.

3 See, e.g., *Matambulire v Kimera* CA No 37 of 1972 (unreported). See also Megarry and Wade, *The Law of Real Property,* supra, p 913.

4 *Northern Counties of England Fire Insurance* Co v *Whipp* (1884) 26 Ch D 482.

5 [1953] VLR 246, at 256

6 See definition of 'proprietor', s. 2, *RTA*.

7 (1937) 57 CLR 302, at 321.

CREATION OF A MORTGAGE[8]

Registered mortgage

Section 114 of the *Registration of Titles Act* empowers a proprietor of land registered under the Act to create a mortgage by signing a mortgage instrument in the prescribed form. The prescribed form is in the Eleventh Schedule to the Act. Upon the registration of the instrument, the land becomes liable as security in a manner set forth in the instrument.[9] The mortgage is protected by s. 61 of the *Registration of Titles Act*, and whoever deals with the land does so subject to the mortgage as an exception to the principle of indefeasibility of title.[10] A registered mortgage is sometimes referred to as a 'legal' mortgage to distinguish it from an unregistered or 'equitable' mortgage.

Equitable mortgage

In equity, a contract to create a mortgage was treated as a promise by the debtor to execute a legal mortgage when called upon to do so. Since equity regards as done that which ought to be done, such an agreement created an equitable mortgage.[11] For example, under the doctrines of equity a deposit of title deeds by way of security whether or not accompanied by a memorandum was equivalent to an agreement to execute a legal mortgage and carried with it the entire remedies incidental to a legal mortgage.[12] Section 138 of the *Registration of Titles Act* specifically enables the creation of an equitable mortgage under the Act by deposit of a certificate of title. The section provides that notwithstanding anything contained in the Act, the registered proprietor may create an equitable mortgage of land by depositing his or her certificate of title with a creditor with intent to create a security thereon whether or not accompanied by a memorandum of the deposit. The section provides further that every such equitable mortgage shall be deemed to create an interest in land. Under this provision an equitable mortgagee is required to lodge a caveat against the mortgaged land.[13]

Several points arising from s. 138 of the *Registration of Titles Act* need to be stressed. First, to create an equitable mortgage the certificate of title must be deposited by the proprietor with the creditor with the object of securing a debt. *Prima facie*, depositing a certificate with a creditor against payment of money raises a strong presumption that the object is to create an equitable mortgage over the entire land described in the certificate and for the whole amount of the debt then due.[14] The presumption can be rebutted by proving, for example, that the object of depositing the certificate of title was merely for safe custody or possessory lien.[15] Secondly, it is not necessary that a note or memorandum accompany the deposit, though, of course, to avoid controversy in the interests of both parties there should be a memorandum setting out the object of depositing the certificate and the terms thereof.[16]

---

8 Under s. 40 of the *Land Act*, 1998, a mortgage over family land is void *ab initio* unless the spouse and or the family of the mortgagor consented to the transaction before it was entered into.

9 Section 51, *RTA*.

10 See *Zafropoulos* v *Recchi* [1978] SASR 5, see also Chapter 5.

11 *Ex Parte Leathes* (1833) Ch 112.

12 *Barclays Bank D.C.O.* v *Gulu Millers* [1959] EA 540.

13 For illustration see *Barclays Bank D.C.O.* v *Gulu Millers* [1959] EA 540. In Australian jurisdictions with a provision similar to s. 138, it has been suggested that though the provision only mentions equitable mortgages created by way of title deposit it does not mean that it is the only way an equitable mortgage can be created over Torrens system land. See Sykes, *The Law of Securities* (4th ed, Law Book Company, Sydney, 1986), p. 315. This may not be so in Uganda, see *Buganda Timber Co Ltd* v *Mulji K Metha* [1961] EA 477, at 481, per Sir Kenneth O'Connor P.

14 *Guaranty Discount Co Ltd* v *Credit Finance Corporation Ltd & another* [1963] EA 345. Also *Byaruhanga* v *Barclays Bank of Uganda Ltd* CS 1327 of 1977 (unreported).

15 *UTC Ltd (in Liquidation) v NZI Securities Australia Ltd and another* [1991] 4 WAR 349.

16 *Guaranty Discount Co Ltd* v *Credit Finance Corporation Ltd & another* [1963] EA 345.

Thirdly, the person named in the certificate, as proprietor, must deposit the certificate. Where two or more persons are registered as proprietors all must be involved. For example, in *De Souza Figueiredo* v *Talbot and another,*[17] two executors were registered as proprietors of the suit property, but only one deposited the certificate as security for a loan. It was held that the deposit was ineffective to create an equitable mortgage. Finally, the section requires an equitable mortgagee to lodge a caveat. On the surface, this requirement appears to be permissive for the equitable mortgagee to protect his or her interest against extinguishment by subsequent registered dealing in the land. However, it seems that lodging a caveat is in fact a requisite for the creation of an equitable mortgage under s. 138.[18] This view is supported by the fact that if lodging a caveat were simply permissive the provision would be superfluous. The reason is that, under s. 148 of the *Registration of Titles Act,* any person claiming an interest in land is entitled to lodge a caveat against dealings in the subject land. A mortgagee is a person claiming an interest in land.

Mortgage of customary land and tenancy by occupancy

Under s. 9(2)(c) of the *Land Act*, 1998, a holder of a customary certificate of ownership of land has a right to mortgage his or her land. Likewise, under s. 35(1) of the Act, a tenant by occupancy (a lawful or *bona fide* occupant) is entitled to 'pledge' or undertake any other lawful transaction in respect of the occupancy.[19] The Act does not prescribe the procedure for the creation of a mortgage over land owned under customary tenure or right of occupancy. Since neither customary land nor tenancy by occupancy are registered under the *Registration of Titles Act*, the provisions of that Act do not apply to them. In the case of *Matambulire v Kimera,*[20] which involved mortgage of a *kibanja,* the High Court held that where the mortgaged land was not registered under the *Registration of Titles Act*, the applicable law was the common law and the doctrines of equity.[21] Similarly, in the case of *Waswa v Kikungwe*,[22] which involved mortgage of customary land, it was held that where a contract 'resembling' a mortgage between 'natives' is sought to be enforced the courts could apply the English law of equity applicable to mortgages.

REMEDIES OF A MORTGAGEE

Subject to any express agreement of the parties, s. 122 of the *Registration of Titles Act* implies certain covenants against a mortgagor in every mortgage made under the Act. The covenants include payment of the mortgage debt, maintenance and repair of the property, and a right of the mortgagee to enter to inspect the premises at any reasonable time.[23] In addition, s. 1(2) of the *Mortgage Decree*, 1974, implies in every mortgage a covenant against a mortgagor in possession to preserve the value of the property.

---

17 [1961] EA 167 (CA).

18 See, for example, *Barclays Bank* D.C.O. v *Gulu Millers* [1959] EA 540, at 550. Also *Jakana* v *Senkaali* CS No 491 of 1984 (unreported); [1988-90] HCB 167.

19 The section does not expressly mention the power to mortgage. However, it is thought that 'other lawful transactions' include a right to mortgage. Before the *Land Act* was enacted there was no doubt that a *kibanja* could be mortgaged just as mailo land. See, for example, *Matambulire v Kimera* CA No 37 of 1972 (unreported); [1975] HCB 150..

20 CA No 37 of 1972 (unreported).

21 Section 9(5) of the *Land Act*, 1998, implies that the provisions of the *Mortgage Decree* No 17 of 1974, apply to a mortgage of customary land made under the Decree. However, the Decree, as presently worded, only applies to registered and equitable mortgages created over land registered under the *Registration of Titles Act.* See the definition of 'mortgage' and 'the Act' in s. 18 of the Decree. In any case, the Decree only deals with remedies, and not with the procedure for creation of a mortgage.

22 (1952-6) 7 ULR 1.

23 Note that any covenant implied by the Act may be negatived by express agreement of the parties, s. 142, *RTA*.

Where the mortgagor is in breach of any term of the mortgage agreement, the mortgagee may pursue the remedies stipulated in the *Mortgage Decree*. There are four remedies that a mortgagee may pursue under the Decree:

i) action on a personal covenant;
ii) take possession;
iii) appoint a receiver;
iv) sale; and
v) foreclosure.[24]

The remedies are cumulative. Therefore, a mortgagee is free to pursue one or all of them.[25]

i) Action on a personal covenant

This is an action for breach of contract and is not unique to the law of mortgages. If the action is successful, the mortgagee may enforce the judgement against the mortgagor's general assets even though they are not comprised in the mortgage.[26] The action on the personal covenant is not a particularly useful remedy whilst the mortgage is still current. However, if the mortgagee sells the mortgaged land, and the proceeds are not sufficient to discharge the costs of the sale and the mortgage debt, the mortgagee may bring an action against the mortgagor based on the personal covenant to recover the balance of the debt.[27]

ii) Possession

Under s. 6(1) of the *Mortgage Decree*, where a mortgagor is in breach of any covenant, the mortgagee may enter into possession of the mortgaged land for the purpose of realising his or her security. The right of possession is enforceable not only against the mortgagor but also against any person who derived title from the mortgagor subsequent to the mortgage, for example, a lessee and an assignee of the mortgaged land.[28] Prior to taking possession the mortgagee must serve the mortgagor notice of not less than sixty days of his or her intention to enter.[29] The Decree does not state how possession may be effected.[30] It is suggested that the mortgagee takes possession by physically entering and taking over control of the mortgaged land from the mortgagor. Where tenants occupy the mortgaged premises, the mortgagee takes possession of the premises by serving them an unequivocal notice to pay rent directly to the mortgagee.[31]

Where a mortgagee enters into possession he or she by law assumes certain powers and duties. The mortgagee's powers include collecting any income from the mortgaged land, including arrears which the mortgagee would have been entitled to had he or she been in possession from the date of the mortgage.[32] The principle duties of a mortgagee in possession are to account not only for income (whether in cash or in kind) he or she actually receives from the mortgaged property but also that which he or she ought to have received by exercise of due diligence. Any such benefits must be set-off from the debt due.[33] Where the mortgagee uses the mortgaged premises for own personal purposes, for example, as an office, he or she will be held accountable for the market rental

---

24 Section 2 of the *Mortgage Decree*.

25 *Barclays Bank (U) Ltd* v *Northcote and another* C.S. No. 1467 of 1974 (unreported).

26 *Burn, Cheshire & Burn's Modern Law of Real Property* (14th ed, London, Butterworths,1988), p. 655

27 *Rudge* v *Richens* (1873) CP 8 LR 358.

28 Section 6(2) *Mortgage Decree*. But see s. 6(6).

29 Section 6 (1), *Mortgage Decree*. It is submitted that the notice must be served after expiration of the period of default stated in s. 115, *RTA*.

30 Under s. 120, *RTA*, which was repealed by the s. 16 of the Mortgage Decree, possession could be effected either by physical entrance or by receiving rents from tenants, if any.

31 See *Mubiru* v *Uganda Credit & Savings Bank* (1978) HCB 109. In addition, under s. 6(5) of the *Mortgage Decree*, the mortgagee has power to collect any income from the mortgaged property.

32 Section 6 (5) of the *Mortgage Decree*.

33 *Matambulire* v *Kimera* CA No 37 of 1972 (unreported); [1975] HCB 150.

of the property.[34] In addition, the mortgagee is accountable for unreasonable damage or neglect of the property due to his or her negligent act or omission. Despite the responsibilities involved, a mortgagee in possession is not entitled to any remuneration for personally managing the mortgaged land.[35] However, the mortgagee is entitled to reimbursement for the costs of repair and improvements he or she carries out to protect or increase the value of the mortgaged land. To the extent that the expenses incurred exceed the income from the mortgaged land, they become part of the mortgage debt at the same level of priority as the principal debt and earn the same interest.[36]

Due to the heavy responsibilities imposed upon a mortgagee who enters into possession, it is not advisable for a mortgagee to exercise this remedy except as a preliminary step towards selling the mortgaged property.[37] Alternatively, a mortgagee may avoid this responsibility by appointing a receiver to enter into possession.

iii) Appointment of a receiver

A receiver is a person appointed to receive income of the mortgaged land and to use the proceeds to reduce the mortgage debt. A receiver may also be charged with a duty to manage the land by, for example, making necessary repairs or carrying out improvements, where so directed in writing by the mortgagee with the consent of the mortgagor or the court.[38] The mortgagee may appoint a receiver if the power to appoint is expressly reserved in the mortgage agreement. In the absence of such powers, the mortgagee may apply to the court to appoint a receiver.[39] Section 5(4) of the *Mortgage Decree* provides that the appointment of a receiver is null and void unless made in writing and in accordance with the provisions of the section.[40] It is submitted that the power to appoint a receiver does not arise unless the mortgagor is in default for a period of at least one month and fails to make repayments following a written demand notice.[41] Where a mortgaged debt is payable on demand, a written demand for payment is equivalent to notice. In that case the mortgagee may proceed to appoint a receiver without further notice.[42]

Primarily, a receiver is employed to protect the mortgagee's interest. He or she directly receives the proceeds from the land instead of the mortgagor receiving them. After payment of rates, taxes and other outgoings relating to the mortgaged land, the receiver must pay the mortgagee what is due under the mortgage debt and hand over the net balance, if any, to the mortgagor. From a legal point of view, the main advantage to the mortgagee of appointing a receiver is that, although the mortgagee appoints the receiver to protect his or her interest, the receiver acts as an agent of the mortgagor irrespective of any agreement to the contrary.[43] The effect is that the mortgagee is not liable to the mortgagor or secondary mortgagees for the receiver's negligence or wilful misconduct.[44]

---

34 Section 6(4). See also *White* v *City of London Brewery Company* (1889) 42 Ch D 237.

35 Section 6 (4)(d).

36 Section 6(4)(d-e).

37 Section 11 (2) of the *Mortgage Decree.*

38 Section 5 (2), *Mortgage Decree.*

39 Section 3, *Mortgage Decree.*

40 See also *Grindlays Bank (U) Ltd* v *Edward Boazi* CA No 23 of 1992 (Supreme Court).

41 Section 115, *RTA*. By virtue of s. 210A(6) of the *Registration of Titles Act*, if a mortgagee attempts to affect service of a notice by post, but the letter is returned undelivered he or she cannot rely on that posting as constituting service under s. 115. In that case, the mortgagee must either effect personal service or apply to the registrar for directions. (See *Uganda Credit and Savings Bank v Eriyazi Senkuba* [1966] EA 500.

42 Section 116, *RTA*, see also *Grindlays Bank (U) Ltd* v *Edward Boazi* CA 23 of 1992, see facts below.

43 Section 4 (1), *Mortgage Decree.* A receiver appointed by the court is not an agent of the mortgagor or mortgagee, but is an officer of the court to which he or she must account for any income he or she receives, s. 4(2) *Mortgage Decree.*

44 *White* v *Metcalf* [1903] 2 Ch 567. In *Grindlays Bank (U) Ltd* v *Edward Boazi*, CA No 23 of 1992, it was held that a mortgagor was not liable for defaults of a receiver who was improperly appointed.

It is mainly for this reason that mortgagees appoint a receiver instead of entering into possession. The drawback is that a receiver has to be paid a commission for his or her work out of the income of the mortgaged property. Indeed, the receiver's remuneration has priority over any other payment due from the income collected.[45] Therefore, where the property does not generate any income, for example, where the mortgaged land is a residential house occupied by the mortgagor, appointment of a receiver may not be economical except as a step towards the sale of the property.

iv) Power of sale

This is the most important and common remedy for realisation of security under a mortgage agreement. The right to sell may be exercised without recourse to court where such right is expressly reserved in the mortgage agreement. Otherwise, the sale must be conducted with the sanction of the court.[46]

Section 9 of the *Mortgage Decree* provides that if a mortgage agreement allows the mortgagee to sell the land without reference to court, the sale must be conducted by public auction unless the mortgagor and subsequent mortgagees, if any, consent to a sale by private treaty. The power of sale arises if the mortgagor defaults in payment of the mortgage debt, or part thereof, for a continuous period of one month (or such other period as is stipulated in the agreement) and the mortgagor fails to pay after a written notice is served on him or her.[47] However, where there is a provision in the mortgage agreement that the loan is payable on demand,[48] the power of sale arises once demand is made and the mortgagor fails to pay.[49] For example, in the case of *Barclays Bank of Uganda Ltd* v *Livingstone Katende Lutu,*[50] the mortgage agreement provided that the debt was payable on demand and that, in the event of default, the mortgagee has a right to sell the land without a court order. It was held that once demand had been made and the mortgagor defaulted in paying the debt, the bank was entitled to sell without recourse to the court. Given the agreement of the parties, s. 9 of the Mortgage Decree sanctions the power of sale without reference to the court.[51] The court held further that if the mortgagee has the power of sale without a court order, the court has no power to order some other remedy or postpone the sale. The only way the mortgagor could redeem his land was to repay the loan.

The mortgagee's power of sale under s. 9 of the Decree is further illustrated by the case of *Barclays Bank of Uganda Ltd v Livingstone Katende Lutu.*[52] The facts of that case were as follows. The appellant bank lent money to a third party. The respondent mortgaged his land to the bank as security for the guarantee he gave the bank for the repayment of the loan. Under the mortgage agreement, the bank had a right to sell the land if the third party defaulted in payment of the loan. When the third party defaulted, the bank, after serving the third party notice of its intention to sell the mortgaged property, advertised the land for sale by public auction. The respondents applied to the court for an injunction to stop the sale. The trial judge held that, notwithstanding the express provision in the mortgage agreement giving the bank the power of sale, that power could not be exercised without a court order. The judge also found that in view of the discrepancy between the money owed and the value of the property, the respondent would

---

45 Section 5(3)(a), *Mortgage Decree.*

46 See ss. 7 & 9, *Mortgage Decree.*

47 Section 115, *RTA*.

48 Many mortgage agreements, though they allow the mortgagor a period within which to repay the loan by periodic instalments, contain a proviso giving the mortgagee a right to demand payment of the full amount at any time.

49 Section 116, *RTA*. See also *Barclays Bank of Uganda Ltd* v *Livingstone Katende Lutu* CA 22 of 1993 (unreported).

50 *Ibid.*

51 Section 9 does not actually state that where a power of sale is reserved the mortgagee may sell without sanction of the court. The provision seems merely to deal with the manner of conducting a mortgage sale.

52 CA No 22 of 1993 (unreported Supreme Court of Uganda).

suffer irreparable loss if his land were sold. On appeal to the Supreme Court, it was held that s. 9 of the Decree makes it clear that if under a mortgage agreement the mortgagee has a right to sell, upon default the mortgagee may sell the mortgaged property without judicial sanction. Manyindo DCJ, Odoki and Platt JJ.SC, in a their joint judgement reiterated the proposition that where a mortgagee has the power of sale without judicial sanction, the 'mortgagor's right to redeem the land is confined to repayment of the loan'. The High Court's decision was accordingly overturned.

Where the mortgage agreement does not empower the mortgagee to sell without recourse to the court, the mortgagee must seek a court order to sell the property.[53] Section 7 (1), *Mortgage Decree*, provides that a mortgagee may apply to the court to 'foreclose' the mortgagor's right to redeem at any time after the breach of any covenant *to pay*.[54] It is submitted that, unless the debt is payable on demand, an application for foreclosure cannot be entertained unless the mortgagor is in default for at least one month and has failed to pay after a written demand.[55] When the application is made, the court will assess the amount due and fix a date, which must not exceed a period of six months from the date of default, within which payment should be made.[56] If the mortgagor fails to pay by the prescribed date, the court must order the mortgagor's right to redeem foreclosed and grant the mortgagee a right to sell the property.[57]

A mortgage sale consequent upon an order of foreclosure must be conducted in accordance with the provisions of s. 8 of the *Mortgage Decree*. Section 8(1) provides that the sale must be by public auction unless the mortgagor and all subsequent mortgagees of whom the mortgagee has notice of at the date of the foreclosure order agree to a sale by private treaty and the court approves the terms of the sale.[58] By s. 8(2) it is further provided that the sale must not take place until after at least thirty days have expired from the date of the foreclosure order.[59] Presumably, the object of this requirement is to prevent the mortgagee from rushing into disposing of the land without sufficient advertisement and preparation. Besides, the delay allows a cooling-off period to allow the mortgagor and mortgagee (and other interested parties) to attain a mutually agreeable alternative arrangement to a foreclosure sale. It should be stressed, though, that unless the mortgagee voluntarily agrees, it seems that a foreclosure order cannot be re-opened to allow the mortgagor to redeem. Finally, s. 8(3) requires the mortgagee to give reasonable notice (not less than thirty days prior to the sale) of the date and place of the sale to the mortgagor and all subsequent mortgagees of whom the selling mortgagee has notice at the date of the foreclosure order. The object here appears to be to give interested parties a chance to attend and observe or participate in the bidding or seek an injunction if there has been an impropriety.[60] Also, as we have suggested, they may come up with some alternative arrangements agreeable to the mortgagee. Failure to notify the mortgagor or subsequent mortgagee does not render the sale void. However, the selling mortgagee would be held liable for any loss suffered by the mortgagor or any subsequent mortgagee as a consequence of the omission to notify them.[61]

---

53 This was also the position at common law. See Megarry & Wade *The Law of Real Property* (5th ed, 1984), p. 936.

54 The fact that the provision only mentions breach of covenant to pay, suggests that a mortgagee cannot apply for foreclosure for breach of other covenants. Under s. 117, *RTA*, (repealed by s. 16(b) of the *Mortgage Decree*), a mortgagee had a right to sell for breach of covenant to pay or for breach of any other covenant.

55 Sections 115 and 116, *RTA*. Also see *Sajabi* v *Amreliwalla and Wamala* [1956] 22 EACA 71.

56 Section 7(2).

57 Section 7(3).

58 Section 8(1) of the *Mortgage Decree*.

59 See also s. 8(3).

60 Section 9(5) provides that the mortgagor and subsequent mortgagees are not precluded from buying the mortgaged land at the sale.

61 Section 8(4).

Duties of the seller

The power of sale is given to the mortgagee to realise his or her security in the event of default. Once the power of sale has accrued, the mortgagee is entitled to exercise it for his or her own benefit at a time of their choosing. It has been established in several cases that, in exercising this power, the mortgagee does not act as a trustee for the mortgagor.[62] Consequently, the mortgagee is entitled to look after his or her own interests where they may conflict with those of the mortgagor. For example, in *Cuckmere Brick Co Ltd* v *Mutual Finance Co Ltd*,[63] the property was allegedly sold below its 'market' value at a badly attended auction. In an action for damages against the mortgagee counsel for the mortgagor submitted that the mortgagee should have postponed the sale because in the circumstances it was not appropriate to sell. Lord Justice Salmon, in delivering his judgement said that the mortgagee has no duty to speculate as to the most appropriate time to sell:

> It matters not that the moment may be unpropitious and that by waiting a higher price could be obtained. He has the right to realise his security by turning it into money when he likes. Nor, in my view, is there anything to prevent a mortgagee from accepting the best bid he can get at an auction, even though the auction is badly attended and the bidding exceptionally low. Providing none of those adverse factors is due to any fault of the mortgagee, he can do as he likes. If the mortgagee's interests, as he sees them, conflict with those of the mortgagor, the mortgagee can give preference to his own interests, which of course he could not do were he a trustee of the power of sale for the mortgagor.[64]

Neither the *Registration of Titles Act* nor the *Mortgage Decree* imposes any duty of care on a mortgagee in exercising his or her powers of sale. However, the common law imposes on a selling mortgagee a duty to act in good faith and with care.[65] The duty of care is based on Lord Atkins' well-known 'neighbour' principle espoused in *Donoghue* v *Stevenson*.[66] The proximity between the mortgagee and the mortgagor gives rise to a duty on the mortgagee to take reasonable care to obtain the true market value of the land at the moment the mortgagee chooses to sell.[67] One of the precautions that needs to be taken by a mortgagee is to ensure that the property is properly advertised before the sale. For example, in *Mubiru* v *Uganda Credit & Savings Bank*,[68] the mortgagee advertised in the newspapers the mortgage sale of the suit property by public auction simply as 'a parcel of land being 4.26 acres'. The advertisement omitted to mention that the land had been developed and a permanent house had been constructed thereon. It was held that failure to state these facts in the advertisement was negligence because the property could have been valued differently. In *Sajabi* v *Amreliwalla and Wamala*, Bacon JA observed that, if a mortgage sale is by public auction, which is duly advertised and to all appearances properly conducted, *prima facie*, it is assumed that the mortgagee's dual duty to sell in good faith and with reasonable care was fulfilled. But where the mortgagee sells by private treaty, it is incumbent upon him or her to make particularly sure that the mortgagor's interests are amply protected.[69]

Where the selling mortgagee fails to take reasonable precautions or to observe preliminary statutory requirements prior to the sale, the mortgagor and any interested party may seek a temporary

---

62 *Mubiru* v *Uganda Credit & Savings Bank* CS 567/65; (1978) HCB 109; *Sajabi* v *Amreliwalla and Wamala* [1956] 22 EACA 71; *Cuckmere Brick Co Ltd* v *Mutual Finance Co Ltd* [1971] Ch 948.

63 [1971] Ch 948.

64 *Ibid*, at 965.

65 *Sajabi* v *Amreliwalla and Wamala* [1956] 22 EACA 71. *Mubiru* v *Uganda Credit & Savings Bank* (1978) HCB 109.

66 [1932] AC 562.

67 *Cuckmere Brick Co Ltd* v *Mutual Finance Ltd*, was cited with approval in *Mubiru* v *Uganda Credit & Savings Bank* (1978) HCB 109.

68 (1978) HCB 109.

69 [1955] 22 EACA 71, at 77, See also Briggs Ag. VP, at 73. As we have seen, sale by private treaty is prohibited unless all interested parties consent, s. 8 (1) & 9 of the *Mortgage Decree*.

injunction to restrain the sale from proceeding. The granting of an interim injunction is of course at the discretion of the court. Normally, the court will not grant an injunction unless an applicant presents a *prima facie* case that the respondent's act or omission is wrongful and that there is a probability that the applicant will prevail on the merits of the case at full trial. Secondly, the injunction will not normally be granted unless the applicant might otherwise suffer irreparable injury, which would not be adequately compensated by the award of damages. Thirdly, if the court is in doubt, it will decide an application on a balance of probabilities.[70] The court may in addition demand that the applicant pay a sum of money into court and or undertake to pay damages to the respondent in the event that the action fails.

Where the sale is completed, the most common remedy available to an aggrieved mortgagor is to institute proceedings for compensation for loss suffered as a result of the unlawful mortgage sale.[71] Damages are awarded in the usual way. For example, in *Mubiru* v *Uganda Credit & Savings Bank*,[72] the mortgagor was awarded damages calculated as the difference between the true market value of the property and the value realised from the improperly conducted mortgage sale. In *Sajabi* v *Amreliwalla and Wamala*,[73] the court found that the mortgagee sold the land by private treaty without serving the mortgagor the statutory notice and conspired with the purchaser to sell the land below its market value. The court awarded damages against the mortgagee and the purchaser, measured as the value of the land at the time of the unlawful sale, less the amount of money due on the mortgage at that date.

Protection of purchasers

Under s 117 of the *Registration of Titles Act*, which was repealed by s. 16(b), *Mortgage Decree*, the title of a purchaser at a mortgage sale was not impeachable merely because the selling mortgagee's power to sell had not arisen or that the sale was otherwise irregular. The section provided further that a purchaser had no obligation to inquire whether or not the condition of sale had been complied with. In contrast, section 8(7) of the *Mortgage Decree,* provides that the title of a purchaser acquired at a mortgage sale consequent upon an order of foreclosure shall not be impeached on the ground that the *order for the sale* was improperly or irregularly made. The scope of this provision is not very clear. It would seem that the provision only protects the purchaser where the court erred in making a foreclosure order. For instance, the purchaser's title will not be affected in a situation where, after the sale, the court overturns a foreclosure order made by a district tribunal on the grounds that the order was misconceived. However, it is submitted that, unlike the repealed s. 117, of the *Registration of Titles Act*, s. 8(7) of the Decree does not protect a purchaser's title where, for example, the sale was not properly advertised or otherwise conducted in a manner which constituted a breach of the selling mortgagee's duty of care to the mortgagor. Nor does it protect the purchaser's title if an irregularity occurred in a mortgage sale which was conducted without judicial sanction. Nonetheless, it is submitted that even in such cases once the transfer is registered under the *Registration of Titles Act,* in the absence of fraud, a purchaser acquires an indefeasible title under section 61 of that Act.[74]

Proceeds of sale

Section 10(1) of the Decree prescribes the priority in which the proceeds from any mortgage sale are to be distributed. First to be paid are the expenses properly incurred or incidental to the sale. Next to be paid are all sums due to the selling mortgagee and any other encumbrances with the same

---

70 *Giella* v *Cassman Brown and Co Ltd* [1973] EA 358 at 360, per Spry VP.

71 Section 8 (4), *Mortgage Decree* provides that where the breach is failure to notify the mortgagor of the sale, the only remedy for the mortgagor is damages.

72 CS No 567 of 1965; (1978) HCB 109.

73 [1956] 22 EACA 71.

74 See *Sajabi v Amreliwalla and Wamala*, Ibid. See also the discussion of indefeasibility in Chapter 5.

order of priority. The remainder of the proceeds, if any, is paid to the mortgagor. The court has the power to order, in the case of a sale consequent upon a foreclosure, that the proceeds be deposited into court for distribution, though the court has no power to alter the prescribed order of distribution.[75] To avoid liability, in most cases it would be prudent for the mortgagee, after paying himself or herself, to deposit the remainder of the proceeds into court.

It should be noted that if the proceeds are not enough to pay for the costs of the sale and to discharge the mortgage debt, that is not the end of the matter. The mortgagee can bring action as an unsecured creditor against the mortgagor for the shortfall based on a personal covenant to pay.[76] In practice, the action is likely to be pointless because the mortgaged land would usually be the mortgagor's only worthwhile asset.

Completion of a mortgage sale

A mortgage sale transaction is completed by registration of the purchaser as proprietor of the land. The purchaser takes the land free from all interests that were created after the selling mortgagee's interest was registered. But the purchaser takes the land subject to any interest which had priority to that mortgage.[77] For example, assume that the land was subject to three mortgages: A, B and C, registered in that order. If B caused the land to be sold, the purchaser would take the land free of B and C's mortgages but subject to A's mortgage unless the latter were paid off.

v) Foreclosure

At common law, if the mortgagor failed to pay the mortgage debt by the agreed date, the mortgagee became the absolute owner of the mortgaged land, irrespective of whether the value of the land far exceeded the money owed. However, the Court of Equity intervened and allowed the mortgagor to redeem, even after the contractual date had long expired, on payment of the mortgage debt and costs.[78] To prevent the mortgagor from redeeming the land, the mortgagee had to seek a judicial order for foreclosure. Thus, foreclosure was the name given to the process whereby the mortgagor's equitable right to redeem was extinguished and the mortgagee was left as the absolute owner of the land both at common law and in equity.[79] By a foreclosure order, the Court of Equity effectively closed its doors in the mortgagor's face.[80] In practice, when the mortgagee applied for a foreclosure order, the court allowed the mortgagor a period of six months within which to pay the money due with interest. At the expiration of the six months, on default of payment, the mortgagee would take possession of the land and the mortgagor's right to the land would end.[81]

The remedy of foreclosure was expressly recognised under s. 130 of the *Registration of Titles Act* as applicable to mortgages created under the Act.[82] However, since s.130 was repealed by s. 16(b) of the *Mortgage Decree*, it is submitted that the only remedies available to a mortgagee of land registered under the Act are those set out in the Decree.[83] Accordingly, the equitable remedy of foreclosure is no longer available to a registered mortgagee.

Remedies of equitable mortgagees

In *Barclays Bank (U) Ltd* v *Northcote and another*,[84] Ssekandi Ag J observed that while s. 138 of the *Registration of Titles Act*, provides for the creation of equitable mortgages by deposit of title

---

75 Section 10 (3).

76 *Rudge* v *Richens* (1873) LR 8 CP 588.

77 Section 8 (6) of the *Mortgage Decree*.

78 *Campbell* v *Holyland* [1877] 7 Ch D 166.

79 The expression foreclosure as used here differs from the *Mortgage Decree*.

80 Megarry & Wade, *The Law of Real Property*, supra, p. 933.

81 *Matambulire v Kimera* CA No 37 of 1972 (unreported); [1975] HCB 150.

82 *Barclays Bank D.C.O.* v *Gulu Millers Ltd* [1959] EA 540 at 550.

83 See also *Barclays Bank (U) Ltd v Northcote and another* CS No 1467 of 1974 (unreported).

84 CS No 1467 of 1974 (unreported).

deeds as security, neither the *Registration of Titles Act* nor the *Mortgage Decree* makes provision for the remedies available to an equitable mortgagee. Accordingly, his Honour felt compelled to look 'elsewhere' for such remedies. The issue had already been canvassed in the judgement of Sir Kenneth O'Connor P, in *Barclays Bank D.C.O.* v *Gulu Millers Ltd Limited,*[85] which was delivered well before the *Mortgage Decree* was enacted. There, Sir Kenneth held that the law applicable to equitable mortgages is to be found in the doctrines of equity. Following this judgement, Ssekandi Ag J held that:

> It would appear that the difference between an equitable mortgage and a legal mortgage as regards remedies is that whereas a legal mortgagee may realise his security under a mortgage by exercising most of the statutory powers conferred upon him without recourse to the courts, an equitable mortgagee must of necessity apply to the courts for exercise of any of these powers. In accordance with the principles laid down in *Barclays Bank* v *Gulu Millers Ltd* ... the court may avail to an equitable mortgagee all the remedies available to a legal mortgagee. The remedies available to a legal mortgagee are now set out in the *Mortgage Decree* 1974 and these are in my view equally available to an equitable mortgagee subject to certain considerations set out in [that] judgement.

Ssekandi Ag J stated that the appropriate procedure to follow for an equitable mortgagee seeking to realise his or her security, was in the first instance to sue the mortgagor and obtain an order for an account of the outstanding mortgage debt. Then he or she should seek a declaration that he or she is entitled to a charge on the land comprised in the certificate of title referred to in the memorandum of deposit to secure the amount outstanding plus interest and costs. The declaration should be followed by an application that if payment is not made within a specified time, the mortgagee may realise the security by pursuing any or all of the remedies provided for in the *Mortgage Decree*.[86]

Remedies of mortgagee of customary land and tenancy by occupancy

In *Jakana v Senkaali,*[87] it was held that the remedies under the *Mortgage Decree*, apply only where a mortgage is created under the *Registration of Titles Act.* In that case the plaintiff advanced to the defendant a sum of money. As security for the loan the defendant deposited the title deeds of his land with the plaintiff's advocate. Under the terms of the contract, if the defendant failed to repay the money within one year from the date of the contract, the plaintiff was entitled to sell the land. When the defendant defaulted, the plaintiff brought proceedings for a court order that the defendant pays the outstanding amount or, in the alternative, that the land be transferred into the plaintiff's name. It was held that there was a binding contract and that the plaintiff was entitled to judgement for the amount of money claimed. With respect to the mortgage, it was held that for a mortgagee to enforce his or her remedies under the *Mortgage Decree*, the mortgage had to be registered under the *Registration of Titles Act,* as either a legal mortgage or equitable mortgage. In the instant case, there was no evidence that the mortgage was registered under the Act.[88] Therefore, the plaintiff could not rely on s. 2 of the Decree to realise his security under the mortgage. It follows from this judgement that the mortgagees' remedies under the Decree do not apply to a mortgage

85 [1959] EA 540.

86 For comments on this case see Bossa, 'Comments on recent legislation: The Mortgage Decree No 17 of 1974' (1975) 1 & 2 *The Uganda Law Focus* 171.

87 CS No 491 of 1984 (unreported); [1988-90] HCB 167.

88 With respect, it is submitted that the judge erred when he said that an equitable mortgage must be 'registered' under the Act. As we have seen, an equitable mortgage is created by deposit of a certificate of title with the mortgagee and the latter must lodge a caveat to protect the mortgage, s.138,*RTA*. It seems in the instant case that the plaintiff did not lodge a caveat. The learned judge did not cite the case of *Barclays Bank of (U) Ltd v Northcote*, supra. But it would seem that the two cases are distinguishable on the ground that the purported mortgage in *Jakana v Senkaali,* was not protected by a caveat.

over customary land or to a mortgage of a tenancy by occupancy.[89] In that case, the mortgagee must resort to the common law for his or her remedies. It is submitted that the common law remedies are the same as in the Decree,[90] except that the mortgagee will require a judicial order to realise his or her security.[91] In addition, the mortgagee may enforce a foreclosure, which, as we have seen, is no longer available under the Decree.

Clearly, there is a need for the legislature to harmonise the law of mortgages. In particular the *Mortgage Decree* needs to be amended to bring it into line with the *Land Act*. For example, at present it is not clear as to the notices and their length that a mortgagee of customary land or tenancy by occupancy must give prior to enforcing a sale. Since the Decree does not apply to such mortgages, the mortgagee is not bound to follow the procedure prescribed by the Decree. However, it is suggested that the mortgagee should, as much as possible, use the procedure as a guideline.

Discharge of a mortgage by payment

We have so far considered situations where the mortgagor defaults in payment of the mortgage debt. In practice, most mortgages are discharged by payment within the prescribed period. Once the mortgagor pays off the mortgage debt, the mortgagee signs a discharge form, which is set out in the Twelfth Schedule of the *Registration of Titles Act*. Upon its registration, the mortgage is discharged and the land ceases to be subject to the mortgage.[92]

EQUITY'S PROTECTION OF A MORTGAGOR

Equity's protection of a mortgagor is summed up in the maxim 'once a mortgage always a mortgage'. This maxim applies in two broad ways: the test for a mortgage is substance and not form and that there should be 'no clogs' on the equity of redemption. The former means that whether a transaction is a mortgage or some other transaction it is not a question of form but of substance. Thus, if the parties enter into a contract of sale of land which in essence is a mortgage, in equity it is regarded as a mortgage and all the consequences of a mortgage will follow.[93] No clogs on the equity of redemption means that the court will not permit any attempt by the mortgagee to exclude the mortgagor's right to redeem his or her property. Lord Lindley, in *Samuel v Jarrah Timber & Wood Paving Corporation*, explained the maxim thus:[94]

> The doctrine 'Once a mortgage always a mortgage' means that no contract between a mortgagor and a mortgagee made at the time of the mortgage and as part of the mortgage transaction, or, in other words, as one of the terms of the loan, can be valid if it prevents the mortgagor from getting back his property on paying off what is due on his security. Any bargain which has that effect is invalid, and is inconsistent with the transaction being a mortgage.

Equity's intervention was justified on the ground that mortgages tend to be entered into by needy people who would accept whatever terms 'crafty' creditors may impose upon them.[95] For example, in *Matambulire v Yosefu Kimera*,[96] the plaintiff, in desperation to go on a pilgrimage to Mecca,

---

89 See also the definition of 'mortgage' and 'the Act' in s. 18 of the Decree.

90 Alternatively, the court could apply the same remedies by statutory analogy. See *Barclays Bank (U) Ltd v Northcote and another* CS No 1467 of 1974.

91 *Ibid.*

92 Section 134, *RTA*.

93 See, e.g., *Grangeside Properties Ltd* v *Collingwood Securities Ltd et al* [1964] 1 WLR 139. See also *Matambulire* v *Kimera* CA No 37 of 1972 (unreported); [1975] HCB 150.

94 [1904] AC 323 at 329. This case was cited with approval in *Matambulire* v *Yozefu Kimera, ibid.*

95 *Samuel v Jarrah Timber & Wood Paving Corporation*, *Ibid*, at 327, per Lord Macnaghten. However, His Lordship cautioned against judicial intervention to defeat bargains freely entered into by persons dealing at arms' length.

96 CA 37 of 1972 (unreported).

mortgaged his land to the defendant on condition that if the plaintiff failed to pay off the loan within a specified period the defendant would become the absolute owner of the land. After the contractual date for payment had expired, the defendant claimed ownership of the land and rejected the plaintiff's subsequent attempts to redeem. It was held that the plaintiff was entitled to redeem until his right to do so was foreclosed by order of court or the land was otherwise disposed of in a mortgage sale. Similarly, a clause in a mortgage agreement that gives a mortgagee an option to purchase the mortgaged property is a clog because it deprives the mortgagor of his right to redeem.[97]

A clause in a mortgage contract may provide that the mortgage shall not be redeemed earlier than, for example, ten years from the date of the contract.[98] Where the mortgagor seeks to redeem earlier a question may arise whether such a clause is a clog on the equity of redemption. The question might be answered by reference to two English authorities, which are often cited in this regard. In *Fairclough* v *Swan Brewery Company Limited*,[99] the applicant/mortgagor had a lease over a hotel for a period of seventeen years. He mortgaged his lease to the respondent (which was a brewery company). The mortgage was subject to the condition that the defendant should not redeem earlier than six weeks before his lease had expired and that during the continuance of the mortgage only beer brewed by the plaintiff should be sold on the premises. The defendant sought an early redemption so that he could be released from the restriction to sell only the plaintiff's beer. The issue was whether a clause postponing redemption was a clog on the equity of redemption. The Privy Council held that the clause was a clog because the right to redeem was illusory or valueless. Lord Macnaghten explained the Privy Council's reasons as follows:[100]

> The learned counsel on behalf of the respondents admitted, as he was bound to admit, that a mortgage cannot be made irredeemable. That is plainly forbidden. Is there any difference between forbidding and permitting it, if the permission is a mere pretence? Here the provision for redemption is nugatory. The incumbrance on the lease the subject of the mortgage according to the letter of the bargain falls to be discharged before the lease terminates, but at the time when it is on the very point of expiring, when redemption can be of no advantage to the mortgagor even if he should be so fortunate to get his deeds back before the actual termination of the lease. For all practical purposes this mortgage is irredeemable. It was obviously meant to be irredeemable.

The above case should be compared with *Knightsbridge Estate Trust Limited* v *Byrne and others.*[101] In this case, a mortgage provided for the repayment of the principal and interest by eighty half-yearly instalments spread over a period of forty years. In view of falling interest rates, the mortgagor sought to redeem early in order to take advantage of a loan elsewhere on better terms. The mortgagor sought a declaration that postponement of redemption for a period of forty years was unreasonable because of its length, and that it was entitled to redeem at any time by serving a six-month notice. It was held that there was no rule of law that postponement of redemption *per se* or for an unreasonable period is a clog on the equity of redemption. Following *Fairclough*, the court said that postponement is a clog if it subsists so as to make the equity of redemption illusory. However, Green MR added that postponement may be one of the factors which the court may take into account in deciding overall whether or not a mortgage agreement should be set aside on the ground that its terms are oppressive and unconscionable.[102] On the facts of this case, the court

---

97 *Samuel v Jarrah Timber & Wood Paving Corporation* [1904] AC 323. It is not a clog if the option is granted in a separate agreement, see *Reeves v Lisle* [1902] AC 461.

98 The advantage of such a clause from the mortgagee's viewpoint is that it provides the mortgagee a secure investment at a favourable interest rate (subject of course to inflation). It has been held that if there is no express provision precluding early redemption, the mortgagor is entitled to redeem at any time, see *G A Investments Pty Ltd* v *Standard Insurance Co Ltd* [1964] WAR 264 at 267.

99 [1912] AC 565 (PC).

100 *Ibid*, at 570.

101 [1939] Ch D 441.

102 *Ibid*, at 457.

found that the parties were of equal bargaining strength, the mortgagor freely accepted the terms, and it could not use the court to breach its contract.

On the basis of these two authorities, it would seem that postponement of the date of redemption by itself is not a ground for judicial intervention unless in the circumstances of a particular case it renders the right to redeem illusory.

Collateral advantage

A collateral advantage in this context refers to any additional benefit to payment of the secured debt and interest which accrues to a mortgagee under a mortgage agreement. For example, in *Fairclough v Swan Brewery Company Limited*, the collateral advantage was the monopoly for the marketing of the mortgagee's product. Prior to the nineteenth entury, the traditional view of the courts in England was that the essence of a mortgage was to secure money lent; therefore any other advantage foreign to this basic object was void.[103] Gradually, this rule was relaxed in line with the subsequent economic developments and the notion of freedom of contract. As a result, more recent cases support the proposition that a collateral advantage is not necessarily a clog on the equity of redemption, especially where the advantage terminates upon redemption.[104]

Other grounds for judicial intervention

The courts have inherent powers to intervene in mortgage agreements, as with any other contract, on the ground that the agreement is in restraint of trade. It is an established common law rule that a contract that operates as an unreasonable restraint of trade is invalid as being contrary to public policy.[105] For example, a provision in a mortgage agreement that for a given period the mortgagor shall only deal in the mortgagee's products may be challenged on grounds of unreasonable restraint of trade. Whether indeed the restraint is unreasonable will depend on several factors including the duration of the restraint and the reasons for it.[106]

Equity may also give relief against terms in any contractual transaction if they are oppressive or unconscionable.[107] It is important to note that the term 'unconscionable' means more than unreasonableness. The court will not intervene in a mortgage transaction merely because the terms are unreasonable, because it is up to the parties to decide what they consider to be reasonable.[108] It will only intervene if the terms are shown to be morally reprehensible, especially where one party seeks unfairly to take advantage of another. For example, in the High Court of Tanzania in the case of *Juma* v *Habibu*,[109] a mortgagor sought a declaration that 60 percent interest rate per annum was harsh and unconscionable. Mapigano Ag J held that the interest rate was evidently unconscionable and extortionate and the respondent had not adduced evidence to show that it was not. In deciding what constitutes excessive rates His Honour refused to follow an earlier case[110] that stated that a contract rate of interest of greater than 48 per cent per annum is *prima facie* excessive. His Honour

---

[103] *Jennings* v *Ward* (1705) 2 Vern S20.

[104] Compare *Biggs v Hoddinott* (1898) 2 Ch 307, and *Noakes and Co Ltd v Rice* [1902] AC 24. However, in *G and C Kreglinger v New Patagonia Meat Storage Co Ltd* [1914] AC 25, the Privy Council upheld a collateral advantage that was stipulated to continue after redemption.

[105] *Giella* v *Cassman Brown and Co Ltd* [1973] EA 358.

[106] See *Esso Petroleum Co Ltd* v *Harper's Garage (Stourport) Ltd* [1968] AC 269.

[107] *Knightsbridge Estate Trust Limited* v *Byrne and others* [1939] Ch D 441.

[108] *Ibid.*

[109] [1975] EA 108 (T).

[110] *Mohamed Mohamedi* v *Athman Shante* [1960] EA 1062.

reasoned that having regard to the prevailing social, political and economic climate of Tanzania where 'the eradication of exploitation is declared policy and where unfair play is frowned on, it was not only interest above 48 percent which may be regarded as exploitative.'[111] Mapigano Ag. J opined that in the prevailing circumstances of Tanzania any interest rate above 20 percent per annum 'could perfectly cause the court to raise its eyebrows and require the party who claims it to prove that it is proper and fair in the circumstances of the case as a whole.'[112]

It should be stressed that all the surrounding circumstances will be considered before the court intervenes in a mortgage agreement on equitable grounds.

---

[111] *Ibid*, at 111.

[112] *Ibid*. Section 13(1) of the *Mortgage Decree*, 1974 gives the minister power to fix from time to time the rate of interest chargeable in any mortgage transaction. To date this power has not been exercised.

8

Servitudes over Land

INTRODUCTION

This chapter deals with the law governing 'servitudes'. The term 'servitude' in Roman law refers to rights of use of another's land in a specified way. The rights considered are: easements, profit *à prendre*, restrictive covenants, customary rights, and licence. With the exception of a licence, the rest of these rights constitute interests in land and, subject to the principle of indefeasibility, are enforceable against whoever is the landowner.

EASEMENTS

An easement is a right attached to a particular piece of land that entitles the owner of that land either to use the land of another person in a particular manner or to restrict that other person's use of his or her land to a certain extent.[1] The land to which the right is attached is called the 'dominant' land and that over which the right is exercised is the 'servient' land. For instance, suppose that A and B are adjoining plots and that the owner of plot A has a right to use a driveway over B's land to reach a public road, that right of way is an easement. Plot A is the dominant land and plot B is the servient land.

Essential features

An easement is an interest in land and, subject to the principle of indefeasibility, is enforceable against any proprietor of the servient land.[2] A right over another person's land does not become an easement merely because the parties said so. It must satisfy certain essential features of an easement prescribed under the general law. These are:

(i) there must be in existence a dominant and a servient land;
(ii) the right must accommodate the dominant land;
(iii) the dominant and servient land must not be owned and occupied by the same person; and
(iv) the right must be capable of forming the subject matter of a grant.

Dominant and servient land

An easement cannot exist in 'gross'. This means that a right cannot be an easement unless it is connected with a dominant land that belongs to the person to whom the right is given.[3] The object of granting the right must be to benefit the use of the grantee's land and not the grantee independently of ownership of land. For example, if X, owner of certain mailo land, gives Y, owner of neighbouring land, permission to use a footpath on her land in order to reach a public road, the right of way is an easement. Suppose X gives the same permission to W. If the latter does not own any land at the material time, the right of way is not an easement but a mere personal licence.[4] A public right of way is not an easement precisely because the right is dedicated to the public at large irrespective of connection with any dominant land. In the case of *Makumbi (Mrs E) & another* v *Puran Singh Ghana & another*,[5] Bennett J said that a plea that a certain road used by members of the public was

---

1 E H Burn, *Cheshire and Burn's Modern Law of Real Property* (14th ed., London, Butterworths, 1988), p. 490.

2 See below.

3 *Makumbi (Mrs E) & another* v *Puran Singh Ghana* & another [1962] EA 331.

4 *Hill v Tupper* (1866) 2 H & C 121, for the significance of the distinction, see 'licence' below.

5 [1962] EA 331 at 333.

a 'customary easement' was unfortunate since an easement enjoyed by the public at large was unknown to law.[6]

The requirement for a dominant land may be excused by statute. For instance, under the *Water Statute*, 1995, the Director of Water Development has the power to create an easement over a person's land for carrying water, drainage or waste under, through or over that land to another person's land.[7] The Act does not require the Water Authority to own the land to be benefited by such easement.

Easement must accommodate the dominant land

A right granted is not an easement unless it confers a benefit on the dominant land or some activity connected therewith, and is reasonably necessary for the better enjoyment of that land. For an easement to accommodate the dominant land, the servient land should be close enough to the dominant land to confer a practical benefit on it, though this does not necessarily mean that they must be adjoining. A classical illustration of this requirement is the case of *Re: Ellenborough Park*.[8] A developer subdivided a block of land into small plots, which they sold to various persons. They left out an inner portion of the block, known as 'Ellenborough Park', to be maintained as a pleasure ground for the full enjoyment, at all times, by the owners of the surrounding plots in common with each other, subject to contribution for its maintenance. During the Second World War, the government requisitioned the park so that the surrounding landowners could not use it. The government paid a yearly compensation rent and an amount for dilapidation. The respective owners of the plots, all of whom were successors in title of the original owners, claimed a share of the compensation money on the basis that they had an easement over the park.[9]

Against their claim, it was contended that the right granted was not an easement but a mere licence granted to the original purchasers. This contention was partly based on the argument that there was not sufficient connection between the right granted to enjoy the park for pleasure and relaxation and the ordinary use of the applicants' land, which was the alleged dominant land.[10] The issue was whether the right accommodated and served the property in question. The court held that whether or not a connection exists between the right granted and the normal enjoyment of the alleged dominant land is mainly a question of fact, which depends on the nature of the land and the right granted. The fact that a right enhances the value of the land, though relevant, was not conclusive; it must be shown that the right was connected with the normal enjoyment of that property. On the facts of the case, the court held that there was sufficient connection because residential property is always improved in character by the availability of a garden and that a garden is a normal attribute of a house. The fact that it was a 'collective garden' was not to be material. However, the court limited its finding to houses neighbouring the Ellenborough Park and not houses which were at considerable distance from the park.[11]

The dominant and servient land must not be owned or occupied by the same person

It is a requirement for an easement that the dominant and servient land must be owned and or occupied by different persons.[12] The reason is an easement is a right exercised over another person's land for the benefit of one's land. Where an owner of *Whiteacre* and *Blackacre* passes over *Whiteacre* to reach *Blackacre* he or she is not exercising a right of way in respect of *Whiteacre*, but rather making use of his or her land to get from one part of it to another.[13] But an easement may

---

6 *Ibid*, at 332-33.

7 Section 36.

8 [1956] 3 All ER 667.

9 If they were the original purchasers, they would have based their claim on contract or licence.

10 The rest of the respondents' argument is discussed below.

11 See also another classical case *Hill v Tupper* [1861-73] All ER 696.

12 *Re: Ellenborough Park* [1956] 3 All ER 667.

13 *Roe v Siddons* (1888) 22 QB D 224 at 236.

be created in respect of land owned by the same person where different persons occupy the 'dominant' and 'servient' land. For example, a landlord can reserve an easement of way over part of the land occupied by a tenant for the benefit of the land he or she retains.

The right must be capable of forming the subject matter of a grant

This requirement embraces several things. Firstly, it means that there must be a capable grantor and a capable grantee. For example, a statutory corporation with no capacity to grant an easement cannot grant an easement.[14] Secondly, it means that the right granted must be capable of reasonable definition. For instance, a right of privacy or a right to a view is incapable of being an easement because it is too wide.[15] Thirdly, the right granted must be within the general nature of rights capable of existing as easements. Though the list of easements capable of being created is never closed, it is customary for easements to fall under one of the well-known categories: right of way, to light, to support, and to water. Newer rights to be recognised as easements include right to a tenant to use a toilet in a flat occupied by a third party;[16] a right to store goods on land;[17] a right to park a car in a defined area;[18] and a right to have a fence maintained by an adjoining owner.[19]

In contrast, the courts have refused to recognise as an easement a right of privacy. For example, in *Hansraj Thakkar* v *The Vanik Mahajan*,[20] the plaintiff and defendant owned adjoining properties, which for over sixty years were separated by a wall. The defendant renovated his house and installed two windows in the wall overlooking the plaintiff's property. The plaintiff brought proceedings complaining that the installation of the windows in the wall interfered with his privacy. He claimed that since the disputed wall had been in existence for over sixty years as a blank wall facing his property, a right of privacy had been attached to the property by prescription. It was held that English law does not recognise any easement of prospect or privacy. Other rights held as incapable of constituting an easement include a right that obliges the owner of the servient land to spend money;[21] and a right to exclusive use of a room.[22]

Creation of easements

Easements may be created by statute, express grant, or reservation and by implied reservation or grant. In addition, easements may be created by way of necessity, implication from the parties' agreement and by prescription.

Easement by statute

A statute may authorise, usually, a public authority to create easements for carrying out their activities. For example, as we have seen, the Director of Water Development has the power to create an easement over a person's land for the purpose of carrying water under or over that land to another person's land.[23] Easements created by statutes need not have all the essential

---

14 *National Guarantee Manure Co* v *Donald* (1859) 4 H & N 8.

15 *Browne* v *Flower* [1911] 1 Ch 219. Compare with the right of full enjoyment of the park, which was held to be an easement in *Re: Ellenborough Park* [1956] 3 All ER 667.

16 *Miller* v *Encer Products Ltd* [1956] Ch 304.

17 *Southern Nigeria* v *John Holt & Co Ltd* [1915] AC 599. See also *Wright* v *Macadam* [1949] 2 KB 744.

18 Megarry & Wade, *The Law of Real Property*, p. 840, note 34.

19 *Crow v Wood* [1970] 3 All ER 425. At 429, Lord Denning said that strictly speaking such a right is not an easement because it involves the servient owner in the expenditure of money. 'But it has been treated in practice by the courts as being an easement ...'

20 [1960] EA 208.

21 For example, an obligation to maintain a road cannot be the subject matter of an easement which runs with the land, and therefore does not bind successors in title: *Jones* v *Pritchard* [1908] 1 Ch 730. See also *Austerberry v Oldham Corporation* (1885) 29 Ch D 750. The only exception to the rule is a right to have one's neighbour maintain a fence. See *Crow v Wood* [1970] 3 All ER 425.

22 *Grigsby v Melville* [1973] 3 All ER 455.

23 Section 36 of the *Water Statute*, 1995.

characteristics of easements. For this reason, such rights created by statute, which have some but not all the characteristics of common law easements, strictly speaking are not easements but statutory rights and should be treated as *sui generis*.[24] The nature and content of these rights is dependent upon the statutes that enabled their creation rather than the common law.[25]

Easement by express grant or reservation

An easement may be created by express grant. For example, assume that Sanyu sells part of her land to Paul and in the transfer, she grants Paul, for the benefit of the land sold to him, a right to use a footpath over her land to reach a public road. The right to use the footpath on Sanyu's land is an easement created by express grant. An easement by express reservation is created where, in our example, Sanyu sells part of her land to Paul and in the instrument of transfer she reserves a right of way over the land sold for the benefit of the land she retains. The right of way is an easement created by express reservation. The legal effect is the same whether an easement is created by express grant or by express reservation.

Easement by implied grant or reservation

Where a landowner grants part of his or her land to another person, the courts will readily imply an intention to grant that other person all 'quasi-easements' pertaining to such land. A quasi-easement is a continuous and apparent easement which is necessary to the reasonable enjoyment of the land, and is at the time of the grant used by the landowner for the benefit of that part.[26] A quasi-easement is best explained by illustration. Suppose Lutaya owns and occupies two adjoining plots of land we shall call A and B. His house is on plot A and plot B is vacant land. Lutaya uses a footpath over plot B as a shortcut from his house to the main road. The footpath would be an easement but for the fact that both the 'servient' (plot B) and 'dominant' (plot A) land are owned and occupied by the same person. Nevertheless, the footpath is regarded as a 'quasi-easement'. If Lutaya sells or leases plot A to Robina, unless a contrary intention is expressed in the instrument of transfer, it is implied that he intended to grant her the right to use the footpath in the same way as he himself was using it prior to the transfer. Quasi-easements are sometimes referred to as easements created under the rule of *Wheeldon v Burrows*.[27]

Where the instrument of transfer does not reserve an easement in favour of land retained by the vendor, subject to two exceptions which we shall presently discuss, courts are reluctant to imply a reservation of an easement in favour of such land. This is because of a well-established maxim that a grantor shall not derogate from his or her grant. The case of *Wheeldon v Burrows* illustrates this rule.[28] T owned two adjoining plots of land, one was vacant, and on the other, there was a workshop whose windows overlooked the vacant plot. T sold the vacant land to the respondent, and, subsequently, sold the plot on which the workshop was erected to the appellant. Following a dispute between the respondent and the appellant, the former erected hoardings near the edge of her land facing the appellant's workshop window thereby obstructing the light entering the workshop windows. The appellant knocked down the hoardings asserting a right to an easement of light in respect of the windows. The respondent sued in trespass. It was contended for the appellant that T impliedly reserved a right of light through the workshop windows in the conveyance of the vacant plot to the respondent, and, therefore the respondent could not build upon her land in a manner, which interfered with his easement. The Court of Appeal rejected this argument. It held

---

24 The *Electricity Statute*, 1999, unlike the previous *Electricity Act* (cap 135), does not anywhere use the term 'easement' in reference to the power given to the Electricity Authority to pass cables etc over any land for the purpose of supplying electricity power to another's land.

25 See for example, s. 36(6) of the *Water Statute*,1995.

26 *Shah Champshi Tejshi and others v The Attorney-General of Kenya* [1959] EA 630 at 638.

27 [1874-80] All ER Rep 669.

28 Supra.

that, with the exception of easements of necessity and an intended easement, a reservation of an easement could not be implied in favour of the land retained by the grantor. If a grantor wants to reserve an easement in favour of the land retained, he or she must do so expressly.

Easement of way of necessity

Where a landowner sells part of his or her land and the part he or she retains is left without any legally enforceable means of access to a public road. an easement of way of necessity will be implied over the land sold.[29] Likewise, where a landowner grants part of his or her land to another and the latter has no legally enforceable means of access to the land then an easement of way of necessity arises by operation of the law over the land retained.[30] The easement arises by operation of law because it is a matter of necessity and vital to the effective ownership of that part of the land that the owner should have access to it, otherwise the land would not be of much use to him or her.

The law is illustrated by the case of *Barclays Bank D.C.O.* v *Patel*.[31] In 1941, Tebbutt, proprietor of certain land in Nairobi, subdivided the land into three plots: A, B and C, and had the three plots registered under the Kenya *Registration of Titles Act* (cap 281). Plot A fronted on Langata Road, a public road, but there was no means of access to plots B and C except via surrounding land with permission of the respective owners. In 1944, Tebbutt sold plots B and C to Moore. Neither the transfer nor the certificates of title issued to Moore mentioned any right of way to the two plots from Langata Road over plot A, which Tebbutt retained. Later, Tebbutt sold plot A to the appellant again without any reference to a right of way, indeed the certificate of title specifically declared that plot A was not subject to any encumbrance. Subsequently, plots B and C were sold to the respondent.

Several years later the respondent brought these proceedings against the appellant claiming a right of way of necessity over plot A. On appeal to the East Africa Court of Appeal, it was contended for the appellant that the circumstances did not support the existence of a way of necessity. Secondly, that in any case the respondent was not entitled to the easement of way of necessity as no reference to such easement was made in the transfer or in his certificates or that of the appellant. The court found that at the time the respondent's predecessor in title, M, purchased the two plots from T, he had no legally enforceable means of access to Langata Road. Accordingly, a right of way of necessity arose by operation of law over the land retained by T. The fact that neither certificate of title mentioned the right of way was not material because the parties do not create an easement of way of necessity. Unlike other easements, the easement of way of necessity arises by operation of the law and, therefore, does not need registration.[32]

A few points need to be noted with respect to an easement created by way of necessity. An easement of way of necessity does not arise if there is an alternative means of access that is practicably available to the claimant as a matter of right. The fact that access is inconvenient, for example, because it is unsuitable for cars or entails travelling a long distance in order to get to a public road, does not entitle the grantee to a way of necessity over the grantor's land.[33] Secondly, the necessity for access must exist at the time of the grant and not merely arise later.[34] For example, suppose at the time of sale the vendor has a legally enforceable right of access over some other

---

29 *Wheeldon* v *Burrows*, supra.

30 *Barry* v *Haseldine* [1952] 2 All ER 317, cited with approval in *Barclays Bank D.C.O.* v *Patel* [1970] EA 88 (CA).

31 *Ibid.*

32 *Ibid*, per Sir Charles Newbold P at 93. Law JA at 94 and 96, said that although a way of necessity is generally referred to as an easement, in his view it was more correct to refer to it as, 'a right inherent to the right of property, comparable to the right of support or the right to light. Such rights are not 'created' but owe their existence to the very nature of things and do not ... require to be registered.'

33 *McLernon* v *Connor* [1907] 9 WALR 141.

34 *Midland Rly Co* v *Miles* [1886] 33 Ch D 632.

land, but later that access ceases to be available because the public road is closed and the vendor has no access to the new road except via the land sold. An easement of way of necessity will not be implied over the land sold because the necessity did not exist at the time of grant.[35] Thirdly, the owner of the servient land is not entitled to compensation because he or she must have envisaged the necessity of way at the time of conveyance.[36] However, since the right of way affects the use of the servient land its owner is entitled to determine exactly where the road shall pass on his or her land and to limit it to no more than the necessity requires. The law does not impose upon him or her any obligation to make the road or to keep it under repair. His or her only obligation is not to obstruct the way and to allow, subject to reasonable notice, the owner of the dominant land and his or her servants to enter upon the servient land to construct or maintain the way.[37]

Intended or implied easement

An easement that is required to carry out the common intention of the grantor and the grantee will be implied even though it is not expressly reserved or granted in the conveyance. Such easement is known as an intended easement. The case of *Wong* v *Beaumont Property Trust Ltd*[38] illustrates this rule. X, owner of a building, leased the basement of the building to T for purposes of carrying on the business of a restaurant. T entered into a covenant to keep the premises open as a restaurant, to control and eliminate all smells and odours caused by such a use of the premises and otherwise to comply with the health regulations. Later, X sold the building to the defendant subject to the lease. Subsequently, T also assigned the lease and the restaurant business to the plaintiff. The plaintiff sought the defendant's permission to construct a ventilation system with an external duct on the back part of the building, but the defendant declined. The issue was whether the plaintiff had a right to put up a duct without the defendant landlord's permission. Denning MR, with the concurrence of the rest of the court, said that the law readily implies the grant or reservation of an easement that is necessary to give effect to the common intention of the parties to a grant. On the facts of the case, his Lordship found that the lease was granted for carrying on a restaurant business subject to an obligation on the part of the lessee to comply with health regulations. In the circumstances, the business could not be carried out at all in the manner contemplated by the parties without the installation of a ventilation system by a duct.

Easements acquired by long user or prescription

At common law, an easement may be acquired by prescription or by long user even though there may not be any actual evidence of grant of the easement.[39] The fact of long user is regarded as sufficient evidence that the easement was once upon a time properly granted. According to strict common law, a prescriptive right was established by proof of continued use from time immemorial, which in England was arbitrarily set at 1189.[40] Gradually, the common law courts developed the doctrine of 'lost modern grant'. Under this doctrine, courts may allow a prescriptive claim by proof of continuous use during living memory, which is arbitrarily set as twenty years. The doctrine is based on a fiction (freely admitted by the courts) that twenty years use provides evidence that a grant was properly made but had since been misplaced and lost.[41] The purpose of the legal fiction is to explain enjoyment of an apparent right that is inexplicable on any other legal basis.

---

35 *Barclays Bank D.C.O.* v *Patel*, supra. But see *Access to Roads Act*, 1969, discussed below in this chapter.

36 *Ibid*, at 93.

37 *Ibid.*

38 [1965] 1 QB 173.

39 Prescription is unknown at customary law. See *Nambalu Kintu* v *Efulaimu Kamira* CA No 26 of 1973; (1975) HCB 221 (unreported).

40 *Statute of Westminster* 1, 1275, C39.

41 *Bryant* v *Foot* (1867) LR 2 QB 161; *Dalton* v *Angus* (1881) 6 App Cas 740.

The general rules for establishing an easement acquired by lost modern grant were authoritatively established in *Dalton* v *Angus.*[42] First, the claimant must prove exercise by him or her (or a previous owner) of the alleged right for at least twenty years. Secondly, the right must not have been exercised with force. For example, if during those twenty years, the owner of the 'servient land' blocked access to a footpath in order to prevent the claimant from using it or protested, but the claimant ignored the protest, a right by prescription cannot arise.[43] Thirdly, the right must be exercised openly and not secretly.[44] Finally, the right must be exercised without licence or permission of the owner of the servient land. Thus, if a landowner gives permission to his or her neighbour to use a footpath on his or her land, the latter cannot claim an easement by prescription even after long user.

Access to public road

At common law, except in the case of an easement of way of necessity already discussed, there is no right of access over another's land. However, a right of access over another's land may be granted under the *Access to Roads Act.*[45] Section 11 of the Act provides that where a landowner fails through negotiations to obtain leave from adjoining landowners to construct a road of access over their land to a public highway, he or she may apply to a land tribunal for permission to do so.[46] The Act gives the tribunal discretion to refuse or grant the application subject to any conditions, such as payment of compensation and the course of direction of the road as it shall deem fit.[47] An order made under the Act must be served on the Registrar of Titles within thirty days from the date of issue, and, subject to payment of any prescribed fees, may be entered on the Register Book as appropriate.[48] Once the road of access is constructed the applicant, or his or her successor in title and any person lawfully going to or from the applicant's land, has a right at all times to use the road.[49] The Act imposes upon the applicant a duty at all times to maintain the road of access at his or her expense. However, where the owner of the land also uses the road of access, he or she should contribute towards its maintenance.[50]

Easements under the Registration of Titles Act

There is no provision in the *Registration of Titles Act* which expressly states the manner of creation of easements under the Act. Section 57 stipulates that a statement in a certificate of title that a person named in the certificate is entitled to an easement shall be conclusive evidence that he or she is so entitled. Though the section quite clearly anticipates the creation of easements under the Act by endorsement on the certificate,[51] it does not indicate whether the endorsement should be on the certificate of the servient or dominant land. Ideally, and consistent with the underlying policy of the Torrens system, the endorsement should be on the certificate of title of the land to be burdened by the easement or on both titles. In any event, it may not make any difference whether the endorsement appears on either certificate. As we have already discussed, s. 61of the *Registration*

---

42 (1881) 6 AC 740.

43 See, e.g., *Eaton* v *Swansea Waterworks Co* (1851) 17 QB 267.

44 The reason is that the underlying basis of a prescriptive claim is acquiescence on the part of the owner of the servient land. It would be unfair to find acquiescence where the interference took place without his or her knowledge. See *Liverpool Corporation* v *Coghill & Sons Ltd* [1918] 1 Ch 307.

45 Act No 2 of 1969, as amended by s. 72(2) of the *Land Act*, 1998.

46 Section 11. In *Barclays Bank D.C.O.* v *Patel*, supra, the court held, with reference to a corresponding Kenya Act, that its provisions do not abolish the common law way of necessity, but merely provide another means whereby a landowner could acquire access over another's land.

47 Section 3.

48 Section 10.

49 Section 7.

50 Section 8.

51 See also s. 58 *RTA*

of Titles Act states that easements created by enjoyment or user or subsisting over or upon any land constitute an exception to indefeasibility.[52]

Extinguishment of easements

An easement may be extinguished by express agreement of the parties. Extinguishment is effected when the owner of the dominant land expressly releases the servient land from the easement.[53] Secondly, extinguishment may come about by merger. Where the dominant and servient land come into a common ownership and occupation, all easements affecting the land are merged and extinguished.[54] Thirdly, an easement may be extinguished by abandonment by the dominant landowner.[55] Abandonment may be express but, more often, it is implied from the acts or omissions of the beneficiary. Because an easement is property, the courts do not lightly infer abandonment and the onus of proof is on a person asserting abandonment.[56] For example, in the case of *Barclays Bank D.C.O.* v *Patel*, Sir Charles Newbold P said that the fact that the dominant landowner for twenty years did not use a right of way was indicative but not conclusive proof of abandonment. It must be clear that such non-use was due to abandonment.[57] Once an easement is abandoned, the dominant landowner cannot reclaim it.

The Torrens Acts in some states in Australia make provision for interested persons in any land affected by an easement or a restrictive covenant, to apply to a court for an order for the easement or restrictive covenant to be modified or extinguished in certain specified circumstances. For example, under s. 129C of the *Transfer of Land Act*, 1893, of Western Australia, the court may order extinguishment of an easement or restrictive covenant if, for example, due to change in land use it is obsolete or deemed to be abandoned.[58] There is no corresponding provision in the *Registration of Titles Act*. Nor does any other statutory provision give the courts in Uganda power to extinguish or modify easements. It is doubtful whether the courts have inherent powers to intervene.

PROFITS À PRENDRE

A profit *à prendre* confers a right to enter another's land to take something off the land.[59] The right must relate to something which either comprises part of the land, such as gravel and sand,[60] or things growing on the land, such as timber, and grass.[61] The right of pasture may be the subject of profit *à prendre*: the taking and carrying away is effected by means of the mouths and stomachs of the animals in question.[62] In addition, a right to catch fish or hunt wild animals on the land can constitute a profit *à prendre*. The grant may be for an indefinite or fixed period.[63] It may confer exclusive right, or it may be a right enjoyed in common with other people including the grantor.[64] Unlike an easement, a profit *à prendre* can be granted in gross. In other words, while there must always be a servient land (land from which something is taken), there need not be a dominant land.[65]

---

52 See Chapter 5.

53 *Waterloo* v *Bacon* (1866) LR 2 Eq 514.

54 *Buckby* v *Coles* (1814) 5 Taunt.311.

55 *James* v *Stevenson* [1893] AC 167.

56 *Ibid.*

57 1970] EA 88, at 94.

58 See also s. 84(1B), *Law of Property Act*, 1925 (England).

59 *Duke of Sutherland v Heathcote* [1892] 1 Ch 475.

60 *Re: Refund under Timber Regulations* [1935] AC 184.

61 *Settlement Fund Trustees* v *Nurani* [1970] EA 562; *Kursell v Timber Operators and Contractors Ltd* [1927] 1 KB 298; *Mills v Stockman* (1967) 116 CLR 61.

62 *White v Williams* [1922] KB 727; *White v Taylor (No 2)* [1969] 1 Ch 160.

63 *Wickham v Hawker* (1840) 7 M&W 63; 151 ER 671.

64 *Toohey and others, Ex Parte Meneling Station Pty Ltd and others* (1982) 158 CLR 327.

65 *S affordshire & Worcestershire Canal Navigation v Bradley* [1912] 1 Ch 91.

A profit *à prendre* incorporates a licence to enter another's land to exercise the right granted. In contrast with a bare licence, unless the parties otherwise agreed, a licence coupled with a grant or profit *à prendre* is irrevocable while the grant remains in existence.[66] A further major distinction between the two rights is that while a bare licence is a personal privilege conferring no interest in land,[67] a profit *à prendre* is an incorporeal hereditament, and therefore it is an interest in land.[68] Being an interest in land, a profit *à prendre*, where validly created, would bind any person dealing in the subject land. However, where the land is registered under the *Registration of Titles Act,* except in case of fraud, a proprietor takes the land free of any profit *à prendre* not created by him or herself and not endorsed on the certificate of title.[69]

In some instances, it may be very difficult to tell whether a contract is for sale of goods or grant of a profit *à prendre*. Part of the reason for the difficulty is that the definition of 'goods' under the *Sale of Goods Act* (cap 79), and of 'land' under the *Registration of Titles Act*, in some respects cover much the same ground. Section 2 of the *Sales of Goods Act* defines 'goods' for the purposes of the Act as including:

> all emblements, industrial growing crops, and things attached to or forming part of the land which are agreed to be severed before sale or under the contract of sale.

Section 2 of the *Registration of Titles Act* defines 'land' as including:

> resources, tenements and hereditaments corporeal or incorporeal, and in every certificate of title ... such word also includes easements anu appurtenances appertaining to land ...[70]

The problem of distinguishing a contract of sale of goods and a grant of a profit *à prendre* is illustrated by the Kenyan case of *Settlement Fund Trustees* v *Nurani.*[71] In that case, Nurani, the respondent, bought from the previous proprietor of the subject land the bark of wattle trees growing on her land with the right to remove it within eighteen months. Before Nurani had removed the bark, the owner sold the land to the appellants who had notice of his right to the bark. The appellants prevented him from removing the bark, whereupon he commenced these proceedings against the appellant. The trial court held in favour of Nurani. On appeal to the East African Court of Appeal, the appellants contended that Nurani's right to remove the bark was a profit *à prendre* and not a mere revocable licence. They submitted that since the right was not registered as an encumbrance under the *Registration of Titles Act* (Kenya), it was unenforceable against them even though they bought with notice.

The issue was whether the transaction between Nurani and the previous proprietor was of sale of goods or sale of an interest in land. Law JA, with whom Spry VP concurred, cited the above definition of 'goods' and 'land' under the corresponding Kenyan statutes. He observed that wattle bark, which is permanently attached to a tree rooted in the soil until the tree is felled and the bark stripped off could come under either definition.[72] However, in the circumstances of this case,

---

66 *James Jones & Sons Ltd* v *Earl of Tankerville* [1909] 2 Ch 440; *In Re: Refund of Dues under Timber Regulations* [1935] AC 184.

67 See below.

68 *Settlement Fund Trustees* v *Nurani* [1970] EA 562; *Duke of Sutherland* v *Heathcote* [1892] 1 Ch 475; *Lavery* v *Pursell* (1888) 39 Ch 508.

69 *Settlement Fund Trustees* v *Nurani* [1970] EA 562; *Mills* v *Stockman* (1967) 116 CLR 61. The *RTA*, like Torrens statutes in most Australian jurisdictions, does not expressly provide for the creation of profit *à prendre.* Nevertheless, according to Whelan, *The Torrens System in Australia,* supra, pp. 106-07, their creation is inferable from the general provisions of the Acts.

70 'Corporeal heriditaments' would include trees, gravel and subjacent minerals, any of which could be granted as a profit *à prendre*.

71 [1970] EA 562.

72 *Ibid*, at 573.

he found that the sale of wattle bark was a contract of sale of goods. His Honour reasoned that the sale was of a single crop of wattle bark, an industrial growing crop to be severed and removed within a limited period. Moreover, the period allowed for its removal was not primarily intended to allow the bark to derive benefit from the land and become altered, but to allow the purchaser to arrange for its removal.[73] Consequently, Law JA agreed with the trial judge that the right of entry on the land conferred by the agreement was no more than a temporary licence not mounting to a registrable interest in land.[74]

RESTRICTIVE COVENANTS

Introduction

Technically, the expression 'covenant' refers to a promise contained in a deed, but in practice, it is used to refer to any contractual promise relating to land whether or not under deed. Covenants made between immediate parties are enforceable in accordance with the ordinary principles of the law of contract. For example, suppose Mukasa subdivides his land into two plots: A and B. He sells plot A to Okello subject to an undertaking by Okello and his successors that he, Okello, will at his sole expense, maintain an access road used by the owners of A and B, and that he will contribute annually 10,000 shillings for five years towards the salary of a local priest. If Okello breaches any of these terms Mukasa can of course sue him for breach of contract.

Enforcement of covenants at common law

Suppose, in the above example, a year later Mukasa sold plot B to Luyiga. If Okello fails to maintain the road or to contribute the money he promised, Luyiga cannot sue him in contract because there is no privity of contract between her and Okello.[75] At common law, however, even in the absence of privity of contract, an assignee of the 'dominant' land (Luyiga) may enforce against the original covenantor (Okello) any covenant provided that it touches and concerns the land. A covenant touches and concerns land if it affects the land as regards the manner of occupation or its value and is intended by the parties to run with the land.[76] In our example, the covenant to maintain the road quite clearly touches and concerns plot A, as its existence and maintenance would affect the value of the land and possibly the mode of its occupation. Therefore, Luyiga can enforce performance of the covenant against Okello, even though there is no privity of contract between the two of them. As regards the covenant to pay the priest's salary, though a worthy cause, it does not touch and concern the land. The covenant is a personal obligation, which can only be enforced by the immediate parties.

So far, we have considered a situation where the dominant land is assigned. Suppose in our example above Okello sells plot B (the servient land) to Aisa, and she buys with notice of the obligations undertaken by Okello. If Aisa fails to perform the obligations neither Mukasa nor Luyiga can sue her for breach of contract, as there is no privity of contract between them.[77] Nor can they sue her under any other common law rule. The reason is that at common law a burden of a covenant, unlike a benefit, does not run with land.[78] Therefore, an assignee of the servient land is not bound by covenants entered into by his or her predecessor in title even if he or she purchased the land with notice.[79]

---

[73] *Ibid*, *Marshall* v *Green* (1875) 1 CPD 35, distinguished.

[74] See also *Mills and another* v *Stokman and another* (1967) 116 CLR 61.

[75] Technically, Mukasa could still sue Okello, but the damages awarded would probably be nominal since he no longer has any benefit in the performance of the contract.

[76] *Smith and Snipes Hall Farm Ltd* v *River Douglas Catchment Board* [1949] 2 All ER 179, at 183, per Tucker LJ.

[77] Okello can however sue her for breach of contract though the damages are likely to be nominal.

[78] The rule is different under the law of landlord and tenant.

[79] *Austerberry* v *Oldham Corporation* (1885) 29 Ch D 750.

Enforcement of covenants in equity

In equity, the burden of a covenant may be enforced against an assignee if it is a *restrictive covenant.* A restrictive covenant is a covenant which restricts the use of the covenantor's land (servient land) for the benefit of the covenantee's land (dominant land). The classical illustration of a restrictive covenant is the case of *Tulk* v *Moxhay.*[80] In that case, Tulk owned a block of vacant land in the middle of Leicester Square in London, as well as several houses adjoining the square. He sold the vacant block to E who entered into a covenant with Tulk that he would keep the square as a garden and not build on it. The subject land changed hands several times until Moxhay, the defendant, purchased it. Though Moxhay bought with notice of the restriction, he did not make any express undertaking to abide by it. Moxhay was preparing to build on the block when Tulk commenced these proceedings for an injunction to stop him. The House of Lords granted the order sought. Lord Cottenham LC said that the court could not permit a party in the defendant's position to use the land in a manner inconsistent with the terms under which the vendor sold the land and of which he had notice. In his Lordship's view, to allow the defendant to disregard the restrictions would be most inequitable to the original vendor who had imposed them in order to protect the value of the land he retained.[81]

Since *Tulk* v *Moxhay,* the rules for enforcing restrictive covenants against assignees have been refined by the courts. First, the covenant must be negative in nature and substance. That is to say, the covenant must restrict the servient owner from doing something and not impose a positive duty to do something. A rule of thumb generally adopted is that a covenant which requires the covenantor to expend money in order to comply with the covenant, is not a restrictive covenant.[82] For example, in *Haywood* v *Brunswick Permanent Benefit Building Society,*[83] Y covenanted to erect a building on the land conveyed to him and to keep the building in repair. Later Y conveyed the land to the defendant, who bought with notice of the covenant. The issue was whether the covenant to keep the building in repair was enforceable against the defendant. It was held that the covenant was not enforceable because it purported to impose a positive obligation against an assignee.

The second requirement is that the covenant must be made for the benefit and protection of the land retained by the covenantee. This means that there must be dominant land owned by the covenantee and servient land owned by the covenantor. If, at the time the covenant is entered into, the covenantee has no land to be benefited, the covenant is a personal covenant, and it only binds the immediate parties. This rule is illustrated by the case of *London City Council* v *Allen.*[84] In 1906, the council granted Mr Allen permission to subdivide certain land subject to an undertaking that he and his successors in title would not build upon a certain part of the land, which it required for future extension of a public road. Three years later, Mr Allen conveyed the land to Mrs Allen, who bought with notice of the said building restriction. The council sought to prevent Mrs Allen from constructing a building on the land in breach of the said covenant. The issue was whether the covenant ran with the land and, therefore, was binding. It was held that it is essential to the doctrine of *Tulk* v *Moxhay* that the covenantee should have at the time of the creation of the covenant, and afterwards, land for the benefit of which the covenant is created. In this case, the court found that though Mrs Allen had notice of the covenant it was not binding because the council had no land to be benefited at the time the covenant was made.

---

80 [1843-60] All ER Rep 9.

81 [1843-60] All ER Rep 9 at 11. In subsequent cases it was held that notice per se is not enough to hold an assignee bound by a covenant, see eg *London City Council* v *Allen* [1914-15] All ER Rep 1008.

82 See Megarry and Wade, *The Law of Real Property*, supra, p. 774.

83 (1881) 8 QB D 403.

84 [1914-15] All ER Rep 1008. The rule does not apply where a statutory provision empowers a public body to impose restrictive covenants, regardless of whether it owns any dominant land. Nor does it apply in the case of 'schemes of development'. See below.

The third requirement for the enforcement of a restrictive covenant against an assignee is that both the original covenantor and covenantee must have intended the burden and the benefit of the covenant to run with the servient and dominant land respectively.[85] In practice, the intention is expressed in the agreement.

Scheme of development

A scheme of development (or a development scheme) is a plan produced by a developer for land in a particular area to be developed and maintained in a particular way consistent with the scheme. For example, assume that D Ltd, a construction and land development company, purchases a large block of land at Tank Hill, overlooking Lake Victoria. D Ltd subdivides the block into ten plots numbered 1-10. The company wishes the land to develop in an orderly fashion and to remain a high-class residential area for an indefinite future. To this end, it plans to extract from each purchaser of the plots a number of covenants. They include an undertaking by each plot owner not to construct any building on the land without first submitting his or her plans to D Ltd and other plot owners for approval. All plot owners agree to extract identical covenants from subsequent purchasers and their assignees. Because of privity of contract, D Ltd could enforce the covenants against each *original* purchaser. However, in practice, after D Ltd has sold off the last plot it is unlikely that they will be all that keen to police the covenants. Their real reason for devising the scheme was to make the plots attractive to buyers to maximise their profits. Once that is done, they cease to be interested. Moreover, if the original purchaser sells to a third party, there would be no privity of contract between D Ltd and that party, therefore, the covenants could not be enforced in contract.

For the scheme to succeed and be effective for an indefinite period, the current owners of the plots themselves should be able to enforce the covenants against each other. This, however, may not be legally possible under the doctrine of *Tulk* v *Moxhay*. As we have seen, the doctrine does not apply unless, at the time the covenant was entered into, the covenantee owned or was in possession of the land to which the covenant relates.[86] In our example, suppose that D Ltd sells the plots 1 to 10 in that order. They sell plot 1 to X subject to the said covenants and the covenants are stated to be for the benefit of lots 2-10, which at the time D Ltd still owns. They sell plot 2 to Y in the same way and the covenants are stated to be for the benefit of plots 1-10 (except 2). It should be noted that by then D Ltd is no longer the owner of plot 1 as they had earlier disposed of it to X.

On the basis of *London City Council* v *Allen*, X cannot enforce the covenants against other plot owners even though the covenant was supposedly entered into for the benefit of all the 10 plots. For the same reason, Y, owner of plot 2, can enforce the covenants against X or his or her successor in title, but not against the owners of plots 3-10. The owner of plot 10, the last plot sold, is in the best position as far as enforcing the covenants is concerned. Since at the time D Ltd sold plots 1 - 9, they were the owners of plot 10, it means that the requirements that the covenant must be for the benefit of the covenantee are satisfied. Therefore, the owner of plot 10 could enforce the covenants against everyone else, but no one else (apart from D Ltd) could enforce the covenants against him or her. However, where the plots form part of a scheme of development, all plot owners are bound by and can take the benefit of the covenants irrespective of the order in which the original purchasers acquired the land from D Ltd.

The rules for the establishment of a scheme of development were prescribed in *Elliston* v *Reacher*.[87] They are as follows. Firstly, the party wishing to enforce the covenants and the party against which it is sought to enforce them must derive title from a common vendor. Secondly, the vendor, prior to selling the land, must have subdivided it into plots with the intention of imposing

---

85 *Federated Homes Ltd* v *Mill Lodge Properties Ltd* [1980] 1 WLR 594.

86 *London City Council* v *Allen* [1914-15] All ER Rep 1008.

87 [1965] Ch 816.

restrictions on all the plots. These restrictions should be consistent with a general scheme of development. Thirdly, the common vendor must have intended the restrictions to be and they are for the benefit of other land retained by the vendor. Fourthly, the parties, or their predecessors in title, must have purchased their lots from the common vendor upon the footing that the restrictions to which the purchases were subjected were made for the benefit of all the other lots included in the general scheme.

Subsequent case law holds that the above rules are just guidelines and not prescriptive for the creation of a building scheme. For example, in *Baxter v Oaks Properties Ltd*,[88] it was held that whether or not there was a building scheme is a question of the intention of the vendor and the purchasers, as gathered from all circumstances. In that case, the second rule in *Elliston v Reacher* had not been fulfilled, as the common vendor had not laid out the estates in lots prior to selling the land. Cross J, nonetheless, found the requisite intention to create a building scheme.

Similarly, in *Dolphin's Conveyance, Re: Birmingham Corporation v Boden*[89] Stamp J said that '[t]he building scheme cases stem, as I understand the law, from the wider rule that if there be found the common intention ... the court will give effect to it ...' In that case, counsel for the defendant sought to attack a scheme on the ground of lack of a common vendor (there having been two vendors) and on failure to lay out the estate in lots. Stamp J upheld the scheme, saying that the equity arose, not by the effect of the four rules, or by the existence of a deed of mutual covenant, but by the existence of a common interest and intention actually expressed in the conveyances themselves.

If the requirements for a building scheme are satisfied, plot owners can sue each other to enforce the covenants in the scheme. Nevertheless, it should be stressed that even with the existence of a scheme of development, only negative covenants are enforceable. Thus, for example, a covenant to keep a building in repair does not run with the land even though the land is part of a scheme of development.[90]

Restrictive covenants and the *RTA*

The *Registration of Titles Act* (cap 205) makes no provision for the registration of restrictive covenants. This is probably because restrictive covenants are equitable interests and the Torrens system generally avoids registration of equitable interests.[91] In some Australian jurisdictions, the practice is for registrars to make notations of restrictive covenants on the certificates of title of the burdened land. The legal efficacy of such notation, unsupported by legislation, has been questioned.[92] Some authorities suggest that restrictive covenants are not enforceable against subsequent registered proprietors, even if they purchased with notice of the covenants.[93] Accordingly, the only certain way to make the covenant bind a subsequent purchaser is for the owner of the dominant land to enter into a fresh contract with the purchaser of the servient land, a task which may not be easy to achieve in most cases.

Remedies for breach of restrictive covenants

Since restrictive covenants have their origins in the courts of equity, the only remedy available to an aggrieved party is by an injunction to prevent the wrongdoer from breaching covenants which

---

88 [1965] Ch 816.

89 [1970] 1 Ch 654 at 663.

90 *Dolphin's Conveyance, Re: Birmingham Corporation v Boden* [1970] 1 Ch D 654.

91 See, for example, s. 46, *RTA*, prohibits notice of trusts to be entered in the register book.

92 Whalan, *The Torrens System in Australia*, supra, p. 110. In Western Australia, s.129A, *Transfer of Land Act* 1893, makes provision for the registration of restrictive covenants.

93 See *Norton* v *Kilduff* [1974] Qd R 47.

he or she had notice of at the time of purchase.[94] Injunctions, of course, are a discretionary remedy, which may or may not be granted by the district land tribunal or the court.[95]

Extinguishment of restrictive covenants

There is no statutory provision that gives the land tribunals or the courts power to order extinguishment of a restrictive covenant, which, for example, is obsolete.[96] However, they may indirectly extinguish such a covenant by declining to grant an injunction against an owner of the servient land in breach of the restrictive covenant. [97]

LICENCE

A licence is permission given to a licensee to enter the licensor's land for some specified purpose or purposes which otherwise would be a trespass.[98] For example, permission given by Makerere University to the students of Makerere College School to train on the university sports grounds is a licence, without which they would be trespassers. A licence differs from a lease in that it does not create an interest in land.[99] This was stated more than three centuries ago in *Thomas* v *Sorrell.*[100] In that case, Vaughan CJ said that:

> A dispensation of licence properly passeth no interest, nor alters or transfers property in anything, but only makes an action lawful, which without it would have been unlawful.

Because a licence does not constitute an interest in land, it cannot be disposed of by will or *inter vivos* or devolve by operation of law.[101] For the same reason, under the general law, a licence only binds a party to the agreement but not a stranger, even if he or she purchases the land with notice of the licence.[102]

Types of licences

There are four types of licences: a bare licence; a licence coupled with an interest; a contractual licence; and a licence protected by estoppel.

Bare Licence

A bare licence is a licence granted without valuable consideration. It is the simplest form of licence. For example, an invitation to a friend to come over to your house for dinner is a bare licence. Because a bare licence is without consideration, it may be withdrawn at any time by the licensor even in the middle of the dinner.[103] An action of trespass would lie against a licensee if he or she remains on the land after the licence is revoked.

---

94 *Tulk v Moxhay* [1843-60] All ER Rep 9.

95 *Serunjogi v Katabira* CS No 547 of 1987 (unreported); (1988-90) HCB 148.

96 The same as with the extinguishment of easements, discussed above.

97 *Gaskin v Balls* (1879) 13 Ch D 324.

98 *Radaich* v *Smith* (1959) 101 CLR 209 at 222. For an excellent discussion of licences , see R.W. James 'Some problems concerning leases and licences' (1967) 3 *East African Law Journal,* pp. 218-51.

99 See also easement and profit *à prendre*, above.

100 (1673) Vaugh 330 at 351; 124 ER 1098, at 1109.

101 *Runda Coffee Estates Ltd* v *Ujager Singh* [1966] EA 564.

102 In *Ashburn Anstalt v Arnold and another* [1988] 2 All ER 147, the House of Lords reiterated this proposition following several years of controversy in English courts. See also *Runda Coffee Estates Ltd* v *Ujager Singh* [1966] EA 564.

103 *Wood* v *Leedbitter* (1845) 13 M & W 838. However, a bare licence may become irrevocable under the principle of proprietary estoppel. See below.

Licence coupled with an interest

A licence coupled with a grant or an interest is a licence to enter upon a licensor's land for the specific purpose of taking something that forms part of the land or is upon the land.[104] Such a licence is irrevocable whilst the grant remains in existence and may be assigned, provided it is disposed of with the interest to which it is annexed.[105] Where a licence involves a right to enter and take away something that forms part of the land or of the soil, for example minerals, gravel, timber or clay, the grant is a profit *à prendre*.[106] A profit *à prendre* constitutes an interest in land. Subject to the principle of indefeasibility, it binds subsequent purchasers of the land to which it applies.[107] In contrast, a licence to take away goods on the licensor's land does not constitute an interest in land. The licensee has a right in the chattel which is on the land, and a licence to enter the land to take away the chattel.[108]

Contractual licence

A contractual licence is a licence granted for a valuable consideration. At common law, a contractual licence, like any other contract, does not bind third parties and its burden does not run with the land. A contractual licence may be revoked, though, if revoked in breach of contract, the licensor would be held liable in damages.[109] At common law, a contractual licence does not bind third parties even if they bought the land with notice of the licence.[110]

Licence protected by estoppel

A licensor may be estopped from revoking a licence in certain circumstances. Where Ouma, a landowner, by his conduct leads Teki to believe that he would obtain an interest in land, and on the basis of this belief Teki alters her position to her detriment, an equity may arise in Teki's favour.[111] The court may force Ouma to adhere to his representation by making such order as is appropriate to satisfy the equity.[112] On the basis of this principle, a court may order that a licence that is revocable at its inception has become irrevocable because of the parties' conduct. For example, in the case of *Inwards* v *Baker*,[113] the plaintiff wanted to buy land on which to build his house, but he could not afford to buy land. Encouraged by his father, the plaintiff constructed a house on the father's land and for several years, while his father was alive, he lived in that house. The father, in his will, devised the subject land to his widow. The plaintiff instituted these proceedings for possession. It was held that the plaintiff's father allowed an expectation to be created in the plaintiff's mind that the house he built was to be his home, at least for his life. In light of that equity, the father could not have revoked the licence nor could his successor in title.[114]

---

104 *Wood* v *Leedbitter*, Ibid. See also *Runda Coffee Estates Ltd v Ujager Singh* [1966] EA 564.

105 *Wood* v *Leedbitter*, Ibid. See also *James Jones & Sons Ltd* v *Earl of Tankerville* (1909) 2 Ch 440.

106 *Settlement Fund Trustees v Nurani* [1970] EA 562.

107 *Settlement Fund Trustees v Nurani, Ibid.*

108 *Settlement Fund Trustees* v *Nurani*, Ibid. As this case illustrates sometimes it is very difficult to distinguish a profit *à prendre* and a licence coupled with an interest in goods.

109 *Wood v Leedbitter* (1845) 13 M&W 838. Also *King* v *David Allen & Sons, Billposting Ltd* [1916] 2 AC 54.

110 *King* v *David Allen & Sons, Billposting Ltd*, Ibid.

111 *Ramsden v Dyson* (1866) LR 1 HL 129.

112 *Plimmer v Mayor of Wellington* (1884) 9 AC 699.

113 [1965] 1 All ER 446.

114 Lord Denning MR, at 37, stated, *obiter dictum*, that any purchaser of the land with notice of a licence protected by estoppel would be equally bound by the equity. It is submitted that in Uganda, because of the principle of indefeasibility of title, except in case of fraud, a registered proprietor would not be bound by such a claim, even if he or she acquired the land with notice. See also *Runda Coffee Estates Ltd* v *Jager Singh* [1966] EA 564.

CUSTOMARY RIGHTS

Local customary rights are ancient rights enjoyed by members of a local community over private land. They do not have the characteristics of an easement in that they are not necessarily appurtenant to any dominant land but any member of the community enjoys them. In England, local customary rights have been upheld as enforceable at common law. For example, in *Mercer* v *Denne*,[115] it was claimed that fishermen who were inhabitants of a parish, had a customary right, which went back to time immemorial, to spread their nets to dry on private land. The court upheld the claim to be a valid legal custom. Other activities that have been upheld as legal customary rights include the playing of sports and pastimes on a piece of land[116] and the use of a footpath to the local church.[117]

In Uganda, there is no doubt that customary rights are enforceable with respect to land owned under customary tenure.[118] As regards land registered under the *Registration of Titles Act*, subject to the *Land Act*, 1998, it is thought that the principle of indefeasibility of title excludes the enforcement of customary rights against registered proprietors. This view is partly based on the High Court of Kenya case of *Obiero* v *Opiyo et al.*[119] The facts of the case were as follows. In 1968, the plaintiff was registered under the Kenya *Registered Land Act* (cap 300) as proprietor of the suit property. She brought these proceedings for eviction of the defendant who claimed to be entitled to the suit property under customary law and to have cultivated the same from time immemorial. The issue was whether the defendant's claim constituted an overriding interest against the plaintiff's title. Bennett J observed that s. 28 of the Act confers upon a registered proprietor an indefeasible title subject to charges and encumbrances shown on the register book and to such other overriding rights listed in s. 30 which are not required to be entered on the register. Having found that there were no encumbrances noted on the certificate of title and that rights derived from custom were not among overriding interests listed in s. 30, His Honour concluded that customary rights were not intended to constitute an exception to indefeasibility of title. Bennet J said:

> Had the legislature intended that rights of a registered proprietor were to be subject to the rights of any person under customary law, nothing would have been easier than for it to say so.[120]

Though sections 28 and 30 of the Kenya Act are not identical with s. 61 of the *Registration of Titles Act*, it is submitted that the reasoning of Bennett J would be of persuasive authority in its interpretation. For example, according to a Baganda custom a mailo owner cannot deny access to a person who wishes to attend his or her relatives' tombs on the land.[121] It is very much doubted that this customary 'licence' to enter constitutes an overriding right to the principle of indefeasibility. However, as we have seen, the provisions of the *Land Act*, 1998, override the principle of indefeasibility in some respects. Relevantly, for the present purposes s. 4(4)(c) of the Act provides that the rights of a mailo owner are subject to the 'customary and statutory rights' of tenants by occupancy. It is thought that the customary rights of such tenants constitute an exception to the principle of indefeasibility of title.

---

115 [1905] 2 Ch 538.

116 *New Windsor Corporation* v *Mellor* [1975] Ch 380.

117 *Brocklebank v Thompson [1903] 2 Ch 344.*

118 See ss. 4(1) and 9(1) *Land Act*, 1998. See above Chapter 1.

119 [1972] EA 227 (K).

120 *Ibid*, at 228. See also *Esiroyo* v *Esiroyo & another* [1973] EA 388 (K). Also in the Papua New Guinean case of *Custodian of Expropriated Property v Tedep* (1964) CLR 318, it was held that unregistered customary rights cannot stand against a registered title.

121 Haydon, *Law and Justice in Buganda* (London, Butterworths, 1960), p. 164.

9

Co-ownership of Land

INTRODUCTION

Co-ownership of land is where two or more persons concurrently own an interest in land. The interest may be a leasehold, freehold or mailo. Each co-owner is entitled to the simultaneous enjoyment or use of the land, claiming not a separate portion but a mutual right in the whole.[1] Co-ownership may be in joint tenancy or tenancy in common.[2]

JOINT TENANCY

There is a joint tenancy where two or more persons together as a group own the entire interest in the property. Co-owners in joint tenancy, unlike tenants in common, do not have *distinct* shares in the land. In the eyes of the law they hold the whole jointly and nothing separately.[3] A joint tenancy has two essential features which distinguish it from a tenancy in common: presence of the four unities and the right of survivorship. Unless these two features exist there cannot be joint tenancy.[4]

The four unities

The four unities are unity of possession; unity of interest; unity of time; and unity of title.

Unity of possession

Unity of possession is a common feature of all forms of co-ownership. It means that each co-owner is entitled to an undivided possession of the whole of the co-owned land and none holds any part separately to the exclusion of the other co-owners.[5] For example, if a husband and wife own their matrimonial house in joint tenancy, one cannot say that the kitchen belongs to the wife and the sitting room to the husband. The house as a whole unit belongs to both of them.

Unity of interest

Unity of interest means that the interest of each joint tenant must be identical in nature and duration. For example, there cannot be a joint tenancy where one co-owner has a leasehold interest in the land and another a freehold. Similarly, there cannot be a joint tenancy where one co-owner is entitled to a greater share of the rent from the land than the other. In these examples, the co-owners would be tenants in common and not joint tenants.[6]

Unity of time

Unity of time means that the interest of each joint owner must vest at the same time. For example, if A and B together purchase land and the land is conveyed to them, there is unity of time because the title vests in them at the same time. Suppose C later becomes a co-owner with them in equal shares, C cannot be a joint tenant with A and B because he acquired his interest after the interest of A and B had vested.[7]

---

1 Megarry and Wade, *The Law of Real Property*, supra, p. 417.

2 The term 'tenancy' means ownership and has nothing to do with leases.

3 Cheshire and Burn, *Modern Law of Real Property*, supra, p. 209.

4 *AG Securities* v *Vaughan* [1988] 3 All ER 1058 (HL).

5 *Bull v Bull* [1955] 1 QB 234.

6 *AG Securities* v *Vaughan* [1988] 3 All ER 1058 (HL).

7 This rule does not apply to dispositions in a will and conveyances to trustees. See Mendes Da Costa, 'Co-ownership Under Victorian Land Law' (1961) 3 *Melbourne University Law Review* 137, at 152.

Unity of title
Unity of title means that the co-owners' title must derive from the same act or document. If they acquired the land by inheritance it must have been under the same will. If they purchased the land it must have been conveyed to them in a single transaction.

The case of *AG Securities* v *Vaughan*[8] illustrates the above points. The appellants owned a four-bedroom house. Under separate contracts entered into at different times, they granted a right to occupy the flat to four individuals referred to as the 'flat sharers'. The contract entitled each occupant to use the premises in common with other people who might from time to time have a similar right. The rent payable by each occupant varied. The Court of Appeal held that the occupants held the flat in joint tenancy. The House of Lords unanimously reversed this decision on the ground that the arrangement was 'notably deficient in the four unities of interest, title, time and possession'.[9] There was no unity of time because each of the flat sharers commenced on a different date. There was no unity of title because each commenced his or her occupation of the flat under a different document. There was no unity of interest because the agreements covered a different period and provided for different payment for that occupation.

The right of survivorship (*jus accrescendi*)
The second essential feature of joint tenancy is the right of survivorship or *jus accrescendi*. Joint tenants as individuals do not have *distinct* shares in the co-owned land; they own the whole as a group. Therefore, upon the death of one joint tenant his or her interest in the land is extinguished and does not form part of his or her estate.[10] For example, if a husband and wife own their matrimonial home in joint tenancy, whoever survives the other automatically becomes the sole owner of the house. Similarly, if there were three joint tenants: A, B and C, and A died, his interest in the land would be extinguished and that of B and C correspondingly enlarged. Upon the death of B her interest would also be extinguished leaving C, the last survivor, as sole owner of the land. This is known as the right or doctrine of 'survivorship'. Because of this doctrine, property held in joint tenancy cannot devolve by will or intestate succession unless the joint tenancy has been previously severed in the lifetime of the deceased joint tenant.[11]

Where joint tenants die in a common calamity in circumstances which render it impossible to determine who survived the other, the doctrine of survivorship does not apply. For example, in *Willcox v McLeroth* a husband and wife executed identical wills each appointing the other sole heir and executor of 'my estate and effects'. They both drowned in a lake in circumstances in which it was not known who survived the other. It was held that according to the common law the estate of each of the deceased must be administered as in intestacy it being presumed that they both died at the same time.[12] In England the common law has been modified by s. 184 of the *Law of Property Act* 1925.[13] The section provides that where two or more die in circumstances rendering it uncertain which of them survived the other, it shall be presumed that the younger survived the older. Since the English Act, of course, does not apply in Uganda,[14] it is suggested that the common law rule espoused in *Willcox v McLeroth* is the appropriate law applicable. The effect of the rule is that in

---

8 [1988] 3 All ER 1058.

9 Per Lord Jauncey of Tullichettle, at 1976.

10 *Wight v Gibbons* (1949) 78 CLR 313; Cheshire and Burn, *Modern Law of Real Property*, supra, p. 209.

11 *Swift and Neale v Roberts* (1764) 3 Burr 1488, 97 ER 941. Severance is discussed below.

12 (1933) KLR 82. See also *The Administrator General of Zanzibar v Khalfan and others* [1963] EA 230.

13 15 Geo.5, c. 20. In Papua New Guinea, if joint tenants die in a circumstances where it is not known who survived the other, the property is deemed to devolve as if it were owned in tenancy in common, see s.7, *Simultaneous Deaths Act* (cap 332).

14 In *The Administrator General of Zanzibar v Khalfan and others*, the High Court of Zanzibar expressly rejected the presumption that the younger survives the older.

the event of death of joint tenants in a common calamity, their respective heirs would inherit the land as if the deceased owned the land in tenancy in common.

TENANCY IN COMMON

Tenancy in common differs from joint tenancy in that tenants in common hold land in individual shares. In other words, each tenant in common has a distinct share in the property. What makes the parties co-owners is that they all have shares in a single piece of land though the land is not yet physically divided amongst them.[15] Because each tenant in common has a fixed share in the land, the doctrine of survivorship does not apply. Hence, if one of the tenants in common dies, his or her undivided share of the land passes under his or her will or intestacy. Although the four unities may be present in a tenancy in common, the only essential one is unity of possession. For example, A and B can be tenants in common even though they acquired their respective interests by different documents at different times and their shares are unequal.[16]

Creation of joint tenancy and tenancy in common

Common law

The common law and equity differed in their approach to the creation of joint tenancy and tenancy in common. The common law leaned in favour of joint tenancy because the operation of the doctrine of survivorship inevitably led to the vesting of the property in one person.[17] Therefore, at common law where a grant was made to two or more persons it was presumed that the grantor intended to create a joint tenancy of the legal interest. For example, in *Re: Murram Murtor*,[18] a testator granted his estate to a trustee to apply for the benefit of G and J. The issue was whether G and J were to hold the estate as joint tenants or tenants in common. It was held that where property is given to several persons concurrently, *prima facie* they take as joint tenants. In this case, since there was nothing to suggest a tenancy in common, it was held that the testator intended G and J to hold in joint tenancy.

The presumption of joint tenancy is discharged either where one of the four unities is missing or where the grant contains 'words of severance'.[19] The words of severance are expressions that indicate the grantor's intention that each grantee should take a separate and distinct share in the property.[20] In *Robertson v Fraser*, Lord Hatherley said, 'anything which in the slightest degree indicates an intention to divide the property must be held to abrogate the idea of joint tenancy, and to create a tenancy in common'.[21] Examples of words which have been held to constitute severance include 'share and share alike', 'amongst', 'in equal share', 'equally' and 'participate'.[22]

Equity

In equity, as at common law, a grant of property to two or more persons without words of severance creates a joint tenancy and a grant with words of severance creates a tenancy in common.[23] However, since equity is concerned with justice and 'prefers the certainty and equality of a tenancy in common to the chance of all or nothing which arose from the right of survivorship'[24], it

---

15 *East African General Insurance Co Ltd* v *Ntende and others* CS No 1387 of 1975; (1979) HCB 225 (unreported).
16 *Bull* v *Bull* [1955] 1 QB 234.
17 *Morley* v *Bird* (1798) 3 Ves. 628; 30 ER 1192.
18 18 KLR 65. See also *Morley* v *Bird* (1798) 3 Ves. 628; 30 ER 1192.
19 Megarry and Wade, *The Law of Real Property*, supra, p. 424.
20 *Robertson v Fraser* (1871) 6 Ch App 696.
21 *Ibid*, at 699.
22 *Ibid*. See also *Morley v Bird* (1798) 3 Ves. 628; 30 ER 1192.
23 *Morley* v *Bird* (1798) 3 Ves, 628; 30 ER 1192.
24 Megarry and Wade, *The Law of Real Property*, supra, p. 425.

leans in favour of tenancy in common. Hence, in certain situations even in the absence of words of severance equity presumes that the co-owners intended to create a tenancy in common and not a joint tenancy unless there is clear evidence to the contrary. Traditionally, there were three such situations in which persons who were joint tenants at law were compelled by the court of equity to hold the legal estate upon trust for themselves as equitable tenants in common. These were:

(i) where the property was purchased with funds contributed in unequal shares;
(ii) where the property constituted partnership assets; and
(iii) where the property was held as security for a loan advanced by the joint tenants.

Property purchased with funds contributed in unequal shares

Where two or more persons together purchase property, the purchase price having been contributed in unequal amounts, equity presumes that the purchasers intended to hold as tenants in common in shares proportionate to their contribution.[25] For example, suppose Adam and Eve take a conveyance of land as joint tenants where Adam contributed two thirds of the purchase price. In equity, it is presumed that they intended to hold the legal estate in trust for themselves as tenants in common in shares proportionate to their contribution. Similarly, where only one pays the purchase price but the conveyance is made to him or her and another in joint tenancy, equity presumes that the sole contributor did not intend the non-contributor to acquire a beneficial interest in the land. In the absence of any evidence to rebut the presumption, it is assumed that the non-contributor holds his or her legal interest in trust for the sole contributor.[26]

Partnership property

There is a presumption that property acquired by partners as part of the partnership assets is held by the partners in tenancy in common and not in joint tenancy. This is irrespective of whether their contribution to the purchase price was equal or unequal.[27] The presumption is justified on the ground that it is inappropriate to apply the rule of survivorship to a business undertaking.[28]

Property held as security

Where two or more persons advance money, whether equally or unequally, to a third person and a mortgage is made to them jointly, at law they are joint tenants but in equity they are presumed to hold the mortgage in tenancy in common. The rationale for the presumption in favour of tenancy in common is that in such a situation it is unlikely that the parties intended that whoever happened to die first would forego his or her interest.[29]

Other situations

The traditional view is that only in the three specific categories mentioned above will joint tenants at law be presumed to hold as tenants in common in equity. However, in *Malayan Credit Ltd v Jack Chia-MPH Ltd*,[30] the Privy Council rejected this view. In that case, the appellant and respondent held a lease in joint tenancy over certain premises where they conducted their separate businesses. The issue was whether in equity they were presumed to be tenants in common. Counsel for the appellant argued that the equitable presumption of tenancy in common did not apply outside the three classes mentioned above. Lord Brightman, delivering the judgement on behalf of the Privy Council rejected the argument and stated:

---

25 *Robinson* v *Preston* (1858) 4 K & J 505; 70 ER 211, at 213.

26 *Calverley* v *Green* (1984) 155 CLR 242.

27 *Lake v Craddock* (1733) 3 P Wms 158; 24 ER 1011.

28 The presumption of tenancy in common to the beneficial interest of partnership assets is now incorporated in the s. 24(1) *Partnership Act* (cap 86). See *Kitiiza v Registrar of Titles* Misc. Appn. No 82 of 1977.

29 *Morley v Bird* (1798) 3 Ves. 628; 30 ER 1192. 'Though they take a joint tenancy, each means to lend his own and take back his own', per Lord Arden MR, at 1199.

30 [1986] AC 549 (PC).

> Their lordships do not accept that the cases in which joint tenants at law will be presumed to hold as tenants in common are as rigidly circumscribed as the plaintiff asserts. Such cases are not necessarily limited to purchasers who contribute unequally, to co-mortgagees and to partners. There are other circumstances in which equity may infer that the beneficial interest is intended to be held by the grantees as tenants in common. In the opinion of their Lordships, one such case is where the grantees hold the premises for their several individual business purposes.[31]

His Lordship reasoned that in a situation such as in the instant case, it was improbable that business people would intend that upon the death of one of them the beneficial interest in the entire premises would vest in the survivor.

Rebuttal of presumption of tenancy in common

Equity's presumption of tenancy in common may be rebutted by evidence that both parties intended to hold the beneficial interest as joint tenants.[32] The presumption may also be displaced in an appropriate case by pleading a counter presumption of 'advancement' or intention to give a beneficial interest. Where the husband pays the whole or most of the purchase price of land, and the property is conveyed to him and his wife in joint tenancy, a presumption of advancement[33] is made in favour of the wife.[34] The effect of the presumption is that the wife takes her legal interest as a gift and not in trust for the husband, as would otherwise be the case.[35] For example, in *Calverley* v *Green*[36] the appellant and respondent lived together as *de facto* spouses. Together they bought a house, which they intended to be their matrimonial home and it was registered in their names in joint tenancy.

Unfortunately, their relationship did not prosper and they separated. The issue was whether they owned the house in joint tenancy or tenancy in common. If they were joint tenants then the proceeds of sale of the house were to be divided equally between them. If they were tenants in common they were to be divided in proportion to their contribution towards the purchase price. The male respondent, who had contributed three-quarters of the purchase price, contended that, though they were registered as joint tenants in equity, they were presumed to be tenants in common because their contribution was unequal. For the female appellant it was argued that the presumption of advancement displaced the presumption of tenancy in common and consequently she took her legal interest as a gift and not in trust for the husband. The High Court of Australia held that the presumption of advancement would have applied, as contended by the appellant, if the parties were properly married.[37] In the event, it was held that they held their beneficial interest in the house in tenancy in common in shares equal to their contribution.

Creation of co-ownership under the *RTA*

Joint tenancy and tenancy in common are created by registration under the *Registration of Titles Act* as joint tenants or tenants in common respectively.[38] Instruments presented for registration that would transfer an estate or interest to two or more persons should set out the manner in which

---

31 *Ibid*, at 560.

32 *Robinson* v *Preston* (1858) 4 K & J 505; 70 ER 211.

33 Dixon CJ, in *Martin* v *Martin* (1959) 110 CLR 297, at 303, said that it is called a presumption of advancement 'but it is rather the absence of any reason for assuming ... that the equitable right is not at home with the legal title'.

34 The presumption of advancement is not made in favour of the husband where the wife is the main contributor of the purchase price, see *Mercier v Mercier* [1903] 2 Ch 98. It also applies where a parent transfers property to his or her children but not where a child transfers property to his or her parents.

35 See *Lumu v Sood* CS No 1541 of 1972, unreported.

36 (1984) 155 CLR 246.

37 See also *Lumu v Sood* CS No 1541 of 1972, Nyamuchonco J said, *obiter dicta*, that the presumption of advancement does not apply where the parties are not legally married.

38 Sections 53 and 93, *RTA*.

the co-owners hold the estate or interest. Where persons desire to hold land as joint tenants, the instrument of transfer should state that the transfer is made to the transferees 'as joint tenants'. If they desire to hold land as tenants in common, the instrument should state likewise and the proportions in which the land is held. The registration of the co-owners as joint tenants or tenants in common is conclusive as far as it concerns third parties who act in reliance upon the register.[39] However, between the parties registration is not conclusive. Evidence may be adduced to establish that, notwithstanding registration as joint tenants, the parties intended to hold the beneficial interest in tenancy in common. The equitable presumptions discussed above operate in appropriate cases to determine the intention of the parties.[40]

Under s. 53 of the *Registration of Titles Act*, where the instrument of transfer to two or more persons is registered without specification of the nature of the co-ownership, the proprietors are presumed to hold in joint tenancy. In the case of *In Re: Foley (Deceased); Public Trustee* v *Foley*,[41] the High Court of New Zealand, interpreting a similar provision, held that its objective is to make registration conclusive, so far as it concerns third parties who act in reliance on the registered instrument. However, as between the registered proprietors the presumption was rebuttable. For example, as illustrated by the case of *Calverley v Green*,[42] evidence may be adduced to show that though the parties were registered as joint tenants, in equity they own the land in tenancy in common.

Right of enjoyment amongst co-owners

Co-owners of land enjoy certain rights and owe each other certain obligations in their dealings with their land. The most important right of a co-owner is the right to possession. In law each co-owner is entitled to possession and enjoyment of the entire co-owned land irrespective of the size of his or her share.[43]

No liabilities for trespass or occupation rent

Because each co-owner has an equal right to occupy the land, neither can sue the other for trespass to the common land.[44] Nor can a co-owner demand occupation rent from the other even if that other occupies the whole. For example, in *Jones (AE) v Jones (FW)*,[45] the defendant and plaintiff were tenants in common of a certain house owning one quarter and three-quarter shares in the property, respectively. For several months the defendant lived in the house alone. In an application for the sale of the house the plaintiff claimed rent from the defendant for sole occupation of the house. The trial judge ordered the defendant to pay three quarters of a fair rent to the plaintiff. On appeal to the Court of Appeal the decision was reversed. Lord Denning MR was emphatic that the common law clearly states that tenants in common are equally entitled to occupation of the land. Consequently, one tenant in common is not entitled to demand rent from a co-tenant even if the latter occupies the whole.

However, where a co-owner is in sole occupation of the common property on the understanding with the other co-owner that he or she will pay occupation rent then he or she is liable to pay rent as promised.[46] The agreement to pay rent may be inferred from the circumstances and conduct of the parties. For example, in *Uganda Thrift Co Ltd* v *J.M. Nnambale*,[47] a group of ten people

---

39 *In Re: Foley (Deceased); Public Trustee* v *Foley* [1952] NZLR 702.
40 See for example, *Calverley v Green* (1984) 155 CLR 242.
41 [1952] NZLR 702.
42 (1984) 155 CLR 242.
43 *Henderson v Eason* (1851) 17 QB 701.
44 *Jacobs v Seward* (1872) LR 5 HL 464; *The Proprietor of Centre Building Units Plan v Bourne* [1984] Qd R 13.
45 [1977] 1 WLR 438.
46 *Leigh v Dickeson* (1881-85) All ER Rep 1099.
47 CS No 550 of 1970 (unreported); [1971] HCB 326.

including the defendant together bought land and constructed thereon several houses for renting. The co-owners incorporated the plaintiff company with a view to transfer to it title to the land. For several months before title was transferred to the plaintiff, the defendant occupied one of the houses and paid rent to the plaintiff. Upon default the plaintiff brought these proceedings for arrears and eviction. The defendant pleaded that as a tenant in common he was neither bound to pay occupation rent nor could his co-tenants evict him. It was held that the partners bought the land for commercial purposes and when the defendant occupied the house in question he did so on the understanding that he was renting it just like a stranger. Therefore, he was bound to pay for his occupation and, if he failed, he could be evicted.

A co-owner may also be liable for occupation rent and or trespass if he or she ousts or evicts another co-owner from occupation of the common property. The co-owner who is ousted from occupation by another co-owner is entitled to sue the person responsible in trespass and to claim occupation rent from him or her for the period he or she was excluded from occupation.[48] For this purpose, exclusion need not be express, it could be implied from the conduct of the offending co-owner. For example, in *Dennis v McDonald*,[49] the defendant and plaintiff lived together in a *de facto* relationship in a house they owned in tenancy in common. After several years, the plaintiff left the house because of domestic violence, leaving the defendant in sole occupation. In an application for sale of the house, the plaintiff claimed occupation rent from the defendant for the period he was in sole occupation. It was held that a co-owner is liable for occupation rent if he or she is responsible for the other being out of occupation. In this case, though, the defendant did not actually oust the plaintiff, for all practical purposes his violence towards her was tantamount to eviction because it would have been unreasonable to expect her to occupy the house in such circumstances.

No compensation for improvements or repair

A co-owner who, of his or her own accord, expends money on improvements or repairs of the common property cannot demand compensation from other co-owners.[50] However, in equity, upon termination of the co-ownership, whether by sale or partition of the common property, a co-owner may claim expenses he or she incurred in carrying out improvements to the property. The reason is that it would be unfair for the non-contributor(s) to take advantage of the increase in value of the property due to the efforts of the other co-owner. But the court of equity allows the improver to recover only to the extent to which the improvements result in the present enhancement of the value of the property, if any.[51] For example, suppose Birungi and Namazzi own a building in tenancy in common or in joint tenancy. Birungi spends 1 million shillings to renovate the house. As we have just stated, if Birungi spent the money on her own accord she cannot demand any contribution from Namazzi. If upon the sale of the property it transpires that because of the renovations its value has increased by 2 million shillings, Birungi would be entitled to reimbursement from the proceeds for her expenses to a maximum of 1 million shillings. If on the other hand the increase in value is only half a million shillings, she would be entitled to recover only half a million shillings. Where, in spite of her expenses, the house does not increase in value she will not be entitled to any reimbursement.[52]

---

48 *Bull* v *Bull* [1955] 1 QB 234.

49 [1981] 2 All ER 633.

50 *Leigh v Dickeson* (1881-85) All ER Rep 1099.

51 *Jones; Farrington v Forrester* [1893] 2 Ch 461. For a good illustration see the decision of the High Court of Australia in *Squire* v *Rogers* [1979] 39 FLR 106.

52 See *Squire v Rogers*, *Ibid.*

No liability to account for profits

At common law, since each co-owner has a right to possession and enjoyment of the entire common property, a tenant who receives more than his or her share of the profit is not accountable to the other co-owners.[53] However, in equity the courts may hold a co-owner accountable for profits either on the basis of equity's inherent jurisdiction to order account between co-owners or as incidental to a partition suit.[54] The liability to account in equity is limited to profits received from a third party's use or occupation of the common property as distinct from income made by the co-owner's investment or use of the common property.[55] For example, where a co-owner leases the common land to a third party he or she must share the rent with the other co-owners, but where a co-owner uses the common land to grow commercial crops he or she has no obligation to account for the profits.[56]

TERMINATION OF CO-OWNERSHIP

Termination of joint tenancy

Joint tenancy may be determined by conversion into sole ownership, severance and partition.

Conversion into sole ownership

As we have seen, on the death of all but one of the joint tenants, the survivor becomes the sole owner by virtue of the rule of *jus accrescendi*. Under s. 201 of the *Registration of Titles Act*, the survivor may apply to the registrar to be registered as the sole proprietor of the land and upon registration he or she is deemed to be the proprietor thereof.

Severance

Severance describes the process whereby joint tenancy is converted into tenancy in common. Though strictly speaking a joint tenant owns no distinct share in the common property equity recognised that each joint tenant had a potential share in the property, which he or she could sever during his or her lifetime.[57] Sir William Page-Wood VC in his celebrated statement in *Williams v Hensman* declared three ways of severance of a joint tenancy: unilateral action, mutual agreement and course of dealing of the co-owners.[58]

(i) Unilateral severance

A joint tenant may unilaterally sever the joint tenancy by engaging in an act that destroys any one of the four unities. For example, where X and Y are joint tenants, if Y during her lifetime transfers her share of the property to Z the joint tenancy is severed because unity of title and time is destroyed. In this regard, Y does not need to seek X's consent let alone inform him prior to granting her interest to Z.[59] At law, a transfer to a third party becomes effective to sever the joint tenancy when the

---

[53] *Henderson* v *Eason* (1851) 17 QB 701. The *Statute of Anne* of 1705 gave the courts power to order an account against a co-owner receiving more than his or her just share.

[54] See Peter Butt, *Land Law* (2nd, Sydney, Law Book Company, 1988) p. 196. Whether a suit to account in equity can be brought independently of a partition suit is not clear see Bradbrook et al, *The Law of Real Property in Australia*, supra, at 317.

[55] *Squire* v *Rogers* [1979] 39 FLR 106, at 124.

[56] *Henderson* v *Eason* (1851) 17 QB 701. See also *Squire v Rogers* [1979] 39 FLR 106.

[57] Megarry and Wade, *The Law of Real Property*, supra, pp. 429-30. Severance cannot be effected by will since a will only takes effect after the death of the testator, see *Re: Caines* [1987] 1 WLR 546.

[58] (1861) J&H 546; 70 ER 862, at 867.

[59] *Williams v Hensman* (1861) J&H 546; 70 ER 862. Note that under s. 40 of the *Land Act*, 1998, the other spouse must consent prior to any transaction affecting family land. Therefore, if in the example X and Y are married and the co-owned property is family land, a purported transfer by Y of her interest, without X's consent, would be ineffective to sever the joint tenancy.

interest of the transferee is conveyed to that party. Hence, where the joint tenancy is registered under the *Registration of Titles Act*, severance becomes effective on registration of the transfer.[60] However, in equity, severance is recognised as operative even before registration of the transfer to the third party provided that there is a contract of transfer (specifically enforceable in equity) between the transferor and transferee.[61] Where the intended transfer to a third party is by way of a gift it will not be effective to sever the joint tenancy in equity unless the grant is completed prior to the grantor's death.[62]

(ii) Mutual agreement

Severance by mutual agreement is where all the joint tenants agree to hold their title as tenants in common.[63] There is valuable consideration for the agreement in that each joint tenant agrees to relinquish the beneficial interest in the common property including the right of survivorship, in a return for a share of a tenancy in common.[64] The fact that the agreement is verbal or otherwise incapable of specific performance does not appear to be important.[65] Once the joint tenants have agreed to sever their joint tenancy, it is immediately and *irreversibly* severed in equity.[66] Where the joint tenants are registered as joint proprietors under the *Registration of Titles Act*, from the moment they agree to sever they will hold the property as trustees for themselves as tenants in common and in equal shares.[67]

(iii) Course of dealing

A joint tenancy is severed by course of dealing where the conduct of the joint tenants towards each other reveals a mutual understanding that the joint tenancy should be severed. Whether this is so essentially is a question of fact depending on the circumstances of each case.[68] Severance by mutual agreement and by course of dealing may in some cases overlap. However, they are separate and distinct methods of severance. The difference is that severance by mutual agreement encompasses express agreement to sever the jointure, whereas severance by course of dealing covers circumstances that may not involve any agreement but where it could be inferred from the circumstances that the parties formed a 'common intention' to hold their property as tenants in common.[69] For example, in *Burgess* v *Rawnsley*, it was held that a court may be entitled to infer a common intention to sever by course of conduct on the basis of negotiations carried on by the joint tenants, even though those negotiations did not result in an agreement.[70]

---

60 Section 51, *RTA*. See also *Wright* v *Gibbons* [1948] 78 CLR 313.

61 *Wright* v *Gibbons*, *ibid*. In Uganda a contract to transfer an interest in land is enforceable even if it is not in writing, section 4 (3) *Contract Act* cap 75, and *Mayanja-Nkangi* v *National Housing Corporation* [1992] 1 ULR 37.

62 *Milroy* v *Lord* (1862) 4 De GF & J 264; 45 ER 1185. In *Sentamu v Nalirya* (CA No 84 of 1959; High Court Digest 538, unreported), it was held that a gift of land is incomplete until registration of the instrument of transfer. However, compare with the High Court of Australia judgement in *Corin v Patton* (1990) 169 CLR 313.

63 *Wright* v *Gibbons* (1948) 78 CLR 313.

64 *Corin* v *Patton* (1990) 169 CLR 540, at 572 per Deane J.

65 *Burgess* v *Rawnsley* [1975] 1 Ch 429.

66 *Burgess* v *Rawnsley* [1975] 1 Ch 429.

67 *Corin* v *Patton* (1990) 169 CLR 540.

68 *Burgess* v *Rawnsley* [1975] 1 Ch 429.

69 *Ibid*, at 447, per Sir John Pennycuick.

70 *Ibid*.

(iv) Other manner of severance

In addition to the three rules of severance declared by Sir William Page-Wood VC, in *Williams* v *Hensman*, there are two other methods of severance. The first one is *severance by court order*. Once the court makes an order which is inconsistent with the continuation of the joint tenancy, the joint tenancy is severed from the date of the judgement though the parties continue to hold as joint tenants until the order is executed and the necessary legal transfers made.[71] For example, if husband and wife hold their matrimonial home in joint tenancy, and in divorce proceedings the court makes an order for a settlement of property, the effect of the order would operate to sever the joint tenancy in equity. Thus, it is submitted that if before the order is implemented one of them dies, the rule of survivorship would not apply in favour of the survivor.

Secondly, severance may occur as a consequence of unlawful killing by one joint tenant of his or her co-owner. It is a rule of public policy of the general law that a person shall not be permitted to profit by his or her own crime.[72] Equity will prevail on him or her to hold the legal interest on a constructive trust for himself or herself and the estate of the deceased in tenancy in common in equal shares. For example, in *Re: Stone*,[73] the respondent and his late wife were registered as joint tenants of their matrimonial house when he strangled her. He was convicted of manslaughter because of diminished responsibility. It was held that the respondent's action in killing his wife caused a severance of the joint tenancy in the land. The court declared that the respondent acquired his interest at law as joint tenant but that he held it on trust for himself and whoever was entitled to it under his late wife's estate, in tenancy in common.

(v) Partition

Joint tenancy may be terminated by partition. The rules for partition are exactly the same as for termination of tenancy in common discussed below.

Termination of tenancy in common

Both joint tenancy and tenancy in common can be determined by sale or by partition of the common land. Termination by sale is where the land is sold and the proceeds distributed amongst the co-owners in accordance with their shares, subject to any appropriate adjustments, such as fees for sole occupation and reimbursements for expenses incurred in improvements. Partition, on the other hand, is the physical division of the land amongst the co-owners. The co-owners may voluntarily agree to sell and share the proceeds or to partition the property, as they so wish, subject to relevant planning regulations. Where one of the parties is unwilling to partition the common property, the courts have inherent equitable jurisdiction to compel a partition if in the circumstances it is just to do so. [74]

The legal position is less clear whether the courts, in an application for partition, can at their discretion order a sale in lieu of a partition. Both at law and in equity the courts could not refuse to decree partition, however inconvenient, where demanded by one of the co-owners.[75] In England, the situation was rectified by the enactment of the *Partition Acts* of 1868 and 1876, which gave the courts discretion to decree a sale and division of the proceeds instead of partition.[76] In the case of

---

71 *Davies v Davies* [1983] WAR 305; *Patzak v Lytton* [1984] WAR 532.

72 *Cleaver v Mutual Reserve Fund Life Association* [1892] 1 QB 147.

73 [1989] 1 Qd R 251. See also *Rasmanis v Jurewitsch* (1968) 88 WN (Pt 1) (NSW) 59. Cf *Public Trustee v Evans* [1985] 2 NSWLR 188.

74 *Mpalikamanya v Sempiira* CS No 571 of 1976 (unreported). See also *Halsbury's Laws of England* (1st Ed), at 834, nt v. At common law, the courts had no such jurisdiction until the enactment of the *Partition Acts* 1539 and 1540.

75 *Mayfair Property Co Ltd v Johnson* [1894] 1 Ch 508. In *Gabriel Michel and another v Khoury* (1944) 10 WALR 286, it was held that the court has no jurisdiction to order a sale in lieu of partition where neither co-owner requests a sale.

76 31 and 32 Vict. c 40 and 39. The Law of Property Act of 1925 repealed both Acts.

Singh v Kaur,[77] it was held that the *Partition Acts* were statutes of general application in Kenya. The argument used in that case would have been of high persuasive value for the application of the Acts in Uganda, but for the fact that statutes of general application do not apply to Uganda.[78] In the event, it is thought that, without a statutory base, the courts in Uganda have no jurisdiction to make a compulsory order for sale of co-owned land where an application is made for partition.[79] A strict application of the common law in this regard might lead to uneconomic land fragmentation. It is arguable that for this reason the courts may, in the exercise of their powers under s. 16(3) of the *Judicature Statute*, 1996, decline to follow the common law rule on the ground that its application is not suitable for the circumstances of this country and its people. In that case, in the absence of any other rule it might make an order for the land to be sold or any such other order as the justice of the case so demands.[80] Ideally, appropriate legislation should be enacted to put the matter beyond any dispute.

PRACTICAL APPLICATION OF CO-OWNERSHIP

Many people who own land in joint tenancy or in tenancy in common are not clear in their minds of the advantages of one form of tenancy over the other. Normally, joint tenancy is best suited for married people because upon the death of either spouse the survivor automatically becomes the sole owner without need of probate. Joint tenancy is also a convenient manner of holding the legal title by administrators of estates and trustees. This is because where there are two or more administrators or trustees and one of them dies, by operation of the doctrine of *jus accrescendi* the survivor(s) would have the legal power to administer the estate.[81] For the same reason, it is advantageous for partners to be registered as joint tenants of their partnership land. Upon the death of one of the partners, the firm normally dissolves and the survivor has a legal obligation to wind up the business, which usually involves sale of the partnership property. By operation of the right of survivorship the remaining partner would have the legal power to dispose of the property without the assistance of the deceased's personal representative who otherwise must be involved if the partnership property were held in tenancy in common. As we have seen, the beneficial interest of the estate of the deceased in the partnership is protected by the presumption that the beneficial interest in the partnership is held in tenancy in common.[82]

Apart from the cases mentioned above, joint tenancy as a manner of holding property can be a trap for the unwary, in particular because of the draconian operation of the right of survivorship.

---

77 (1936) 17 (1) KLR 1.

78 *Uganda Motors Ltd v Wavah Holdings Ltd* CA No 19 of 1991. On the basis of this authority, the High Court holding in *Mpalikamanya v Sempiira* CS No 571 of 1976 that the *Partition Acts* were applicable to Uganda, is no longer good law.

79 Cf *Gabriel Michel and another v Khoury* (1944) 10 WALR 286.

80 See s. 16(2)(c) of the *Judicature Statute*, 1996.

81 Section 186, *Succession Act* (cap 139), provides that 'When probate has been granted to several executors, and one of them dies, the entire representation of the estate accrues to the surviving executor or executors'. See also s. 275 of same Act. Also see s. 19 (1) *Trustees Act* (cap 142) provides that where a trust is given to two or more *jointly*, the same may be exercised by the survivor(s) for the time being.

82 See also see s. 13 of the *Administrator Act* (cap 140), which requires the surviving partner to furnish a sworn statement of account to the administrator.

10

Expropriated Property

(This chapter was written by Mr Peter Walubiri, Senior Lecturer, Faculty of Law, Makerere University.)

HISTORICAL BACKGROUND

In August 1972, President Idi Amin announced an economic war, the net effect of which was the massive expulsion of persons of Asian extraction from Uganda. Thousands of properties belonging to these Asians were expropriated by the government and placed under the management of the Departed Asians Property Custodian Board. After Idi Amin's fall from power, legislation was enacted under which most of these properties have either been returned to the former owners or sold off.

Asians' economic dominance

In spite of its economic, political and social magnitude, this expulsion and expropriation was not entirely unexpected. The Asian community first made a serious presence in Uganda in the aftermath of the construction of the Uganda railway where hundreds worked as indentured labourers. After the construction of the Uganda railway several of them settled to a life of commerce. By the mid-forties, the Asians had established themselves as a dominant force in the retail trade, cotton ginning, coffee hulling, produce buying, transportation, import and export trade.[1] Almost all major towns, including trading centres, had Asians as the dominant trading community and real property owners.

The Africans to whom a cash economy was just being introduced for the first time were largely relegated to peasant farming and labouring in plantations, factories and shops owned by the Asians and Europeans. There was no significant African presence in commerce or industry. Over time, discontent grew among the African communities. They started agitating for a more significant share in the economy in terms of cotton ginning, coffee curing rights, marketing of their agricultural produce and participation in commerce. They were in effect demanding more political and economic space. They organised strikes and trade boycotts.[2]

Corrective measures

The colonial government responded to this agitation by several measures such as the setting up of the cooperative movement to enable Africans to engage in organised production and marketing of their own produce.[3] In 1949, the Lint Marketing Board was set up to handle all cotton exports and to ensure a greater return to the farmers.[4] A price stabilisation scheme was set up to ensure that fluctuations of export prices did not result in large yearly variations in peasants' incomes. The following year, the Uganda Credit and Savings Bank was set up with the object of facilitating loans to Africans in furtherance of agricultural, commercial, building and co-operative society purposes.[5]

---

1 They were in part assisted financially by the foreign banks like the Bank of India, which were the first to be established in Uganda.

2 These strikes and boycotts targeted Asian merchants.

3 *Cooperative Societies Ordinance No. 5 of 1946.*

4 Lint Marketing Board Ordinance No. 33 of 1949 and subsequently Ordinance 16 of 1959 (Cap. 234, Law of Uganda, 1964].

5 See long title to the Uganda Credit and Savings Bank Ordinance 20 of 1950.

Other measures included the setting up of the Uganda Development Corporation in 1952 to facilitate the industrial and economic development of Uganda, promote and assist in the financing, management and establishment of new undertakings, schemes for the better organisation and modernisation of and the more efficient carrying out of any undertaking and the conduct of research into the industrial and mineral potentialities of Uganda.[6]

Provision was also made under the *Acquisition of Ginneries Ordinance*, for the government to acquire compulsorily privately owned ginneries and sell them to Africans.[7] Several of these were sold to African-run cooperative societies. In 1953, the Produce Marketing Board was set up to perform a similar role in relation to other produce such as maize, simsim, and groundnuts, to the role that was being performed in respect of cotton by the Lint Marketing Board.[8] The board assumed a near monopoly of the export of these products and was able to guarantee a stable income for the producers.

Other initiatives included the setting up of the African Loans Fund to facilitate loans to Africans in furtherance of agricultural, industrial, commercial and building purposes.[9] These economic and legislative measures, coupled with other political initiatives to give Africans more say in the running of the colonial government, though positive in themselves, did not fully satisfy the Africans who continued to agitate for more economic and political space. Eventually, political independence was won on 9th October 1962. The post independence government continued to strengthen those institutions set up in the colonial era to integrate Africans into the economy.

To accelerate urban development, the National Housing Corporation was set up in 1964 to undertake the development, building and management of housing estates.[10] As part of its programme to integrate Africans into the towns, the corporation had special programmes, especially in Kampala (Ntinda, Naguru, Kiswa, Nakawa, Kataza), to enter into agreements for the sale of houses on terms of deferred payment for a period not exceeding 20 years or for the grant of a lease of any such house[11]. Under the *National Trading Corporation Act*,[12] the corporation was mandated to promote or aid any person being a citizen of Uganda in business.[13] The promotion or aid could take the form of financing.

All the foregoing measures made significant contributions to the integration of Africans into the economy but the dominance of the Asians in commerce and industry still remained. It remained a contentious political issue in the country and between Uganda and Great Britain since most of the Asians were British citizens or British protected persons.

In 1969, a new *Trade (Licensing) Act* was enacted with one of its aims being to limit the operational area of non-citizen traders.[14] The minister was empowered, from time to time by statutory order, to declare any trading centre to be an area in which a person who was not a citizen of Uganda was prohibited from trading.[15] Pursuant to these powers, the minister issued statutory orders prohibiting non-citizens from trading in most rural trading centres.[16] Under section 4(1) of the Act, it became illegal for any person who was not a citizen of Uganda to trade outside any city, municipality or town or to trade in prohibited goods. This law put considerable pressure on the Asian trading community to move to the city or other large urban centres. By 1969, there were open political calls

---

6 *Section 4(1) The Uganda Development Corporation Act, Cap. 319.*

7 Ordinance 7 of 1952.

8 See Ordinance 1 of 1953 (now repealed Cap. 243).

9 *Long title to The African Loans Fund Act, Cap. 164.*

10 *The National Housing Corporation Act, Cap. 321.*

11 *Ibid* s. 3(1)(c).

12 No. 18 of 1966.

13 *Ibid* s. 4(1)(c).

14 Act 14 of 1969.

15 *Ibid* s. 2(b).

16 See ss. 196 of 1969, 227 of 1969, 12 of 1970, 13 of 1970, 119 of 1970.

on Britain to repatriate its Asian citizens. Thus, when the expulsion of Asians finally took place in 1972, it was not entirely unexpected.

The laws enacted to give effect to the expulsion of the Asian community, the expropriation and management of their properties and the subsequent return of those properties have had a far reaching impact on the law of Uganda. The most effected law was undoubtedly the law of real property, since the most valuable form of property affected was immovable property.

THE EXPROPRIATION

Cancellation of entry permits

The first stage of the expropriation was the expulsion of non-citizen Asians from Uganda. On 9 September 1972, a decree was published to cancel entry permits and certificates of residence held by certain persons in Uganda.[17] Under this law, and notwithstanding the provisions of the *Immigration Act, 1969*, all entry permits or certificates of residence issued to any person of Asian origin, extraction or descent and who was a citizen of the United Kingdom of Great Britain and Northern Ireland, the Republic of India, the Republic of Pakistan, or the Republic of Bangladesh were cancelled.[18] By a subsequent amendment to the Decree, the cancellation was extended to 'any other person who is of Indian, Pakistan, or Bangladesh origin, extraction or descent'[19] regardless of his citizenship.

Prohibition of new liabilities

Persons who had to leave Uganda due to cancellation of their entry permits or certificates of residence were prohibited from transferring or mortgaging their immovable property or, in the case of companies, from issuing new shares or appointing new directors.[20] However, those transfers and mortgages that had been properly done before 6 October 1972, when Decree 27 of 1972 was published, were saved.[21] In the case of immovable property, these restrictions were the first step of expropriation, in as much as registered proprietors were prevented from freely dealing with their properties as provided for by law.

Declaration of assets

Every departing Asian was obliged to declare his or her assets and liabilities and supply such other particulars and information relating to his property or business on the forms specified in the schedule to the decree.[22] The forms submitted to the minister had, *inter alia*, to be accompanied by a list of title deeds, debentures, loan agreements and contracts or other agreements entered into by the departing Asians.[23] Once the assets were declared, the minister would list them in a register of declared properties and businesses.[24]

---

17 *The Immigration (Cancellation of Entry Permits and Certificates of Residence) Decree No. 17 of 1972.*

18 *Ibid*, s. 1.

19 *Section 1 The Immigration (Cancellation of Entry Permits and Certificate of Residence) (Amendment) Decree No. 30 of 1972.*

20 *Section* 1 The *Declaration of Assets (Non-Citizen Asians) Decree*, No. 27 of 1972; Re-enacted as s. 1 of Decree 27 of 1973.

21 Section 1(1) & (3) of Decree 27 of 1973.

22 S ection 2(1) of Decree 27 of 1972. Re-enacted as s.2(1) of Decree 27 of 1973.

23 Ibid s. 2(2)(c). Re-enacted as s.2(a) (a) of Decree 27 of 1973.

24 *Ibid* s. 3.

Agents for sale of properties to Ugandan citizens

Initially, it was conceived that departing Asians would nominate persons to act as their agents to sell their property or businesses. To that end, every departing Asian was obliged to give to the minister notice in writing nominating a person to act as his or her agent.[25] The agent had to ensure that the property or business was properly looked after until it was transferred by sale to a Ugandan citizen.[26] The agent had powers, subject to the directions and approval of the Abandoned Property Custodian Board, to sell or transfer the property or business to any person, let any premises, convey by way of gift to any person the property or business, or to acquire the property or personally carry on the business.[27] However, these powers of agency were short-lived since the following year Decree 27 of 1973 repealed Decree 27 of 1972.[28] All acts done by agents in the performance of their duties on or after 24 October 1972 for the purposes of managing any declared assets were deemed to have been done by the government.[29]

Vesting of the properties in the board and government

The first category of properties to be expropriated was that of non-citizen Asians who departed Uganda without declaring the same. Such property could not be sold or purchased and it automatically vested in the government.[30] When Decree 29 of 1972 amended Decree No. 27 of 1972, the Abandoned Property Custodian Board was created and the property hitherto vested in the government was vested in the board without further assurance.[31]

The second category of properties to be expropriated was property abandoned by departing Asians or left in such a way that no adequate arrangements were made for the proper and efficient management of such property. The board could, by statutory order, declare such property to be vested in the board.[32] Under statutory instruments Nos. 169 and 174 of 1972, a total of 14 properties, mostly industrial properties, and one hotel were vested in the board in this manner. The powers of the board to vest property were subsequently assumed by the minister who could by statutory order vest in the government any other asset of a departed Asian.[33]

The third category of properties was property expropriated by the *Properties and Business (Acquisition) Decree,* 1972.[34] Under this Decree, all properties specified in the Schedule to the Decree were vested in the government and deemed to have been so vested and acquired by the government as from 18 December 1972.[35] Most of the scheduled properties were industrial establishments and tea estates owned by British nationals. The list was amended by several statutory instruments[36] and subsequently replaced by a single instrument appended to Decree 12 of 1975, which was itself amended by a number of statutory instruments.[37]

The last category was property simply taken over by the Custodian Board or other government officials without either being declared or abandoned and no order made in respect thereof or acquired under the *Properties and Business (Acquisition) Decrees.* Though not founded on any law this expropriation had serious legal consequence, as we shall discuss later.

---

25 *Ibid* s.2(2)(d).

26 *Ibid* s. 2(3).

27 Section 1(a) of the *Declaration of Assets (Non-Citizen Asians) (Amendment) Decree, 1972.*

28 Section 36(1)(a).

29 *Ibid* s. 4(4).

30 s. 4(5) Decree 27 of 1972.

31 s. 8 and 12 (1) of Decree 27 of 1972 as amended.

32 s. 12(2) of Decree 27 of 1972 as amended.

33 s. 4(2) of Decree 27 of 1973.

34 No. 32 of 1972.

35 *Ibid* s. 1(1).

36 See s.1 Nos. 4 of 1973, 20 of 1973, 58 of 1973, 129 of 1973, 47 of 1974, 76 of 1972.

37 See s.1 Nos. 44 of 1976 and 88 of 1978.

Constitutionality of the expropriation

At the time of the expropriation, the Constitution of the Republic of Uganda, 1967, which was then in force, provided for protection of private property. Article 13 of the Constitution provided that:

(1) No property of any description shall be compulsorily taken possession of, and no interest in or right over property of any description shall be compulsorily acquired, except where the following conditions are satisfied, that is to say,

(a) the taking of possession or acquisition is necessary in the interest of defence, public safety, public order, public morality, public health, town and country planning or the development or utilisation of any property in such manner as to promote the public benefit; and

(b) the necessity therefore is such as to afford reasonable justification for the causing of any hardship that may result to any person having any interest in or right over the property; and

(c) provision is made by a law applicable to that taking of possession or acquisition,

(i) for the payment of reasonable compensation,...

Decree No. 1 of 1971 under which Idi Amin assumed office suspended several parts of the Constitution but Article 13 was not affected. Although Amin was afforded legislative powers under that legal notice, those powers had to be exercised in conformity with the surviving provisions of the Constitution, including Article 13.

In our opinion, the various decrees that made provision for expropriation were beyond Amin's legislative powers in as far as they violated Article 13 of the Constitution. The taking of possession of these properties was not in the interests of defence, public safety, public order, public morality, public health, town and country planning or the development or utilisation of any property in a manner so as to promote public benefit. There was no necessity for the scale of hardship occasioned to the Asian community and the decrees did not provide for payment of reasonable compensation.[38]

Unfortunately, the constitutionality of these decrees was not challenged until after the fall of Idi Amin's government and after the enactment of the remedial *Expropriated Properties Act* in 1982. The issue of the constitutionality of expropriation was in effect overtaken by events. It was nevertheless raised in *Hudda & Ors v Nyanza Saw Mills (1947) Ltd & Ors*[39] but was abandoned at the hearing. The issue was also raised in *United Assurance Co. Ltd v Attorney General*[40] but was never determined.

Management of expropriated property

The law for the management of expropriated properties was eventually consolidated into the *Assets of the Departed Asians Decree*, 1973.[41] All assets and liabilities vested in the government by virtue of s. 4 of the Decree were transferred to the Departed Asians Property Custodian Board,[42] which had itself been established under s. 5(1) of the Decree.

The board was established as a body corporate with perpetual succession and a common seal with capacity to sue and be sued in its corporate name.[43] The board was mandated to take over and manage all assets transferred to it.[44] This included the responsibility to discharge all the liabilities transferred to it by the Decree[45] and the discharge of mortgages or other debts owed by a departed

---

38 Provision for compensation was made by Decree 12 of 1975 long after the expropriation in 1972.

39 High Court Miscellaneous Application No. 46 of 1987, unreported.

40 Civil Appeal No. 1 of 1986, unreported.

41 No. 27 of 1973.

42 *Ibid* s. 13.

43 *Ibid* s. 5(3).

44 *Ibid* s. 7(1)(a).

45 Section 7 (1)(b).

Asian in relation to expropriated property. The board was also empowered to collect all debts or other monies due to the departed Asian in respect of expropriated property.[46] However, debts claimed by or against a departed Asian were exempted from bearing any interest whatsoever, notwithstanding anything to the contrary contained in any agreement.[47] Effectively then, the contractual relationship between mortgagors and mortgagees was interfered with.

The board was specifically empowered to sell or otherwise deal with such assets in the same way that a departed Asian could do.[48] The board could and actually did sell, mortgage, lease, sub-lease and let several of the properties it was managing. In other instances, the board released mortgages, surrendered leases or re-negotiated the terms of leases such as the annual rent payable. In all these transactions, third parties acquired legal rights which were subsequently affected by the provisions of the *Expropriated Properties Act, 1982* and which have resulted in considerable litigation.

Compensation to departed Asians

Decree 27 of 1973 was amended in 1975 to clarify the issue of compensation to departed Asians.[49] Under the amendment new sections 15, 15A, 15B and 15C were introduced in Decree 27 of 1973 to provide for compensation, its mode of determination, time of payment and appeals to an arbitration tribunal respectively.

The government committed itself to pay compensation, in respect of any property or business declared under s. 2 of the Decree, to the departed Asians.[50] The compensation was to be determined by the Board of Valuers appointed under s. 2(1) of the *Properties and Business (Acquisition) Decree*, 1975.[51]

The compensation had to be paid within such period as the minister may determine having regard to the period within which the property or business may generate sufficient income to effect the amount of compensation payable.[52] The value of compensation, as determined by the Board of Valuers, had to be communicated to the responsible minister of the government of the departed Asian's country of origin.[53] If the government of the departed Asian was not satisfied with the valuation, it had a right, exercisable within 30 days of the notification of the valuation, to inform the government of Uganda of its objection together with its reasons. Unless the two governments reached a settlement within 60 days from receipt of the objection, the matter would be referred to an Arbitration Tribunal appointed under s.15C of the Decree. Notwithstanding any other Ugandan law to the contrary, the award of the Arbitration Tribunal was final and binding on the two governments.[54]

Provision was made under s.15B for departed Asians, who had not declared their properties, to declare them belatedly and to supply other information to the minister. Where such information was not forthcoming, the government could nevertheless pay compensation as deemed appropriate. These compensation provisions were repealed by the *Expropriated Properties Act*, 1982[55] before

---

46 Section 7(1) (d)

47 Section 7(3) as inserted by S. 1(a) of the *Assets of the Departed Asians (Amendment) Decree No. 12 of 1975.*

48 Section 7(1) (e).

49 See s.1(b) of Decree 12 of 1975.

50 Section 15 (1) of Decree 27 of 1973.

51 Section 15(2) Decree 27 of 1973.

52 Section 15A (1) Decree 27 of 1973.

53 Section 15A (2) Decree 27 of 1973.

54 Section 15A (3). Under s. 15C the tribunal was to be chaired by an advocate of at least 5 years standing. The tribunal had to have 3 members appointed by the Uganda government and 3 other members appointed by the governments of the departed Asians concerned. The six members would appoint the chairman failing which the Chief Justice of Uganda would appoint one.

55 Section 16(1)(d).

they were implemented. Some compensation was paid to the governments of former owners but there is scanty information on the amounts involved and the procedures followed.

REVERSING THE EXPROPRIATION

The pressure for repossession

Upon the fall of Idi Amin's regime in 1979 foreign governments, notably Britain, that had supported the anti-Amin war effort and to whom the post-Amin governments looked for donor support to rebuild the ruined economy, called upon the government in Uganda to redress the wrongful expropriation of Asian properties in 1972. The expropriation was but one of the many wrongs of the Amin regime which had to be redressed.

Not all Ugandans were unhappy with the expropriation. Many had expressed joy at the departure of the Asians. The departure actually opened up many business opportunities to Ugandans, opportunities that they would never have dreamt of before the expropriation. This section of the population did not favour the repossession and actively campaigned against it in the 1980 general elections. However, the new government fulfilled its electoral promise to return the expropriated properties to the former owners by enacting the *Expropriated Properties Act,* 1982.[56]

The purpose of the Expropriated Properties Act, 1982

The long title to the Act stated that its purpose was to provide for the transfer of the properties and businesses acquired or otherwise expropriated, during the military regime, to the Ministry of Finance and to provide for their return to their former owners or disposal of the same by the government. The interpretation of the Act had to be guided by its express object and intention. The Supreme Court has held that this is a remedial statute aimed at putting right what the legislature in 1982 thought had been unfortunately decreed or done. It was aiming at returning property to former owners and accordingly it had to be given a liberal interpretation.[57] The mischief which the Act intended to rectify was the appropriation of property by the military regime and the remedy was to return the property to former owners. The Supreme Court emphasised that, if the statute were construed restrictively the mischief intended to be redressed would be perpetuated, thereby failing to provide a remedy to the injustice which was occasioned by the military regime to former owners.

Properties to which the Act applies

Provision is made in s. 1(1) of the Act for the following properties or businesses to remain vested in the government and to be managed by the Ministry of Finance. These are properties or businesses which were:

(a) vested in the government and transferred to the Departed Asians Property Custodian Board under the *Assets of Departed Asians Decree, 1973.*

(b) acquired by the government under the *Properties and Business (Acquisition) Decree,* 1975.

(c) in any other way appropriated or taken over by the military regime, save property which had been affected by the provisions of the repealed *National Trust Decree,* 1971.

The properties provided for in s. 1 (1)(a) & (b) were those that were expressly taken over under the respective decrees and have not been the subject of any controversy. However, properties covered

---

[56] Act No. 9 of 1982. The Act came in force on 21/02/83 pursuant to statutory instrument No.5 of 1983 made under s. 18 of the Act.

[57] *Registered Trustees of Kampala Institute v Departed Asians Property Custodian Board* Civil Appeal No. 21 of 1993 per Platt J.S.C. at p. 13.

under s. 1(1) (c) have generated controversy and litigation since they were not taken over under any known law. In *Lutaya v H.G. Gandesha & Anor*[58], the plaintiff claimed to be a lawful tenant by allocation of expropriated property and was entitled to quiet enjoyment of the property until the property was returned to the former owner or otherwise disposed of under the *Expropriated Properties Act,* 1982. The first defendant argued that he was a Ugandan citizen whose property was not expropriated. The learned Chief Justice who tried the suit made finding on the three issues he framed in the suit. Of particular interest was that since the first defendant and his wife, who were the only shareholders of the second defendant company, were all Ugandan citizens the property of the second defendant was not taken over under the Act.

He then considered the interpretation of the phrase 'in any other way appropriated or taken over by the military regime' occurring in s. 1(1)(c) of the *Expropriated Properties Act,* 1982 and concluded that anyone who wished to bring any kind of appropriation or taking over of the property during the military regime as falling under s. 1(1)(c) of the *Expropriated Properties Act,* 1982 must show that the appropriation or the taking over of that property was in the first place, 'lawful.'

Masika CJ's judgement was followed by the High Court in *Registered Trustees of Kampala Institute v Departed Asians Property Custodian Board.*[59] However, the Supreme Court reversed the latter judgement on appeal. Taking into account the mischief intended to be cured by the *Expropriated Properties Act,* 1982 Wambuzi CJ concluded that the words 'in any way appropriated or taken over' must mean whether by law, as in paragraph (a) or (b), or not. Since in this case, the evidence indicated quite clearly that the suit property was forcefully taken over or used by the government, it would be absurd to suggest that because the taking over was illegal, the property in effect could not be returned to the former owner.[60]

What is important, then, is to show that one owned property at the time of the 1972 expropriation which was expropriated, regardless of the lawfulness of such action. However, the former owner must prove that at the time of the 1972 expropriation he or she owned legal or equitable property capable of expropriation. In *Onapa v Mohammed Hussein Rashid Punjani,*[61] the respondent held a 3-year lease over a property in Kampala, which expired on 31 October 1972. In September 1972, he applied to the lessor for an extension of the lease with effect from 1st November 1972. On 28 March 1973, the Commissioner of Lands, as agent of the lessor, wrote to the respondent that his application for extension of the lease by a further period of 12 months with effect from 1st November 1972 had been approved and required the respondent to accept the offer and fulfil certain conditions. In the meantime, the respondent's certificate of residence was cancelled and he left Uganda without declaring his assets and before he received the offer of extension of the lease. Later, in 1984, the appellant obtained a lease in respect of the property and was issued with a certificate of title. The lease was extended a number of times until 1988 when he obtained a lease of 97 years.

In 1992 the respondent obtained a certificate of repossession in respect of the suit property. The appellant contested it on grounds that the respondent did not have property to repossess. The Supreme Court held that there was no lease or agreement for a lease when the respondent left Uganda in 1973. Therefore, the property did not fall under the operation of the Act.

In *Kulani v Satwant Kaur,*[62] the appellant, who was the mailo owner of the disputed property, contested a repossession certificate issued to the respondent on the grounds that the respondent

---

[58] High Court Civil Suit No. 860 of 1982; [1986] HCB 46.

[59] High Court Civil Suit No. 610 of 1992, unreported.

[60] Supreme Court Appeal No. 21 of 1993. Judgment of Wambuzi C.J. at p. 10 & 11. Other members of the Court concurred. The High Court has since followed this judgement to hold that properties of citizens actually taken over fall under the Act. See *Shamsudin Hussein Ismail v. Attorney General* Misc. Appeal No. 358 of 1994.

[61] Civil Appeal No. 5 of 1995, Supreme Court, unreported.

[62] Civil Appeal No. 22 of 1995, Supreme Court, unreported.

had executed a surrender of his lease with effect from 7 July 1972 before he was expelled from Uganda. This surrender had only been registered in 1977. The Supreme Court held that the unregistered surrender conferred on to the mailo holder a right to the reversion of the lease and extinguished the respondent's lease. The property had reverted to the mailo owner on 7 July 1972 when the lease was surrendered. Therefore, the *Expropriated Properties Act* did not apply to that property which was never expropriated.[63] Similarly, in *Jaffer Alibhai and 2 others v Nandala H. Kaira and another*,[64] the Supreme Court held that a departed Asian, who had sold his property and received part payment before leaving Uganda and the sale had subsequently been completed by the Custodian Board, could not reclaim his property, since the purchaser acquired an equitable interest in the property at the time of sale, which sale was completed by the Custodian Board.

Re-vesting of property in the government and nullification of dealings

As pointed out above, all property vested in the government under Decree 27 of 1973 or in any other way appropriated or taken over by the military regime was re-vested in the government to be managed by the Ministry of Finance.[65] The minister could by statutory order appoint any other person or body to manage any such vested property.[66] Until such appointment, the Departed Asians Property Custodian Board continued to manage the properties.[67]

To ensure that the expropriated properties remained vested in the government and that they were dealt with under the provisions of the *Expropriated Properties Act,* 1982 all purchases, transfers, grants or any other dealings of whatever kind in such properties were nullified.[68] This nullification even affected leases or tenancies which had expired or were terminated. Such expired or terminated leases were deemed to have continued in force and to continue until the property had been dealt with under the Act.[69]

This nullification interfered with the lawful transactions that had been concluded by the Departed Asians Property Custodian Board in respect of these properties. Purchases or leases or surrenders lawfully effected by the Custodian Board were nullified. Equally nullified were foreclosures and sales of mortgaged properties by mortgagees.[70] Re-entries by lessors on expropriated leases were also nullified and such forfeited leases reinstated to be dealt with under the Act.[71] Thus, this law interfered with existing legal relationships between vendors and purchasers, mortgagors and mortgagees, and lessors and lessees.

The nullification, on the face of it, was intended to be retrospective, that is, to affect those dealings that had taken place before the *Expropriated Properties Act,* 1982. This was the earlier view held by the High Court.[72] According to this view, after the coming into force of the *Expropriated Properties Act*, the normal legal relationship would obtain, for example, between a lessor and a lessee. In *Bidandi Ssali v Attorney General*,[73] the High Court held that a lessor could, after the coming into force of the 1982 Act, re-enter upon the land and terminate the lease if there were any breach of the terms of the lease by the Departed Asians Property Custodian Board.

---

63 Per Manyindo D.C.J at p. 8 of his judgement.

64 Civil Appeal No. 53 of 1995, Supreme Court, Unreported.

65 *Section 1(1) Expropriated Properties Act, 1982.*

66 *Ibid* s. 1(3).

67 *Ibid* s. 1(4).

68 *Ibid* s. 1(2)(a).

69 *Ibid* s. 1(2)(b). Under regulation 13 of s.1 No. 6 of 1983 these leases were deemed to continue after the property was dealt with under the Act for a further period of 2 years or a period equivalent to the unexpired period of the lease or tenancy at the time of expropriation whichever was the greater period.

70 *See Gokaldas Laximidas Tanna v SR Rosemary Munyinza* Civil Appeal No. 12 of 1992, Supreme Court [1994-5]; HCB 53.

71 *See Nordin Charania Walji v Drake Semakula* Civil Appeal No. 40 of 1995, Supreme Court, unreported.

72 *Bidandi Ssali v Attorney General*, Civil Suit No. 834 of 1989.

73 *Ibid.*

This retrospective view of nullification is no longer good law. In *Victoria Tea Estates Ltd v James Bemba & Anor*[74] the Court of Appeal re-considered the true import of s.1(1) & (2) of *Expropriated Properties Act* 1982 in view of a purported re-entry by a lessor registered on 29 May 1991 and a certificate of repossession issued in respect of the same property on 28 November 1991. The court held that since the government in 1973 expropriated the suit property, it followed that Act 9 of 1982 applied to it. The suit property became the statutory property of the government, until the Minister of Finance dealt with the property as provided for by Act 9 of 1982. Any other purported dealing in such property was null and void.[75]

Accordingly, even if there were breaches of rental payments the lessor could not re-enter. The lessor's only remedy was to sue the government for arrears of rent.

Dealings by the minister

The expropriated properties re-vested in government had to remain so vested until the minister dealt them with in any of the following ways:

(i) return to former owners (repossession)
(ii) government entering a joint venture with the former owner.
(iii) sale
(iv) disposal in any other manner.

Repossession by former owners

Former owners of expropriated property were entitled within ninety days of the commencement of the Act to apply to the minister in the prescribed form to repossess their property.[76] If the minister was satisfied with the merits of the application and the property was one in which the government did not wish to participate, the minister could issue a certificate authorising the former owner to repossess such property.[77] A 'Certificate Authorising Repossession' was sufficient authority for the Chief Registrar of Titles to transfer title to the former owner.[78]

Under s.15 of the Act, the minister was mandated by statutory instrument to make regulations prescribing forms of application and to facilitate the better implementation of the provisions of the Act. Pursuant to these powers, the minister enacted the *Expropriated Properties (Repossession and Disposal) Regulations*, 1983.[79] Under regulation 10(3), a 'Certificate Authorising Repossession' was in the form set out in the Second Schedule to the regulations.[80]

After the High Court decision in *Lutaya v H.G. Gandesha & Anor*[81] which held that properties of Uganda citizens were not lawfully expropriated and were not subject to Act 9 of 1982, the Custodian Board developed a special form under which they returned those properties to the former owners. In substance, this form, which differed from that prescribed by the regulations, disclaimed the Custodian Board's interest in the property and stated that the former owner was free to repossess his or her property. This form would be copied to the occupants of the property.

The legal status of this new form, which did not comply with the regulations, was challenged in the High Court and two of their lordships handed down conflicting judgements. In *Jani Mohammed*

---

[74] Civil Appeal No. 49 of 1996, Supreme Court, unreported.

[75] Per Twinomujunu J.A. at p. 10.

[76] S.3 of the Act. The Minister, by General Notice No.20 of 1993 issued in the Uganda Gazette vol. LXXXVI of 13.5.93 together with S.I No 1 of 1994 extended the deadline for lodging applications to 30.10.93. This extension was held legitimate by the Court of Appeal in *Jaffer Brothers Ltd v Bagalaliwo*, Civil Appeal No. 43 of 1997, unreported.

[77] S. 5(1) of the Act.

[78] S. 6(a) of the Act.

[79] S. 1 No. 6 of 1983.

[80] Form 3

[81] Supra

Jaffer Ltd v Khemisa Senya.[82] Rajasingham J. held that this letter was in effect a 'Certificate Authorising Repossession'. Byamugisha J. using the literal rule of interpretation came to a contrary conclusion.[83] which was subsequently followed by Kato J. (as he then was).[84] This issue was re-visited by the Court of Appeal which having regard to the purpose of the Act, held that a letter of repossession was in effect a 'Certificate Authorising Repossession'.[85]

Joint venture between the government and a former owner
Where the government is interested in property which a former owner has applied to repossess, the minister notifies the applicant of the government's interest and invites the former owner to enter into joint venture negotiations.[86] Where the negotiations are successfully concluded, a joint venture company is incorporated and the minister issues a certificate transferring the property or business to the company.[87] The minister can also validate any existing joint venture arrangements which are in the best interests of Uganda, without having recourse to the above procedure, by merely issuing a certificate validating the transfer.[88]

Sales by the minister
The minister is empowered by s. 8(1) of the Act to make an order that the property be sold in the following circumstances:

a) where the former owner fails to apply for repossession within the prescribed time
b) where the minister is not satisfied of the merits of the application
c) where negotiations for a joint venture fail, or
d) where a former owner fails to physically return and reside in Uganda within a period of 120 days from date of repossession.

The minister has used these powers to sell hundreds of largely unclaimed properties.[89] The purchaser is issued with a certificate of purchase, which has the same effect as a certificate of repossession.[90]

Disposal by any other manner
Other than ordering the sale of a property, the minister can, under s.8(1) of the Act, order any other form of disposal, depending on the circumstances of the particular property. He or she can, for example, order that a property be subdivided into separate titles, each to be leased to a particular person.[91] He or she can revalidate leases granted by controlling authorities before 1982 and make provision for the compensation of the former owner.[92] He or she can also revert a property to a planning authority for replanning and order the authority to compensate the former owner.[93] In one instance, the minister ordered a resale of properties to purchasers whose purchases had been nullified by the Act.[94] In another instance, the minister validated an earlier sale by an agent of the former owner.[95]

---

82 High Court Civil Suit No. 829 of 1992, unreported.
83 *Nazarali Hassanali Sayani v Edward Mperese Nsubuga*, High Court Civil Suit No. 364 of 1993 unreported.
84 *Jaffer Brothers Ltd v Bagalaliwo*, High Court Civil Suit No. 31 of 1995, unreported.
85 *Jaffer Brothers Ltd v Bagalaliwo*, Civil Appeal No.43 of 1997, unreported.
86 Section 4(1) of the Act.
87 Section 4(2) of the Act.
88 Section 4(3) of the Act.
89 See the *Expropriated Properties (Sale and disposal) order s.1. No.18* 1994 replaced by s. 1 No. 17 of 1995 and supplemented by s.1 Nos. 18 of 1997 and 12 of 2000. Under regulation 11 the property is sold by competitive tender on the basis of reserve price set by the Board of Valuers.
90 Section 8 (3) of the Act.
91 E.g., The *Expropriated Properties (Management)Order s.1 No.57 of 1995.*
92 The *Expropriated Properties (Management & Disposal) Order s.1 No.32 of 1996.*
93 E.g. *The Expropriated Properties (Reversion) Order S.1 No. 33 of 1996.*
94 The *Expropriated Properties (Repossession and Disposal)* Regulations s.1 No. 67 of 1998.
95 The *Expropriated Properties (Management) Order s.1 No. 78 of 1998.*

Dealing with incumbered properties

Where a property applied for by a former owner is subject to a caveat, lien, loan, charge, mortgage, or other registered incumbrance in favour of any lender, the minister must first hold consultations with the former owner and the lender with a view to securing a mutually acceptable arrangement for the discharge of such incumbrance.[96] Where no such arrangement is reached, the minister is then empowered to make such arrangement as he or she considers fit.[97] The minister has similar powers in case of properties that he orders to be sold.[98] It is submitted that where no arrangement is reached and no directions are made by the minister then the incumbrance remains to be discharged according to the ordinary law governing such caveat lien, loan, charge or mortgage.[99]

Present tenants

Persons who at the commencement of the Act were legitimately occupying or managing property affected by the Act are allowed to continue to occupy or manage the property until it is dealt with under the Act.[100] After disposal of the property by the minister, such occupants are entitled to not less than 90 days notice to vacate residential property.[101] The law is silent on notice in case of non-residential properties.

Compensation

Provision is made in the *Expropriated Properties Act* for compensation to be paid to various categories of people. Where the minister orders a property to be sold, the former owner, not being a citizen of Uganda, is entitled to compensation from the government of Uganda.[102] Where the property is returned to a former owner or transferred to a joint venture company or retained by the government, the former owner or the company or the government is obliged to pay for the value of any improvements on such property to the person who effected such improvements.[103]

Where the property has been transferred to any person for value and it is subsequently returned to a former owner or otherwise dealt with under the Act, the government is liable to pay compensation to such person.[104] The compensation payable to such a person is the purchase price paid for the property less the income derived or which ought to have been derived from the property from the date of transfer.[105] The provisions relating to compensation are not compatible with the Constitution.

Firstly, the measure of compensation is not the present market value of the property. Secondly, compensation has to be paid over such a period and in such a manner as the minister may determine or negotiate with the person to be compensated.[106] In *Pyrali Abdul Resul Esmail v Adrian Sibo*,[107] the issue of whether these provisions met the constitutional requirement for adequacy and promptness of compensation was raised but only two of their lordships attempted to address the issue. The majority of the court for one reason or another declined to decide this issue.

---

96 Section 5(2) *Expropriated Properties Act, 1982.*

97 Ibid. s .5(3).

98 Ibid s 8 (2).

99 See for example *Standard Chartered Bank (U) Ltd v Grand Hotel (U) Ltd* Civil Appeal No. 13 of 1999, Court of Appeal, unreported.

100 Section 9(1) of the *Expropriated Properties Act, 1982.*

101 Ibid s 9(2).

102 Section 11 (1) of the Act.

103 Section 11(2) of the Act. According to s.12 of the Act the minister in Matters of Valuation [of Compensation] is guided by the Board of Valuers established under s. 2(1) of the *Properties and Business (Acquisition) Decree,* 1975.

104 Section 11 (3) of the Act.

105 Section 11(4) of Decree 11 of 1975.

106 Section 11 (6) of the Act.

107 Constitutional Petition No. 9 of 1997, Constitutional Court, unreported. See commentary in Peter Walubiri(ed) *Uganda, Constitutionalism at Cross Roads*, Uganda Law Watch, Kampala, 1998, 187-91.

Appeal from the minister's decision

Persons aggrieved by any decision made by the minister under the Act have a right to appeal to the High Court against the minister's decision. The right is exercisable within 30 days from the date of communication of the decision.[108] Written decisions are deemed communicated fourteen days after date of posting to an address in Uganda or twenty-one days to an address outside Uganda.[109]

The minister's decision cannot be challenged in an ordinary suit since there is no statutory provision for appeal.

CONCLUSION

The expropriation of properties of persons of Asian descent had economic, social and historical origins that had

raged on for over three decades. Government attempts to redress the economic imbalance between the Asians and the native Ugandans seem not to have been fully appreciated by the people. The indigenous people who had hoped that, following independence, the economy would change in their favour felt impatient with the slow pace of change. Legislative attempts to drive the Asians out of the rural economy came too late. When a barbaric soldier seized political power, he resorted to the crude expulsion of the Asian community.

While the law was able to cope with the expropriation, albeit with several distortions of the existing legal order, the economy miserably failed. The inexperienced natives had no managerial skill to run the properties and businesses of the departed Asians. This coupled with the strained international relations with major donor and trading countries, brought the economy to its knees. By the fall of Idi Amin there was need for massive foreign aid and investment. Again the laws have been quick to make provision for repossession of properties and promotion of foreign investment but economic progress has been slow. Moreover, the issue of who should dominate the economy remains dangerously alive today. One hopes there will be no repeat of nationalisation or expropriation in future.

---

108 Section 14(1) of the Act.

109 Section 14(2) of the Act.

Index

Acquiescence, 67
Adverse possession
Lapse of time, 65
Limitation period, 62, 63
Power to evict squatters, 61
Prescription and acquiescence, 66
Certificates of title, 2
Colonial administration land policy, 3
Communal Land Associations, 30
Co-ownership, 144, 154
Customary law, 1
Customary rights, 142
Doctrine of estates
Estates less then freehold, 48
Estates of freehold, 48
Doctrine of tenure, 48
Doctrines of equity, 1, 2
Easements
Creation, 130, 131
Dominant land, 128, 129
Extinguishment, 135
Features, 128
Intended, 133
Necessity, 132
Public road, access to, 134
Servient land, 128
Under *Registration of Titles Act*, 134
User or prescription, 133
Equitable interests, 55, 56, 57, 58, 59, 60, 61, 72, 76, 83, 97
Equity, 55, 56
Expropriated property,
Expropriation, 157, 158, 159, 160
History, 155
Reversing the expropriation, 161, 163, 164, 165, 166
Fixtures, 51, 54, 113
Government land, 7, 33
Joint tenancy
Creation, 146
Definition, 144
Doctrine of survivorship, 145
Termination, 151, 153
Unity of interest, 144
Unity of possession, 144
Unity of title, 145
Land administration
District Land Boards, 34
Land Committees, 15, 19, 23, 24, 26, 26, 29, 35, 47
Land fund, 33
Uganda Land Commission, 33
Land (Amendment) Act 2000, 47
Land Bill, 7
Land disputes, settlement of,
District Land Tribunals, 30, 42, 43, 45
Sub-county Tribunals, 44
Transitional jurisdiction, 47
Urban and City Division Land Tribunals, 45
Land Reform Decree, 1975, 5, 6, 7, 8, 9, 10, 12, 15, 23, 30, 33
Land registration pilot schemes, 3
Land Tenure and Control Bill *see* Land Bill
Landlord, 97, 104
Landlord and Tenant Law 1937, 3
Leases
Assignment, 101
Breach of covenant, 104
Conditions, 97
Covenants, 97, 98, 100, 102
Creation, 94
Distinguished from licence, 91
Duration, 91
Exclusive possession, 92
Fixed term, 90, 110
Forfeiture, 106, 108, 110
Periodic, 90
Reversion, 103
Sublease, 101, 102
Tenancy at sufferance, 90
Tenancy at will, 90
Tenant by occupancy
Termination, 110
Legal interests, 55, 56, 57, 58, 59, 60
Licences, 141, 142
Lukiiko, 2
Mortgagees
Appointment of a receiver, 118, 120, 122, 123
Collateral advantage, 127
Foreclosure, 123
Mortgaged property, purchase of, 126
Personal covenant, 117
Possession, taking, 117
Remedies, 116, 123, 124
Mortgages
Creation, 115
Customary land, 116
Discharge by payment, 125
Equitable, 115
Judicial intervention, 127
Nature, 113
Mortgagors, 113, 114, 115, 116, 117, 118, 119, 120, 121, 122, 123, 124, 125, 126, 127
Ownership of land
Compulsory acquisition, 38, 40, 41
Government regulation of land use, 38
Non-citizens, 32, 36
Restrictions on family land, 37
Prescription, 67
Priority *see* Legal interests; Equitable interests
Profits a prendre, 135
Public Lands Act 1969, 4, 5, 9, 23, 35
Registration of titles *see* Torrens System
Restrictive covenants
Enforcement at common law, 137
Enforcement in equity, 138
Extinguishment of, 141

Remedies for breach of, 140
Schemes of development, 139
Servitudes, 128, 135, 137, 141
Sources of law, 1
Tenancy in common
Creation, 146
Definition, 146
Termination, 153
Tenant by occupancy
Certificate of occupancy, 19
Payment of rent, 14, 15
Registrable interest, 22
Termination, 21
Tenure systems
Customary tenure, 1, 4, 5, 7, 23, 25, 26, 27, 32
Freehold tenure, 3, 5, 7, 8
Leasehold tenure, 8, 9
Mailo tenure, 2, 10, 12, 14
Toro Agreement 1900, 3
Torrens Systems
Indefeasibility of title, 73, 74, 81, 82, 83
Origins, 69
Register Book, 29, 69, 70, 71, 73, 74, 76, 79, 80, 82, 86, 87, 134, 143
Remedies for deprivation of land, 86, 87
Title by registration, 70
Unregistered instruments, 71
Uganda Agreement 1900, 2

www.ingramcontent.com/pod-product-compliance
Lightning Source LLC
LaVergne TN
LVHW082332200926
848481LV00012B/3327
* 9 7 8 9 9 7 0 0 2 2 8 7 8 *